MAIKO MASQUERADE

MAIKO MASQUERADE

CRAFTING GEISHA GIRLHOOD IN JAPAN

Jan Bardsley

UNIVERSITY OF CALIFORNIA PRESS

University of California Press
Oakland, California

© 2021 by Jan Bardsley

Library of Congress Cataloging-in-Publication Data

Names: Bardsley, Jan, author.
Title: Maiko masquerade : crafting geisha girlhood in Japan /
    Jan Bardsley.
Description: Oakland, California : University of California Press,
    [2021] | Includes bibliographical references and index.
Identifiers: LCCN 2020037052 (print) | LCCN 2020037053 (ebook) |
    ISBN 9780520296435 (cloth) | ISBN 9780520296442 (paperback) |
    ISBN 9780520968943 (epub)
Subjects: LCSH: Geishas—Japan—Kyoto—History—21st century. |
    Popular culture—Japan—History—21st century. | Kyoto
    (Japan)—Social life and customs—21st century.
Classification: LCC GT3415.J3 B37 2021 (print) | LCC GT3415.J3 (ebook) |
    DDC 792.702/80952—dc23
LC record available at https://lccn.loc.gov/2020037052
LC ebook record available at https://lccn.loc.gov/2020037053

30 29 28 27 26 25 24 23 22 21
10 9 8 7 6 5 4 3 2 1

For my students, with gratitude for your insights, enthusiasm, and dedication, and for all that you have taught me.

CONTENTS

ILLUSTRATIONS

PREFACE

Why Study Maiko Stories?

"What kinds of geisha stories exist these days in Japan? Are Japanese reading novels and seeing movies about geisha, too?" My students raised these questions in spring 2002 at the end of our first-year seminar, "Geisha in History, Fiction, and Fantasy." Our entry into Geisha studies had been diverse, taking us into discussions about constructions of gender and beauty, race and sexuality, Orientalism and fantasy. We explored shifting representations of geisha in Japanese woodblock prints (ukiyo-e), Kabuki, film, and short stories from the profession's inception in the Edo period (1603–1867) through modern times. Turning to "geisha girl" fantasies abroad, we analyzed Victorian souvenir photographs, the 1896 British musical comedy, *The Geisha: A Story of a Teahouse*, and Hollywood geisha movies such as Shirley MacLaine's 1962 comedy *My Geisha*. Understanding this historical context helped us analyze Arthur Golden's 1997 *Memoirs of a Geisha*, a global best seller still much in vogue at the time, and reception to it as indicated by hundreds of reader responses posted on Amazon. It was the phenomenal response to Golden's novel that had inspired me—and other colleagues in the United States—to create this college course on geisha to investigate the dynamics and effects of cultural representation. By the end of our seminar, we knew that the geisha's profession and social position in Japan were not monolithic, but encompassed shifting labor conditions, geographical differences, various arts, and changes in social status. We saw how Japanese representations, though often different from Euro-American ones, spoke equally to their cultural moment. But what was the case in Japan now?

Searching for the answers to the question of current geisha representations became a quest. Over many trips to Kyoto, I realized that the geisha figured little in the contemporary cultural landscape. It was her teenage apprentice—the *maiko*—who was the twenty-first-century star. Fictional maiko played the lead in films, novels, TV dramas, and manga. It was the maiko who inspired tourist experiences and souvenirs. Her celebrity aura was motivating teens from around Japan to venture to Kyoto to try to become maiko themselves—or at least to cosplay as one. To find out "what kinds of geisha stories exist these days," we best begin by analyzing the meanings attached to this millennial maiko and the multiple representations of her. In turn, this emphasis points to competing views of the geisha—and the geiko, as she is known in Kyoto—and more broadly, to visions of girlhood in Japan.

This book is an interdisciplinary cultural studies project long in the making. Drawing from my years of teaching "Geisha in History, Fiction, and Fantasy," I concentrate on textual and visual analysis of works produced mainly in Japan in the 2000s. Using the same critical lens with which my students and I viewed, for example, the Cold War geisha girl in American media, I explore the maiko's cultural weight in Japan. To learn about the production of these texts and their subject, I sought out firsthand experiences and interviews in Kyoto from 2003 to 2019, having the most extended research time for five months in fall 2011. In Kyoto, I strolled the five districts that are home to geiko and maiko, attended dance performances and festivals, saw museum exhibits, and collected materials. I indulged my fan-girl curiosity, following Japanese guidebooks to sweets shops favored by maiko, visiting Kyoto sites featured in maiko fiction, and shopping for maiko goods in souvenir stores. In 2011 and later in 2017 and 2019, I was able to have conversations with those who in some way create maiko images, talking with authors, a painter, a photographer, Kyoto boosters, and business owners. This research has given me opportunities to talk with a small number of maiko, geiko, their clients, and other members of their community. Nevertheless, it is the *textual* maiko that draws my attention here. I intend *Maiko Masquerade* to contribute to conversations on representation, specifically the construction and influence of cultural icons. This is not an ethnography or a view behind the scenes, but a study of how diverse cultural texts in Japanese—guides, histories, fiction, film, narrative manga, and comics—variously represent maiko, geiko, and their world, mainly in the first two decades of the twenty-first century. By focusing on representation, we see how maiko stories of all kinds construct notions of girlhood in Japan, connect gender roles to Japaneseness, and frame Kyoto as a site of touristic and historic Japan. Analyzing maiko stories takes us past the individual experience of a relatively few young women to the creation of local and national narratives, which, in turn, shape those individual experiences.

I hope my students in "Geisha in History, Fiction, and Fantasy" will enjoy getting an answer to their questions—even though this arrives almost twenty years later. Yet, as I complete this book in spring 2020, so much has changed. Covid-19 has wreaked havoc on Kyoto's teahouse culture. All the spring dance productions, the year's major activity for geiko and maiko, were cancelled. The Kyoto International Manga Museum, which houses the *100 Maiko Illustrations* discussed in this book, is temporarily shuttered. Eirakuya, the textile firm that produces funny maiko prints also discussed below, is making cloth face masks. Geiko and maiko will face challenges in restoring their careers and their associated enterprises in the wake of the pandemic. But, as history shows, this is a resilient, creative community, which has overcome enormous setbacks in the past, to thrive again. Already, there are experiments with Zoom parties and other virtual performances. I look forward to seeing the spring dances again, walking in all five districts, and contemplating the new twenty-first-century stories produced about maiko and geiko.

NOTES ON JAPANESE TERMS AND CURRENCY

I italicize Japanese words at initial use only and append a glossary of recurring Japanese terms. The term *geisha* refers broadly to all women in this profession in Japan; *geiko* is the preferred term for those in Kyoto. With few exceptions, Japanese nouns do not have plural forms; thus maiko, geiko, kimono, and so on may indicate singular or plural depending on context.

Following East Asian custom, I give Japanese names in order of surname preceding given name, except for authors who publish in English. When citing a Kyoto geiko's book, I use the author's name as indicated in the book's copyright information, whether that be her professional name, as in the case of Komomo, or her legal name, as with Yamaguchi Kimijo.

I use macrons to indicate long vowel sounds in Japanese except in cases of well-known places (Tokyo, Osaka, Kyoto) and terms commonly used in English. When citing artists' names (Kojiroh, Osugi Shinji, Ono Kosei, Sato Masao), I use their preferred romanization which omits macrons.

All translations from Japanese are my own unless otherwise noted.

During the years most discussed in this book, 2005 to 2019, the average yen-US dollar exchange rate was 104. There were peaks at 122 in both 2007 and 2015, and the lowest rate was 77 in 2011.

Introduction

The Maiko, Kyoto's Apprentice Geisha

Arrive in Kyoto by train and you will see all manner of *maiko*—apprentice geisha—before you even leave the station. The quintessential Kyoto girl, she is the city's mascot and character brand, literally, its "dancing girl," as the characters *mai* and *ko* indicate, and her likeness appears everywhere. Perky maiko grace maps, menus, and posters of the city's ancient gardens and temples. Milky maiko smile at you from the foam atop steaming cups of cappuccino and matcha latte (figure 1). In the station's souvenir shops, doll-like maiko in bright kimono morph into kawaii Post-it notes, hand towels, key chains, and candy wrappers. With luck, you may even catch sight of a real maiko, her distinctive hairstyle making her instantly recognizable, as she embarks on her own travels.

In April 2008, apprentices made the news when their numbers rose.[1] For the first time since 1955, Kyoto had one hundred maiko. Of course, other Japanese girls in unusual garb captured media attention at home and abroad around this time, too—sporting Lolita fashion, costumed for maid cafés, or uniformed for singing in AKB48—but the maiko stood for the traditions of Kyoto.[2] No wonder the so-called "maiko boom" occurred in tandem with a surge in domestic tourism to Kyoto. Driven by excitement over the purported thousand-year anniversary of Murasaki Shikibu's legendary *Tale of Genji*, Japan's most celebrated work of fiction and poetry, tourists flocked to Kyoto in 2008 to experience the "old capital."[3] Maiko numbers fell somewhat in succeeding years but steadied at about eighty in 2012, where they hover in 2020. Enchantment with the maiko in the 2000s has sparked new Kyoto tourist activities and inspired popular media nationally. Maiko blogs, interviews,

FIGURE 1. Maiko Cappuccino at Caffè Ciao Presso in Kyoto Station, 2018. Courtesy of Kintetsu Retailing, Inc.

and dance performances, maiko-related goods, and even maiko movies and television dramas extended the boost in maiko numbers to a broader cultural moment. Photo studios offering maiko costume play mushroomed in Kyoto, attracting domestic and international tourists to don maiko wigs, makeup, and garments, creating the vogue for strolling in the old capital as a faux maiko. Clearly, representations of the maiko far exceeded her numbers in 2008 and continue to do so in 2020, suggesting that the millennial maiko as an emblem of Kyoto girlhood has struck a chord reaching far beyond her actual presence. Investigating this fascination as it took shape in early twenty-first-century Japanese media and popular culture is the subject of this book.

Exploring this phenomenon, I examine representations of the maiko as a cultural icon of Japanese girlhood for a national audience. This focus takes us to an appealing variety of popular books, films, TV series, and visual texts, generally aimed at broad audiences, produced in Japan mainly in the 2000s, and largely created by women.[4] Certain themes surface across the textual field, shaping these millennial representations of the maiko. Most importantly, we find active efforts to erase past interpretations of the maiko as a victim, observing how 1950s films, for example, commonly depicted her as an innocent with a limited future and inferior social status, whose sexuality was for sale. Banishing this stigma released the maiko's image for a host of new stories appropriate to late twentieth- and twenty-first-century Japan. Fundamentally, the maiko came to symbolize the hardworking young artist, the chaste keeper of traditions, and the exemplary Japanese girl. This transformation, which appears to have occurred over the postwar period, also elevated the maiko's Kyoto community as a site of deeply rooted cultural values. Occurring near the end of Japan's Lost Decades, a long recessionary period rocked by bank failures, natural disaster, and horrific crimes, the maiko boom elicited reassuring images of the past preserved and renovated with playful flourish.[5] Amid a conservative backlash in the 2000s in Japan against the nation's gender-equity initiatives of the 1990s, the maiko as quintessential Kyoto girl may have calmed anxieties about the blurring of gender identities.[6] As we will see, the maiko also stood in contrast to media hype over high school girls in the late 1990s, whose alleged delinquency and promiscuity, critics charged, threatened the health of the nation.

Millennial maiko narratives stress agency, underscoring that the apprentice has chosen this path of her own accord, largely due to her love of kimono and dance, and not because anyone pushed her into it. As the stigma of sexual servitude receded, replaced by emphasis on girls' agency, the notion of the exemplary *maiko-rashii maiko*, that is, the impeccably comported "maiko-like maiko" arose. As I suggest throughout the book, the perfection inherent in "maiko-likeness" has motivated various tropes of masquerade, inspiring maiko narratives of "ordinary Japanese girls" and even one ordinary boy in disguise striving to meet this ideal. Such narratives of masquerade speak to the effort and pleasure of performing femininity in millennial Japan, reinforcing the boundaries of gender while posing possibilities for subverting them. Comic interpretations, ones that spoof the pretensions of "maiko-likeness" and Kyoto as a world-heritage city, proliferate too, playing with the maiko image to produce a lighter, even satiric look. Lastly, we also see how the maiko as exemplar of millennial Japanese girlhood motivates contrasting visions of the "ordinary Japanese girl"—the maiko's hometown girlfriend or sister, the maiko before her transformation, or even the maiko incognito on her day off. In the book's conclusion, I argue that constructions of both maiko and ordinary girls tell us much about girlhood in Japan, illuminating narratives of personal choice, gender-appropriate roles, regional and ethnic identity, and the performance of idealized and contradictory femininities.

This favored attention to the maiko piques curiosity about *geiko*, the preferred appellation for geisha in Kyoto, and the one that I shall use for them in this book. After all, she has long been a cultural icon of Japan and exists in greater numbers today in Kyoto than the maiko. Small numbers of geisha are still active in Tokyo and other parts of Japan, but this book concentrates solely on Kyoto, geiko, and maiko.[7] As an arts professional, the geiko may pursue a lifetime career and develop as a leader in her community. Regarded as an expert in kimono and Japanese etiquette, the geiko can also exemplify Japanese femininity and *iki*, an insouciant chic.[8] Some millennial books about maiko, especially photo essays, may follow a woman's transition to becoming a geiko, but, rather like romances that end with weddings, the story tends to stop there. Personal accounts published in the 2000s by former geiko emphasize their years as maiko even though they spent many more as geiko. Maiko narratives in films, fiction, and narrative manga in the 2000s represent the geiko as an ambiguous figure, uncomfortably associated with accumulated wealth, independence outside marriage, and single motherhood. It is one thing to cheer on the hardworking, chaste girl, whose future remains open, but another to root for the geiko. Anthropologist and expert on geisha culture Liza Dalby writes, "As Japanese women, the most important social fact about geisha is that they are not wives. Geisha and wives are mutually exclusive categories because of the way women's roles have traditionally been defined in Japan."[9] Wives are defined as keepers of home and children, while geisha "inhabit a space where men get together on neutral territory to socialize."[10] Throughout this book, we will encounter different portraits of the geiko in Kyoto and geisha in the rest of Japan. In the conclusion, I argue that the ambivalence evident toward the geiko in millennial texts speaks to a broader discomfort in Japan with financially independent, career-focused single women.

What kinds of maiko stories preceded and attended the maiko boom? I introduce diverse narratives here by showing how they shape this book's chapters. I begin by describing the three chapters that I base on nonfiction books. This literature, comprised of popular histories, photography books, tourist guides, and academic studies, extols the *hanamachi* (the "flower districts" where geiko and maiko reside) and aims to preserve the community as a cultural site relevant to all Japanese.[11] Chapter 1, "The Maiko's Hanamachi Home," shows how such books introduce the history of the hanamachi, the community's values, the teahouse system, and the roles of women in leadership and men as clients. Chapter 2, "The Well-Mannered Career Path," explains the maiko-geiko career path and the values underpinning each stage, including maiko-likeness, by examining hanamachi etiquette guides and autobiographical books, all mainly authored by women. Moving to personal accounts, chapter 3, "Life in the Hanamachi: Voices of Maiko and Geiko," explores how three women—former geiko Kiriki Chizu, geiko Yamaguchi Kimijo, and maiko Kamishichiken Ichimame—all maiko in different decades, ranging from the 1960s to the early 2000s—reflect on performing their public roles, developing as dancers, and their lessons learned.

Turning to fictional maiko narratives in chapters 4, 5, and 6, we encounter a range of stories from tragedy to comedy, fantastical adventures, and even absurd maiko portraits. Genres include film, TV, manga, light fiction, and comic art. Exploring mass-mediated stories, we take up five narratives produced in Japan from the 1950s through 2020, analyzing changing perceptions of the maiko's social status and mission. Chapter 4, "From Victim to Artist: Maiko Stories in Movies and Manga," opens with the 1950s maiko characterized as an impoverished girl in need of rescue in two quite different films: the 1953 drama *Gion bayashi* (released in the United States as *A Geisha*) and the 1955 musical comedy *Janken musume* (released in the United States as *So Young, So Bright*). The fraught life of a maiko in the late 1960s, based on former geiko Iwasaki Mineko's 2001 autobiography, informs Yamato Waki's manga, *Kurenai niou* (Crimson fragrance, 2003–07), a lavishly drawn story of a fiercely independent young artist, who fights against stigma.[12] Two other narratives of maiko produced in the 2000s take a much gentler approach, casting the maiko as an innocent artist and the hanamachi as her protective home. The 2008–09 series *Dandan* (Thank you), an NHK-TV morning drama broadcast nationally, follows the escapades of maiko Nozomi and her rural twin, Megumi, who meet for the first time as eighteen-year-olds, exploring how they mature over the next several years, growing up loyal to their hanamachi and countryside families. Koyama Aiko's manga *Maiko-san-chi no Makanai-san* (Miss Cook for the maiko girls)—begun in 2016 and still running in 2020—revolves around home-cooked food, girl friendships, and ordinary girls' struggles to manage appetites while striving to perform as maiko-like maiko. Moving to an imaginary boy's experience of maiko life takes us to chapter 5, "Adventures of a Boy Maiko." In her 2002–14 light novel series, *Shōnen maiko: Chiyogiku ga yuku!* (Boy maiko: There goes Chiyogiku!), Nanami Haruka reimagines the maiko as an icon for gender play. Creating tall tales, Nanami depicts the boy Mikiya alternating between the language, behavioral codes, and sentiments of a middle school boy and his weekend masquerade as maiko Chiyogiku. This fantastical view of maiko continues in chapter 6, "Hit a Homer, Maiko! Maiko Visual Comedy," as we consider humorous visual texts found in two prominent Kyoto sites: the legendary textile firm Eirakuya and the Kyoto International Manga Museum. Here we find maiko pictured in absurd situations, even engaging in sports in full costume, or their masquerade extended by morphing across different species and with other icons. We observe how artists tease us to guess who is behind the mask, positing both an ordinary teenage girl and interlopers embracing the guise of girl consciousness. The conclusion, "The Ordinary Girl in the Maiko Masquerade," wraps up *Maiko Masquerade* by reflecting on the alternate portraits of girlhood in Japan represented by fictions of the maiko and her foil, the ordinary Japanese girl, and considers the ambivalence directed toward geiko.

Having sketched out the book's chapters and maiko sources, I use the remainder of this introduction to set the stage for *Maiko Masquerade*'s journey into representation. I begin with a historical overview of the maiko—her current position, her changing legal and social status, her relationship to other stigmatized girl figures, and, briefly, her role in modern art. Moving to her iconic costume, I show how the maiko's distinctive look extends to the touristic commerce of cosplay, character branding, and the souvenirs of millennial *Japonisme*. Despite its anachronistic quality, the maiko's look confirms her as a *shōjo*, the girl-character long associated with the self-expression of girls' culture in modern Japan. The maiko's shōjo resonance inspires millennial fiction and manga, and brands Kyoto itself as shōjo territory. Turning to academic research on geisha, I connect *Maiko Masquerade* to a wealth of English-language scholarship on geisha, especially on the history of their representations. All this leads me to what I find most interesting in maiko texts—the themes of masquerade. I trace the concepts of masquerade relevant here, opening a new perspective on millennial maiko stories.

WHAT IS A MAIKO?

Contemporary maiko are young women, typically between fifteen and twenty years of age, who have chosen to train in an arts profession with roots in the merchant culture and pleasure quarters of the Edo period (1603–1867). Their archaic hairstyles and kimono link them to this artistic past, easily identifying them as maiko. Although other geisha communities in Japan once had apprentices, too, the maiko is famously a Kyoto phenomenon today.[13] Chapters 1 and 2 discuss the maiko's community and her career path in detail, but here, in brief, are the defining features of her life in the 2000s. Maiko live and work with geiko in one of Kyoto's five hanamachi, neighborhoods that are the historic and current sites of exclusive teahouses. True to their title as "dancing girls," maiko spend their days in rigorous training in traditional Japanese dance, music, and other arts, joining geiko at evening teahouse parties where they may dance for small groups of mostly male clients. Maiko also perform in spectacular dance productions open to the public in spring and fall and take visible roles in Kyoto festivals. They often promote Kyoto products and tourism by appearing in commercials and booster events in Japan and abroad. Although over 90 percent of maiko in the 2000s hail from outside Kyoto, all must master the lilting Kyoto dialect of Japanese used in the hanamachi—uniformly described by maiko as the hardest part of their training, even for Kyoto-born girls. They must become adept in the customs, dress, and etiquette of these communities. Eligibility requirements are not strict, but the training is, and succeeding in this training can mean going from ordinary teen to a kind of Kyoto celebrity.

Photographs of maiko taken over the past hundred years document the continuity of her costume. But the nature of the maiko's apprenticeship has changed radically over time in terms of her age and obligations. The origins of the role are somewhat hazy. Andrew Maske, an expert on Japanese art, finds few references to maiko in documents of the Edo period, and observes that the maiko "came to specifically mean 'an apprentice geisha dancer,' usually from Kyoto, in the Meiji period (1868–1912)."[14] Author and photographer Kyoko Aihara, who has documented the hanamachi in several books, writes that the practice of inviting local girls who studied dance to perform at banquets in the Pontochō hanamachi near the Kamo River in the 1800s may have been one of the origins of the maiko.[15] By the late 1800s, we observe maiko emblemizing Kyoto in modern art. For one example, the 1893 painting *Maiko* by Kuroda Seiki, designated an Important Cultural Property, features an intent maiko as she sits

FIGURE 2. *Maiko*. 1893. Kuroda Seiki. Important Cultural Property, Tokyo National Museum. Wikimedia Commons.

in front of a window open to the Kamo River (figure 2). By the early twentieth century, maiko "had already come to symbolize the romance of Kyoto," and in the 1920s, we find maiko featured in souvenir color postcards.[16]

We can learn about the lives of maiko in the 1920s and 1930s by referring to Kyoko Aihara's work on their prewar history based on her interviews with former geiko and archival research. Poignantly, she notes that photographs

FIGURE 3. This photograph, likely taken in the Taisho era (1912–26), depicts child maiko. This picture is cited with permission from Kyoto Institute, Library and Archives Website.

of the era, such as the one reproduced in figure 3, show that maiko were mere children.[17] She describes how girls between eleven and thirteen, dressed in colorful maiko finery, would attend teahouse parties. Expected to look pretty and stay quiet, maiko developed a kind of sign language for communicating with each other at parties to relieve their boredom.[18] Girls as young as nine or ten in training to become maiko had a role, too. They would attend parties to serve sake, a custom that also functioned to give clients a glimpse of the future maiko. In an interview with Aihara, the manager of the Tamika teahouse and former geiko Masuda Kazuyo remembered participating in one of these "Maiden Parties" (Shōjo-san no kai) in 1938. She showed Aihara a photograph of herself in costume for the event. Her finely patterned kimono, bright red collar, and hair ornaments emphasize her tender age.[19] Many maiko in this era and well into the postwar period were likely daughters of geiko or others associated with Kyoto's hanamachi. It was not unusual to see these girls already wearing the maiko's formal hairstyle at their graduation from elementary school. Their youth helped establish the maiko's persona as childlike, an image of innocence idealized even in the 2000s when teens take on the role. Publicly displayed photographs of maiko celebrated their youthful appearance in this era. Aihara recounts how the photography shop Bijindō (Hall of Beauties) across from the famed Minamiza Theater in Kyoto used to display approximately fifty photographs of the prettiest maiko and geiko of the day. Among the beauties was one who had debuted as a maiko in 1934, the eleven-year-old Kosue.[20] Empathizing with the maiko of the 1930s, Aihara writes, "Whenever I look at Kosue's photograph, I am keenly aware of how the maiko of the past were still children, small in frame, and *obokoi*, that is, cherubic and charming."[21] This public display of maiko in the 1930s points to acceptance, and even civic pride in Kyoto's young maiko.

The age of the maiko and the legal terms of her apprenticeship changed after the war. No longer could children assume the role. The Labor Standards Law of 1947, with some caveats, stipulated fifteen years as the minimum age for full-time employment. This meant that prospective maiko would typically finish middle school before their debut, as is still the case. At this point, too, the apprenticeship no longer had the power to bind a girl to the geisha house. Before the war, when it was not uncommon for parents to receive payment from a geisha house in return for indenturing their daughter, the girl was reduced to debt bondage, required to fulfill her contract or repay the money. Finding a suitor with enough funds to buy her contract was one way out. Many popular Japanese films and novels of the 1920s and 1930s dramatize tales of girls' self-sacrifice for their families as they volunteer—or are pushed—to geisha houses in various parts of Japan.[22] In her 1957 memoir, translated as *Autobiography of a Geisha*, Masuda Sayo describes the suffering, abuse, sexual servitude—and later stigmatization—that she endured after her indenture to a rural geisha house in Nagano in the late 1930s.[23] In marked contrast, since 1947, girls not raised in the hanamachi but enamored of the maiko role must approach a hanamachi elder for permission to become her apprentice. Their parents or guardians must give their consent, since the girl is a minor. No money is exchanged, and the girl may quit at any time. Chapter 2 details the contemporary apprenticeship, but suffice to say here, many prospective maiko in the 2000s quit the apprenticeship after only a few weeks due to its rigor and the stringent hierarchy of the hanamachi. Those that do complete the apprenticeship, which may take five or six years, emerge ready to become self-supporting, artistically accomplished geiko.

The issue of the maiko's control over her sexuality remains the most sensitive aspect of her history. Concerns about the exploitation of maiko and young geiko and geisha linked them to prewar and early postwar anti-prostitution protests, legal initiatives, and sympathetic film depictions. At some point in her apprenticeship, the maiko was expected to perform the *mizuage* in which a longtime client paid to be the first man to have sexual intercourse with her.[24] After the mizuage, the maiko would wear a new hairstyle, a sign of her sexual initiation, and hence, her adulthood.[25] Considering this practice in view of the custom of arranged marriage through the 1950s makes the maiko's experience less unusual, if no less painful, as others have pointed out. Many a bride had sex for the first time in her life with the groom she met on her wedding day. Yet, as a commercial transaction that occurred outside marriage, the mizuage stigmatized the maiko—and geiko, too—as women of the *mizu shōbai*, literally, the "water trade" of entertainment and sex for purchase, separating them from the propriety of wives.

Former Gion geiko (Gion is one of Kyoto's geiko districts) and prolific author Mineko Iwasaki strenuously disagrees with any association of the maiko as prostituted, even in the past, and Yamato Waki stresses this point, too, in her manga series, *Kurenai niou*.[26] Histories of the hanamachi published in Japan in the 2000s, however, acknowledge the sexual victimization of maiko, casting the discredited custom as "prewar." But they state at the outset that, despite the mistaken impressions "many Japanese" may continue to hold, the hanamachi no longer engages in the sex trade. It is an arts community. All millennial texts state that the contemporary mizuage is only a sartorial transition, a sign of a maiko's maturity in the apprenticeship. Nonetheless, the stigma—associated with maiko, geisha, and their community—has endured. In 1983, Liza Dalby observed: "Would one boast of one's connection with geisha or proudly present an evening of their entertainment to the visiting Queen of England? Most certainly. Would one want one's daughter to become a geisha? Probably not."[27]

Tracing the lingering effects of this stigma, one finds evidence in millennial literature of parents from the 1960s into the 2000s opposed to their daughters becoming maiko, as we see in the personal accounts discussed in chapter 3. While most authors do not give the reason for this opposition, we can imagine that the maiko's past association with sex work is one factor. It is also likely that a girl's decision to forego high school to become a maiko would concern parents in a society that values academic achievement. As well, parents of maiko might fear appearing financially unable or unwilling to raise their daughters to adulthood. Siblings may object, too. One maiko remembers how her sister warned that the apprenticeship would harm her chances for marriage.[28]

How did the maiko, once stigmatized as a victim of sexual prey, become a positive icon of Japanese girlhood and Kyoto artistry in the 2000s? It is difficult to name a single turning point for even after the legal changes of the early postwar, including the law banning prostitution that took effect in 1958, the stigma held. In the 1950s debates leading to the prohibition on prostitution, anti-prostitution activists argued that the geisha system provided a kind of loophole for sex work to continue in Japan in the guise of entertainment. Investigating this debate, Caroline Norma discusses how the anti-prostitution crusader Kanzaki Kiyoshi and feminist Yamakawa Kikue charged in the 1950s that claims of hanamachi artistry served to obfuscate and legitimate sex work at elite levels.[29] Influential films for mass audiences in the 1950s, as we see in chapter 4, charged that the maiko's youth and artistry veiled a sordid reality of victimization that failed to abide by the new Constitution; one movie suggested that autograph-hunting high school girls who chased after maiko for photographs on their Kyoto field trips had no awareness of this.[30] But charming portraits existed in the early postwar, too. The April 1954 issue of the girls' magazine *Shōjo* ran the funny illustrated fantasy of a fully costumed maiko enjoying a day in New York city.[31] In 1959, writer A. C. Scott observed the maiko image on all kinds of Kyoto souvenirs, "on postcards, posters, brochures, towels, crockery and anything else that is available to put pictures on."[32] Cynically, Scott adds that tourists to Kyoto so expected to see maiko that even young geiko dressed in maiko finery to meet their expectations.[33] In 1961, the bittersweet film *Maiko no kyūjitsu* (Maiko holiday), produced in Kyoto and inspired by *Roman Holiday*, portrayed the budding romance of a maiko, who masquerades as an ordinary girl, and a Tokyo university student visiting Kyoto. Although the film does not mention sexual servitude, it implies that the unbridgeable gap in their social status forces them to part; she is destined to become a geiko, not a wife.[34]

It appears that the maiko's reputation transformed in tandem with Japan's growing domestic affluence in the 1960s and emergence as an economic power on the global stage. National magazines featured articles on Japanese entertainers at maiko parties in the 1960s and visitors to Japan like the British model Twiggy posed in Kyoto for photographs with maiko in 1967.[35] Maiko danced at the 1970 Japan World Exposition, Osaka (Expo '70), and welcomed high-profile visitors, greeting President Ford in 1974 and Queen Elizabeth in 1975. Yet, as discussed in chapter 1, financial downturns, changing entertainment tastes, and expanding educational and employment opportunities for young women made recruiting maiko increasingly difficult. By the 1980s, Kyoto tourist concerns hired high school girls to dress and stroll as maiko to meet visitors' expectations about the sights of the old capital. In 1985, the phenomenon of *kankō maiko* (tourists' maiko) even figured in one of writer Yamamura Misa's murder mysteries.[36]

Controversies over sexual exploitation in the 1990s likely influenced requirements for the maiko's representation as Kyoto's girl mascot. In the late 1990s, Japan became embroiled in controversies surrounding international movements against the sexual exploitation of children, emerging as "a pariah among the advanced industrial countries."[37] David Leheny explains that "critics claimed (with questionable accuracy) that by the late 1990s as much as 80 percent of the world's child pornography originated in Japan."[38] To show adherence to international norms, the Japanese Diet approved with unanimous support in 1999 The Law for Punishing Acts Related to Child Prostitution and Child Pornography and for Protecting Children. Leheny observes that critics in Japan saw this law as intended to eradicate compensated dating (*enjo kōsai*), a phenomenon of high school girls spending time with men for money which had stirred moral panic.[39] At the same time, as Sharon Kinsella has argued, Japanese politicians sought to dampen rising criticism abroad of Imperial Japan's wartime enslavement and prostitution of "comfort women" (*ianfu*) by making the delinquent high school girls a convenient decoy.[40] I assume that amid these controversies, representations of the millennial maiko required resonance with purity and virtue. Although none of the maiko texts I have seen locates the maiko in this historical context, my sense is that near the end of the twentieth century, the maiko was distinguished from other girl types in Japan as being especially mannered and contained. The maiko had long been Kyoto's mascot, her image emblazoned on souvenirs, as we have seen; in the late 1990s, however, I do not believe this usage could have continued had the maiko's image not been pristine.

The visibility and sexuality associated with the delinquent high school girl of the 1990s no doubt contributed to the elevation of the maiko as the millennial good girl and bears discussion here. Known colloquially as *kogal*, these teens became associated with urban youth territory such as Tokyo's Harajuku and Shibuya districts.[41] Media hype about kogals missed the transgressive creativity of girls' culture, which, Laura Miller shows, extended to inventive handwriting, slang, and "print club" photographic fun with girlfriends.[42] It was their apparent defiance of feminine codes that first incited concern. Kogals stood out for their bleached hair, heavy makeup emphasizing large, round eyes, tanned skin, and rolled-up school uniform skirts, provoking waves of media attention.[43] Christine Yano reads their style against the minutiae of school regulations stipulating correctness in attire and behavior, and the long-held ideals of Japanese beauty that valued "black hair, pale skin, almond-shaped eyes."[44] She also highlights how kogals reflected "girls gaining control of their consumer lives and in-group expression."[45] In contrast, the maiko's equally eye-catching appearance modeled traditional, even anachronistic features of feminine beauty and deportment. She spoke the old language of Kyoto, not the new slang, and as an apprentice, she towed the line. As we see in chapter 6, Sato Masao's cartoon of a "high school graduate maiko" creates humor by imagining the unlikely blend of kogal-like effrontery and the maiko's costume. Sharon Kinsella contends that much of the moral panic surrounding the kogal focused on her connection to compensated dating and materialism, disparaging the teens as unfit future mothers who would cause the downfall of Japan, fueling racialized diatribes against them and their tanned skin as non-Japanese.[46] Vitriol about compensated dating landed on the girls, not the men soliciting them. Although the maiko, too, participates in entertainment for older men, she works within a heavily supervised, codified environment, and as an apprentice, she keeps only tips. These circumstances mute the maiko's own imbrication in materialism and the sexualization of the girl. The maiko's trajectory as a geiko, an independent single woman, however, leads her into delinquent territory, too, underscoring why maiko narratives tend to revolve around the girl, not her potential geiko future.

Discussion of the maiko and commodified sexuality and intimacy inevitably circle back to the mizu shōbai. As Liza Dalby explains, "For the most part, geisha manage to float near the top of mizu shōbai society," a broad, diverse industry which "has its sordid undercurrents . . . [but] also holds undeniable glamor."[47] The industry has earned much scholarly attention in Japanese studies. Social scientists have studied hostess bars, host clubs, and the more recent phenomenon of maid cafés.[48] They have examined the status and labor of Filipinas as hostesses and the labor conditions of Japanese sex workers.[49] Scholars have also shown how the mizu shōbai includes clubs that welcome gender variance—gay bars and transgender clubs.[50] The literature on maiko, especially interviews in the 2000s with women leaders in the hanamachi, as we see in chapters 1 and 2, explicitly distances the geiko's community from the mizu shōbai, pointing to hanamachi artistry, etiquette, exclusivity, and preservation of fine Japanese traditions as marking this difference. Nonetheless, one can see some broad commonalities between the teahouses and other venues, including maid cafés, in creating welcoming, "healing" fantasy spaces between work and home, establishing rituals, building relationships, and nurturing clients' sense of belonging.

Before leaving this historical overview, I should say a few words about the maiko's renowned role as the subject of artwork. The apprentice has figured as an artist's subject in various modern formats—Western-style painting, modern prints, illustration, photography, and nihonga (neo-traditional Japanese paintings). It is not unusual to encounter paintings of maiko in museums in Japan, and some artists are most admired for their maiko portraits. Twentieth-century artists and illustrators much discussed in Japanese studies today such as Yumeji Takehisa, Takabatake Kashō, and Nakahara Jun'ichi, known for their popular illustrations in girls' magazines, created many maiko images. Their distinctive styles make each artist's maiko easily identifiable. Amid this history of men creating maiko art, nihonga painter Morita Rieko stands out as a woman who became a trusted hanamachi insider in the 2000s and has earned acclaim for her luminous, even goddess-like paintings of maiko.[51] *Shou II* (Attire II, 2002), reproduced here (figure 4), features a maiko costumed for her misedashi debut. Standing tall and gazing assertively at the viewer, she holds out the long sleeves of her kimono. An enormous pine tree reminiscent of the Noh stage rises behind her. Natural elements—flowers, maple leaves, an ocean wave blend into the patterns on her kimono, framing the maiko as heir to ancient Japanese aesthetic traditions.

Contemporary art creates humorous and fantastic maiko, too, underscoring the millennial maiko's representation as a playful girl figure, not a victim. In the 2000s, Osugi Shinji, a well-known artist in Kyoto, paints primitive-looking maiko with enormous eyes, big hair, and a profusion of hair ornaments creating crowns of color atop their heads.[52] His work adorns coffee mugs, cell phone covers, and even a Kyoto city bus. Tamura Yoshiyasu, a manga artist, painter, and illustrator depicts magical maiko-like girls with piercing blue eyes.[53] In 2018, collaborations with high-profile women artists Mika Ninagawa and Yayoi Kusama lent Kyoto's hanamachi some edgy visual cool and color.[54] Although beyond the scope of this book, it would be intriguing to follow this visual history of the maiko, investigating whether changing art trends mirrored her shifting social status.

FIGURE 4. This nihonga painting depicts the maiko as a goddess at her *misedashi* debut. *Shou II* (Attire II). 2002. Courtesy of Morita Rieko.

CAPTURING THE MAIKO LOOK: TRADITION, COSPLAY, GENDERED FANDOM

The maiko's distinctive look most defines her millennial role. What she wears and how she wears it, how she talks and moves when in formal dress—produce her public image (figure 5). Each element of the maiko's look has a history, and in turn, each serves to enhance narratives and artwork about maiko, emphasizing her role as Kyoto's quintessential girl. Former geiko Kiriki Chizu ascribes the maiko's appeal as an "invitation to an extraordinary world," writing, "One reason everyone adores maiko is that they can wear the gorgeous, charming outfits that others can't."[55] Dressing as a maiko invests a girl with the glamour and weight of tradition. She wears fine things, many of museum quality and exorbitant in price. The lore associated with every aspect of her appearance grounds each component in Kyoto craftsmanship. Wearing them, the ordinary girl becomes the Kyoto maiko, enacting tradition, and in turn, she gives new life—immediacy and relevance—to these talismans of the past. Producers of photography books, tourist brochures, and guides to the hanamachi take pleasure in conveying the visual appeal of the maiko. They zoom in on discreet elements of her wardrobe, explaining the history, craftsmanship, and dress codes for each. Authors of maiko novels and manga weave this lore into their narratives and graphics, too, often as a focal point for moving their story ahead.

Maiko in formal garb wear heavy clothing that is not easy to manage, but many prospective apprentices find the chance to dress as maiko the enticing aspect of the role. Stiff hairstyles must be maintained for days at a time, requiring the use of a pillowed stand that elevates the neck and protects the hair at night. For formal occasions, maiko apply cosmetics that signal past customs, too, and a tradition of performance makeup. Although elements of every maiko's formal dress are uniform, such as the *darari obi* that hangs down her back and high *okobo* sandals, for instance, the patterns of each kimono and obi are unique. Dressed by her *okiya* mother, the maiko gradually learns how to express creativity and personal taste within these traditions. Since the maiko's unique dress blurs the lines among uniform, costume, and fashion, I will use these terms interchangeably in this book. As we see in chapter 3, maiko have a heightened sense of being "on duty" when in uniform. We may also say that the maiko wears a costume. That is, when in full formal regalia, the maiko wears a complete ensemble that re-creates the past, references sartorial traditions no longer practiced, and suggests the flair of theatrical

FIGURE 5. Off to an engagement in Pontochō, the maiko wears the long *darari obi* and *kanzashi* hair ornaments, classic symbols of her attire. 2015. Courtesy of Diane Kaczor.

performance. Fashion comes into play here, too, as the maiko's dress reflects continual change within tradition. Her clothing responds to changing seasons and maturity in her role and encompasses newly designed kimono and *kanzashi* hair ornaments. It is the maiko's relationship to the expectations surrounding her dress—as uniform, costume, and fashion—that mark her involvement in the "maiko masquerade."

The masquerade—as tourist fun reduced to costuming alone—has created a veritable cottage industry of studios specializing in costuming and photographing tourists as maiko. The vogue responds to what Jennifer Prough identifies as the "recent focus on the personalized and participatory in tourism branding."[56] This maiko makeover experience (*maiko henshin taiken*) offers travelers a cosplay experience like others at popular tourist sites in Japan.[57] For the equivalent of $80 to $120, dressers will apply classic maiko cosmetics, help the client into the kimono and obi chosen from among their offerings, and finish with a wig and kanzashi ornaments. The client pulls on *tabi* socks, slips on high okobo sandals, and learns to hold the maiko's formal carrying case as instructed. The studio takes photographs of the transformed client, and for an extra fee, allows the client to walk outside in Kyoto in her maiko finery. Former geiko Kiriki Chizu speculates that "if such studios had existed in my youth, I may have satisfied my curiosity" that way rather than becoming a maiko.[58]

The maiko makeover experience appeals to young and old, domestic and international tourists alike. Experts on maiko, management professor Kumiko Nishio and *Chiyogiku* series writer Nanami Haruka, have both written about their photo-studio experiences.[59] Japanese students on high school field trips are fans. Groups of friends, mother and daughter pairs, do the activity together and post their photos on social media. One former geiko who ran a studio in Kamishichiken told me that before the Great Tohoku Earthquake of 2011, she used to costume groups of older women from the area who included the maiko makeover on their trip to Kyoto. Aimee Major Steinberger's 2007 manga sketchbook, *Japan Ai: A Tall Girl's Adventures in Japan*, captures the fun of a six-foot tall American girl becoming a maiko for a few hours.[60] In 2014, one Chinese blogger described traveling to Kyoto with a friend mainly for this experience: "The whole time we were outside in costume, we felt as if we really were maiko." To her surprise, she and her friend found themselves surrounded by a group of Chinese tourists excitedly snapping photos as their guide told them how lucky they were to have this unusual chance to see a maiko. Finally, in a small voice, she confessed, "I am Chinese."[61] It is the convincing look of these makeovers and the eagerness of tourists to take photos, even if they suspect the girl may not be an actual maiko, that worries some in the hanamachi.[62] It makes it difficult to manage the maiko's image, styled as the epitome of fine deportment, amid the improvisations of nearly identical "maiko."

I do not consider these faux maiko examples of "yellow face" or akin to the geisha girl get-ups in the United States that demean Asians and Asian Americans. As a tourist industry run by Japanese in Japan, maiko cosplay confirms Japaneseness as play, as a desirable masquerade, and as an experience in which Japanese are in control. Studios apply maiko cosmetics to everyone identically. If there were non-ethnically Japanese maiko, they would wear this makeup on the job. This cosplay calls attention to the homogeneity of maiko, imagining any person of other ethnicity, age, or gender becoming a maiko only as a funny costume experience. We can also see how this frankest of maiko masquerades elevates the bar for actual maiko. After all, if any girl can fool tourists simply by getting in costume, what makes the real apprentice any different? Is this all just a range of costume experiences? The emphasis on training maiko in etiquette, language, and deportment, as we see in chapter 2, not only distances the apprentice from past stigma, but also distinguishes her from the contemporary faux maiko tourist. The maiko may feel an imposter at times, too, but she must never give her public that impression.

The popularity of maiko costume play points to the gendered differences in maiko fan practices. Tourist activities encourage girls and women to identify with maiko femininity through makeovers, buying maiko charms and cosmetics, and dining in maiko-themed cafés.[63] But men are positioned as maiko observers, most often as photographers. Few men have the wherewithal to become teahouse clients, but anyone can become a fan photographer. Male fans—both Japanese and those from abroad—most support maiko by taking photographs of them in public spaces and posting these online. On the day of a maiko's debut, for example, crowds comprised largely of amateur male photographers take pictures as they follow the maiko making her ritual greetings to local teahouses. The 2007 slapstick film *Maiko Haaaan!!!* satirizes one man's obsession with maiko and his competition with other amateur photographers to upload the choicest shots.[64] Many professional photographers—Japanese and international, men and women—have established close relationships with maiko and geiko, publishing books of their work.

THE MAIKO AS SHŌJO, KYOTO AS GIRLS' PLAYGROUND

The maiko's look, as we have seen, telegraphs her status as a Japanese girl, a shōjo. Generally glossed in English as "girl," the shōjo as cultural icon of modern Japan has generated much scholarship in Japanese studies. In brief, the shōjo has been symbolic of girlhood freedom since the advent of modern girls' schools in the late 1800s. In the 1970s, the shōjo became associated with consumer pleasures and the kawaii culture of toy-like characters. Both roles inform maiko representations: she is the shōjo artist and, as Kyoto character brand, she is also the shōjo object. What interests me most here in pondering the maiko as shōjo is the way her image works in Kyoto to create spaces of female pleasure, sites and things that particularly welcome girls and women, domestic and international, to play, eat, shop, do makeovers, and engage in romantic fantasies of the maiko's shōjo girlhood. The historical maiko, on the other hand, emerged in a world of play for purchase, it was a hanamachi world geared to providing pleasure to Japanese men, and not a general tourist destination. Contemporary maiko fantasies, however, shift the concern from pleasing men to inviting girls to have fun, and extend this girlish play into all kinds of small consumables and sweet experiences, erasing the maiko's past associations with child labor and gendered servitude. While we are always aware of the maiko as a figure who points to the past in the present, her past has been renovated to produce romantic notions of an authentic Japanese girlhood and even a kind of maiko chic.

A caveat is in order here. Fetishized representations of the shōjo as a Japanese girl in a sailor-style uniform in popular culture and pornography are well known. But I am referring here to the shōjo as a nostalgic figure for women, one with deep roots in fiction, manga, and other entertainments reminiscent of girlhood, emblematic of a world apart from adult men. By the same token, many women in Japan treat their high school uniform as a keepsake, a sentimental reminder of their youth.[65] I should say that shōjo aesthetics do not appeal to all girls and women in Japan.[66] They do attract some boys and men who embrace the release of gender constraints the shōjo embodies. Indeed, literary critic Takahara Eiri posited the notion of adopting "girl consciousness" as a claim to psychic freedom that exceeds the boundaries of gender and age.[67]

Since the late 1800s, the shōjo has associated girlhood with sentiment, free expression, and friendship. Connected to the advent of sex-segregated girls' schools, modern uniforms, Western learning, and dormitory life free of parental supervision, the shōjo marked a new stage in the privileged woman's life course. Neither child nor adult, the shōjo enjoyed freedom from the pressures to (re)produce. Illustrated magazines for girls, replete with sentimental stories, established the narrative lines and aesthetic codes of girls' culture.[68] This literary and visual world proved formative to girls' culture throughout the twentieth century. In an influential 1982 essay on shōjo, scholar Honda Masuko encapsulates the shōjo aesthetic as *hirahira*, that is, the "fluttering" of ribbons and bows in girls' fiction that communicates the "ephemerality" of girls' culture. Honda envisions this realm as a hidden space vibrant with the "lush 'colors, fragrances, and sounds' that resonate uniquely with the aesthetics of the girl."[69] The shōjo's realm was a marginalized one, but it was this very marginality, according to Hiromi Tsuchiya Dollase, that allowed girls to lay claim to an imaginative territory all their own.[70] The hirahira elements of the maiko's costume with its glittering kanzashi and dangling obi, her chaste life within the closed, feminine world of the hanamachi, and her vocational identity as a Japanese girl, all make her heir to these utopian notions of the shōjo.

As Kyoto's shōjo mascot, the maiko also aligns with late twentieth-century fascination with the girl. Her image links to the explosion of kawaii aesthetics, fancy character goods like Sanrio's Kitty-Chan, and shōjo consumerism of the 1970s and 1980s. In affluent Japan, as Anne Allison remarks, the shōjo epitomized freedom from adult pressures, representing "the counterweight to the enterprise society: a self-indulgent pursuer of fantasies and dreams through consumption of merchandise."[71] New fashions, fiction, innovations in manga for girls, and the continuing popularity of the Takarazuka Revue displayed these girl fantasies. Moreover, the shōjo as a figure of escape generated all kinds of childlike goods for adults, extending kawaii aesthetics beyond girls' culture and across the country. Charming mascots for townships, baseball teams, corporations, and even the Self-Defense Forces became commonplace. Christine Yano speaks to this multibillion-dollar character industry as transforming "urban Japan [into] a kind of visual theme park of kawaii as an embodied, commodified world."[72] Yano highlights the comforting presence of these characters, writing that cute characters "transform the adult world—fraught with responsibilities, dangers, and global matters—into a haven of play and nostalgized childhood."[73] The maiko, as shōjo mascot, performs the same functions for Kyoto, casting the old capital as a "haven of play," too. She, too, becomes the kind of kawaii "enchanted commodity" which Allison argues transmits pleasure, intimacy, and identity.[74] As a road sign, the maiko greets drivers on their way to Kyoto. As a plastic souvenir doll, she makes Kyoto small, inexpensive, and vulnerable. Costumed as maiko, other well-known characters—Pikachu (figure 6), Kitty-chan, and Disney's Minnie Mouse—suggest that even they enjoy touristic escape into the character fantasy of Kyoto's pretty girl.

Consider this poster published by the Kyoto Municipal Transportation Bureau in 2011 to attract female consumers to Kotochika, a new underground

FIGURE 6. Popular Pokémon character Pikachu attired as a maiko at newly opened Pokémon Center at Shijō/Karasuma in Kyoto, 2019. Courtesy of Jennifer Prough.

shopping area in Kyoto (figure 7).[75] The poster frames a wave of young women wearing ordinary clothes, but adorned in maiko makeup, hairstyle, and kanzashi ornaments as they head to Kyoto for fun. It imagines a space of nearly identical young women and no one else, trading on associations of shōjo consumerism, dress-up play, and friendship. The poster beckons women to come to a city where girl-pleasures are central. Characterizing shopping as a women's activity, branded by maiko, the poster promises a doubly feminine enjoyment of Kyoto. Contemporary maiko advertisements like these switch the focus from pleasing men to imagining girls at play, as though it is their turn to have fun. As Yano writes about Hello Kitty fans, "This temporary return to the land of kawaii is

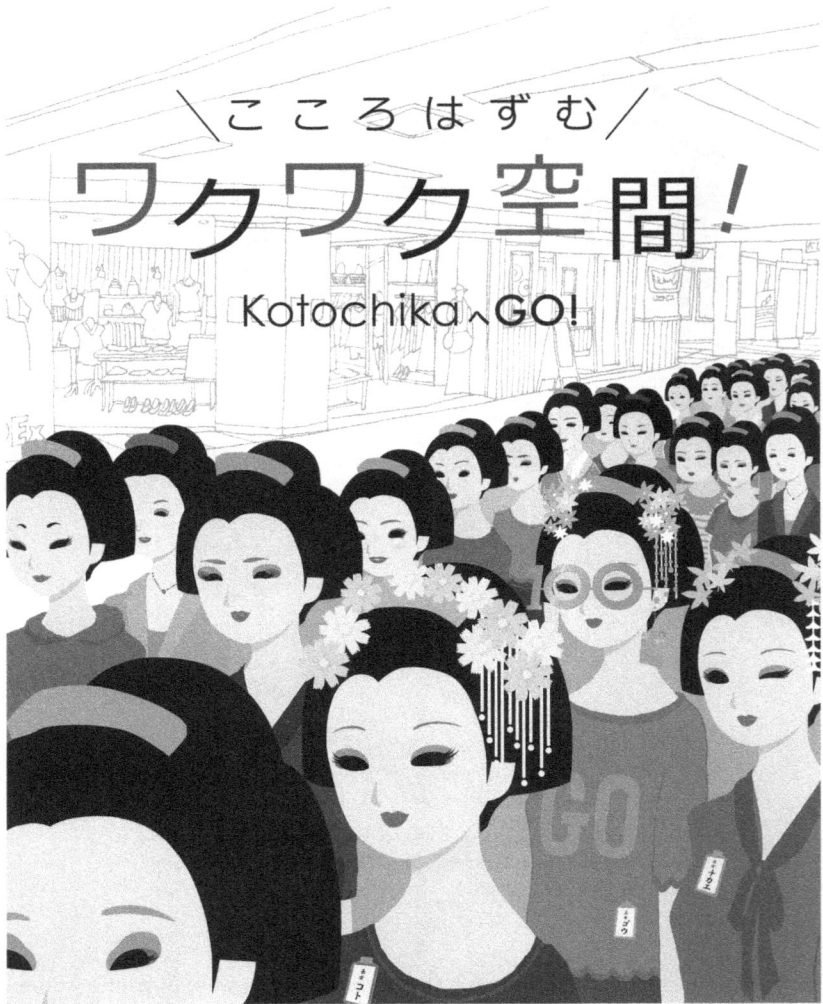

FIGURE 7. This 2011 poster promotes Kotochika, Kyoto's underground shopping arcade, using maiko imagery to communicate a women-friendly experience. Courtesy of Kyoto Municipal Transportation Bureau.

part of the masquerade of adult women as shōjo."[76] That many consumers have the sense of deliberately choosing to act beneath their station by embracing Kitty-Chan becomes what Yano calls "the wink on pink" that makes these acts transgressive. Casting this within a broader Japanese cultural context, Yano considers how "*asobi* [play] forms an important part of the cultural frame in Japan: far more than child's play, asobi forms an integral part of adult creativity," that can be seen "as frame, as performance, as game, and as sly pleasure."[77] In the same way, consuming maiko kitsch and doing maiko makeovers takes girls and women into equally resistant territory, transforming the maiko from plaything for older men to the maiko as girl seeking her own pleasures, often with girlfriends, and without men—although many men may imagine being-this-girl-themselves quite seductive.

Maiko fandom also translates into curiosity about elements of her wardrobe that girls and women may adapt to create their own tradition-inflected chic. Fans' affection for Japanese crafts related to maiko and maiko accessories as signifiers of girls' culture put a new spin on Japonisme. Old-fashioned parasols, fans, inexpensive kanzashi, and maiko-style name cards—the material culture of maiko—offer consumers another means of borrowing the maiko's aura. It recalls the nineteenth- and twentieth-century passion abroad for the fans, screens, and vases that connoted a whiff of the exotic. As Susan Napier has explained, this was a desire connected to notions of leisure, fantasy, and play, and it is a passion revived in Japan and abroad.[78] Whether women consuming maiko-related objects in the 2000s believe they are helping to preserve crafts, buying tradition, or making a sly "wink on pink," they are engaging in a campaign, as we see in the Kotochika poster, to make Kyoto a place inviting to women as consumers. The cute maiko as Kyoto character brand blends Old Japan with Cool Japan, turning the esoteric capital into a welcoming touristic playground.[79]

GEISHA STUDIES

My research on millennial representations of the maiko draws on an abundance of scholarship on geisha. I introduce the three strands of Geisha studies here to give a sense of the subject's transnational richness and complexity. First, we take up examinations of geisha history and their representation in Japan; secondly, analyses of geisha fascination abroad; and finally, college courses in the United States that employ research from both these areas to explore broad social issues and the dynamics of representation.

Research on geisha in Japan shows that no single definition of the geisha captures the shifts in her role and cultural status over time and geographical location. Even a quick snapshot of junctures in geisha history shows enormous changes over time. Geisha history stretches back to the pleasure quarters of the Edo period when the original geisha, which means "arts person," were men known as *taikomochi* (drum carriers) who entertained wealthy clients with music, dance, and comedy in the seventeenth century.[80] By 1800, the geisha was recognized as a woman talented in the arts and adept in playing the samisen, a string instrument.[81] In their heyday in the 1890s, geisha turned heads in celebrity-style photographs and as fashion leaders in major urban centers.[82] Groups of geisha cheered on public speakers in the 1890s, launched patriotic activities during the Russo-Japanese War (1904–5), and figured in picture postcards sent to men at the front. Meiji intellectual men praised geisha as exquisite, highly cultivated national symbols.[83] At the same time, geisha were maligned by the Japan Women's Christian Temperance Union and supported by infamous New Women in the 1910s.[84] In 1935, over seventy-four thousand women in Japan identified as geisha; a few worked at the glittering heights of the profession in major cities, while many more labored in exploitive conditions of indenture and sexual servitude.[85] After the war, hanamachi in Kyoto and Tokyo quickly revived, attracted American men stationed in Japan, and later thrived in the growing affluence of the 1960s. By the end of the twentieth century, geisha were largely associated with Kyoto, refined etiquette, and traditional arts, and were only about two hundred in number.[86]

Research on the geisha encompasses a wealth of English-language scholarship on the performing and visual arts, labor history, and feminist research on gender and sexuality. Scholars have considered geisha as subjects on stage in Kabuki, Bunraku puppet theater, and modern plays. Other research takes account of representations of geisha in the visual field of photography, various modes of painting, and printmaking. Analyses of geisha as characters in twentieth-century films and literature reveal the changing valence of the geisha and differences of regional and socioeconomic status among geisha. My work is in many ways inspired by and benefits greatly from earlier English-language studies but departs from their largely ethnographic approach. Liza Dalby's influential 1983 book *Geisha*, based on her mid-1970s fieldwork in the Pontochō hanamachi, pioneered academic studies of geisha culture. Dalby explains how the communities work, their customs and rituals, and the arts that geisha practice and their aesthetic codes. Most interesting for this study is Dalby's historical analysis of the changing characterizations and status of geisha from the Edo era to the 1970s. Kelly M. Foreman, an ethnomusicologist and samisen artist who did fieldwork in the hanamachi in the 1990s, took the study of the geisha arts and community culture into the 2000s. Foreman's 2008 book, *The Gei of Geisha: Music, Identity and Meaning* offers an excellent in-depth analysis of performance structure, the geisha's relationship to arts masters, and contemporary patronage. Trained in Japanese literary and cultural history, I have focused my work on investigating how disparate texts in Japan, often authored by women, from the 1910s to the present have variously imagined Japanese women's lives. I bring this textual approach to exploring representations of the millennial maiko. This approach examines how popular media identify the maiko for a national audience. After all, very few Japanese will ever meet a maiko or geiko firsthand and even fewer will attend a party in the hanamachi, but mass audiences have encountered maiko-related films, fiction, and visual images. What maiko stories are available to the public imagination in contemporary Japan? How do they compete or reinforce other notions of Japanese girlhood in the public sphere? These are the questions I wish to bring to Geisha studies.

Research on geisha fascination outside Japan surveys an almost equally large field of cultural production. This scholarship stresses that most narratives created in Europe, the United States, and Australia have little to do with actual geisha and everything to do with the changing domestic concerns of various historical moments. Dalby writes, "What we see here is an idealized geisha, excised from its Japanese context to float culture-free in the global imagination."[87] Analysis of the geisha icon in *Madame Butterfly* tales, musical comedies and films, novels, fashions, painting, advertising, and rock music—cultural texts produced from the late 1800s to the present—have uncovered messages about sexuality, gender identity, women's rights, racialized hierarchies and interracial romance, and imperialism.[88] Masquerades occur frequently. Instances abound of "yellow face"—Anglo actors in Asian roles—and more recently, "white-washing"—cases in which Anglo actors play characters originally established as Asian. Scholars show how the geisha, cast variously as the feminine submissive, femme fatale, artist, and/or symbol of decadent sexuality, could conflate with Japan in the popular imagination. In the 1950s and early 1960s, for instance, when movie stars and fashion models were becoming the postwar icons of femininity in Japan, high-profile Holly-wood movies and TV comedy gave new life to geisha in American popular culture. Arthur Golden's 1997 novel *Memoirs of a Geisha* and its film adaptation in 2005 revived global attention to geisha.[89]

College courses on geisha, the third area in Geisha studies, creatively employ both strands of existing scholarship to open fresh questions on the construction and symbolic weight of cultural icons.[90] Most arose in response to the revived fascination with geisha instilled by *Memoirs of a Geisha*, guiding students' critical analysis of popular texts. Incorporating methods and building on knowledge from all three strands of Geisha studies, I focus on close readings of Japanese written and visual texts. I want to understand how these represent Kyoto's geiko, their community, and most importantly their maiko apprentices in the twenty-first century to audiences in Japan. In taking this textual approach, I adhere to Sarah J. Pradt and Terry Kawashima's advice on representation to students in their 1998 geisha course. Although initially concerned that a class on geisha might reinforce Orientalist stereotypes, Pradt and Kawashima found that, on the contrary, most students expressed eagerness "to learn about the 'truth' behind the geisha stereotype."[91] The sense of the stereotype as a concealment rather than a social dynamic opened the door for Pradt and Kawashima to explain the main questions driving the class, "What are 'truth' and 'authenticity'? How are cultural boundaries and definitions drawn, and by whom? Why are certain groups of people represented in particular ways at different times and places? Where does gender enter into this picture?"[92] In raising these broad questions, Pradt and Kawashima underscored the politics of representation itself, emphasizing "representations must also be constantly contextualized."[93] They instructed their students to work with icons as "cultural constructions specific to a time and place," mindful that "Japanese textual discussions of the geisha are not necessarily 'more true' than an American one."[94] Following Pradt and Kawashima, I also strive to build the context for twenty-first-century Japanese representations of the maiko, seeking to understand the cultural dynamics and gender politics to which the maiko, as artist and icon, gives visibility. We will find here, too, that no one maiko narrative is truer than another, but all point to certain values and social locations, often playing with notions of concealment, too.

Embarking on a course, and now a book, about maiko and geiko/geisha, I take to heart the concern Pradt and Kawashima raise about reinforcing

Orientalist stereotypes simply by taking up the topic, but like them, I have found students hoping for more. I also share with Pradt and Kawashima an interest in "bridging the divide between Asian and Asian-American studies" in their geisha course. I find the American and Japanese contexts different, and hence, the politics of the geisha masquerades differ, too. For one example of this contextual difference, consider San Francisco artist Scott Tsuchitani's 2004 public artwork, *Memoirs of a Sansei Geisha*, an intervention in the publicity surrounding the massively popular San Francisco Asian Art Museum's exhibit, *Geisha: Beyond the Painted Smile*. Replicating the exhibit poster with a satiric twist, Tsuchitani made two notable changes: he replaced the face of a young geisha with his own, complete with his dark-rimmed glasses, and changed the text to read, "Orientalist Dream Come True. GEISHA: Perpetuating the Fetish."[95]

Tsuchitani's masquerade provokes attention to the ubiquity of Orientalist stereotypes in the American landscape and the attendant diminution or erasure of Asian American men. His satire challenges the cultural assumptions evident in the United States. In this book, however, we move to Japan. While satiric masquerades occur here, too, as we see in chapter 6, they respond to the cultural politics of Japan in the early 2000s. Maiko masquerades and the literature on maiko do launch critiques of Japanese men, but they do so in an environment where Japanese men hold power. Images of maiko, geiko, and their Japanese clients emerge among innumerable other depictions of Japanese, unlike in the United States. The maiko and geiko may function as a cultural other in Japan, too, but in this context, they do not stereotype Japanese.

Analysis of representations of exoticism and Orientalism produced in twenty-first-century Japan must take account of a different context. Geisha have long used mystery to their advantage; as Dalby remarks, "Exoticism is a geisha's stock in trade."[96] Further, the postwar marketing of maiko and geiko/geisha is complicated by Japan's own nation-branding strategies, which often incorporate fantasies of young women. Nancy Stalker observes how Japan's efforts in the 1950s and 1960s to promote its national identity as "feminized purveyor of cherry blossoms and geisha, ikebana and tea ceremony," became "deeply internalized by both domestic and international audiences," and functioned to "erase its wartime image as imperialist aggressor and ameliorate its emerging image as ruthless economic competitor."[97] In the 1970s, maiko dancing at Expo '70, at the government's behest, and greeting foreign dignitaries upheld this artistic, feminine image of Japan. Updating the brand to enhance its Cool Japan tourist campaign in 2009, Japan's Ministry of Foreign Affairs (MOFA) deployed *kawaii taishi* "Ambassadors of Cute"—a trio of young women posing as a Schoolgirl, Lolita, and Harajuku teen—to boost overseas curiosity in Japanese youth fashion.[98]

In tracing maiko narratives produced in Japan mainly in the 2000s, I am interested in how the maiko, geiko, and her hanamachi community are promoted to Japanese audiences. We find nation branding operating here, too. Many fiction and nonfiction narratives communicate mystery, Kyoto traditions, and the maiko as a cultivated form of girlhood to Japanese readers. But we also encounter gently subversive moments and images that push back at these portraits. I should add that, like Dalby, I see maiko and geiko as "embedded in Japanese culture," but neither "a marginal subculture" nor "a microcosm, a symbol, or a typification" of Japan.[99]

MASQUERADE: BECOMING THE MAIKO-LIKE MAIKO

Tropes of masquerade are pervasive in maiko texts of the 2000s. By saying this, I do not mean that apprentices or geiko are fake or the hanamachi is a sham. Rather, I call attention to themes prominent in the narratives. The recurring references to the pleasures of transformation and the dangers of disguise; allusions to the maiko's costume rendering her unrecognizable; and fears of slipping up in maiko uniform—all suggest a kind of masking. Following these dynamics of masking and unmasking offers a useful strategy for linking disparate maiko narratives. Like the history of Western philosophies of masquerade that Efrat Tseëlon distills, we find these Japanese narratives also reveal two approaches to identity. "One assumes the existence of an authentic self. This approach views the mask—real or metaphoric—as covering, on certain occasions, and even deceiving by pretending to be the real self. The other approach maintains that every manifestation is authentic, that the mask reveals the multiplicity of our identity."[100] To unpack the dynamic of masking and authenticity in maiko narratives, I explain the concept of "maiko-likeness" and adjacent notions of acting "like a woman" and "like oneself." I highlight insights from some relevant critical work on masquerades, showing how these prove productive in reading maiko texts in their historical and cultural context.

We begin with the expression "maiko-likeness" (*maiko rashisa*), which comes up frequently in the hanamachi literature of the 2000s. To be called "maiko-like" is high praise for an apprentice. But how could a maiko be anything other than "like a maiko?" Understanding the use of the Japanese adjective *rashii*—and its noun form *rashisa* and adverbial *rashiku*—makes this clear. As linguists Eric McCready and Norry Ogata explain, there are two uses of *rashii*. The first is evidentiary. To put this in the context of maiko, let's say the speaker sees two girls strolling in Kyoto, assumes that their costumes indicate that they are maiko, and exclaims that they are "girls who appear to be maiko (*maiko rashii onna no ko*)." The second use of *rashii* expresses confirmation of the speaker's expectations. A maiko's graceful movement, for example, may prompt the observer to exclaim "how *like a maiko* she is (*maiko rashii*)." In this case, the speaker's expression compliments the young woman on meeting the expectations for maiko performance. By the same token, a maiko caught behaving badly and failing to meet the speaker's standards might be criticized as "unlike a maiko" or, in a stronger translation, even "unworthy of a maiko (*maiko rashikunai*)." This usage of *rashii* clarifies that simply garbing as a maiko is not enough; rather, an apprentice must fully embody maiko-likeness to satisfy observers' expectations. As McCready and Ogata point out, this usage of *rashii* indicates that an "object or situation exemplifies an image the speaker takes to be characteristic of something else."[101] In the maiko's case, this challenges the apprentice to reduce the distance between her "ordinary self" and the "something else" of idealized maiko conduct.

Challenging the maiko to perform in certain ways that satisfy observers' expectations indicates that maiko-likeness encompasses a series of codified behaviors. By cleverly manipulating the codes that confirm observers' expectations, even a boy may earn compliments for maiko-likeness (see chapter 5). This emphasis on codes recalls Judith Butler's work on gender as performative, as iterations of socially constructed gender-appropriate acts.[102] Jennifer Robertson has discussed how actors' manipulation of *kata* ("stylized gestures, movements, intonations, and speech patterns that signify gender") enacts femininity and masculinity on the Takarazuka Revue stage.[103] Descriptions of learning kata in maiko texts, as in other Japanese traditional arts, speak to the importance of daily repetition, observing others, and accepting correction, as one gradually internalizes codes (chapter 2).[104] This internalization reduces the sense of distance between the apprentice and maiko-likeness, and the feeling of artifice.

The demands of maiko-likeness closely resemble the conservative expectations for women to perform *onna rashii*—"feminine" or "woman-like"—behaviors. Historian of Japanese language Nanette Gottlieb remarks that, unsurprisingly women in Japan find the expression annoying, as it "carries very strong overtones of traditional Japanese gender roles for women."[105] Onna rashii behavior calls to mind the virtues of modesty, self-sacrifice, and docility, and cedes qualities such as assertiveness and leadership to the *otoko rashii*—"man-like"—realm of masculinity. In the case of the maiko, there is no masculine equivalent. In maiko texts, a youthful display of femininity—*onna no ko rashii* (like a girl) behavior—is prized. While some maiko find the need to be girlish (or some would even say childish) constraining, as discussed in chapter 2, it is a large part of the maiko's appeal. Embracing a girl persona, the maiko appears free of adult responsibilities, even the womanliness required of onna rashii ideals. Maiko Ichimame, who we meet in chapter 3, takes pleasure in her maiko rashii moments and shows no rush to grow up.

Another concept of likeness is critical here, too—the ideal of *jibun rashii*, living in a manner that suits and expresses one's own self. Popularized in Japanese discourse since the 1980s in women's magazines and state policies alike, jibun rashii presumes an authentic self and the freedom to nurture that self.[106] In her 1998–2000 research in Tokyo, Ayumi Sasagawa discovered that young mothers understood jibun rashii as emancipation from fixed notions of motherhood and the freedom "to determine their own lives—to choose their own sense of how to live."[107] In the 2000s, maiko and geiko narratives, too, celebrate the jibun rashii life, but imagine achieving this as a process. As an apprentice, a girl must endeavor to project maiko-likeness, all the while trying to master the arts and conventions of the hanamachi. But, as a geiko, she must abandon this girlish behavior to act like an adult, "like oneself." Even as this path endorses contemporary belief in attaining the jibun rashii life, it also mirrors to some extent expectations for growth in traditional Japanese arts, where originality flows from internalizing existing conventions. Former geiko Kiriki Chizu, as discussed in chapter 3, found this true in her years of ikebana study.[108] Steeped in hanamachi customs through her apprentice-ship, the young geiko is expected to express individual flair. Stressing her performance as jibun rashii underscores that the contemporary geiko has chosen her life. As one Gion geiko commented in a 2016 interview, "During my days as a maiko, I always kept in mind how a maiko should act, and I felt happy whenever I was told that 'you are maiko-like.' But once I became a geiko, I realized that it was fine to be more like myself (*jibun rashiku*)."[109] Varied notions of likeness in maiko texts inspire moments of masquerade, feelings of authenticity, and quests for self-discovery. The pursuit of likeness inevitably creates conflict between characters and their aspirations to be "like" an idealized self. But moments of feeling whole, as though perfectly resolving this conflict, occur, too. Notably, the self, no matter what ideal likeness it approximates, is gendered in maiko texts.

The sense of femininity itself as an obligatory masquerade of one kind or another extends far beyond maiko texts and maiko-likeness. Literary scholar Gitte Marianne Hansen argues that femininity as masquerade occurs in contemporary Japanese texts of all kinds. Drawing on a host of storylines in media produced in Japan since the 1980s, she identifies cultural messages about normative femininity.[110] Hansen coins the term *contradictive feminin-ity* to illuminate the conflicting messages women in Japan receive about the various roles that a "normal" Japanese woman should be able to perform. These roles encompass traditional femininities such as caregiving and extend to ones appropriate to new roles such as in corporate leadership. Hansen argues that the frequent use of female doppelgänger motifs in popular texts dramatize the fragmentation women may feel in moving among the contra-dictive subject positions in their lives that comprise normative femininity. Maiko masquerades, too, display struggles to accommodate contradictive femininity, employing the doppelgänger motifs that Hansen identified. We see the "transforming woman," a character Hansen defines as extending her abilities to navigate among a range of femininities, in maiko and geiko's per-sonal accounts of their multiple roles (which we will see in chapter 3). We see Hansen's "doubles," too—that is, a character split into two people or compet-ing selves, which together perform the range of contradictive femininities, as exemplified in the twins' tale in *Dandan* and the best friends in *Maiko-san-chi no Makanai-san* (see chapter 4). Such masquerades are entertaining, giving audiences the sense of peeking behind the scenes or the comfort of knowing the real story when watching girls fooling others with their disguises. They show girls making choices between two possible paths. The narratives call attention to the artifice and performativity of maiko-likeness, value jibun rashii goals, but rarely question the social structures and conventions driving multiple expectations for femininity.

Analyses of geisha masquerade in American fiction and films give still other perspectives for approaching Japanese maiko texts. Interpreting the popularity of *Memoirs of a Geisha* and its numerous tropes of masquerade, Allison speculates on readers imagining "play with the border between the exotic and the self."[111] The artifice associated with the geisha creates the sense of the reader trying on a role, too, appropriating "the geisha's performativity and desirability as a fantasy woman," which Allison links to the geisha-inspired fashion that arose in the wake of the novel's success.[112] Film scholar Gina Marchetti's analysis of *My Geisha* and *An American Geisha*, a 1986 TV drama very loosely based on Liza Dalby's geisha research, offers insights into masquerade, too.[113] Marchetti observes how both films depict Anglo adventurers who lose themselves in geisha identity, discover their true femininity, sacrifice their ambitions, and return to their expected position as heterosexual Anglo women in romantic relationships with Anglo men. As geisha impersonators, both characters skillfully traverse "national and cultural borders to create an entirely new self-identity."[114] Marchetti points out that "each film deals with the fantasies that make explicit the potentially radical notion of femininity as a masquerade."[115] Following Gaylyn Studlar, Marchetti sees how the geisha masquerade, as a display of "excessive femininity" and "female transvestism," refutes notions of gender as natural.[116] Rather, these acts of masquerade open opportunities for homoerotic pleasure in gazing at the self-invented geisha and subversive possibilities inherent in displays of race and gender as culturally and historically crafted constructs. Female spectators may enjoy "a fantasy of self-definition and the paradoxical power this put-on femininity has in the male world."[117]

Bringing these critiques of American geisha stories to analysis of the maiko masquerade shows parallels and differences. Japanese audiences for maiko narratives may well feel that they, too, are playing at the border of self and exotic other since the maiko occupies an unusual position in Japan. Female readers may delight in imagining their own transformation, self-invention, "put-on femininity," and homoerotic pleasure. Unlike the American narratives, however, Japanese maiko stories in the 2000s do not create the maiko as alluring, except in the case of the boy maiko. Even the geiko in millennial Japanese narratives is not a femme fatale. Also, unlike in *My Geisha* and *American Geisha*, the maiko never crosses ethnic or national boundaries, only regional ones. I have not found any evidence of mixed-heritage, minority, or non-Japanese girls becoming maiko, in either reality or fiction. Most narratives encourage their readers, assumed to be Japanese, to take pride in the hanamachi as a wellspring of Japanese culture and admire maiko-likeness as an elegant performance of traditional girlhood. They assume that any "ordinary Japanese girl," with effort, can become a maiko. Defining this ordinary girl as a non-Kyoto, ethnically Japanese girl reveals as much about cultural politics in twenty-first-century Japan as her maiko masquerade, as discussed in the conclusion.

Tales of maiko masquerades and the transformation or concealment of ordinary girls recalls public curiosity about other masked icons of Japanese femininity. Symbols of modernity since the late 1920s, the bus guide and elevator girl, discussed by Alisa Freedman and Laura Miller, respectively, continue to inspire nostalgia.[118] This scholarship, too, proves useful for interpreting maiko texts. Like the maiko, bus guides and elevators girls have been fashioned "into figurines and featured in popular songs, novels, uniform fashion shows, films, parodies, and more."[119] Visible in their public roles guiding people on new forms of transport, smart in their modern uniforms, scripted and poised, these "modern girls on the go" underwent training to express carefully cultivated femininity. No wonder they, too, motivated cultural texts about the ordinary girl behind a masquerade.

The transformation of ordinary young women from various class and regional backgrounds into these recognizable urban, public figures compares well to hanamachi training in the 2000s. Millennial maiko recruits, too, represent different regional identities, dialects, and (likely) class backgrounds. They, too, experience transformation through behavioral training and dress. Yet training in codified ways of behaving and interacting with the public often provokes charges of stifling originality, a criticism leveled against the perfect performances of bus guides, elevator girls, and maiko alike. Miller suggests, however, that such codes can also extend freedom, the woman's professional façade enabling "a liberating metamorphosis . . . as her vulnerability in the public gaze is masked or protected by the uniform and scripted speech."[120] This sense of masking, however liberating to the uniformed woman, inevitably fuels public intrigue about a hidden authentic self.[121] But, as Miller reminds us, social scientists "are quick to note [that] all human actions are culturally constructed and performative," even those conducted in private.[122] We find the same tensions between codified performance in public and authenticity offstage framing the literature on maiko. Maiko texts, amid their interplay between maiko rashii and jibun rashii personas, call into question the relationship among a range of identities, not only within a maiko or geiko's public/private path to self-discovery, but in her connection to the hanamachi, her hometown, her family, and Japan.

Maiko masquerade takes many forms in twenty-first-century texts. They communicate a host of competing messages about the self, the other, and others within the self. We may ask how these masquerades, whether revealing a hope for authenticity, liberation in disguise, or an embrace of performativity and many masks, each as authentic as the next, speak to hopes for girlhood in Japan in the 2000s.

CHAPTER I

The Maiko's Hanamachi Home

Elegance. Grace. No place better fits such description than Kyoto's five hanamachi. The charming townscapes, heartfelt hospitality, brilliant dance. It is in these hanamachi that an exquisite culture endures, both material and spiritual, one nearly forgotten in our nation.

—Kyoto Traditional Musical Art Foundation, (Ōkini Zaidan), website 2020

Dazzling in her formal costume, the maiko embodies an unusual vision of Japanese girlhood. Inseparable from her community, this vision continually reminds viewers that the maiko exists to represent the hanamachi, its customs and values. It is her hanamachi home that molds the maiko, provides her wardrobe and training, manages her career, and guides her performance of maiko-likeness. In turn, the maiko offers the hanamachi a youthful face, connecting the old districts to the vitality of contemporary fascination with girlhood and Kyoto tourism. What is the history of this community and its artistic and commercial practices? How do its advocates strive to make the community relevant in the twenty-first century? We turn to the contemporary literature on the hanamachi to explore these questions, learning how it sets the stage for idealizing the maiko.

To understand the millennial maiko's role in representing her community as a site of cultural heritage, this chapter delves into the literature (popular guides, academic studies, and photo books) published about the hanamachi in Japanese in the 2000s. Created mainly by a handful of prolific authors based in Kyoto, whom I will introduce in this chapter, these books offer a wealth of insider information on the hanamachi, appealing to a popular audience. Although they form a relatively small body of literature and take somewhat different approaches, these volumes all aim to communicate the value of the hanamachi as a cultural treasure that offers lessons relevant to Japanese readers' everyday lives and work. Close readings of these books lead me to argue that hanamachi literature defines the community as a wellspring of Japaneseness at its finest, firmly rooted in locale, history, and tradition. As the Kyoto Traditional Musical Art Foundation website asserts, the hanamachi accords respect for "nearly forgotten" modes of Japanese hospitality and the arts.[1] Authors endorse the hanamachi as a restorative site of "slow beauty" in a world bent on speed, and a community that values enduring relationships and face-to-face communication among artists, craftspeople, business owners, and clients.[2] It is a literature that acclaims women's leadership, the increase in women as teahouse clients, and the evolving reputation of the hanamachi as a female-friendly place, but it also prizes gentlemanly clients. Nostalgia for the hanamachi life during the rising affluence of the 1960s emerges in asides in many of these works, too, recalling the Kyoto of trolley cars, literati and merchant culture, tipsy maiko and stylish geiko, and the familiarity of conventional gender roles.

The emphasis on rootedness and nostalgia in hanamachi literature offers an appealing antidote to the sense of social dislocation experienced by many in Japan in the Lost Decades and precedes the emphasis on national bonds (*kizuna*) championed after 3.11 (as the March 11, 2011 earthquake, tsunami, and nuclear plant meltdown has come to be called). In her influential 2013 book, *Precarious Japan*, based on fieldwork conducted in the summers from 2008 through 2011, anthropologist Anne Allison describes sensing "a widely shared uneasiness over an instability and insecurity in life" that was leading to "pain of social loneliness."[3] She cites labor economist Genda Yūji's assessment that having an *ibasho*—"a space and place where one feels at home"—counters this pain, giving rise to feelings of self-worth and hope for the future.[4] As if responding to this concern, hanamachi literature frames the community as an ibasho par excellence, one firmly grounded in geographical and cultural space, a world with enduring rituals of belonging. Authors praise the community as the site of Japanese traditions of hospitality (*o-motenashi*). Using this language creates an expansive ibasho, one that invites readers, assumed to be Japanese, to claim membership in this imagined community as part of their national identity, even if they never experience it personally. The language of healing, prominent in popular discourse in the 2000s, also comes to the fore in expressions of gratitude for the hanamachi and the capacity of maiko to restore good cheer. As Koito, former geiko and mother of the

Miyagawa-chō okiya Kaden, remarks, the "hanamachi were created as places of healing . . . and it is the job of a maiko . . . to learn how to lift hearts simply by her presence."[5]

Contemporary writing on the hanamachi explicitly distances this community from the mizu shōbai, despite its long association with this marginalized world of nighttime entertainment (see the introduction). Authors do not ignore, however, its historical connection to the pleasure quarters of the Edo period. They assume readers are familiar with maiko as Kyoto's mascot, but have no knowledge or experience of the hanamachi. They state that Japanese are as likely as foreigners to hold mistaken stereotypes of the hanamachi as being involved with sex work. Authors intend to dispel this assumption while giving readers an in-depth view of the richness of hanamachi culture. Like promoters of ballet and opera, these experts hope that this arts community, as a unique cultural site, will remain sustainable despite its expense and the challenges of supplying new recruits who will become its future leaders.

My goals for discussing hanamachi literature in this chapter are two-fold. To set the stage for all the chapters that follow, I want to establish familiarity with the hanamachi and the teahouse system. To this end, this chapter functions in part as an armchair tour of the hanamachi, drawing from the literature introducing it to Japanese readers. Since my primary concern is representation, I also draw attention to how the hanamachi experts present this community and its values, especially in discussions of the teahouse system, which underpin expectations of the maiko. This is a celebratory literature; the only criticism turns on prewar treatment of the maiko as a sexual pawn. I begin by briefly introducing the most prominent authors on the hanamachi, and then show how their work depicts each hanamachi as a unique neighborhood. Here, I extend and update their narratives by including comments from other hanamachi insiders, the districts' websites, English-language scholarship, and my own research. Discussing hanamachi financial health, I show how the literature represents the community's commercial viability over the past hundred years. Turning to the teahouse system, we consider representations of its business model, the role of the manager, the physical space of the teahouse, and the rituals of belonging that clients must follow. I also consider here what I term "salon masculinity" to discuss characterizations of the ideal male client that arise in the literature. In conclusion, I return to my argument about the literature's themes of rootedness and conventional gender roles, analyzing them in view of millennial discourse in Japan.

INTRODUCING THE HANAMACHI EXPERTS

Looking at the books on the hanamachi lined up on the shelves in my office, I am struck by the sense of trust that they represent. That is, the authors and photographers most engaged in educating Japanese about this world have developed an abundance of friendships within the hanamachi that has paved the way for their interviews, photographs, and attendance at myriad events. Japanese-language readers can learn much about the hanamachi from the work of two women, experts Kyoko Aihara and Kumiko Nishio. Over decades of research, both became enthusiastic insiders, appreciating the hanamachi as a world ever more open to women as consumers. They have published mainly in Japanese, but also in English. Along with their comprehensive books on the hanamachi, both have written books on the community's forms of etiquette, as discussed in the next chapter.

Prolific Yokohama-born author, photographer, and student of art history, Kyoko Aihara describes how her initial encounter with the hanamachi came unexpectedly in the late 1990s when she accepted an assignment to write about geisha for a British publisher and made her first forays into the community, which in turn inspired her to write in Japanese.[6] She enrichens her accounts with short interviews, photographs, astute references to Japanese art, fashion, history, and literature, connecting readers to the hanamachi's women leaders, various shop owners, and the work of related craftspeople. Aihara's interviews with elder hanamachi women offer an invaluable record of life in the districts from the 1930s through the 1970s. Kumiko Nishio, associate professor at Kyoto Women's University and a scholar of business administration, wrote her Kobe University dissertation on the hanamachi as a business community, analyzing its training methods, client relations, and maiko-geiko career path, later publishing this as a book in 2007, and in 2010–11, in English translation.[7] Although a Kyoto native who had studied Japanese dance as a child and was familiar with the hanamachi, Nishio did not know it well until she began her research. Her book also mentions her own long path to earning a PhD as a single mother, a journey that no doubt gave her empathy for the women carving out lifetime careers in the hanamachi, many as single mothers, too. Nishio argues that the training methods and other business skills developed in the hanamachi offer models relevant in the twenty-first century.[8]

Photography books, perhaps the most numerous of all publications on the hanamachi in Japanese and English, tantalize readers with photographs of elaborate costumes, dance productions, and ceremonies while also offering views of hanamachi life backstage. Often accompanied by only minimal text, photo books present the hanamachi as a lovely visual story, displaying the continuity of hanamachi dress and rituals over decades, and casting the community as nearly timeless in its distance from changing city tastes. They depict a world almost entirely filled with women. Photos take the viewer to the rituals of hairdressing, kimono dressing, and dance lessons, pairing shots of annual community gatherings with those of casual encounters among insiders in the hanamachi neighborhoods. Photographer Mizobuchi Hiroshi stands out as one who began taking pictures of the hanamachi in 1972, eventually retiring to pursue this documentary work full-time. He has published over twenty books—artistic photo-books and guidebooks—on the hanamachi; one of his most recent, the 2015 bilingual English-Japanese book, *Kyoto no kagai: The Kagai in Kyoto*, gives a long view of the hanamachi by including black-and-white photos of the 1970s and early 1980s.[9] Like Aihara, Mizobuchi began this journey with mere curiosity and a few amateur photographs after moving from Tokyo to Kyoto for work. He did not expect documenting the hanamachi to become his life's work, but clearly, he, too, has become a trusted insider.[10]

In contrast to Aihara, Nishio, and Mizobuchi, author Ōta Tōru, the owner of Oimatsu, a Japanese confectionary established in 1904 in the Kamishichiken hanamachi, is a longtime insider and lecturer. He organized academic symposia in 2007 and 2008 on the hanamachi. In 2009, he coedited *Kyō no kagai: Hito, waza, machi* (Kyoto's hanamachi: People, arts, towns) with Hiratake Kōzō. This volume seeks to initiate *kagaigaku* (hanamachi studies).[11] Including short interviews with geiko and other hanamachi insiders, the book introduces hanamachi history, the maiko-geiko career path and sartorial signs, annual festivals, various arts, hanamachi architecture, and preservation efforts. The volume also attends to architecture, offering explanations about buildings in the hanamachi and the layout of teahouses.

With this introduction to the prominent hanamachi authors in mind, we move to learning about the community, its five districts, commercial enterprises, and leaders.

SNAPSHOTS OF THE FIVE HANAMACHI (GO-KAGAI)

Tourists to Kyoto may easily visit the five small districts where geiko and maiko work, appreciating their distinctive architecture and unique flavor. All the districts invite the public to purchase tickets to view their dance performances held annually in the spring and fall. Known as hanamachi, literally "flower towns," each of these districts has ochaya (teahouses) where exclusive parties with geiko and maiko take place, and where guests commonly consume sake and beer along with tea. The hanamachi are home to okiya, also known in Kyoto and in the literature as *yakata*, where maiko and young geiko reside.[12] Many establishments combine the functions of the ochaya and okiya in one.[13] Each hanamachi also has a *kaburenjō* which serves as a theater for its public dance performances; arts training spaces where maiko and geiko take lessons; and administrative and financial affairs offices (*kenban*), with which all maiko and geiko are affiliated.[14] As Kyoto guidebooks such as Mizobuchi's advise, one can also find in each hanamachi eateries of various kinds (coffee shops, Japanese-sweets cafes, bars, and restaurants) as well as stores selling stationery, small goods, and other things associated with the atmosphere of the hanamachi.[15] Photo studios offering the maiko cosplay experience (see the introduction) are located around the hanamachi, but are not affiliated with them. This commerce points to the districts' transformation from a locus of men's leisure to a tourist-friendly place inviting to girls and women, too.

These five districts, known collectively in Japanese as *go-kagai* (literally, the five flower-districts), use the same business model and, as discussed in the next chapter, offer the same training and career path to prospective maiko. Women play significant leadership roles in each district, as heads of the ochaya and okiya, as senior geiko, and as leaders of their respective professional associations (*kumiai*). The five districts collaborate in one annual public dance production, *Miyako no nigiwai* (Prosperity of the capital), an event initiated in 1994 as part of the year's celebrations of the twelve-hundredth anniversary of the capital's transfer to Kyoto. In this sumptuously costumed production, selected geiko and maiko from each hanamachi display their district's characteristic dance style; the finale brings together four maiko from each district in a single dance.[16] For all their similarities, each hanamachi takes pride in possessing a distinct community. Writers point out slight differences in the way the maiko and geiko wear their hair or kimono, for example, in a certain district, noting small variations in their practices and common expressions.

Even short descriptions of the hanamachi emphasize their centuries-long history, their grounding in the cultures of medieval pilgrimage, commerce, samurai politics, and the artistic culture of early Kabuki and modern literature. We also learn how Kyoto maiko and geiko memorialize the city's cultural past through public dances, ceremonies, and appearances at major religious and theatrical events, and major spectacles such as Jidai Matsuri (Festival of the Ages) in fall and Gion Matsuri (Gion Festival) in summer. Here, I give some highlights from the literature to provide context for the books and films discussed in chapters ahead that take place in these districts.

Let's start with the oldest and smallest hanamachi, Kamishichiken, located in northwest Kyoto several miles from the other four hanamachi. Kamishichiken is located near the ancient Kitano Tenmangū Shrine.[17] The name Kamishichiken, ("seven upper houses") refers to the original seven teahouses built from materials left over from a medieval reconstruction of part of the shrine after a fire. In the mid-seventeenth century, on receiving official license from the authorities, Kamishichiken formally became a hanamachi and further expanded.[18] Aihara reports that the district's geiko may have evolved from Kitano shrine maidens (*miko*) who, on reaching adulthood, took on work near the shrine as fortune tellers and tea-servers.[19] Closely identified with the shrine, Kamishichiken geiko and maiko participate in its various public ceremonies; their spring dance is *Kitano Odori* (Kitano dances).

Kamishichiken has also had a long, close relationship to Nishijin, the merchant area nearby that is famous for its fine handwoven textiles. In the past, busy merchants used to conduct business in its teahouses as though their "second homes."[20] In the twenty-first century, Kamishichiken has initiated new collaborations with Nishijin, such as kimono festivals, as both communities attempt to maintain their old-style businesses in a contemporary world. Since 2010, Kamishichiken has operated a summer beer garden at its kaburenjō, making it possible for visitors to meet its maiko and geiko in a relaxed, inexpensive setting. The hanamachi maintains a website in Japanese, enlivened with photographs of its maiko and geiko performing on stage and greeting visitors, and posts news about its activities on its Facebook page.[21] A former maiko savvy about social media, Kamishichiken Ichimame promoted the hanamachi and the life of a maiko by keeping a blog in 2007. She also authored a short book about her maiko experiences, which I discuss in chapter 3.

One must travel to the eastern side of the city to visit the other four hanamachi. They are close to the Higashiyama hills and within ten minutes walking distance of each other near the intersection of the Kamo River and Shijō Avenue. The largest hanamachi in terms of area and numbers of teahouses, and the most famous is Gion Kōbu. Known simply as Gion, this hanamachi originated in seventeenth-century teahouses near Yasaka Shrine.

Gion figures regularly in modern stories about maiko. For instance, we learn about Gion in personal accounts penned by Gion geiko Kiriki Chizu (retired) and Yamaguchi Kimijo (chapter 3) as well as in the 2008–09 NHK-TV drama *Dandan* and the 2003–04 manga series *Kurenai niou* on the Gion career of geiko Iwasaki Mineko (retired) (see chapter 4). The influential Inoue dance school and its present head or *iemoto*, Inoue Yachiyo V, form an essential part of the hanamachi leadership and influence the aesthetic codes of Gion.[22] As photography books of Gion by Mizobuchi and others document, several annual festivities and hanamachi ceremonies, such as New Year's and summer greetings to the iemoto, revolve around Inoue Yachiyo V.[23] Almost every year since 1872, the hanamachi has held its annual *Miyako Odori* (Dances of the capital) in April, a major event that Kyoto continues to promote.[24] As we see in chapter 3, Gion maiko and geiko view participation in *Miyako Odori* as their main dance event of the year, and they take most pride in their professional identity as students of the Inoue school. In October, Gion's six-days of public dances known as *Onshūkai* or *Saraikai*—literally, the rehearsal or recital—are geared toward connoisseurs of dance.

The prosperity Japan enjoyed following World War I caused Gion to flourish, becoming home to over one thousand active geiko and maiko.[25] The expansion of Imperial Japan in the 1930s meant profits for Gion, too, as newly wealthy "high-level officials and men in munitions production and trading companies" indulged in ozashiki.[26] As former Gion geiko Nakanishi Miyo told Aihara in an interview, the Gion association purchased two airplanes for the military. She also recalls how in the 1940s when money for ozashiki became scarce, teahouse managers were sewing insignia and buttons on military uniforms.[27] Near the end of the Pacific War in 1944, the Gion kaburenjō was "commandeered and transformed into a munitions factory where geiko and maiko who had not fled to the countryside were conscripted to sew parachutes and uniforms for the army."[28] Soon after the war and despite the lack of food and other resources, Gion rebounded. Occupation forces requisitioned part of the kaburenjō as a dance hall and patronized its teahouses.[29] Old clients returned, too. By 1949, according to Nakanishi, cited above, Gion had revived. In 1950, Gion staged *Miyako Odori* after a six-year hiatus.

Famous for its picturesque central street, Hanamikōji, which opens on to Shijō Avenue, Gion Kōbu is now a major tourist destination (figure 8).[30] Indeed, in 2019 Gion residents and shop owners complained of being overrun by hordes of tourists, their unruly behavior captured on videos uploaded to the

FIGURE 8. Hanamikōji, the main street of Gion Kōbu, home to exclusive teahouses. 2015. Courtesy of Diane Kaczor.

internet. Sometimes maiko must take taxis even a short distance from their okiya to the teahouse to avoid the exuberance of the crowds. Many visitors to Kyoto come to the hanamachi in the evening to attend Gion Corner, a theater located next to the Gion kaburenjō. Its website proclaims, "Enjoy the dances performed by maiko right before your eyes." Established in 1962 by the mayor of Kyoto and civic leaders, Gion Corner was intended to introduce various Japanese art traditions and offer an evening function in the city for tourists from abroad.[31] The nightly hour-long performance includes a pair of maiko, selected from different hanamachi on a rotating basis, performing the tea ceremony and dancing.[32] Another landmark, the Ichiriki, the most exclusive, profitable, and well-known Gion teahouse, known for its red walls and located on the corner of Shijō and Hanamikōji takes pride in its association with the much-romanticized tale of the Forty-Seven Rōnin.[33]

Gion Higashi, the small hanamachi north of Gion, affiliates with Kankame-Inari Shrine in its neighborhood, housing its administrative office there and participating in the shrine's public ceremonies.[34] In the past Gion Kōbu and Gion Higashi comprised one hanamachi but the local government divided them in 1881, making the smaller hanamachi seem lesser by calling it "Gion B" (*Gion otsubu*). Mizoguchi's 1936 film *Gion no shimai* (Sisters of the Gion) laments the exploitation of geiko laboring in this so-called second-rate "B" area—a portrait that incited the ire of the hanamachi (see chapter 4). In 1955, the hanamachi took the name Gion Higashi.[35] Since 1952, its single annual dance performance, *Gion Odori* has taken place in November at Gion Kaikan Hall. Rendered in English as *Maple Dance*, the event marks peak maple-viewing season in Kyoto and displays Gion Higashi's prowess in the Fujima dance school.[36] Gion Higashi is the hanamachi favored by Nanami Haruka, author of the boy-maiko *Chiyogiku* series (see chapter 5).

Miyagawa-chō, the hanamachi closest to the Minamiza theater and near the banks of the Kamo River, has a long association with Kabuki. It is said that those who wanted to see Izumo no Okuni, the founder of women's kabuki in the early 1600s, and actors, too, would rest at its teahouses. Actors eventually took their stage names (*yago*) from the names of the teahouses that they frequented.[37] The government officially permitted teahouses here in 1751.[38] Tucked away from Shijō Avenue, Miyagawa-chō is a quiet neighborhood, designated as a Kyoto City Historical Scenery Preservation District in 1999.[39] Miyagawa-chō was the first to experiment in recruiting maiko through online publicity, expanding its maiko numbers. Its spring dance *Kyō Odori* (Dances of the old capital) held in April at its kaburenjō gives a prominent role to maiko. Mizobuchi's 2013 book on Miyagawa-chō captures the district's festivities and its elegant teahouses. Starting in 2014, Miyagawa-chō has set up a tented beer garden in July and August, where maiko in summer yukata greet and serve customers.[40]

Crossing the Kamo River to the west brings you to the narrow main street of the Pontochō hanamachi. Originally associated with trade in the nearby waterways, the area received permission from the authorities in 1712 to establish teahouses.[41] Anthropologist Liza Dalby, who did her fieldwork here in the mid-1970s, recounts a lively history of the district. She explains that the Pontochō kaburenjō, completed in 1927 and still standing, was the site of modern experiments where geiko tried out new forms of western dance, from ballroom dance to "Rockette-style revue numbers." By 1930, its top floor had become a dance hall where geiko danced with customers.[42] While Gion Kōbu prided itself on training maiko born in its district, Pontochō has been known since the Meiji era for accepting prospective geiko from all over Japan. Aihara explains that the district's early practice of inviting local girls, who studied dance, to perform at banquets may have been one of the origins of the maiko.[43] We can also learn about Pontochō from the 1954 book of black-and-white photography *Geisha of Pontocho*, a collaboration by P. D. Perkins and photographer Francis Haar, which documents the early postwar life of the hanamachi, the attire and arts practices of its geiko and maiko, the families who lived there, and the merchants and teachers who also worked there.[44] I find striking one Haar photo of a meeting of the "Directors of the Pontocho Geisha Association." It shows eight kimono-clad geiko of various ages, intent on discussion as they sit in a u-pattern on tatami mats behind small tables topped by business papers.[45] Unlike the scenes recorded in contemporary photo books, this one may speak to interest in Japanese women as leaders in the 1950s in the wake of postwar constitutional reforms.[46] Contemporary references to Pontochō highlight the district's restaurant verandas, open in spring and summer, that give full view of the Kamo River and where one may catch sight of maiko and geiko attending parties. Pontochō holds its annual spring dance *Kamogawa Odori* (Dances of the Kamo River), first performed in 1872, in May. The district recruits prospective maiko and musicians (*jikata*) online.[47]

COMMERCIAL VIABILITY: HANAMACHI EBB AND FLOW

Hanamachi writers all comment on shifts over time in the number of teahouses, geiko, and maiko. They do not remark on the larger implications of the modern times of boom or bust, whether they were due to the wealth produced during the expansion of Imperial Japan in the 1930s, the bubble economy of the 1980s, or the collapse of both; rather, the concern remains on the viability of the hanamachi. As Dalby writes, "The *mizu shōbai* is called the 'water trade' precisely because its fortunes ebb and flow depending on larger economic tides."[48] The history of the hanamachi demonstrates this flux, flourishing in good times and shrinking during economic downturns. Although women of the hanamachi once led lives as precarious as floating rafts, they now make careers in locales regarded as venerable places, each tied to important historical moments of religious and political (male) power exchanges. Changing tastes and forms in entertainment also have affected their popularity. The reasons girls and women enter the hanamachi have changed over time. As we have seen, books published in the 2000s on the hanamachi express hope for its preservation as a vital cultural site rooted in Kyoto history. Authors seem to breathe a sigh of relief that the numbers of its teahouses, geiko, and maiko appear to have stabilized in the 2000s. Looking back at this literature in spring 2020, however, when Covid-19 has led the hanamachi to cancel all spring dances and most ozashiki, we can imagine the economic challenges the community will face in its wake.

Giving a broad overview of the early twentieth-century geisha population, Dalby notes that there were over 80,000 geisha in Japan in the 1920s even as they faced competition from the new and more accessible entertainment offered by café girls; geisha numbers declined to 74,200 by 1935.[49] Nevertheless, Iwasaki describes the 1930s as "a time of flourishing abundance for Gion," when wealthy, powerful men "competed with each other to help support the most popular geiko."[50] In 1944, all hanamachi in Japan were closed due to the war, but reopened in 1945 in the early occupation, making a robust comeback.[51] Uemura Hideko, a former Gion Higashi geiko interviewed by Aihara, describes the years from postwar recovery in the early 1950s through the mid-1960s as a "rush hour" of activity in the hanamachi, where one continually saw clients and their favorite geiko coming and going, and the busy round of ozashiki left geiko with little time off.[52] The so-called "Golden Sixties" of economic prosperity were good for the hanamachi. In 1965, over 500 geiko and just under 100 maiko were active in Kyoto.[53] When former Gion geiko Iwasaki Mineko debuted as a maiko in 1965, Gion had over 150 teahouses.[54] In the 1960s, most maiko came from Kyoto and many were the daughters of teahouse managers or geiko.[55] In her memoir, former Gion geiko Kiriki Chizu recalls how much media attention maiko earned in the mid-sixties, much like young pop stars experience today.[56] Similarly, Gion teahouse manager Arai Mameji writes how the teen magazine *Yangu redei* (Young Lady) ran a photo-story on her April 1969 maiko debut.[57]

But over the next ten years, a sharp decline ensued. The oil crisis of 1973 hit the hanamachi hard. Apprentice numbers sank to their lowest point, with only 28 maiko active in 1975. Geiko numbers had also decreased to 372.[58] Photographer Mizobuchi recalls worried Gion leaders asking him for help in finding prospective maiko.[59] This decline in the hanamachi occurred amid Japan's growing prominence on the global stage, young women's increasing years of education and employment opportunities, and the rise of different entertainments such as rock music and disco dance clubs. The emergence of a new era of women's activism and Japanese feminists' vigorous participation in the UN Year of the Woman in 1975 likely made a hanamachi career seem outmoded in contrast. Nonetheless, manga artist Yamato Waki, in her collaborative manga with Iwasaki based on the geiko's life, visualizes the changing scene of the 1970s as prosperous (see chapter 4). She draws young people decked out in hip fashions and trendy haircuts filling the shopping streets of Kyoto. The narrator adds, "The 1970s were surely the midpoint of the era of high-speed growth. As ever, clients came to Gion in droves, but concerns abounded over who would assume its leadership, the dwindling numbers of those who wanted to become geiko and maiko, and the numerous closings of old teahouses, okiya, and shops."[60] Yamato depicts shopkeepers, crafts people, and kimono makers worried about the ripple effect on their businesses.

Moving to hanamachi accounts of the 1980s, we find memories of conspicuous consumption and clients lavishing gifts on maiko and geiko, as former geiko Kiriki recalls (see chapter 3). But the collapse of the bubble economy in 1991 led still more ochaya and okiya to close.[61] From 1985 to 1998, Kyoto geiko numbers stabilized at about 200 while the maiko population ranged between 50 and 80.[62] Maiko numbers improved when Gion and Miyagawa-chō made recruiting efforts between 2003 and 2008, aiding the spike in maiko numbers to 100 in 2008—the "maiko boom." In fact, by 2001, over 90 percent of maiko came from elsewhere in Japan. Aihara imagines this influx of non-Kyoto girls speaks to the increasing popularity of Kyoto as a national tourist destination and the growing impression of Kyoto's hanamachi as female-friendly.[63] In April 2020, the Kyoto hanamachi were home to 122 teahouses, 165 geiko, and 81 maiko.[64] Writing in 2004, Liza Dalby mused that others may worry over the future of the hanamachi, but geisha "pay little attention to alarmed reports of their imminent demise."[65]

Nevertheless, the Kyoto hanamachi have collectively taken measures to ensure government and corporate financial support for their artists. In May 1996, the Association of the Kyoto Hanamachi (Kyoto Kagai Kumiai Rengōkai) collaborated with the Tourist Board of Kyoto City to establish the Kyoto Traditional Musical Art Foundation (Dentō Gigei Shikō Zaidan), nicknamed Ōkini Zaidan (Thank You Foundation).[66] Since its founding, the Ōkini Zaidan has also received support from Kyoto Prefecture and Kyoto city governments, Kyoto Chamber of Commerce and Industry, and corporate donations.[67] The foundation, managed by Gion's kumiai office, organizes events such as the annual *Miyako no nigiwai*; assists with Gion Corner; helps in recruiting and booking maiko; and can provide members with the introductions required to attend ozashiki.[68] It gives awards to outstanding geiko for preserving the traditional arts (*dentō gigei hojisha*).[69] According to

Kelly Foreman, the foundation initially aimed to aid the older geiko musicians, who were finding it difficult to bear the financial cost of "mastering several genres of traditional music."[70] She views the founding of the Ōkini Zaidan as signaling that the Kyoto hanamachi "is increasingly considering itself akin to the larger arts community, in seeking support beyond the private personal style of patronage upon which it has long relied."[71] In *Kyō no kagai*, Hamasaki Kanako briefly introduces the Ōkini Zaidan, inviting readers to join its *Tomo no kai* (Friends' group). Assuring women readers that they will enjoy its activities, Hamasaki describes how "teahouse customs, geiko and maiko attire, cuisine, dance, and so on, fascinate women, too."[72] In 2020, women comprise half the membership of the Friends' Group.[73]

Even with Ōkini Zaidan support, hanamachi survival rests largely on the continued profits of the teahouses and the skill of the women who run them. In the next section, we see how the literature explains the business practices and values of the teahouse system, extolling the roles of its skilled managers and gentlemanly clients.

THE OCHAYA: TEAHOUSE SYSTEM

Exploring the literature's explanations of the business structure of the hanamachi introduces us to the powerful women of the hanamachi, the teahouse managers, and the elite establishments that they run. The ochaya, literally "teahouses," are exclusive spaces within the hanamachi where parties (*ozashiki*) with clients, geiko, and maiko take place.[74] As Aihara explains, these are households run and inhabited almost solely by women.[75] The managers (*okami-san*) are all women and addressed by maiko and geiko as mother (*okāsan*). The hanamachi—as an enterprise and an arts community—depends on the success and leadership of the managers. Many are former geiko, while others have been trained by a relative who has passed on the business to them. All must cultivate their business by nurturing long-term relationships with clients for whom they plan ozashiki. Their work encompasses a host of social, touristic, and arts activities. They may plan large events for clients at Kyoto hotels and elite restaurants (*ryōtei*), procure tickets to special events, and arrange seasonal outings such as to see maple leaves in fall.[76] More broadly, they book maiko and geiko as models for artists and photographers, arrange for them to perform for high school students on field trips, and manage their Kyoto-related promotional appearances in the city, other parts of Japan, and overseas.[77] As one okami-san told Nishio, "Our business resembles that of an event-planning agency."[78] The manager's mentorship of maiko and geiko likens her business to a talent agency, too. Writing from the perspective of a management scholar, Nishio recognizes the okami-san's essential role in public relations, business relationships, training, and quality maintenance.

How do ochaya managers see this work? Although maiko remain the focus of most attention in the hanamachi, recent literature points to the role of the managers in training them and keeping the hanamachi running. In the 2010s, interviews, books, and a TV special have sought individual women's insights into this position.[79] For example in her 2012 book, Aihara intersperses conversations with maiko with short interviews of seven managers of different ages and hanamachi.[80] Four of the managers had been geiko. Only one of the managers had opened her own teahouse/okiya; others had assumed second-; third-, or even fourth-generation leadership of their respective teahouses. Aihara's book, like the other accounts, communicates respect for the responsibility that these managers shoulder. These and other accounts show how the managers strive to maintain exclusivity by delivering top-flight service while keeping the hanamachi relevant to the broader public in Japan—a kind of public relations tight-rope act. Most stress their role in training the next generation of maiko, ochaya staff, and clients. The managers do not discuss the financial details of running the teahouse or their income. This omission removes the image of managers from commercial concerns, framing them as preservationists. Within each community, however, annual awards ceremonies in January recognize the top-earning teahouse, geiko, and maiko.[81]

Teahouses as architectural spaces are prized for their distinctive Edo-era style. As we see in the chapters ahead, films, fiction, and manga make use of these spaces to build their fictional worlds. Teahouses are elegant, pristine spaces with tatami mats and classic tokonoma alcoves for displaying scrolls and flower arrangements, as Mizobuchi documents in his photo book on Miyagawa-chō.[82] As the largest teahouse in Gion, the Ichiriki can hold up to one hundred guests, but most teahouses have a maximum of twenty at any one time. Most have three to four rooms of different sizes available for ozashiki.[83] A relatively recent addition is the "ochaya bar" where regular clients may casually and less expensively enjoy a teahouse visit and conversation with the okami-san.[84] The TV drama *Dandan* takes viewers through its fictional ochaya/okiya, showing the strict demarcation between the elegant spaces upstairs for ozashiki—and the lively, cluttered communal space where maiko and geiko live—and the private space downstairs for the okami-san's office. Personal accounts by maiko often describe visiting the manager's space before and after attending ozashiki upstairs. There is also a kitchen downstairs, a garden, and the manager's living space. There may also be a small adjacent building (*hanare*), as imagined in the *Chiyogiku* stories (see chapter 5).

Ozashiki—parties with geiko and maiko—figure importantly in the literature on the hanamachi and related fiction. Guides to the hanamachi describe in detail the typical ozashiki and the manager's role in planning and overseeing them, and their method for billing clients. Arranging the ozashiki begins with the client contacting the ochaya manager with preferred dates. The client discusses the budget, the purpose of the party, and the number of guests to be invited. The client may make special requests, such as asking for a favorite geiko, to have a certain dance performed, or suggestions for after-party entertainment such as a karaoke bar. The okami-san takes care of everything. She may make hotel and taxi reservations, and even arrange for Kyoto souvenirs for the guests. If the client wants a meal served, she will order this from a local caterer; an ochaya is not set up for food preparation other than for light snacks and beverages. The okami-san plans the flowers and selects the art for the room, specifically tailoring them to the guest's event and the season. She will arrange for geiko and maiko, who will talk with the clients, may perform dances, and can play light-hearted games associated with the ozashiki. She will hire and manage a female staff (*nakai*) that helps with preparation and serving and may take part in conversation. At the ozashiki, greeting and talking with client and guests, the manager will make sure that everything goes well. She initially absorbs all costs of the ozashiki—food, beverages, taxis, fee and tips for the geiko and maiko, and tax—and hotel and bar expenses, sending her client a single bill for the entire event the next month.[85] Nishio explains that vendors value the teahouse business since they have a reputation for prompt payment, and this motivates them to keep their own service high in quality.[86]

Hanamachi literature gives little information on the client's costs for an ozashiki. Costs vary, for instance, depending on the teahouse, the length of the party, the number of guests, the number of geiko and maiko booked, and food and drink, among other factors. Maiko and geiko earn the same pay for their time, despite their difference in seniority.[87] Tips are also expected. In 2019, the Ōkini Zaidan informed me that hiring one maiko or geiko for an ozashiki might run between 40,000 and 50,000 yen (US$375–470).[88] On occasions when demand for ozashiki is high, such as on the day of a maiko's debut or a special holiday, clients must pay the full fee even though maiko and geiko may not be able to stay the entire time.[89]

This exclusive teahouse system, with its elegant spaces and skilled managers, caters to an elite, largely male clientele. Hanamachi literature explains how one becomes a favored client, both welcoming readers to *ochaya asobi*— "teahouse fun"—and defending the practice of exclusivity, as we see in the next section.

SALON MASCULINITY: COOL CLIENTS, NAJIMI FAVORITES, AND NO FIRST-TIMERS

Contemporary hanamachi literature concentrates on the maiko and the importance of her deportment as community mascot, but some attention turns to men as clients, too.[90] We can observe how an idealized man—the embodiment of what I term "salon masculinity"— emerges in this literature, authored mainly by women, and inspires fictional portraits. Maiko, geiko, and teahouse managers alike all speak highly of their favorite clients. To maintain privacy, they do not name them (apart from stories about prominent men long deceased), rendering the ideal man an anonymous figure.[91] They describe how preferred clients behave respectfully, dress well, make clever conversation, and have mastered the unwritten rules of the ozashiki.[92] These clients appreciate the traditional arts and may even practice one. Young Miyagawa-chō geiko Komomo describes how she enjoys knowledgeable clients who "can play with the lyrics of a song, for example, altering the lines to make them funny, or make up their own dances in time with the song."[93] Most importantly, favored clients generously support maiko and geiko's careers. Clients as idealized characters appear in hanamachi fiction and film in the 2000s, usually as avuncular elders, but sometimes as love interests. *Dandan*, for one example, introduces the suave Sawada Yūichi, the "charismatic company president" of an online tech company; this sophisticated thirty-something client appreciates refined ozashiki, even having his own kimono tailored. In stark contrast to this cool customer, the slapstick film *Maiko Haaaan!!!* features boors who drink too much and expect sexual favors but see themselves as teahouse connoisseurs. These disparate client portraits resonate with the amusing stories about the pleasure quarters in the eighteenth and nineteenth centuries that recounted the escapades of an urbane sophisticate (*tsū*) and his clueless counterpart (*hanka-tsū*). Like fictional tales of clients in the 2000s, these Edo-era stories entertained readers with fantasy tours of the pleasure quarters while fashioning amusing guides to the best and worst of masculine deportment.[94]

Approval of salon masculinity in hanamachi literature of the 2000s does not assume the best guests are young men. Far from it. As hanamachi guides and geiko memoirs indicate, the teahouse offers a world where older men tend to predominate, and age associates with wisdom, wealth, and career achievement—company presidencies, artistic accomplishment, leadership of a Buddhist temple, and even Nobel Prizes. Although contemporary Japanese etiquette guides for men encourage adopting the cosmopolitan habits and tastes of the global elite, and avoiding at all costs becoming another stereotypical, cranky old Japanese dad (*oyaji*), hanamachi literature never faults a client's predilection for old-fashioned Japanese tastes.[95] In fact, it is his knowledge of older Japanese customs that will win him fans in the hanamachi. The client may also take comfort in knowing that young women in the hanamachi will not disparage him as trend-setting office ladies might, a predicament also discussed in men's etiquette books.[96]

Hanamachi tales of clients of old communicate a strong sense of belonging and some nostalgia for the Showa days of the 1950s through 1970s. Teahouse manager Yoshimura Kaoru observes, "I feel there were many clients in the past who participated in training maiko and geiko"; they knew the arts, had an eye for dance, and would admonish young ones to study harder. "But now, even at ozashiki, clients are just fooling with their cell phones."[97] Aihara quotes another teahouse okami-san saying how much she enjoyed it when regular clients in the past used her teahouse as their second home. "That's the way it was in the old days. Some clients would even drop by in the middle of the day."[98] Gion manager Higaki Miyoko, who finds contemporary clients rather quiet, exclaims over the clients of the 1950s through 1970s, calling them "men of ambition," who loved to debate, followed geiko's arts performances closely, and attended *Miyako Odori* out of true love for the production. Commenting on Higaki's memories, Aihara explains how "up until recently, Gion was spoken of as a place that raised men. Being a favored client recognized a man as trustworthy."[99] Iwasaki describes how even in the early 2000s "regular customers, many of whom host ozashiki at least once a week, if not more often" form strong bonds of loyalty with the teahouse and geiko.[100] These men become the *najimi*, the favored, familiar clients. Such loyalty may even carry over generations, linking one family to a single teahouse.[101]

Such stories from the "good old days" flourish in hanamachi literature. Comic anecdotes turn the spotlight on famous najimi, such as Nobel Prize winning author Kawabata Yasunari who popped in his favorite Gion teahouse late at night for a bowl of udon noodles. Although the manager retorted that she did not run a noodle shop, she quickly ordered a bowl delivered for him.[102] Such tales humanize teahouse culture, displaying a range of acceptable masculinities. But they also point to the gendered nature of the hanamachi even now, and the labor required of the managers who "mother" the clients and maiko who perform as surrogate daughters. They further show how clients developed loyalty to certain teahouses. These long-term relationships with managers and geiko extended to requests for help with a client's major family events, even with a client's funeral.[103]

Ochaya managers cultivate long-term client relationships, but they are notorious for refusing "first-timers" (ichigen-san). According to this custom, the teahouse manager will not book an ozashiki for a new client, no matter how prominent or wealthy, without first obtaining a recommendation from one of her regular clients. The regular client must take responsibility for educating prospective clients about teahouse etiquette and payment.[104] As Nishio explains, managers will complain directly to a client if a recommended guest behaves badly, which may well damage a man's professional reputation outside the hanamachi, too.[105] Many Japanese find this rule pretentious and off-putting. *Maiko Haaaan!!!* satirized teahouse snobbery with a catchy song about a rejected Mr. First Timer—ironically, its lead character was the buffoon who proved the rule. But books on the hanamachi and accounts by former geiko invariably defend the custom as essential to ensuring the sophisticated atmosphere of the ozashiki. The managers pride themselves on knowing their clients well, even to the point of distinguishing which brands of beer their umbrella corporations support and serving them accordingly.[106] The fact that the managers also live at their ochaya makes them cautious about new clients, and this concern increases when the ochaya doubles as an okiya with young geiko and maiko living there. Of course, managers also want assurance that the new client will pay the bill when it arrives the following month. The Ōkini Zaidan, hoping to make the hanamachi somewhat more open, can now obtain introductions to teahouses for its members. Elite hotels and Japanese-style inns in Kyoto may also provide introductions.[107]

Rituals of patronage are key to affiliation with the hanamachi. For their part, clients may frequent only one teahouse in any one hanamachi. In other words, a client may have a favorite ochaya in Kamishichiken and another in Pontochō but may not have more than one in either hanamachi. It is only acceptable to request an ozashiki at another teahouse in the same hanamachi if one first asks one's regular okami-san to arrange it. Clients can go to parties at other teahouses when invited by regulars there. With a wink, Aihara likens client loyalty to a parishioner's allegiance to their place of worship.[108] For her part, the manager promises to protect the privacy of her clients and guests. While retaining their exclusivity and bonds of trust with regular clients, managers must still cultivate new ones to stay in business.

Both Aihara and Nishio address the role of the geiko's patron (*danna*). Remarking that they frequently get asked about this, Aihara explains that most Japanese assume the danna-geiko relationship is a sexual one.[109] Nishio mentions that when asking her whether danna still exist, people tend to hesitate asking about this sensitive topic, but also show keen interest.[110] Both authors define the contemporary danna as one who offers financial support to the geiko as an artist, acting as a kind of sponsor. Not all clients become danna. According to Aihara, the danna is an essential ally of the hanamachi; one who appreciates the arts, frequents ozashiki, has engendered trust, and along with the community's leaders has created the culture of the hanamachi.[111] The patron will support lessons, the purchase of kimono and obi, buy tickets to the hanamachi dance performances, and may invite geiko to events and on trips.[112] Both Aihara and Nishio emphasize the danna's role as a true patron of the arts. Aihara affirms that it is no longer necessary, and likely nearly impossible for a geiko to rely on a wealthy danna's support as in the past. Films in the 1950s, however, portrayed maiko as forced to take a danna (*mizuage danna*) as their initial sexual partner to pay off debts (see chapter 4). According to the literature, intimate relations between a geiko and her danna may still occur in the 2000s, but only should they both choose, and as Aihara explains, there are hanamachi protocols for arranging and ending the relationship.[113] Nishio leaves the situation ambiguous, writing: "Well, I asked people involved in the hanamachi, 'Are there still *danna-san* today?' But they gently pointed out to me that the question itself does not have much meaning, saying, 'If there weren't any, there would be no way to answer, and even if there were, what goes on inside the hanamachi is absolutely not discussed outside, you know.'"[114]

Women may also host ozashiki, and well-known authors such as Ariyoshi Sawako and Hayashi Mariko have written about their ochaya visits.[115] Iwasaki recalls, "Since most women who visited Gion Kōbu had achieved their status under their own steam, they expressed appreciation for our work and talking with them was easy."[116] But women appear only rarely as clients in all the texts—film, fiction, memoirs, and manga—discussed here. Iwasaki remembers entire families attending ozashiki, joking that the ochaya can be "high-class 'family restaurants,'" and she recalls cases where a "husband might be presiding over a stuffy ozashiki of business executives in one room while his wife and her girlfriends were laughing it up in another," and attending both parties.[117] But in these accounts, too, it is still a man who is the client. There is no indication anywhere in this literature that a woman might become a danna, even in the sense of acting as a major patron of a geiko's artistic career.

CONCLUSION

This chapter has explored the maiko's hanamachi home, focusing on its history, values, and teahouse system, as defined in books published mainly in Japanese in the 2000s. This discussion highlights major themes in hanamachi literature that will continue to reverberate—whether endorsed, questioned, or parodied—in representations of the maiko discussed ahead. Books by Aihara, Nishio, Ōta and Hiratake, and Mizobuchi communicate the sense of hanamachi life as deeply rooted in Kyoto's past. Whether attention turns to language, relationships, clothing, landmarks, or even superstitions, each element contributes to identifying the hanamachi as a unique environment, steeped in local lore and custom. This perspective continually—and selectively—looks back, suggesting any forward motion must be firmly grounded in the past. At the same time, the authors passionately argue for the relevance of this world—its slow beauty, nurturing of social networks, business practices, and training methods—even for Japanese who may never step foot in the hanamachi. The authors urge readers as Japanese to take pride in this institution, learn about it, take pleasure in it, and advocate for its preservation. Nishio remarks how "in our hearts, we Japanese feel deeply attracted to the elegant customs of Kyoto's hanamachi."[118] Aihara describes how she came to believe that the hanamachi offered Japanese a unique space of Japaneseness (Nihon rashisa).[119]

We may consider this celebration of the hanamachi as national heritage site in view of the "nation branding" discourse of the 2000s. Anthropologist Koichi Iwabuchi has observed how national stories like the one constructed around the hanamachi must reassemble "selective narratives, symbolic meanings, and widely accepted stereotypical images of that nation" to fashion a "coherent entity."[120] Although deeply informed by interviews, archival research, and expert knowledge gained over decades, hanamachi literature tends to emphasize coherence in the community at the expense of criticism and shies away from revealing internal discord or problems within the system. Moreover, it extends that coherence to a national audience, assuming that all readers, by virtue of being Japanese, should feel some degree of ownership of this cultural site. This appeal to readers' inherent Japaneseness can stimulate ethno-culturalist sentiment, veering into what Iwabuchi terms "the exclusionary reconstruction of a narrative of the nation."[121]

Much of hanamachi literature motivates nostalgia, giving the feeling that almost nothing today can ever quite capture the pleasures of the past. But nostalgia always tells us more about the present than the past. Although the literature acclaims women as leaders, clients, and consumers, it implies that men will always be clients and never the service providers, except in adjacent supporting roles such as catering or kimono-making. The literature praises ideal "salon masculinity," framing this as Japanese, as easily the province of older men, and as worthy of a certain amount of indulgence. All in all, these values position maiko-likeness as a catalyst to retrieve the past in the present. This creates contradictions that the maiko must attempt to resolve, as we shall see in chapters ahead. Although costumed in anachronistic fashion and performing traditional arts, the maiko must embody the millennial Japanese girl who has freely chosen her career, works diligently, and may become a leader in her community one day. At the same time, the maiko must learn to project the girlish spontaneity and innocence that will delight a clientele largely comprised of older men and managed by older women. In a sense, her vitality shows the hanamachi is still alive and has a future.

Although the hanamachi literature prizes the face-to-face communication of teahouse culture, we see many indications of virtual communities establishing, too, in 2020. Facebook pages; Instagram accounts; insiders' blogs; online recruiting; and, in the face of Covid-19, Zoom ozashiki all speak to an audience for hanamachi culture extending well past Kyoto. It will be intriguing to see how the hanamachi might employ its virtual fans to thrive in the twenty-first century.

In the next chapter, we turn to the maiko's career path. Again, drawing on hanamachi literature, we observe how concerns for etiquette inform each stage in her path from trainee to geiko. This literature shows how the hanamachi concerns for community, aesthetic codes, and Japaneseness take form in shaping the maiko's training program.

CHAPTER 2

The Well-Mannered Career Path

A maiko in full costume closely approximates the Japanese ideal of feminine beauty.

—Iwasaki, *Geisha, a Life*

Ōta Kimi, the manager of the Gion Kōbu teahouse Tomiyo, addressed all the maiko in a letter, reminding them, "You are the symbol of Gion Kōbu. You must always speak in the gentle dialect of the hanamachi and pay attention to your demeanor."

—Ōta Kimi, interviewed by Shiromoto Satomi, in Ōta and Hiratake, *Kyō no kagai.*

In venues large or small, even strolling in Kyoto, apprentices know that performing photo-worthy maiko-likeness forms the core of the maiko's mission. They must not forget that their demeanor represents Japanese femininity and symbolizes their hanamachi, as Iwasaki and Ōta express above. How do they learn to do this? What does their apprenticeship entail? What aspects of maiko training do experts champion for all Japanese? This chapter explores these questions by examining the okiya as a value-charged training and living space, the okiya mother as its lead teacher, and maiko training strategies. We also learn about the skills expected at different stages of the maiko-geiko career path. I show how hanamachi books published in the 2000s, and etiquette guides particularly, idealize the maiko as a model of an elegant Japanese deportment worth preserving. These books imagine her apprenticeship as a passage indelibly marked by her expression of maiko-likeness. Once a geiko, the young woman must abandon her girlish maiko behaviors, expressing more mature, womanly, and individualistic ones.

Tracking this training regime and the maiko-geiko career path familiarizes us with the protocols of the maiko apprenticeship and the okiya structure, an important foundation for understanding the narratives discussed in this book. We see how texts on hanamachi etiquette and maiko training reveal an aestheticized vision of Japanese girlhood, one in which the language of disciplined deportment frames the hanamachi and its vigilant okiya mothers as stalwarts of traditional Japanese values. This narrative divorces the hanamachi from the mizu shōbai and the maiko from trendy characters like café maids or Lolitas, and even ordinary girls. Focusing on training and preservation deflects attention from okiya profits earned from maiko labor. For all the stress on correctness, a readerly pleasure is available in this literature too, as one may imagine navigating exclusive worlds and public attention with equal ease, while performing Japanese femininity well. The pleasurable aspects of expressing maiko-likeness and the hanamachi as championing an ethics of care inspire many authors, as we see in the succeeding chapters.

Respect for etiquette informs all contemporary books on the hanamachi. This chapter draws mainly on five published from 2005 to 2018. Hanamachi etiquette guides based on interviews with hanamachi elders, geiko, and maiko by Kyoko Aihara and Kumiko Nishio, the experts whom we met in chapter 1, explain maiko training—the attitudes instilled and the behaviors learned—as offering a model for all young Japanese and for business success. In 2005, Aihara published *Kyoto hanamachi motenashi no gijutsu* (The art of hospitality in Kyoto's hanamachi), including interviews with four senior hanamachi women about maiko training; in 2012, Nishio authored *Maiko no kotoba: Kyoto hanamachi hitosodate no gokui* (Maiko language: Training secrets from the Kyoto hanamachi), based on interviews and her observations. Memoirs by two Gion elders—okiya mother and former geiko Arai Mameji's *Gion Mameji: Chotto mukashi no Gion machi* (Mameji of the Gion: The Gion of recent past, 2015) and teahouse mother Yoshimura Kaoru, as presented in Taniguchi Keiko's *Gion, uttoko no hanashi: "Minoya" okami, hitori katari* (Gion, stories of our place: Thoughts from the manager of the Minoya, 2018)—offer perspectives on maiko training in the early 1970s and, from a supervisory perspective, in the 2010s. The 2008 photo essay, *A Geisha's Journey: My Life as a Kyoto Apprentice*, published simultaneously in English and Japanese versions, a nine-year collaboration by photographer Naoyuki Ogino and Miyagawa-chō geiko Komomo (figure 9), traces Komomo's path from trainee to maiko to geiko, illuminating her improving grasp of hanamachi codes and values.[1]

Reading about maiko etiquette and training, one cannot ignore the specter of an ordinary girl badly in need of polish. Interviews with okiya and teahouse

FIGURE 9. Maiko Komomo's first time performing in Miyagawa-chō's *Kyō Odori* (Dances of the old capital) in April 2001. ©2008. Courtesy of Naoyuki Ogino.

managers quoted in hanamachi guides reveal how much training she will need to become a maiko. These managers are not alone in taking this view. In her research on corporate etiquette training for new recruits in Japan, Cynthia Dickel Dunn cites evidence that "company executives complain that young people fail to greet others properly, lack motivation, do not express themselves well, do not know how to behave when entertaining clients, and do not know how to use honorific language correctly."[2] For its part, the hanamachi rectifies these faults by starting from scratch, teaching the maiko manners that reflect an older style of Japanese femininity training.

Remarks across the literature speak to the effectiveness of maiko training in the eyes of many adults. One maiko recalls being complimented by an ozashiki client who said, "My, but you are charming. I have a daughter about your age, but her manners are hopeless. Well, I guess that we have to take some responsibility for that, but in that area, you maiko are impressive."[3] Similarly, *Chiyogiku* author Nanami Haruka recalls feeling giddy when greeted by a trainee on her visit to an okiya. Her hair in a ponytail and wearing a simple sweater, the girl impressed Nanami as a "hospitality industry pro."[4] She delighted in the trainee's graceful movement and speech. Nishio recounts bringing her sons, both college students, to an ozashiki for their "high-society debut (*shakōkai debyū*)," explaining that, "What most impressed them was the hospitality (o-motenashi) of the maiko."[5] In comparison, her sons felt that they did not measure up even though they were close in age. Her sons' reaction motivated Nishio to write *Maiko no kotoba* (Maiko language) to encourage young people to hone their social skills to win compliments for professionalism in their own chosen field one day. Aihara offers the example of seeing a maiko riding a bus in Kyoto, observing that, "Maiko are surprisingly different from the girls that you see on trains or in town. It is pleasant to see their precise manners and courteous behavior. I feel that it's not only their appearance, but their sensibility, too, that sets them apart. This makes me wonder what kind of training these young girls received to become maiko."[6] Thinking about the maiko's well-trained deportment prompts Aihara to recall her own youth in the Showa 40s (1965–1974) when she feels that Japanese schools erred in teaching shallow notions of independence (*jishusei*) and freedom.[7] Hanamachi training points in a different direction.

Accounts from anthropologist Takie Lebra's 1984 book, *Japanese Women: Constraint and Fulfillment*, suggest that maiko training as represented in contemporary guides resonates with the femininity training found in middle-class families before and during the war. Many of Lebra's interviewees grew up in homes that taught daughters' modesty, compliance, reticence in speech, neatness, and graceful body movements "according to the culturally standardized codes of propriety."[8] Reminiscent of the maiko's skill in greetings, Lebra describes expectations for daughters: "If the family was hosting a guest, the daughter would be called upon, either as part of the training or to display her already accomplished femininity, to serve tea and offer *aisatsu* (formal greeting), which included bows and stylized polite speech. . . . When the situation was reversed and the girl visited someone else, she was supposed to be able to follow the codes for guests."[9]

Despite fears that these old forms reported by Lebra had faded, Brian McVeigh's study of a Japanese women's junior college based on research in the early 1990s shows the same ideals driving the school's goals and conflating ladylike behavior with ethnic identity. The college, which promoted myriad rules for deportment, reinforced the assumption that, "if one is born a female Japanese, then one should not only act Japanese but should also be feminine *because* one is born Japanese."[10] McVeigh observed, "Japaneseness and ladylike behavior mutually construct and reinforce one another."[11] Thus, the maiko is not alone in her mission to embody Japanese femininity or in mastering behaviors based on older forms. Commonly cast as a quintessentially Japanese girl, the maiko may be held to even stricter and more anachronistic forms of femininity and Japaneseness in the 2000s.

The maiko's aesthetic labor builds on a training regime infused with Buddhist notions of cultivation (*shugyō*), an approach that integrates mind-body learning, and emphasizes the mastery of prescribed movements (*kata*). Kabuki and Noh actors, ikebana and tea ceremony practitioners also learn by observing kata performed by masters, imitating them, and improving with the master's corrections. Although such cultivation entails a lifelong, never-ending pursuit, internalization of kata gradually enables the student's own creativity. Aihara remarks, "Form sustains spirit. Spirit sustains form. I sense that is what constitutes cultivation (*shugyō*) in the hanamachi."[12]

Again, the maiko and these other artists are not alone in following this method. Returning to Dunn's study of corporate training seminars, we find attention to corporate kata for "voice, gesture, movement, facial expression, grooming, and use of space."[13] Dunn observes how this training aims to transform the quotidian, creating "aesthetic performances in which the focus is primarily on correctness of *form*."[14] It is this emphasis on form coupled with notions of cultivation that render maiko-likeness a highly visible sign of hanamachi propriety, Japaneseness, and aestheticized girlhood. According to Kelly M. Foreman, this code becomes naturalized in the hanamachi as "common sense" that is "transmitted by observation, oral instruction, and teacher-student relationships."[15]

With this emphasis on manners as markers of Japanese femininity and notions of proper familial training in mind, we turn to the business of the okiya. I should note here that in the 2000s when over 90 percent of prospective maiko come from outside Kyoto, the literature does not mention class, educational, or regional differences among them. As non-Kyoto girls, they are uniformly, as teahouse manager Yoshimura Kaoru refers to them, "girls who came from elsewhere (*yoso kara kita ko*)."[16] Praising the "quality-controlled maiko training system [that] takes non-Kyoto novices firmly in hand," Liza Dalby notes how the "system of training girls in the arts, appearance, and behavior" fashions the maiko to meet "demanding standards."[17] Everything starts with the girl's move to an okiya.

THE OKIYA: TRAINING AND LIVING SPACE

Unless you think of them as your own children, you cannot raise [a maiko]. It truly warms my heart when even those who have left Pontochō to marry come back for a visit, still calling me "Mother."

—Masuda Kazuyo, Pontochō, quoted in Aihara, *Kyoto hanamachi: Maiko to geiko no uchiake-banashi*

The okiya plays an indispensable role in training maiko and managing their careers until they become independent geiko. Each okiya is headed by a woman addressed as its mother or okāsan. Like Masuda Kazuyo, okāsan typically describe developing maternal bonds of affection for their young charges. Aihara observes that okiya "each have their own atmosphere," a diversity true of fictional okiya, too.[18] Maiko stories of the 2000s cast the okiya as bustling with activity and backstage drama. Kindly mothers, varying in strictness, guide the maiko and geiko, and interact with tradespeople and their hanamachi colleagues. All the stories educate audiences about the okiya's basic purpose and familial structure, which we take up in this section.

Viewing the okiya as a model for on-the-job training, Nishio characterizes it as akin to "performing arts production agencies," since the okāsan has responsibility for training maiko, overseeing their arts progress and their relations in the community, and scheduling their work assignments.[19] All maiko and geiko must remain affiliated with their okiya while they are active in the hanamachi. In most cases, the okiya is also an ochaya, which means that the okāsan simultaneously manages the maiko and young geiko living at her okiya and takes on the work of the teahouse manager (see chapter 1). The okāsan will hire staff to help this home-business run smoothly. Geiko Komomo describes how her mother Koito, still a full-time geiko herself, hired three women to assist in her small Miyagawa-chō okiya. They arranged flowers, mended kimono, cleaned house, and prepared meals, and one acted "as a kind of back-up" who helped with serving snacks and fixing drinks for customers at their home bar.[20] Similarly, Iwasaki Mineko recounts the busy days of her okiya mother and her assistant in the 1950s through the 1970s: they paid courtesy calls in the district, managed accounts, accepted engagements for maiko and geiko, and coordinated and recorded the ensembles worn by the women.[21]

In hanamachi guides and fictional narratives alike, the okiya comes across most strongly as a home and a women's world. Rooted in its hanamachi network and traditions, the okiya lavishes time and attention on its young charges. References to everyone eating home-cooked meals together are routine. Manners count. This, too, makes the hanamachi appear as a site of older Japanese values. Impressed, Aihara finds that "the most basic, vital home education lives on in hanamachi maiko education."[22] In the okiya, maiko must internalize the etiquette for addressing their seniors as a daily practice. They learn to address all okiya and ochaya managers as okāsan. They address all geiko and maiko who are senior in years in the hanamachi as Elder Sister (onēsan). An oft-told anecdote that shows the depth of this sense of belonging imagines two elderly geiko meeting for the first time, one asking, "Elder Sister, you're the child of which okiya?" Examining okiya custom, Nishio describes in detail its familial structure, affective bonds, and the naming system of the okiya that formally links the maiko and geiko; since Liza Dalby also gives detail on this in Geisha, I will not repeat that here.[23]

Okiya mothers' training strategies and care earn high praise from Aihara and Nishio. Aihara lauds Pontochō okāsan Nakanishi Noriko for her sensitivity to the dispositions of the present generation. Nakanishi views hanamachi learning as spirituality (seishinsei) born of the "daily accumulation" of learning.[24] She strives to produce a positive atmosphere to build resilience in "today's girls." "Unless it's enjoyable for them, they can't try, and they can't learn. If they go through the motions grudgingly, they won't make any progress."[25] Frequent praise makes a difference, and in the end, parents thank Nakanishi for "having taught their daughters 'such beautiful manners even to the finer points.'"[26]

The only man involved in the okiya is the *otokoshi*, the dresser, who comes to assist maiko and geiko with their kimono, using his strength to fasten the obi well. It takes him only about ten minutes to dress a maiko or geiko. Busiest on days of major events when all the maiko and geiko require formal dress, he may dress twenty-five or more in one day.[27] In Gion Kōbu and Gion Higashi, the dresser escorts maiko and geiko on their round of greetings to teahouses on the day of their debut. The otokoshi used to be a position handed down over generations in families; Hamasaki and Ōta interviewed one fourth-generation Gion dresser in his fifties who had been doing the work since his early twenties.[28] Before the war, when maiko were children or young teens, the dresser acted as a kind of father figure to them. In 2015, Arai Mameji wrote that there were four otokoshi working in Gion at that point; one had joined during open recruitment for dressers in the early 2000s.[29] Iwasaki writes that, "Being a dresser is a highly skilled profession, one that takes years to master. A good dresser is critical to a geiko's success."[30] Dressers often figure as characters in fictional maiko narratives of the 2000s, ranging in age and personality from the cool young dresser who assists with Chiyogiku's disguise to the curmudgeonly dresser in *Maiko-san-chi no Makanai-san* who scolds an errant trainee, reminding her that the maiko's pleasant demeanor motivates all in the hanamachi to work so that "you maiko flowers can show your best face."[31]

Moving into the okiya, the prospective maiko must learn how the household operates, the duties of all concerned, and most importantly, her own role in making it work. A series of clearly defined stages and protocols await her, and even hold the opportunity for a lifetime career. Most applicants, however, arrive with no dance training and the relatively short-term goal of becoming a maiko. In the next section, we track the career path by examining three major stages—trainee, maiko, and geiko—as explained in the literature on life in the hanamachi. Along this path, the apprentice must learn to find her way beyond her okiya, mastering the customs, arts, and human relations of her community. We observe how expectations for deportment increase at each stage of the maiko's career path, highlighting the performative nature of her work. The maiko learns on the job by observing others and being observed and corrected herself. "I was always told that you can't learn by having the mother tell you 'do this, do that,'" manager Nakanishi explains, "rather, 'watch and learn (*mite manabinasai*).'"[32]

THE SHIKOMI TRAINEE

The trainee must greet the other person as an adult human being. She must be able to assess their position, and her own, and speak accordingly. Her demeanor—or as we say here in Kyoto, her *motenashi*—must be perfect at all times.

—Koito, okiya mother, quoted in Komomo and Ogino, *A Geisha's Journey*

The path to becoming this perfectly attuned apprentice begins by persuading an okiya mother to take one on as a *shikomi* (trainee). Girls can become shikomi fresh out of middle school, which marks the end of compulsory education in Japan, and forego high school to pursue this training full-time. Typically, they should not be older than twenty, the official age at which one becomes an adult and fully-fledged citizen in Japan.[33] This is also the age when maiko may well become geiko. This age range shows that maiko are considered girls, not young adults. Applicants must agree to switch to contact lenses if wearing glasses, and let their hair grow to shoulder-length to accommodate the maiko hairstyle. (We may assume that stylishly bleached, permed, or colored hair would not be welcome).

The okiya interview is the first step. In the past, girls arranged an introduction to an okiya through someone connected to the hanamachi such as a local kimono shop owner or client. But today, responding to the new recruiting efforts, many simply contact an okiya or the Ōkini Zaidan by email. Komomo tells readers how her journey started by initiating contact in 1997 with Koito, the geiko hailed for creating her own website.[34] Their correspondence lasted for three years. Born in Mexico, going to elementary school in Tokyo, and traveling to Beijing with her parents for middle school, Nasu Ruriko (her legal name) adored kimono, and had some study of Nihon buyō (literally, "Japanese dance"). Her plan to become a maiko met her desire "to be a Japanese person who could explain her own country and culture to others," overcoming a lack of knowledge on Japan she had felt acutely abroad.[35] A short stay at Koito's okiya the summer before middle school graduation, an increasingly common stage in maiko recruitment, confirmed the girl's decision—she became a trainee at age fifteen, and six months later, a maiko in 2000. Supportive of her decision, Komomo's parents cautioned her about the challenging training; indeed, Komomo found it "pretty tough."[36] One okāsan told Aihara that most girls, just like Komomo, know that apprentice life can be hard, but "they have no idea exactly what makes it difficult" and nothing in their education at home or school has prepared them for it.[37]

The shikomi period typically lasts from ten months to one year, but in cases where the teen already has proficiency in Japanese dance, this may take only six months. The relationship with the okiya begins with the girl, her parents or guardian, and the okiya okāsan meeting to discuss the apprenticeship. If things go forward, they make a verbal agreement. There is no written contract. Since shikomi may quit at any time, and many do quit after only a few weeks, the okāsan try their best to understand an applicant's motivation and determination in this interview. Pontochō okāsan and former geiko Masuda Kazuyo told Aihara that many girls nowadays come for their interview infatuated with the idea of becoming maiko, "imagining they can become maiko without any training. But it's essential to absorb what you are taught without complaint."[38] They must ascertain whether they truly have interest in learning the traditional arts. Similarly, former geiko Tanaka Hiroko, who has managed the Gion ochaya/okiya Tsurui since 1974, stressed the importance of the initial meeting. Tanaka insists that mothers accompany their daughters to the interview, since "if you meet the mother, you will understand what kind of daughter" she has raised.[39] She tells Aihara that since parents and teachers coddle children these days, few young people are prepared for the rigor and continual correction of their every move.[40] Komomo's mother Koito comments, "Training as a maiko is unimaginably hard for the spoiled children of today's society," so she devised the trial stays in the okiya to help girls "get a taste for the life."[41] Reflecting on mothers' high expectations for shikomi, Aihara surmises, "Compliance, seriousness, and an attitude of precision in daily life are key."[42]

Taking on a new shikomi represents a significant commitment—personal, educational, and financial—for the okāsan, as the literature emphasizes. By agreeing to accept the applicant, the okāsan welcomes the girl into her okiya family. Again, narratives emphasize the importance of the okiya as home; in this case it offers a substitute home for teens who may be away from their family homes for the first time. As her hanamachi "mother," the okāsan will train her in etiquette, hanamachi language, how to wear kimono, and the arts, and ensure that she obeys curfew. The okāsan promises to bear all expenses for the teen's lodging as well as her dance and other arts lessons, an investment that will continue throughout the apprenticeship. As the teen progresses on the maiko path, the okāsan will assume the considerable expense of providing her kimono, accessories, and weekly hair dressing. Nishio calls attention to the okāsan's knowledge of the kimono to dressing the maiko well, remarking that a poorly turned out maiko, no matter how talented, will not impress clients.[43] Once the trainee debuts as a maiko, she starts to earn money for the okiya, and hence, creates a loss for the okiya if she quits soon after. Although the literature stresses the financial investment required to train a maiko as the equivalent of thousands of dollars, there is no mention of how much the okiya earns from her assignments.[44] Thus, the okāsan's guidance and investment shine in the literature, sidestepping discussion of income earned from maiko bookings. The shikomi receives pocket money as a trainee and later as an apprentice, but she does not draw a salary. (Sumo wrestlers also undergo a long-term apprenticeship along these lines). As a maiko, she will receive tips from clients, which she may keep.[45] The maiko's distance from her labor as income-producing reinforces her image as one of a nonmaterialistic young artist aided by her benefactors.

Becoming a shikomi requires quite an adjustment. The trainee may be unfamiliar with kimono, have no knowledge of Japanese dance or music, and little experience even sitting on the floor. She may have had her own room at home and likely will not at the okiya. Various okāsan tell Aihara that trainees must adapt to taking meals with others, learning how to share food and pace themselves to finish with the group.[46] As the lowest-ranking member of her okiya, the shikomi must adjust to long days of arts lessons, running errands and helping with housework, and being on hand in the wee hours of the morning to help maiko and geiko returning from parties by folding and storing their kimono. She will have little time or space to herself. Most of all, shikomi will feel the weight of adjusting to hierarchy, absorbing all the correct protocols, learning the names of numerous people associated with the hanamachi, and keeping up with her lessons in the various arts, which in Gion are listed on a chalkboard as in figure 10.

Shikomi must learn to take criticism well and correct their behavior. One okiya mother explained to Nishio that this prepares the shikomi to act on trained instinct as a maiko. If a shikomi kept asking "why do I have to do this," persisting in arguing for a rationale, she would never develop the quick reactions necessary—in effect, failing to grasp the mind/body integration of shugyō. She would be unable to "do maiko rashii work at an ozashiki."[47]

The shikomi must always show deference. Nishio recalls the saying that shikomi "even bow to telephone poles" in the hanamachi, meaning that the youngest owe respect to everyone in the district "higher" than themselves. As

FIGURE 10. Maiko and geiko will consult this publicly posted chalkboard in Gion to learn the schedule of their arts teachers' upcoming lessons. Photo by author.

an example, Nishio explains that when she visits the hanamachi in kimono, the shikomi that she encounters will always stop, bow, and greet her as their elder, assuming Nishio must have some connection to their district.[48]

Speaking from experience, Komomo, too, describes the difficulty of adapting to shikomi life, "losing all the freedoms I'd taken for granted in my old life." She never knew when she could see her family or have a day off.[49] She concentrated on greetings, assisted Koito with her kimono, and did household chores. "I soon realized that the main point of my existence as a shikomi was to help people."[50] Arai Mameji, recalling her shikomi experience decades earlier in Gion in 1968, remembers the tough training, and takes great pride in having undertaken an apprenticeship. A chance sight of a 1958 picture in a photo book brings it all back to Arai— the shot of a small shikomi anxiously scrambling after a tall, formally clad maiko; the shikomi nearly falls out of her sandals as she struggles to keep a parasol over the maiko on a hot summer's day. "I felt as though that single photo encapsulated the girl's entirety."[51]

THE MAIKO: DEBUT AND APPRENTICESHIP

There was so much I had to learn as a *maiko*, and so many duties to perform. Every day
I was faced with things I didn't understand . . . It was like being at school twenty-four
hours a day, seven days a week.

—Komomo, *A Geisha's Journey*

About two weeks to one month before her maiko debut, the shikomi takes on
a new position, becoming a *minarai maiko*, literally, a maiko who is "learning
by observing." At this point, one ochaya in her hanamachi, termed her *minarai-
jaya*, will assume responsibility for guiding her initial forays into the world
of ozashiki. She will wear formal makeup, have her hair styled according to
convention, and wear a kimono with somewhat shorter sleeves than a maiko's.
Her *han-darari* obi will be half as long in back as that of a maiko. She will meet
clients and attend ozashiki for the first time, guided by the geiko and maiko
that she accompanies. Komomo remembers her two-week minarai period
passing "in a whirl" as she went nightly to one teahouse after another with
Koito, making "appearances at lots of ozashiki in front of people I had never
met."[52] Even more nerve-racking was the test in dance performance, taken in
view of her hanamachi elders, required for becoming a Miyagawa-chō minarai.
"Everything from my manners to my way of walking was under scrutiny."[53]

The minarai must make a good impression on clients to ensure getting
assignments after she formally debuts. Appearing at ozashiki allows her a
chance to get to know the clients and their names and motivates them to take
interest in her budding career.[54] Okiya and teahouse mothers repeatedly tell
Nishio, minarai must remember that, even when attending a party, they are
still working. As one mother reminds her minarai, "Since you are so inexpe-
rienced, it's essential that you adopt the attitude of trying to blend in with all
the people who are kind enough to be there with you. Do your very best to
try fitting in with your surroundings."[55] The minarai must also obey the geiko
and senior maiko at lessons and ozashiki. Even as a maiko, Komomo recalls
fear of her *sempai* (those senior to oneself) as "they were always getting mad at
me for one reason or another, and it seemed as if I couldn't do anything right
around them." This anxiety led Komomo to greet her sempai at ozashiki even
before welcoming the clients, provoking still more scolding.[56]

The maiko debut (*misedashi*) is an important public event, often captured in
documentaries, and announced in the local news.[57] Dalby describes the misedashi as signaling that the girl "has been tested and judged ready by the larger

community, which has a collective stake in her success."[58] Geiko speak of their misedashi as exciting and nerve-racking. Komomo remembers the thrill of feeling like a movie star, even though she "spent the whole day stressed out about silly little things."[59] After having her hair formally styled, getting her distinctive makeup applied, and being dressed in special kimono and the maiko's darari obi, the new maiko will perform a sake ritual that bonds her to the geiko who will be her closest Elder Sister. In the afternoon and in all her finery, she will be escorted to the teahouses in the hanamachi for her first greetings to the okāsan as a maiko—a reminder that she needs these managers' support to establish her career. Amateur and professional photographers will crowd around her to take pictures of the procession. In the evening, the maiko will also attend a round of ozashiki, again hoping to make a good impression and win future requests from the clients. Followed by cameramen all day, Arai Mameji remembers visiting so many ozashiki on the night of her 1969 debut that she stayed only ten or fifteen minutes at each.[60] Films as different in time as Mizoguchi's 1953 drama *Gion Bayashi* and Suo's 2014 *Maiko wa redi* (*Lady Maiko*) dramatize the maiko's misedashi from her costuming and ceremonial rounds to evening ozashiki.[61]

As a maiko, the teen is no longer expected to perform the errands and chores of the shikomi. But, as Komomo found, she will feel as though actively learning "twenty-four hours a day, seven days a week." As a maiko, Komomo saw her time consumed by formal lessons and informal afternoon practice, realizing that, "Dance practice was the one I had to concentrate on most."[62] A typical maiko day might entail lessons from 10 a.m. to 2 p.m. and ozashiki from 6 p.m.[63] The maiko may also be booked to perform at events promoting Kyoto, speak and perform for students visiting Kyoto on field trips, visit senior residences, and serve as a maiko model for commercials or paintings. Clients may offer to "take her out for a nice meal (*gohan tabe*)" to give the maiko a break from hanamachi hierarchy and work. No matter what her professional duty, the maiko will earn income for her okiya from the time she leaves for an assignment to the time she returns. She will have two days off per month. No surprise that one maiko commented to researchers, "A maiko's greatest wish is to have free time."[64]

The maiko will obey codes of deportment in her public role, as trained by her okiya mother. Arai, who admits that she is strict, forbids her maiko to use cell phones. She forbids them to buy beverages from a vending machine or to walk while drinking. "They are maiko, so following the old ways is good. I want them on their best behavior as members of the hanamachi who attract attention."[65] Arai believes that she must exert herself to train apprentices. Since they come from all over Japan, they have not internalized hanamachi etiquette, unlike in the old days when most Gion maiko came from Gion homes.[66]

The maiko as an apprentice continues her on-the-job training.[67] In her free afternoon time, she must make the rounds of teahouses in the hanamachi, greeting the managers and building her relationship with them. In the evening, she must follow the lead of geiko and senior maiko at ozashiki, mastering the balancing act of pleasing clients as a maiko rashii maiko. We will find more stories about the meanings of maiko-likeness in the personal accounts of maiko and geiko in chapter 3, but etiquette guides give insights, too. I find teahouse manager Tanaka Hiroko's comments to Aihara most telling. Tanaka describes clients, who may be older than the maiko's father, as needing escape from their responsibilities and hoping to feel refreshed by the maiko's girlish spontaneity. Tanaka assumes that the client may have a daughter at home who likely goes to her room when she comes home, making no effort to talk with her father. "I don't believe that clients want to have adult conversations with maiko. On the contrary, drawing clients into her youthful world is a maiko's hospitality."[68] Komomo, too, feels her job is to lift clients' spirits: "I love making people happy. Seeing the smiles on their faces when we walk into the room makes all the hard things about the life worthwhile."[69] The maiko becomes the perfect daughter.

The maiko's changing costume and hairstyle signal her growing maturity within the apprenticeship. After two or three years as a maiko, she will have a kind of coming-of-age ceremony termed *mizuage*. At this point, her hairstyle will change from the *wareshinobu* to the *ofuku* style. She will wear smaller kanzashi hair ornaments and the color of the straps of her high sandals will change from red to aqua, among other sartorial markers of this transition. But the experienced maiko must also show developing prowess. Writing about maiko maturity, Nishio defines the role of the experienced maiko at ozashiki as *maiko no shachō*, using the same term *shachō* as used for a company president. A maiko in this position is a kind of maiko team captain. According to Nishio, she does not arrive at this position simply through years as a maiko. Rather, she must demonstrate professionalism and leadership, assuming a sense of responsibility in her hanamachi in ways that extend past her own okiya.[70] Nishio imagines that this is the kind of maiko immediately recognizable on stage among the others as having matured in her art, too.[71] She has also developed *zamochi*, a skill in entertaining clients and making an ozashiki convivial.[72]

Many maiko will end their career in the hanamachi without becoming geiko. They may seek other work, continue their schooling, or get married as do other young women their age. Nishio knew one case of a maiko quitting to become a *tayū* in Shimabara, that is, becoming a kind of reenactor of the artistic courtesan role of the Edo era.[73] When a maiko or geiko decides to leave the hanamachi, she may participate in retirement rituals. These include giving out a kind of formal announcement—fine white paper folded in a large, triangular shape that bears the characters *hiki iwai* (retirement congratulations) in the center, and to the right, her professional name and her legal name to which she will return. Once the retiree gave symbolic gifts of white steamed rice to those in the hanamachi who had supported her career—teahouse and okiya mothers, her teachers, her geiko sempai and colleagues—often mixing in some red azuki beans that hinted at her possible return one day by muting the stark farewell indicated by the white. Recently, retirees have given gifts of white sugar or white tenugui (cotton hand towels) rather than rice.[74] Aihara mentions that some younger geiko and maiko have dispensed with the ritual altogether. Frankly sad to see the custom fade, Aihara appreciates the rituals of belonging and gratitude that have formed hanamachi culture, but realizes that generational change happens here, too.[75] Hiratake notes that former geiko resuming their careers in the hanamachi will hand out formal announcements of their return.[76]

"TURNING THE COLLAR" TO BECOME A GEIKO

Whenever one mentions the hanamachi, it is the image of the maiko that most powerfully comes to mind. Yet, it is the geiko who are its mainstay. Becoming a geiko is the goal of the maiko's apprenticeship. Only when she has finally become a geiko, perfectly internalizing her art and a sense of hospitality, will she be a fully-fledged adult in the hanamachi.

—Hiratake and Hamasaki, "Hanamachi wa ima"

Being a geiko is a professional identity, and it can be a lifetime career. Even though geiko do not function as Kyoto mascots, they are, as Hiratake and Hamasaki affirm, the "mainstay" of their community. Typically, when a maiko is around twenty years old, after four or five years as an apprentice, she will decide whether to pursue a career as a geiko. The ceremonial transition for this is known as *erikae*, "turning the collar." The changing color and pattern of a maiko's collars mark her progress in the apprenticeship.[77] As a geiko, she will

FIGURE 11. The maiko, standing behind the geiko, wears the apprentice's signature *kanzashi*, patterned collar, and long-sleeved *furisode* kimono. Photographed in Kyoto, 2009, by Claudia Bignion. Wikimedia Commons.

wear a pure white silk collar (figure 11).[78] The maiko's appearance may play a role in the timing of her erikae. A tall, more adult-looking maiko may graduate to geiko status sooner, while a "baby faced" maiko like Komomo spends longer in the apprentice role, because, as Komomo explains, "First impressions matter a lot in our world."[79] Aihara uses the adjective *ezukuroshii*, a word denoting maturity and adult sexuality to describe the maiko who has matured past childlike colors suiting her, a sign that she is ready for her erikae.[80] Some young women have remained maiko longer than usual because their hanamachi had too few apprentices.[81] *Maiko wa redī* satirizes this, imagining a woman well into adulthood and still a maiko, albeit a ridiculous one, since she was the only one left in her okiya.

On the day of her erikae, the new geiko is dressed in a formal black *kuro-montsuki* kimono. She exchanges cups of sake with the women from the okiya and ochaya who have supported her career, requesting their continued guidance. As happened at her misedashi, she is escorted about the hanamachi for rounds of greetings at ochaya and other establishments.[82] Once again, she can expect to see crowds of professional and amateur photographers, reporters and TV crews eager to document her geiko debut. Ideally, she feels new confidence. Komomo remembers, "At my misedashi, I'd had no idea where my life would take me. But by the time of my erikae, I had experienced so much and thought so hard about my decision to become a geiko that I had no reason to feel worried."[83] The new geiko must communicate maturity. Nishio writes, "The appearance of the geiko represents a complete change from her maiko days, there is the beauty of an adult woman, the aura of iki . . . far from the adorable maiko she'd been up to yesterday, her stance projects glamour and captivating charm."[84]

Everything about the geiko's appearance signals that she has become an adult. Her makeup aims for sophistication rather than cuteness. She has traded her high okobo for more comfortable zori and her long maidenly sleeves for the shorter adult-length. She no longer wears the long darari obi. Although the geiko wears her kimono with flair, her "usual kimono does not differ greatly from what any other Japanese woman might wear—if anything, it may be more subdued."[85] But the most pronounced and welcome change may be that she now wears a wig rather than having her own hair elaborately fashioned. Most geiko have two wigs—one to wear and one available to be restyled. The more dramatic change occurs in the geiko's professional status. After turning the collar, the young geiko continues to live at the okiya for one or two more years until completing her apprenticeship and becoming a fully independent geiko (*jimae geiko*). At that point, she will move out of the okiya and into her own place near the hanamachi. This is a sudden transition to adulthood. For the first time in her life, she must manage all her expenses such as paying the mortgage or rent, utility bills, groceries, taxes, and the like. Even small expenses can be a surprise, since young geiko tend to have little experience with money; as apprentices, they never dealt with living expenses. One geiko reports, "At the time I became a geiko, I had no idea how the world worked. I didn't even know that I should pay the taxi fee by myself."[86] As an adult, the geiko must also cover the costly expenses of her professional life—her arts lessons, kimono and accessories, and gift-giving rituals. She takes charge of her schedule and keeps the income from her work at ozashiki and other assignments. As a maiko, she could expect only two days off per month, but now, she is free to take more time for herself. The more ozashiki she attends, of course, the more income she earns. In her 2007 book, Nishio estimated that a geiko with a robust schedule of ozashiki and some additional work such as promotional tours might earn a total yearly income before taxes of well over 28 million yen or almost $250,000, given a 2007 exchange rate of approximately 115 yen to the US dollar.[87] Rather than drawing attention to the geiko's potential income, however, the literature emphasizes her devotion to arts training, an expensive pursuit, and her considerable work-related expenses. Some women who choose to become geiko describe the transition from maiko to adult as a liberating psychological transition. They are happy to graduate from maiko-likeness. Komomo puts it this way:

> Becoming a maiko was a big relief. . . . I also soon realized that ozashiki are completely different for geiko and maiko. Maiko are often just seen as stereotypes; nobody bothers to look beyond the make-up to the real person beneath. A geiko, on the other hand, is seen as an individual with a name and a unique personality. For a maiko, the most important thing is to match the image that people have of us, but as a geiko it's okay for us to let our own character show. After all my worry about becoming a geiko, I finally felt liberated.[88]

In her interview with a geiko, Aihara discovered the same sentiments of constraint and liberation:

> There was once a geiko who looked back on her apprenticeship as a terrible time in her life since all she was supposed to do was to hold herself back in a *maiko rashiku* way. . Since she had to act childlike as a maiko, not only her costume but her behavior too could not be adult. When she became a geiko, however, she enjoyed being able to express her individuality. She sensed that she had returned to her "real self (*honrai no jibun*)." She felt that to act like a maiko meant that she had to suppress who she really was, making her feel uneasy at times.[89]

Yet, some new geiko find the transition distressing. Becoming a Gion geiko in 1975, Arai, found the abrupt change in expectations astonishing.

> Strange to say, but when I was a maiko, I used to stand taller, wanting people to see me as even a little more adult. But now that I turned the collar, becoming a geiko, all I heard was, "You don't even know that sort of thing?" I felt that from

one day to the next only my dress had changed, and I was the same as always inside. Despite feeling just as I had as a maiko, the instant that I became a geiko, I was treated as an adult, making me feel that the adult world was very strict. This made me realize how tolerantly I'd been treated as a maiko since everyone thought of me as a child.[90]

As Arai learned quickly, a geiko will be expected to take charge at ozashiki, provide leadership to maiko, and make sure that the party flows well. To keep relying on others like a maiko would, as Aihara writes, be *geiko rashiku nai* (unworthy of a geiko).[91] As hanamachi literature attests, if the new geiko resists taking on this new responsibility, longtime clients and teahouse managers will push her toward it. As a professional artist, she should continually strive to develop her artistic skills. She may take on the training of maiko herself. Some hanamachi allow geiko to marry and continue in the profession, but references to married geiko in the literature are few and vague. Gion Kōbu does not sanction marriage for active geiko but has long supported single motherhood. Even if their hanamachi permits marriage, few geiko try to combine career with marriage. The late nights and hours devoted to arts lessons conflict with the expectations for family life. The aura of the geiko and her association with luxury also put her at odds with the frugality and practicality expected of the wife. According to Hiratake and Hamasaki, it is not unusual for women to move in and out of the geiko profession.[92] Former geiko Kiriki Chizu writes that the Gion welcomes back geiko who divorce.[93] Hiratake and Hamasaki and Foreman both find that longtime geiko tend to lose interest in marriage and enjoy their arts career.[94] Some geiko open their own bars or shops in the hanamachi, whether or not they intend to remain geiko, making use of their social skills and networks.

Before concluding this discussion of the maiko-geiko career path, I should mention the *jikata*, or musicians, as they form another important part of the arts community. According to Hiratake and Hamasaki, in the first decade of the 2000s some maiko were choosing this path rather than becoming geiko.[95] Jikata are women proficient in the samisen who play at ozashiki and the public dance performances. References to their roles in the hanamachi do not lead to comment about their deportment, only their musical skill. Foreman finds that many geiko move from *tachikata* (dancers) to jikata later in their careers.[96] Kiriki describes how around 2007, the time of her writing, there were between twenty and thirty jikata in Gion. Among these were graduates of four-year universities who majored in classical Japanese music. According to Kiriki, some of the newer jikata were donning wigs, coming to ozashiki, and attending major events with geiko where they helped serve sake.[97] Since few clients hire jikata for ozashiki performances, however, it is hard for the musicians to find steady work in the hanamachi; in turn, the hanamachi leaders worry about having sufficient jikata available for the spring and fall dances.[98] In 2020, the Gion and Pontochō websites both invite prospective jikata to contact them.[99]

CONCLUSION

Hanamachi literature, and especially hanamachi etiquette guides, depict the apprentice as sheltered within a world of classic arts and old customs. They define hanamachi aesthetics and sensitivity to social interaction as distinguishing this world from the commercial decadence of the mizu shōbai and the numbness of ordinary life. Entering the hanamachi as an ordinary girl, unaware of her own overly casual behavior and individualistic ways, the trainee hopes to emerge as a maiko. She must exemplify Japanese femininity and artistry while exuding youthful charm around clients, becoming the perfect daughter. Supervised closely by numerous female mentors, this idealized maiko experiences a significantly extended, aestheticized girlhood, apart from politics, material concerns, and sexuality. Trained to become the maiko-like maiko, the girl must internalize the codes learned from observing and being observed.

The rhetoric of manners in hanamachi literature not only divorces the maiko from the mizu shōbai, it mitigates the impropriety of the girl valued as entertainment for older men. This distances the maiko from tales of kogals meeting men on the streets of Shibuya and pocketing cash. Rather, the maiko emerges as the good girl who labors to learn the arts and etiquette, without concern for income, in an environment supervised by older women. Clients, also schooled in hanamachi manners, wish to support her career. Thus, readers and observers may root for the maiko, a chaste girl working hard in a demanding world of Japanese tradition, since her future remains vague. After all, she may decide to give it up to become a wife and mother and/or assume a mainstream vocation.

The literature on hanamachi training and etiquette in the 2000s does not devote as much space to the geiko. As a single, self-supporting artist, with hints that she has intimate relationships, the geiko is an ambivalent figure in the Japanese cultural landscape. As Foreman writes, "geisha are often cast as the epitome of woman on her best, most feminine Japanese behavior," but devotion to the performing arts rather than husbands makes them somewhat suspect.[100] Adulthood, individualistic expression, independent sexuality, and the potential to earn high incomes take the geiko figure in different directions. In contrast, maiko training and maiko-likeness contain the girl in a privileged space of innocence. Performing the maiko brand frees her from having to stamp her role with uniqueness. Yet some maiko find this containment can be too confining.

In the next chapter, we move from hanamachi guides about the maiko's training to consider women's personal accounts of their maiko and geiko lives. All stress personal agency, pride in dance achievement, and the demands of performing competing selves. They show what it means to walk a hanamachi career path, striving to embody its celebrated etiquette.

CHAPTER 3

Life in the Hanamachi

Voices of Maiko and Geiko

The Gion taught me everything important in life.

—Kiriki Chizu, retired geiko

It was *Hassaku*, the August 1st ritual of paying summer greetings to one's teachers and teahouse managers. Despite the sweltering heat, Gion maiko and geiko wore full makeup and dressed in their most formal black linen kuro-montsuki kimono. Maiko adorned their hair with bright kanzashi while geiko appeared in heavy wigs. Eagerly snapping pictures, crowds gathered to watch the procession. Reporters were on hand to capture the story for the evening news. Hours later, relaxing in her air-conditioned room that evening, geiko Kokimi watches herself and others in the spectacle on TV, marveling at its elegance, murmuring, "Gion is really something. Geiko are so beautiful."[1] But she also gives a comically different picture of the day's procession, complete with emoji-like punctuation and asides.

> My body rebels, as though crying "Water! Waaater! Now or I will die!"
>   It's that hot.
>   But onward we must walk, as if refreshed.
>   After all, we're what you might call, "Kyoto Arts and Crafts in Motion[?]."
>   I don't expect anybody wants to see a whole bunch of sweaty maiko and geiko traipsing along and fanning themselves to death, tucking up the hems of their kimono, their white makeup getting all patchy. (Even if that's the reality, we're keeping it under wraps).[2]

Firsthand accounts of hanamachi life like Kokimi's, conversational in style and often entertaining, entice readers by promising an insider's view of an unusual world. The disparity between public perception and personal experience, which Kokimi aptly communicates, often comes to the fore. Autobiographical books by modern geisha, though rare, date to the 1910s, depicting their experiences and the customs of their communities.[3] As though writing for curious but disparaging middle-class women locked out of the hanamachi as clients, twentieth-century geisha writers defend their character against stigma. In contrast, geiko accounts published in the first two decades of the 2000s endorse the Kyoto hanamachi as a site of cultural heritage, feminine polish, and refined etiquette. Bringing immediacy and the flair of individual voice, their books document continuity in women's progress on the maiko-geiko career path across postwar decades while revealing the impact of changing economic times and trends in the cultural landscape.

But generational differences abound among 2000s writers.[4] Boomer-generation authors who became maiko in the late 1960s regale readers with stories of hanamachi life amid the increasing affluence of the 1960s and 1970s and the opulence of the 1980s bubble economy. Their choice to become maiko rather than going to high school was somewhat unusual given the steadily expanding postwar rate of girls' high school graduation nationally. Maiko of this era benefitted from positive coverage in popular national magazines and at major events such as the first world's fair held in Japan, Expo '70 in Osaka. Their choice to remain single and make long-term careers in the hanamachi departed radically from other women in their baby-boomer cohort, many of whom became full-time homemakers and mothers, and often returned to work on a part-time basis to supplement family income.[5] Maiko and young geiko establishing careers in the first decade of the 2000s encountered a different social landscape. They benefitted from Kyoto's surge in tourism near the end of the decade and the promotion of maiko as retro-cute shōjo. Foregoing high school was an atypical choice but did not prevent profitable careers for those successful in the hanamachi. Despite their differences, boomer and millennial authors publishing in the 2000s express pride in their hanamachi careers, inviting Japanese women readers to see aspects of maiko-geiko training as engaging and even relevant to their own lives.

To explore this autobiographical genre in the era of the maiko boom, I have selected three books to discuss in this chapter. Elsewhere in the book, I explore two more renowned personal accounts published in Japanese and English in the 2000s, taking up the photo essay *A Geisha's Journey* (chapter 2) and Iwasaki Mineko's story (chapter 4). The three books examined in this chapter appeared only in Japanese, all published in 2007 close to the rise in domestic tourism to Kyoto and the boost in maiko numbers. Different in length, tone, and format, all three appear aimed at a readership of Japanese girls and women. Authored by a retired geiko, active geiko, and active maiko respectively, these accounts reflect hanamachi experiences among women born in different postwar decades and at different stages in their professional lives. Former geiko, Kiriki Chizu retired in 1988 after twenty years in Gion, but remains close to the hanamachi. Recounting stories of her eventful days as a maiko and geiko in affluent times, Kiriki offers lifestyle advice to her readers, too, in *Aisare jōzu ni naru Gion-ryū: Onna migaki* (The Gion way to skill in becoming loveable: A woman's polish). Next, we turn to Gion geiko Kokimi's humorous book, *Suppin geiko: Kyoto Gion no ukkari nikki* (Bare-faced geiko: My haphazard diary of Gion, Kyoto). Publishing under her legal name, Yamaguchi Kimijo narrates a year in her geiko life as she turns twenty-eight in 2007, thrives in her career, and wonders whether she will ever marry or become a mother. We conclude with the maiko's view as presented by Kamishichiken Ichimame's *Maiko no osahō* (Maiko etiquette). In 2007, teenage Ichimame was embarking on her fourth year as a maiko, with plans to become a geiko. Although none of these books became well-known nationally (unlike much of the fictional work discussed in this book), I found all readily available in Kyoto bookstores in the early 2010s.

Together, these three books offer valuable insiders' perspectives on hanamachi life. As scholars of autobiographical genres remind us, of course, even personal accounts do not present transparent reality. Like the films, novels, and manga discussed in chapters ahead, they are representations, too. Highly crafted, often collaborative, geiko- and maiko-authored books of the 2000s create the fiction of a unified, authorial voice, as first-person accounts conventionally do.[6] Still, they show how three women embrace hanamachi values, learn how to adopt public roles, and experience life in their unusual world.

What themes stand out among Kiriki, Yamaguchi, and Ichimame's books? How does their work relate to the literature on community values we explored in chapter 1 and the maiko-geiko training in chapter 2? All three books cohere in stressing personal agency, pride in dance achievement, and the demands of performing competing selves. Each woman in her own fashion expresses satisfaction in meeting challenges and overcoming personal setbacks. Portraits of maiko-likeness and the sense of masquerade emerge differently in the three books. Geiko Yamaguchi and maiko Ichimame present the difference between onstage and offstage personas in endearing ways, as though revealing that they are ordinary women after all. Yamaguchi shows her reader how quickly she can go from slacker to pro, "switching on" her geiko identity by donning her wig. Trading her maiko look for comfortable boyish fashion on her day off makes Ichimame unrecognizable. Yet both women delight in performing their hanamachi selves, too. In contrast, retiree Kiriki depicts self-management of her maiko and geiko roles as steps on a long path to mature femininity and social dexterity, drawing lessons from her experiences for her readers. For Kiriki, maiko-likeness may be a pose, but it is one suited to the apprentice as a young person with a specific role to play in the success of ozashiki.

We may step back for a moment to consider what readers will *not* hear from these three authors. Contrary to stereotype, none describes learning to wield feminine guile or erotic allure, as popularized in Arthur Golden's *Memoirs of a Geisha*. In fact, sex and romance do not figure in these narratives at all. We hear little about individual clients, unsurprising given the privacy valued in teahouse culture. As Kiriki writes, "I've seen and heard all sorts of things in Gion. But I will never divulge anything other than what I've written here."[7] Although we learn much about the geiko's professional work and expenses, we find out almost nothing about geiko incomes or the lucrative possibilities of the long-term hanamachi career. Nor do we hear much about discord within the okiya or the community. Rather, the authors represent the hanamachi as a familial community, where most insiders, including supportive clients, collaborate to nurture maiko as artists well-schooled in Japanese etiquette and social skills, and where everyone is too courtly to mention money. In fact, it seems as though there are no downsides at all in these books to becoming a maiko or a geiko. Even continual work carries the reward of adventure, and strict discipline yields personal and professional growth. Reflecting on this positivity, we must bear in mind the authors' close affiliation with their hanamachi at the time of their writing. Their books enhance the reputation of the hanamachi as a refined arts community with the geiko as its lead artist, and distinct from the commercialism of the mizu shōbai. The only critical geiko voice emerges in the work of Iwasaki Mineko, which I analyze through its interpretation in a popular manga in chapter 4.

We may also view these hanamachi books through the wider lens of popular genre. The values advocated here—discipline, gratitude, and resilience—dovetail with the motivational life stories published in the 2000s by other achieving Japanese women. Figure skaters, ballerinas, soccer players—many young celebrities have published their first-person books for general audiences. They, too, accentuate how ordinary people can step out of their comfort zone to set and achieve goals. Popular femininity guides by the transgender beauty IKKO and Miss Japan beauty queens, also conversational in style, seek to motivate and entertain.[8] Taking a broader view, we can see how the personal success story as a genre complements the neoliberal climate of the 2000s in Japan where the responsibility for one's lifelong health and financial stability rests on one's own shoulders. These kinds of success stories tend to translate forms of discrimination and structural inequities into personal hurdles that one must overcome. One must steel individual resolve, not buck the system. Narratives of life in the hanamachi, however, differ in emphasizing the authors' commitment to community. Here, they push back at the neoliberal call to invest only in oneself. Although the independent geiko becomes a freelance contractor in some sense, responsible for generating her income, she is always affiliated with an okiya and depends on the teahouse network. She remains a student of her arts masters. The geiko and her community depend on each other for identity and income, and together, they must attract and train prospective maiko. The maiko's entire mission revolves around developing the skills and inner strength necessary to represent her hanamachi in a maiko rashii manner.

RETIRED GEIKO KIRIKI CHIZU: CULTIVATING CHARM AND WISDOM

How pleased I'd be if my stories should serve as a useful touchstone for your own daily life and work.

Kiriki Chizu, *Aisare jōzu ni naru Gion-ryū*

Retired Gion geiko Kiriki Chizu's 242-page book, the longest of all three discussed here, mixes personal accounts of her twenty-plus years on the maiko-geiko career path with motivational advice.[9] She takes readers behind the scenes to lively ozashiki, quirky customers, events for visiting royalty and heads of state in the 1970s and 1980s, challenging dance lessons, and long hours of modeling for artists as a maiko. Proud of "being raised in the Gion," Kiriki suggests how her readers may enhance their own beauty and style, communication skills, and positivity by adapting Gion strategies. They, too, can learn to follow their teachers, quickly assess the dynamics of social gatherings, and improve their relations with others through greetings, thoughtful gift giving, and teamwork. Although she advocates resilience and

FIGURE 12. Cover, *Aisare jōzu ni naru Gion-ryū: Onna migaki* (The Gion way to skill in becoming loveable: A woman's polish) by Kiriki Chizu. Copyright © 2007. Courtesy of Kōdansha.

effort, Kiriki avoids perfectionism. After a few years as a geiko, she decided to do her best without competing for top honors or expecting perfection in every performance. Rather, by going at "my pace" (*mai pēsu*), she learned to aim for good work, not flawless results. Kiriki writes that if she were to name her personal philosophy, she'd say, "I've become an advocate of going for 80 percent."[10] Even the promotional sash (obi) around her book (figure 12) reads, "*Going for 80 percent* can make you happy" (emphasis in the original). A remarkable statement in a society that challenges people to give everything to work.

Born in Osaka in 1951, Kiriki grew up in a family that ran a kimono shop. Near the end of the occupation at this point, Japan still struggled to recover from the war, plagued by scarcities in food and shelter. We do not learn whether Kiriki faced such difficulty herself; she only mentions her childhood to explain how her interest in becoming a maiko developed. She began dance lessons on June 6 in her sixth year—the customary "6-6-6" start date favored in Nihon buyō, taught by an aunt who was a dance instructor in the Fujima school. Becoming a maiko allowed Kiriki to pursue her passion for dance. Even though Gion follows the Inoue school, Kiriki's experience must have stood her in good stead. She recalls that Gion acceptance rates were not high. "I came to Gion because I'd had lessons in Nihon buyō since I was a child, and by the time I turned fifteen, I wanted to become a maiko more than anything else. . . . For a young woman in her teens who adored dance and wanted to establish herself as an artist, what better place than Gion?"[11]

Kiriki's decision to become a maiko put her at odds with her family and her generation. Over her parents' objections, which she does not explain, Kiriki moved to Kyoto after middle school, taking up residence in a Gion okiya. She also enrolled in a local Kyoto high school, but quit after one semester, finding it impossible to maintain both her schoolwork and her shikomi duties. As a baby boomer, Kiriki had grown up amid Japan's efforts to implement a new postwar coeducational system.[12] Schools were built to meet demographic demand, and as we have seen, girls were graduating from high school in increasing numbers. For example, 73.7 percent of girls in Japan in Kiriki's cohort went on to high school in 1967; of that group, 23.5 percent entered college or university in 1970.[13] Choosing a different path, Kiriki recalls her strong determination: "I wanted to become a fully-fledged maiko quickly."[14] In April 1968, after one year as a shikomi, devoting most of her time even then to dance and adapting to okiya life, the sixteen-year-old debuted as the maiko Toyochiro.[15] In 1972, she "turned the collar," becoming a geiko at age twenty-one. During Kiriki's early maiko and geiko years ensconced in Gion, students on college campuses protested Japan's role in the Vietnam War and other social issues, and the 1973 oil crisis had devastating effects on the Japanese economy. Youthful tastes from miniskirts to excitement over the Beatles' 1966 Japan tour affected the cultural landscape. Gion was not immune to these changing tastes and financial effects. Maiko numbers dropped from over forty in 1965 to fewer than twenty by 1975; similarly, slightly over 150 geiko remained in Gion in 1975, down from almost 250 in 1965.[16] Nonetheless, Kiriki's narrative rarely mentions contentious current events; instead she describes herself as fortunate that her hanamachi career occurred in prosperous times.

Proud of her choice to pursue dance professionally in the hanamachi, Kiriki still shows the need to justify her lack of formal education. She asserts, "Gion taught me everything important in life."[17] One of the promotional captions on the book's obi promises that readers will learn "what Gion teaches you that high schools do not." Kiriki argues that in Gion, "the most distinguished are middle-school graduates," explaining that the earlier one starts full-time arts training, the more proficient one becomes.[18] Indeed, she recalls how Gion people even express pity for those who went on in school rather than getting an early start in the profession, scoffing, "What were you thinking? Going to high school!"[19] This does not mean that Kiriki devalues formal education; rather she argues for her Gion training as equally valuable. The short biography on her website shows that Kiriki takes pride in her invitations as an older person to speak at Kyoto University about Gion and to have coauthored an academic paper on the hanamachi with a professor there.[20]

Somewhat tongue in cheek, Kiriki also credits media attention to maiko in the late 1960s as a motivating factor in her own decision to join Gion. "Everything seemed to glitter in the 1960s and '70s during the era of high-speed growth—with events like the Tokyo Olympics and the Osaka Expo. And in those days maiko were part of the glitter."[21] Weekly magazines ran regular features, showing photos of big stars surrounded by maiko and giving the same kind of attention to individual maiko that young pop stars (*aidoru*) enjoy today. Kiriki recalls, "I would get ahold of those magazines and lose myself in them."[22] An impressionable middle school student, she dreamed of her photo running in a magazine, too. In fact, glitter and celebrity did envelope Kiriki's life as a maiko and young geiko. She describes how "maiko had a special existence; we were privileged" in her day and even more so in the opulent 1980s—pampered by clients with gifts of the trendiest gourmet foods, fancy dinners, golf dates, and first-class trips to Hawaii and Europe.[23] Kiriki stresses that clients had to pay for the maiko's time and for the chaperones required to accompany maiko on every outing. Sexual contact was strictly forbidden.

This glittering life for maiko in the late 1960s extended to public events, too. As "the face of Kyoto," Kiriki and other maiko traveled within Japan to local events and department store promotions, dancing for enthusiastic audiences.[24] "Events were always packed, mainly with members of the general public coming to catch sight of maiko, an extraordinary event for them. We would pay courtesy calls to the area's local newspaper and city hall. We'd promote Kyoto by participating in parades, handing out fliers, and things like that. Everyone was overjoyed about maiko coming to town. It was a unique privilege for us."[25]

Enamored of Kyoto, Kiriki was eager to promote the city, but as an admittedly shy person who lacked self-confidence, she found public performance no easy task. Troubled when paparazzi and zealous fan photographers hounded her, Kiriki disliked feeling "as though I had become an exhibit (*misemono*) myself."[26] But she credits the demand that maiko meet the challenge of continual display in public and at ozashiki as the way to gain feminine polish.

"Since I always had to stay alert to being on display, a sense of self-awareness naturally developed in me. My posture, the way that I moved, my manners, and so forth became refined."[27]

Kiriki experienced celebrity moments. Immediately following her debut, she appeared in TV commercials and modeled for the famous nihonga painter Ishimoto Shō (1920–2015), a specialist in maiko paintings.[28] The June 1972 special Gion issue of *Taiyō* (*Sun*), a national magazine, features photos of Kiriki at her erikae and as a geiko.[29] In 1975, she earned national celebrity by starring in a kimono campaign for PARCO, the department store, which was turning heads in the 1970s for its enigmatic ads. Her PARCO poster depicts Kiriki in a navy blue kimono as a calm young woman, seated, her eyes cast downward as though lost in thought, her hair pulled back, and her makeup minimal. As though in reaction to the second-wave feminist movement brewing at the time, the poster catch-copy reads, "I want to be a woman until I die" (*shinu made onna de itai no desu*).[30] Without comment on this line, Kiriki remembers what a sensation the poster caused, being stolen from subway station walls as soon it was put up. Copies for sale soon sold out, too. She muses, "Had I not been a geiko, this job certainly would not have come my way."[31] Modeling requests from other major companies soon followed. Modestly, Kiriki recalls how PARCO wanted to book her among all other Gion geiko precisely because of her average looks, assuming she'd inspire "ordinary women" who'd think, "Since it looks good on her, I'll give it a try too."[32]

Unlike Ichimame and Yamaguchi, Kiriki does not narrate moments of public performance as a comic disparity between onstage/offstage selves. Perhaps because her book functions in part as a beauty and lifestyle guide, Kiriki presents her maiko training as a gradual, holistic maturing, available to her readers, too, should they decide to take care with their deportment, aware of being on display in their own lives. Kiriki credits a sense of alertness (*kinchōkan*) as the key to beauty. Adopting the discourse of the day, Kiriki promises that "anyone can attain polish and shine (*kagayaku*)," claiming that the most successful maiko and geiko are not born beauties (*bijin*). Rather, their "secret" lies in developing beauty through dance training, ozashiki conversational experience, and most importantly "by being on daily display in front of many people at ozashiki and attracting attention from those around them, experiencing continual alertness."[33] Assuring readers how much a maiko may improve in a single year, Kiriki claims that the sheer visibility of the maiko role engenders the vigilance and discipline that "can transform a potato into a diamond."[34] Kiriki argues that producing beauty or "elegance" (*hannari*) is best seen as developing skills in conversation, dance, and special interests rather than relying on physical attractiveness. In this regard, Kiriki uses herself—a woman of "average looks"— as an approachable model for producing elegance.

When Kiriki turns to memories of maiko dance training, however, a much different maiko-geiko life comes to the fore, overshadowing the excitement of public celebrity and pampering by wealthy clients. Stories of her Inoue dance lessons reveal exacting teachers and methods. From the outset, Kiriki knew that as a maiko, she was on a strict professional track.[35] But she was shocked to receive an *otome* one day at her dance lesson, a teaching tool that maiko find devastating. The otome—a serious reprimand—happens when the teacher finds the student lacking and orders her to *stop* dancing and immediately return home. In fact, custom holds that the student must sit quietly for the rest of the day closely watching all the other students' lessons one after another. The teacher keeps ordering her to leave, but she must stay, always on the point of tears.[36] Sensing the problem, her okāsan came to fetch her at the end of the day. At that point, Kiriki gave one more performance for her teacher who gently praised her improved effort. "See, look at you now. You can do it if you try, right?" Kiriki cried all the way back to the okiya with her okāsan, but she believes that the discipline worked. "I knew deep down inside where my own dance that day had not been up to par."[37] By meeting this and other challenges as a dancer, Kiriki believes that she took critical steps in "maturing as a fully qualified maiko" and gradually developing "a sense of myself as a professional."[38] The teacher never scolded her again. Although this kind of training may depart from contemporary teaching methods, Kiriki writes, or seem illogical, she maintains that this kind of nonverbal experiential training produces significant learning and resilience. Kiriki devoted herself to dance in many venues, meeting one challenge after another. At thirty, she earned the *natori* designation for dance proficiency in the Inoue School, an honor that made her eligible for select roles.[39] Kiriki credits her dance training for nurturing her resolve never to give up when tested in arts lessons or at work.

Although Kiriki describes how she developed grit in her dance training, when it comes to the maiko's role at ozashiki, she stresses the importance of projecting girlishness and naivete. Anecdotes on maiko-likeness appear in a section on many ways to show consideration for guests. Kiriki deems that, "It is the job of maiko, as girls in their teens who know nothing, to sit quietly, with the sense of themselves as novices. With the charm and gentleness of a doll, the maiko becomes a real asset."[40] By "asset (urimono)," I take Kiriki to mean that the maiko must contribute to the lighthearted atmosphere of the ozashiki, lifting her elders' spirits by performing an innocent girlishness, as we saw described in chapter 2. Kiriki notes that while it is important to engage in ozashiki conversation, "it is not appropriate for a maiko to put forward her own opinion or talk on and on about things she knows."[41] "Should a client remark, 'What a well-informed maiko,' then that is a sign that she has actually been a wet blanket."[42] "There are places where a know-it-all is not welcome," writes Kiriki, and she asks, "Isn't this true in other social situations, too?" Rather a maiko should respond to what clients are telling her with, "'Oh, is that true? I didn't know that,' as that creates a more pleasant mood."[43]

As an example of developing sensitivity to maiko-likeness, Kiriki relates anecdotes about proper responses to a client's offer to give a maiko a gift. Once, when a client asked what she might like, one maiko, failing to "read the room," blurted, "a Kelly bag"—an exorbitant request, as the luxury French handbag costs thousands of dollars. On a different occasion, another maiko "spoiled the moment" by replying, "a motorcycle helmet"—not understanding that the client and teahouse manager, who would likely be the one purchasing the gift, would have no idea how to get one. Although Kiriki says this request would be fine if the client were a motorcycle enthusiast, it is better to ask for something modest and within the expected desires of a maiko such as new sandals or a fresh supply of calling cards (hanameishi). Kiriki most approved of a maiko who requested a Hello Kitty plush toy, praising her as a "smart girl" for coming up with a maiko rashii item.[44] Not only does this toy befit the childlike image of a maiko, but the request shows that she knows "how to read the room"; that is, she understands the situation and her role in it. Such stories coupled with accounts of Kiriki's dance training underscore the complex role the maturing maiko needs to play, one of walking a fine line between girlishness in some instances and intensity in others. Performing maiko-likeness requires juggling both personas.

Near the end of her book, Kiriki writes at length about her agonizing decision to retire at age thirty-six at the top of her career after over twenty years in Gion. Little did she know, she writes, that this also coincided with the peak in the bubble economy. She began to feel her motivation ebbing away but did not know what do next. "Saying that I would retire was one thing, but it wasn't like I had skills in all kinds of fields. To quit meant not attending ozashiki, giving up my job."[45] In choosing her next career, Kiriki wanted to work in a field that would introduce international tourists to Japanese culture. Embarking on a fresh career in ikebana, a passion of hers, proved a rewarding path that gave her opportunities for work-related travel abroad, even though it meant starting at the bottom of a new hierarchy.[46] "For me, who had hardly been out of the hanamachi, one culture shock followed after another. . . . It was a world 180 degrees different from ozashiki."[47] It took Kiriki ten years to establish herself in this second field, one led at the top entirely by men, but she feels proud of taking on the challenge of a new career at thirty-six.[48]

For several years in the early 2000s, Kiriki ran the small shop Kasai in Gion, where she sold various petite goods and served tea and sweets. Here, she could also make special arrangements for maiko to come by to meet customers, giving them a taste of the ozashiki, and fulfilling her dream of helping people understand the "true character of Gion."[49] Although Kiriki discusses her career choices, she makes no reference to decisions about marriage and motherhood. Still involved with Gion in 2020, Kiriki maintains a Japanese website and blog, advertising her services as a speaker, event planner, and guide to Gion.[50] Although Kiriki's life course as a single career woman departs from most Japanese of her boomer generation, her passion for Korean TV dramas and Korean language lessons, golf, and travel abroad as an older person puts her in league with many affluent women in her cohort.[51] For Kiriki, her willingness to follow the lead of her dance and ikebana teachers led ultimately to self-discovery. It may be counterintuitive, she writes, but absorbing the teacher's instruction enables the student to produce art *in her own way*—jibun rashiku style. Following the teacher's direction, "you may doubt whether you can express yourself, but even so, your jibun rashisa will fully be expressed."[52] She advises that readers take this approach, too, when starting work in any new field. As maturity develops, one grows into one's own style and talent. Kiriki also advises her readers to follow their teacher patiently, rather than insisting on doing everything in their own way from the start.[53]

GEIKO KOKIMI: FINDING HUMOR AND JOY IN HANAMACHI LIFE

Turning to our next author, Yamaguchi Kimijo, the geiko Kokimi, takes us up to the 1990s and a different social climate. High school education was routine in Yamaguchi's day; over 96 percent of the girls in her cohort entered high school, almost half went on to some form of college.[54] But, after the bubble burst in 1991, new graduates faced "the ice age of employment," finding it so difficult to get a foothold on a career ladder, they became known as the "Lost Generation."[55] From the 1990s through 2000s, changes in demographics and mores related to young women in Japan incited fears over the collapse of the family: the numbers of single career women increased, birth rates fell, and divorce rates rose. In the mid- and late 1990s, media attention turned to deviant schoolgirls, fascinating for their sexual and financial independence, cheeky style, and consumerism (see the introduction). An escape from current events and the concerns of her day, Yamaguchi's witty book focuses closely on her daily life in Gion and her relations with her family. Although the end of the bubble economy did impact the hanamachi, Yamaguchi portrays Gion as busy and flourishing. In 2007, Gion had seventy-four teahouses, half the number operating in the mid-1960s, and twenty-eight maiko. Its geiko population had dwindled to eighty-six.[56]

"A must read for anyone who dreams of becoming a maiko or geiko. Whether you live in Kyoto or are just a fan, you'll be surprised by what this guided stroll through Kyoto with a Gion expert teaches you." This exuberant copy on its sash entices readers to buy Yamaguchi Kimijo's *Suppin geiko: Kyoto Gion no ukkari nikki* (Bare-faced geiko: My haphazard diary of Gion, Kyoto). The title plays with both meanings of the word *suppin*—a face "free of makeup" and writing "free of pretense and formality."[57] *Suppin* also evokes a rebellious streak. As Mikiko Ashikari points out, adult women appearing in public without makeup arouse suspicion for transgressing Japanese femininity codes.[58] The cartoon image on the book jacket holds a surprise. At first glance, you see a geiko looking back over her shoulder as her purple kimono dips far down her back, exposing the erotic nape of her neck. But unfold the cover, pulling it all the way out, and you see her impishly flashing the peace sign—a common gesture in Japan when snapping photos (figure 13).

The funny cover captures the irreverent voice of *Suppin geiko*. In one tale after another, Yamaguchi gives comic behind-the-scenes views of maiko and geiko. Clearly, Yamaguchi takes her work seriously and enjoys performing, but humor keeps her from seeing herself as a model geiko. Recalling wishes made at a summer festival, she jokes about having "too many," mixing the blithe and serious. She hopes for "a life without regrets; health and happiness for my family, friends, and clients; and . . . and my dance getting better; becoming a good geiko; losing three kilos; and world peace."[59] Her maiko days passed easily, and she still retains good relations with her okiya. While she admires the beauty of hanamachi conventions, she also laughs at the gap between the

FIGURE 13. Cover, *Suppin geiko: Kyoto, Gion no ukkari nikki* (Bare-faced geiko: My haphazard diary of Gion, Kyoto) by Yamaguchi Kimijo. Copyright © 2007. Published by LOCUS. Courtesy of Kanbara Kunie.

performers and their elegant display, revealing the chaos backstage at dance productions, the stickiness beneath kimono in summer, and lapses in manners.

Organized as a series of anecdotes grouped together by the four seasons, *Suppin geiko* takes readers through a year in Yamaguchi's life, weaving in stories from her childhood and maiko days. Spring comes first—the season when trainees join the hanamachi and everyone in Gion gets caught up in preparations for *Miyako Odori*. We learn about her first days in the hanamachi, her funny slip-ups and successes, the up-and-down relations with her family members, and her reflections on life in Gion. The collaboration of Kimijo's elder sister, Yamaguchi Yukiko, in writing the 159-page book based on conversations with Kimijo no doubt shaped the narrative's breezy, conversational style. Adorned with charming watercolor images by illustrator Obika Kazumi and peppered with emoji-like parenthetical comments (Tears! Sweating it! Laughter!), *Suppin geiko* is a delightful read. As an active geiko, Yamaguchi needed to obtain permission from the Gion leadership to publish the book, making the edits that they deemed necessary. Since the first-person authorial voice is the geiko's and the book credits her as its author, I will refer to Yamaguchi Kimijo as the author in my discussion.

Suppin geiko gives readers a sense of how maiko and geiko plan their lives from month to month. Their schedules revolve around annual Kyoto festivals and major dance performances, hanamachi ceremonies, their arts lessons, and evening ozashiki. In a sheepish way, Yamaguchi confesses to taking account of the lucky and unlucky days noted on the calendar, too.[60] She describes her misedashi debut as a critical turning point in her life, making her feel that she truly and proudly *belonged* to her new community.[61]

Born in 1978 in Tokushima Prefecture on the island of Shikoku where her parents owned a clothing shop, Yamaguchi entered her Gion okiya/ochaya after middle-school graduation in 1992. She spent one year as a shikomi and a month as a minarai. She debuted as the maiko Kokimi in 1993 at age fifteen and became a geiko five years later in 1998. She had been an independent geiko for several years when she published *Suppin geiko* at about age twenty-nine. A die-hard Hanshin Tigers baseball team fan, Yamaguchi made the news in 2003, when the team won the pennant, as the Tiger Geiko (*tora geiko*), commissioning an expensive tiger-themed kimono and obi which she wore at ozashiki. In 2019, I was excited to observe Yamaguchi, still an active geiko, dancing a major role in the year's *Miyako Odori*, a swaggering male part that she carried off with aplomb.

What prompted Yamaguchi's decision to enter maiko training? It had much to do with the "push" of disliking school, especially mathematics, and the "pull" of kimono and dance. Unlike her elder sister, a stellar student, she hated studying, could never hope to ace a test, quit piano lessons after just one day, and played hooky from cram school. At the same time, she had always adored kimono. She wryly recalls how even as a child, "I loved kimono more than anything else in the world. After the Shichigosan Festival,[62] I cried and fussed, and wouldn't take off my kimono for three days. As soon as I came home from school, I would put on my kimono. . . . Guess you could say I had a real rough childhood."[63]

Her childhood interest in becoming a maiko stirred when an adult once suggested, "You know, if you became a maiko, you could wear a kimono every day." Yamaguchi recalls an instant captivation with hanamachi dance. She describes feeling "spellbound" as a ten-year-old when she first saw Gion master teacher Inoue Yachiyo IV dance on TV. "I learned that only maiko and geiko in Kyoto's Gion could study that."[64] Even as she entered middle school, she resolved to become a Gion maiko as soon as she graduated.[65]

At a loss about what to do with their "eccentric daughter," Yamaguchi's parents suspected that she would quickly lose her "infatuation with Gion" once she experienced its rigor. Reflecting on her youthful rebellion, Yamaguchi writes how her parents chuckled when she warned, "I am going to Gion, and if you try to stand in my way, I will run away from home."[66] Having no knowledge of Gion, her parents arranged for their daughter's introduction to an okiya through an acquaintance of another dress shop owner. Going to Gion for the first time for her interview, Yamaguchi fell in love with its ambience. "So far, this had been nothing more than a dream I'd had from watching TV, but here was the world of the maiko."[67] Right after graduation, she moved into the okiya and, as her parents expected, she realized how little she knew about her new world. "No one among my family or friends was associated with the hanamachi. I had jumped into a completely unknown world. . . . All I can do is give it my best every day."[68] Even as others in her cohort of trainees quit, Yamaguchi remained undeterred because, like Kiriki, she owned her choice. "I was the one who had *decided* to become a maiko" (emphasis in the original).[69] Her dislike of school figured here, too. Yamaguchi laughs when recounting her mother's teasing words when she left her daughter at the okiya: "You can come home anytime, you know. Come home, take the high school entrance exam, get your life back on track. . . . I've already bought the math flash cards for you, so I'll be waiting."[70] Yamaguchi realized that her mother knew "there was nothing I despised more than the idea of math drills !"[71]

Anecdotes about her parents' initial hesitation and gradual acceptance of their daughter's decision also recall stigmatizing perceptions of the maiko-geiko career path that Yamaguchi encountered. Often clients at ozashiki, who, she assumes, had daughters of their own about her age registered surprise that her father had permitted Yamaguchi to become a maiko.[72] Her only response is to tell her readers that she understands how some might worry about letting one's daughter forgo high school for an unusual occupation in an unfamiliar world, knowing that if she failed, it would be hard to get back on an academic track again.[73] But she does not ask why the men felt comfortable being there themselves if they had these doubts. Talking with these clients gives Yamaguchi fresh perspective on her father's support for her decision; poignantly, she realizes that he probably would have preferred his daughter take a more conventional, less risky path because he is protective. "Having accomplishments in art instead of academic degrees, I just keep giving it everything I've got, here in Gion, apart from Dad."[74] She takes pride in her work, exclaiming that as the characters for *geiko* indicate, she is "a woman (ko) supported by art (gei)." Quickly taking the drama down a notch, Yamaguchi quips, "But even if I came home at this point, wouldn't he say, 'Time for you to get back to high school' (laughter)?"[75]

Yamaguchi expresses some wistfulness about missing out on the fun of ordinary teenage life and young romance. One summer evening as she nears her thirtieth birthday, she imagines what she gave up: hanging out with classmates at fast-food places, getting excited about the annual school festival, trying out part-time jobs, and crushes on boys. All her old friends have graduated by now and gotten jobs, following a conventional path. While mocking her tendency toward self-dramatization, she muses, "First as a maiko and then a geiko, I had forbidden myself such things. . . . Things that any ordinary young person (*futsū no ko*) could do would be considered poor manners for a maiko or geiko."[76] Seeing young couples sitting together on the banks of the Kamo River makes Yamaguchi envious. How charming it would be to walk along the river wearing a pink-and-red yukata, holding hands with a boy, she muses, and then just as quickly, she says, "but a geiko cannot do that, especially this close to Gion. But then I have no boyfriend (tears), anyway, so it's a moot point."[77] Yet, "all the same, if I had it to do all over again, I would still choose this life of mine."[78]

In *Suppin geiko* Yamaguchi writes about her dance and drum performances with both pride and humor, emphasizing that maiko and geiko, no matter how long they have been in the hanamachi, are always students of the arts.[79] Like Kiriki, she values the sense of alertness (kinchōkan) engendered by performance. She enjoys performing at ozashiki, "the quiet tension of dancing" in that intimate space, but finds "a far different kind of tension and excitement when one is called out to dance on stage."[80] She recounts many tales about the excitement surrounding the public dances, especially the *Miyako Odori*, on stage and backstage in the green room where family, friends, and clients gather, and a constant supply of gourmet food gifts arrives. Reveling in the camaraderie, Yamaguchi paints an amusing picture of exhausted maiko and geiko—the beauties of Kyoto's cherry blossom season—secretly yearning for muscle-pain relief ointment. Whether a new maiko or a veteran geiko, no one in Gion gets to take a pass at this busy time. Yamaguchi explains how everyone is up early in the morning, on stage in the afternoon, guzzling protein drinks after that, and then off to evening ozashiki, finally topping off the evening with a flurry of vitamin supplements.[81] She expresses how happy she feels when clients compliment her dancing and she gets the added boon of "losing weight without even dieting."[82]

Turning to the Gion's fall dance production, Yamaguchi describes the preparations for the sober *Onshūkai*, which may be translated as "recital," held on the first six days in October. She explains how many connoisseurs know these famous dances well and likely notice any mistakes. Their high expectations make Yamaguchi feel anxious as she rehearses but satisfied when she performs well. Sometimes new dances are choreographed, too. She writes, "I feel such a sense of accomplishment when I pull off a difficult dance. I can't even express in words how good it feels when my clients and others at the event praise my dancing. But caring this much also makes me very anxious. Like when I wake up in the middle of the night having dreamed of dancing on stage with everyone else and being the only one making mistakes. That makes me leap out of bed and start practicing right then and there."[83]

Ever the self-deprecating narrator, Yamaguchi recounts her lapses as an artist, too. She gives the example of resolving to practice well in advance for the summer *Yukata-kai* dances—so named because all wear matching cotton yukata—in Gion, even putting her samisen in the living room to coax herself to practice every chance that she had some free time. But she cannot bring herself to practice at all. "Sure enough, I end up practicing all night on the last day before the event. The same thing I do every year before *Yukata-kai*."[84] She readily admits that she has her bad days like everyone else when nothing seems to go right. "There are days when I regret that I couldn't make the guests very happy. There are days when I just didn't give my all to the lesson and got chewed out by the teacher. My sister was put out with me and then I got into a fight with our mother. Just when I ended up wondering if I could do anything right, the Hanshin Tigers went and lost, too (smile). Those sorta days."[85]

Resilient, Yamaguchi can scoff at her self-pity, vow to get her act together, and resolve to "live life always brimming with self-confidence." But even the fervor of this resolution makes her laugh at her "immature self." She jokes that she is likely to end up in the same boat all over again, popping into the bar near her condo for a nightcap to ease her sorrows.[86]

Yamaguchi reveals how she gets ready for her performance and how costuming helps her switch on and off. Her tale of a typical afternoon affirms her ordinariness yet shows how she can snap into character. Yamaguchi relates how she likes to stretch out in front of the TV, making an "afternoon ally" out of a variety show. She ends up sluggish, feeling as though it is impossible even to imagine how she will make it to the ozashiki that evening. But getting into costume makes all the difference. "I take a bath, sit down at the mirror on my makeup table. I pull back my hair and begin with cosmetics. I put on the white foundation, doing my face. My slack facial muscles tense instantly. At the appointed time, the dresser arrives."[87] When the dresser pulls her obi tight, Yamaguchi feels an immediate transformation. "The moment that my obi is fastened, it seems that I can't have been that afternoon slacker at all. It's like I am a totally different person. And just to prove it, I pick up the trash that I had kicked out of the way just moments ago (smile). I clean up the wreckage of my afternoon snacks on the table and down a quick cup of tea. I am ready for work!"[88]

All systems go, Yamaguchi now relishes going to the ozashiki. Donning her geiko wig adds the final touch. "When I put on my wig, the switch is on. I become the Kyoto Gion geiko, Kokimi."[89] By the same token, when she gets back home after midnight, tired and tipsy from ozashiki, getting out of costume relaxes her. "I take off my kimono and put it away. Once that is done, I take off my heavy wig. In fact, I really want to take that off first thing. . . . When the wig comes off, the switch is off!"[90] This tale makes Yamaguchi realize, "My geiko switch seems to be inserted in that wig."[91]

Yamaguchi's satisfaction with her career choice comes across throughout the book and especially in the following story. One day in May, she overhears students from her native Tokushima chatting in their local dialect on their field trip to Kyoto. Their uniforms look like those of her old school. Memories of her own elementary school trip to Kyoto rush back. She remembers how her family laughed over the souvenir she brought home—a plastic replica of Kyoto's legendary Golden Temple. Recalling her childhood dream of becoming a maiko, Yamaguchi feels as though she is in a time warp. "And what do you know—I really did become a maiko and a geiko. . . . Even though I'd been the one to decide on this, I still felt surprised that I had actually pulled it off."[92] Yet, nearing thirty, Yamaguchi wonders about her future. When seeing off a geiko sister who is leaving the hanamachi to get married, she asks, "Can you really do the whole wife thing in Tokyo?"[93] Yamaguchi imagines that one day she, too, will want to become a mother, as her own mother advises, "but for now I just don't have enough resolve."[94] She does not give any further detail on what marriage or motherhood might mean to her or for her career. Rather, these remain merely expected stages in the conventional life course, put off for now. She concludes her book looking forward to the coming spring and *Miyako Odori*.

MAIKO ICHIMAME: FASHIONING A DOUBLE-LIFE OF PERFORMANCE AND PLAY

Taking up the maiko story of our third author, Kamishichiken Ichimame, turns our attention to girls joining the hanamachi in the early 2000s. We find that girls' educational attainments in Japan remain high, many of the same demographic concerns persist, and fashionable girls are making news. Around the time of Ichimame's publication, mainstream media was turning attention to AKB48 idols and quirky images of Japanese girlhood in Lolita fashion, maid cafés, and schoolgirl chic (see the introduction). Among this costumed line-up of girl types, the maiko appeared uniquely conservative. Yet, Ichimame's self-presentation as a hardworking girl-next-door resonates with the AKB48 idol's imagined persona.[95] When Ichimame joined her okiya, financial concerns still lingered in the second of the Lost Decades, the numbers of teahouses had dropped, but the five hanamachi still managed to prosper. In 2007, Kamishichiken, the smallest hanamachi, was home to eighteen geiko and ten teahouses, but only seven maiko.[96]

"If reading my book makes you even a little bit curious, then please do visit Kamishichiken. You might start just by looking around the shops in the area. If that inspires you to attend the Kitano Dances or come to our beer garden, I will be delighted. And if you happen to see me, please feel free to say hello. I look forward to being able to meet you all."[97]

With this cheerful invitation to her readers, Kamishichiken maiko Ichimame opens *Maiko no osahō* (Maiko etiquette). This inviting 125-page guide (figure 14) takes readers through Ichimame's maiko life from her decision to realize her childhood dream through her training and debut to her new status as a senior maiko. Although her use of the elegant term *sahō*, which I translate as etiquette, resonates with the courtly conduct codes expressed in classical Japanese literature, Ichimame's voice comes across as fresh and enthusiastic. *Maiko no osahō* grew out of a popular blog about maiko life that Ichimame created in 2007 with the encouragement of her okiya, the Ichi teahouse.[98]

FIGURE 14. Cover, *Maiko no osahō* [Maiko etiquette] by Kamishi-chiken Ichimame. Copyright © 2007. Courtesy of Daiwa Shobō.

Her "elder brother," a son in the Ichi family, helped her get the blog started and took photos for it.[99]

Maiko no osahō focuses on Ichimame's maiko life, giving few details about her background. Her legal name is not used in the book. A February 2007 interview with Ichimame posted online gives her age as eighteen, which places her birth around 1989.[100] As *Maiko no osahō* went to press, Ichimame was "embarking on her fourth year as a maiko."[101] According to one Italian website, Ichimame became a geiko in spring 2009.[102] In 2011, I learned from a former Kamishichiken geiko that Ichimame had left the hanamachi to pursue other work.

A lighthearted look at an unusual teenage life, *Maiko no osahō* offers photos and comic illustrations of Ichimame on and off the job. She tells readers all about how a maiko must speak, dress, behave, and train. She often laughs at herself, especially about her naivete—she thought early on, for instance, that she would need a passport to fly to another part of Japan.[103] Her first-person voice gives readers direct experience with the hanamachi dialect. Ichimame even includes her "maiko's beginner vocabulary," a list of numerous hanamachi terms and phrases at the end of her narrative. Like Ichimame's former blog, *Maiko no osahō* aims to intrigue prospective maiko, providing information on how readers may contact her okiya for an interview and a trial stay.[104] In her conclusion, Ichimame reiterates how wonderful it is to be a maiko, meeting all kinds of people and learning the arts: "I have written openly about my daily life and thoughts in this book. Could you sense the joyful life of the maiko and the atmosphere of the Kamishichiken district?"[105]

Writing effusively about how happy she is to be a maiko "fulfilling her dream," Kyoto-native Ichimame describes having her heart set on becoming a maiko since her first visit to the district's *Kitano Odori* around age ten.[106] Inspired by the dance performances, she thought, "I want to become a maiko and dance on this stage, too."[107] She became even more motivated to join the hanamachi after talking with a geiko one summer day when someone took her along to the Kamishichiken Beer Garden. Like Kiriki and Yamaguchi, she takes responsibility for her decision. Her only reference to hearing disapproval of the maiko role in some quarters is quickly muted by gratitude to her parents for supporting her decision: "I have heard that some girls face opposition from their parents when they say that they want to become maiko, but mine didn't say a word. Maybe it's because they understood how I felt. All they said was, 'This is your decision, so give it your all.'"[108]

Ichimame joined Kamishichiken immediately after her middle school graduation, becoming the Ichi's only shikomi trainee at the time. She imagines that she would have become a hair stylist or nail artist, if not an apprentice, both of which would have required much less training than becoming a maiko.[109] Unlike Kiriki and Yamaguchi, she does not comment on her decision to forgo high school. Ichimame's modest ambitions and her lack of attachment to academic pedigree show her readers that you do not have to be a star student to make your way in the hanamachi. Of all the personal hanamachi narratives published in the 2000s, Ichimame's book concentrates most on the present, communicating immediacy as she gives readers a peek into her daily life as a Kamishichiken maiko in 2007. She does not discuss long-term personal or career goals other than making passing reference to someday becoming a geiko. Hers is truly a narrative that concentrates on the life of the maiko, as though capturing girlhood as a time unto itself.

Evidence of dedication to arts training forms an essential part of maiko personal narratives, as we have seen, and *Maiko no osahō* is no exception. Ichimame takes her arts lessons seriously. Since her short book delves into many aspects of maiko life, and she is still a dance novice, Ichimame has less to say about her dance practice than the much more experienced Kiriki and Yamaguchi. Nonetheless, moving from shikomi to maiko, she realized how arts "lessons are a maiko's job," and the most important for maiko are dance lessons.[110] After her debut, she increased the number of lessons that she took each weekday. Even in her free afternoon time, Ichimame practices new dances, asking her okiya mother to observe and guide her. She realizes that learning dance is a lifelong endeavor.[111] Photographs in the book of Ichimame at her dance lessons and performing show her deep in concentration.[112] Remarking on her growing awareness of the role of the maiko's arts, Ichimame writes, "I am gradually coming to understand how much the lessons in each performance art contribute to the ozashiki. It is important for me to work hard at my lessons."[113] While essential to her life as a maiko, the rigor of dance assumes less space in her book than others published in the 2000s, a factor contributing to the lighter tone of Ichimame's writing.

Ichimame's enjoyment of her double life as diligent maiko most of the time and typical teen on her few days off makes *Maiko no osahō* accessible, assuring readers that she is no different from ordinary girls. Moving between personas seems to come easiest and even be fun for maiko Ichimame, leaving no sense of contradiction. She describes in detail the different attitudes she adopts on her days in uniform as a maiko and her days off when she can slip into a Kyoto crowd unnoticed. She gives the impression of enjoying each persona equally. Like Yamaguchi, Ichimame feels that getting into costume is an important switch-on moment. Costuming as a maiko readies her to perform. "Whenever my obi is tightly fastened, somehow this focuses my mind, too, and I feel like beaming. Off to the ozashiki."[114] Exploring both her personas, we look first at her work to become a "dignified maiko" (*hinkaku aru maiko-san*), comprising three chapters, then flip to the single chapter that presents her life as an ordinary teen, "Ichimame's Day Off."

The importance of maiko-likeness is front and center in *Maiko no osahō*. For Ichimame, embodying this ideal—that is, meeting expectations that she

ノエビア
舞妓さんの
白粉

リキッド
ファンデーション

おでかけ時の
お化粧

ピンク or
ベージュの
アイシャドー

赤に
近い
ピンクの
リップ

ピンク系の
チーク

筆の
数々

マックの
コスメいろいろ

FIGURE 15. Pink highlights at her eyes and pink lipstick complete Ichimame's maiko look for a daytime outing (*odekaketoki no okeshō*). Copyright © 2007. Courtesy of Katsuyama Keiko.

is a proper maiko—is in many ways a visual task that requires coordinating movements and costume. The performance rests on how properly she wears her kimono, how she moves, and how she wears her makeup (figure 15), recalling the stress on aesthetic labor as good manners discussed in chapter 2. Ichimame extends the performance past the stage and the ozashiki, and even the hanamachi, to any time or place that a maiko appears in uniform. Each element of her costume and behavior must be "like a maiko."

As Ichimame takes her reader through all the ways that she has learned to produce the maiko persona, she does so with a kind of childlike wonder and joy. Performing maiko-likeness, according to her book, lies in the details from the nuance of her kimono pattern to her ready smile, and even to her handbag. For example, when going out in kimono, she carries a "pale pink maiko-san rashii purse." Revealing what she carries in a more casual bag to her lessons, Ichimame points to her childlike Disney-character accessories, admitting that "I guess you could say that I am still a kid."[115] Elsewhere, too, she describes herself as "10 percent adult, 90 percent child."[116] Characterizing herself as childlike in nature and fond of adorable goods would appear to connect her effortlessly with maiko charm. But Ichimame's book shows that even for her, producing maiko-likeness is determined emotional and aesthetic work—she feels that she must maintain an appealing, upbeat, and kawaii demeanor. This mission shapes her affective interaction with clients at ozashiki where she employs dance, games, and conversation to lighten the mood. She writes that "my job is to make guests have fun" so that they can "forget life's cares."[117]

Yet, maintaining this girlish role does not come easily. Ichimame communicates how producing maiko-likeness requires constant vigilance. Like Kiriki, she describes how the maiko must be ever on the alert, ever respectful of her position as a representative of Kyoto and her hanamachi. Ichimame advises, "It is necessary to keep in mind that you are always on display. When you let your guard down, your posture will slip, and your way of standing and walking will be all off. So, the trick is to be alert, even to be somewhat overly self-conscious, mindful that, 'Everyone is paying attention to me, so I have to behave properly.'"[118]

Performing maiko rashisa in public also means making tourists happy by agreeing to their requests to take photos. Again, Ichimame frames this as more privilege than duty: "After all, whenever we say Kyoto, it calls up the image of the maiko, right? It makes me so happy that people feel lucky to see us. I love it when they say, 'Oh, I was able to make such a wonderful memory.' It's times like those that really make me feel, 'I am so glad that I became a maiko.'"[119]

Even a maiko's privilege to travel and take on celebrity duty comes with responsibility. Ichimame likes her trips outside of Kyoto for events and promotions but keeps foremost her duties to perform. Wherever her location, she feels the weight of maintaining the hanamachi's reputation. She views proper behavior as a way of "paying back" her hanamachi for all their guidance. "I am always advised to remember that I am a representative of Kamishichiken and must behave properly."[120] Happily, there are moments when all her efforts to adapt to the hanamachi succeed and she feels the ease of mastery. The sense of fumbling as a novice drops away. For example, even though it took her a month to learn how to put on a kimono, when she finally got the hang of it, she realized, "I had become maiko rashii."[121]

The maiko's day off, when she dons street clothes and blends into the crowd, often serves to reveal a character's interior life and ordinary self in narratives of maiko masquerade from the 1950s to the 2000s (see chapter 4). In *Maiko no osahō*, the chapter on Ichimame's day off lends an air of comic relief, a refreshing break from descriptions of effort, precision, and feminine duty. As if winking at her readers here, Ichimame identifies herself as an ordinary teenager, musing, "If we happened to meet on my day off, I don't expect you'd recognize me at all."[122] The cartoon of Ichimame in blue jeans, parka, and baseball cap on her day off in figure 16 shows the wide gap between her maiko persona and her typical teen clothing. She sees herself as a "sporty type" who prefers boyish clothing (*otokoppoi sutairu*) in neutral colors and twists her hair in a bun atop her head.[123] As though laughing at her day-off look, the maiko adds, "Not a very girlish look (*onna no ko rashii*), is it?"[124] Another manga shows how Ichimame likes going to movies, shopping for clothes, relaxing at Starbucks, and dining out with friends.[125] She relishes her days off, when she sleeps in, goes out as she likes, and has no schedule until she is due back for curfew at 9 p.m. "It's so different from when I am dressed as a maiko. No one pays any attention to me, so I feel that I can behave however I like. It's comfortable."[126] For all the ease of her days off, Ichimame asserts that she prefers attending ozashiki, expressing gratitude for the opportunity, "I feel the good fortune of being a maiko every day."[127] Returning to the okiya on her day off, she is often consumed with thoughts about work the next day.[128] Ichimame makes no comment on the gendered aspect of her role switching as she moves from boyish garb to the demure outfit of Kyoto's quintessential girl.

Casting herself as a typical teen privileged to have become a maiko, Ichimame narrates a personal story of gradual maturation thanks to her hanamachi experience. A self-described crybaby (*nakimushi*), she also admits to being strong-willed (*ki ga tsuyoi*), desiring to follow through with what she sets out to do, and not giving in to her weaknesses.[129] Her authorial persona in *Maiko*

FIGURE 16. Maiko Ichimame enjoys her casual day-off fashion (*kyūjitsu no fasshon*). Copyright © 2007. Courtesy of Katsuyama Keiko.

no osahō remains just young enough to express an appealing maiko-likeness. Crafting girlishness as on the cusp of adulthood, but still safely within the space of the shōjo, Ichimame experiences moments where she fully identifies as a maiko-rashii maiko. As she says in the Q &A section with an anonymous interlocutor at the end of her book, she is reluctant to embrace the "completion" of adulthood, preferring to keep "chasing her dreams."[130] Yet, sensing the responsibility to act as a role model at this point in the fourth year of her maiko career, Ichimame exclaims elsewhere in her book how much it would mean to hear a junior maiko say, "I want to be like elder sister Ichimame-san."[131]

CONCLUSION

These personal accounts of life in the hanamachi by Kiriki Chizu, Yamaguchi Kimijo, and Kamishichiken Ichimame, although diverse in voice and format, help us understand the individual journeys of three ordinary girls rising to the demands of an extraordinary career. Appearing open and unpretentious, these authors may reassure readers that they, too, do not need academic pedigree, social status, or beauty to cultivate polish. Reflecting on the privileged life of maiko and young geiko in the late 1960s and early 1970s, Kiriki describes learning to fulfill the maiko's public role as "the face of Kyoto," developing skill and grit as a dancer, and attaining sophisticated social skills—all abilities not "taught in high school." She connects the challenges of maiko-likeness to the novice position generally, urging readers to follow their teachers humbly as the means to ultimately realizing their own jibun rashii way of doing things. Kiriki also uses maiko-likeness to illustrate the importance of understanding one's position in a work-related social situation. Kiriki frames her narrative as the achievement of skillful femininity over years of experience. Taking up her career in the Gion twenty-five years later in the early 1990s, Yamaguchi Kimijo escaped the difficulties facing many of her Lost Generation in the "ice age of employment." Having passed through her maiko stage easily, she flourishes as a dancer and values her Gion friendships but still feels some pressure to leave for marriage and motherhood. Yamaguchi's comic style plays with the disparity between her elegant geiko performance and the relaxed procrastinator that she is backstage. Like Kiriki, she marshals pride in her arts training and economic independence to rebuff stigmatization of the geiko and lack of academic pedigree. Becoming a Kamishichiken apprentice in the early 2000s, ten years after Yamaguchi's misedashi, Ichimame narrates her maiko years as an adventure. The recessionary climate of the second Lost Decade apparently has no effect on her apprenticeship. Unlike Kiriki and Yamaguchi, this young author does not defend her choice to forgo high school; rather, she concentrates on describing all that she must learn as a maiko. Perhaps to appeal to potential recruits, Ichimame emphasizes the dress-up fun of changing clothing, hair, and makeup. Like Yamaguchi, she plays with the comic difference between her proper maiko rashii role and her tomboyish day-off comfort, in effect, presenting maiko deportment as a highly crafted performance of femininity and even a way to bask in the pleasures of girlhood.

All three authors contribute to our understanding of the maiko masquerade, albeit in different ways that reflect their personalities and life stages. All three talk about switching on and off their public hanamachi self. Yet we see that learning the performance of maiko-likeness is a process. It requires walking a fine line between appearing naively girlish while developing a mature understanding of her role in the okiya, at lessons, and at ozashiki. As Kiriki advises, the maiko must learn to read the room, understanding the role expected of her. But, as Ichimame and Yamaguchi show, the maiko and geiko can take days off from this vigilant mode, falling back on casual postures, clothing, and tastes. Moving back and forth between these personas with the authors, perhaps readers, too, identify with the pleasure and duties of performing different roles.

In the next chapter, we move from personal accounts to examine representations of maiko in five popular films and narrative manga produced over seven postwar decades. These fictional works overlap most of the decades in which the authors discussed here worked in the hanamachi. Like their personal accounts, these fictional narratives show a remarkable continuity in maiko training, rituals and costuming, and work. But they differ radically in their presentations of the maiko's motivations and her changing connections to sexual labor. As we move from the 1950s to the later twentieth century, we see the maiko character evolve from powerless victim of commodified sexuality to determined young artist encouraged by kind clients and hanamachi elders. These films and manga show that as the stigma of sexual labor recedes, the demand to perform refined maiko-likeness in the 2000s increases, much as we have seen here in the personal accounts published by a maiko, geiko, and retired geiko in 2007.

CHAPTER 4

From Victim to Artist

Maiko Stories in Movies and Manga

As you know, when foreigners come to Japan, they all praise "Fujiyama and geisha girls" as symbols of the beauty of Japan. The most beautiful and most representative of these geisha girls are Kyoto's Gion maiko.

—*Gion bayashi*, 1953

We maiko are not your *geisha girls*. Don't assume that we are for sale.

—*Kurenai niou*, 2003–07

Maiko characters—as victims, brave hearts, mambo dancers, and fast-food fanciers—have starred in a variety of postwar Japanese movies and narrative manga. Scouting for all things maiko, I watched every film and TV program on the topic that I could and added narrative manga to the visual mix. Familiar patterns and clear shifts emerged in major works. Films of the 1950s to TV drama and manga of the 2000s costume the maiko identically, style her as an accomplished dancer, and imagine her as a famous symbol of Kyoto. But the plots they spin about her backstory—how she came to be a maiko, what her future holds, and what is important to her—differ radically over the decades. Famous films of the 1950s depict maiko as impoverished girls at the mercy of greedy managers and lecherous men. Performing maiko arts comes easily for these maiko, but avoiding sexual exploitation appears impossible. In contrast, narratives of the 2000s associate the maiko firmly with refinement. Yet this turn brings demands of another sort. The millennial maiko struggles with the unruly "ordinary girl" inside as she endeavors to embody maiko-likeness. This chapter explores this dramatic shift in representations of the maiko through analyzing five popular narratives produced over nearly seven decades. Each develops maiko stories, sometimes expanding to link the maiko to the health of Japanese society, other times moving in closer to see her connection to a sentimental world of girls' friendship. Considering these narratives, we notice how the geiko character goes in and out of the spotlight as interpretations of her position change, too, revealing a certain uneasiness about unmarried adult women's financial and sexual independence.

Moving chronologically, we begin with two 1950s films that emphasize the maiko's path as yoked to sexual servitude: director Mizoguchi Kenji's 1953 critically acclaimed black-and-white drama *Gion bayashi* (known in the United States as *A Geisha*) and Sugie Toshio's 1955 hit, the teen musical comedy *Janken musume* (*So Young, So Bright*).[1] Although completely different in tone, both films depict maiko requiring rescue, but do not question the girls' performances as maiko. They focus on the maiko's precarity while taking account, too, of her identification with the postwar assertiveness associated with the rise of teenagers as a cultural force and consumer market. Moving to narratives of maiko life as experienced in the mid-1960s through the early 1970s, we consider legendary manga artist Yamato Waki's serialized girl comic *Kurenai niou* (Crimson fragrance). This well-known manga dramatizes retired geiko Iwasaki Mineko's 2001 autobiography. Influential in shaping early 2000s readers' notions of Gion life decades earlier, Yamato's manga depicts maiko "Sakuya" as a pioneer in standing up for women's independence, fighting harassment in many forms. Although proud of her skills and a supporter of Gion arts, Sakuya chafes against the duties to perform maiko-likeness. Moving ahead, we encounter the 2008–09 NHK-TV serialized morning drama *Dandan*, which means "gradually" in standard Japanese and "thank you" in the Izumo dialect featured in the drama.[2] *Dandan* tells the story of a chaste, independent-minded maiko who after much travail decides to make Gion her lifelong career. *Dandan* rejects any association of the hanamachi with sex work or commercialism, lauding Gion geiko as artists. Our last and most recent narrative, Koyama Aiko's girls' comic *Maiko-san-chi no Makanai-san* (Miss Cook for the maiko girls), serialized since 2016 and still running in 2020, blends the preparation and consumption of ordinary comfort food with stories of maiko. Koyama's maiko wrestle with their teenage appetites, idealizing maiko-likeness while struggling to perform it. These maiko immerse themselves in the vitality of girl culture backstage at the okiya.

Examining these narratives, we cannot miss how many maiko characters are orphans or girls with only one parent in their lives. This loss makes them vulnerable to varying degrees. In the 1950s films, the loss of parental protection drives girls to the hanamachi seeking a home and a vocation as a maiko. They literally have nowhere else to turn. In the narratives produced in the 2000s, the parental loss is chiefly psychological, making the maiko uncertain about her identity and yearning to replace that affection with a father-figure client, a lost father's return, or the friendship of another girl or elder sister. Parental loss also positions the maiko as more available to adventure than a girl with two parents in the home, as though the lack opens a door to the world and the fictive family of the hanamachi. These maiko crave a sense of belonging.

GION BAYASHI: THE MAIKO AS VICTIM OF FEUDALISTIC POSTWAR JAPAN

I will start the discussion by taking up the case of filmmaker Mizoguchi Kenji. A critically acclaimed director, Mizoguchi made many films sympathetic to the plight of women victimized by patriarchy. The fact that his own sister was indentured to pay for his education gave Mizoguchi a vested personal interest in such narratives. Hypocritically, however, he frequented brothels, and, as Catherine Russell notes, his "womanizing was as notorious as his bullying of women on the set, and yet he thought of himself as someone who had special insight into women's lives."[3] Japanese critics see *Gion bayashi* as a postwar remake of his landmark 1936 film, *Gion no shimai* (Sisters of the Gion), which laments the exploitation of geiko laboring in the second-rate "B" area, later known as Gion Higashi.[4] The film so irritated those in the hanamachi that, according to Aihara, they made it known that anyone participating in the film was unwelcome "east of the Kamo River."[5] As Keiko McDonald observes, entrenched in a neighborhood of cramped, dark alleyways, Mizoguchi's 1936 geiko inhabits a "world . . . so structured that none of her decisions or desires can alter it."[6] The film concludes with a young geiko, aptly named Omocha (toy), lying bandaged in a hospital after nearly being killed when her vengeful boyfriend tossed her from a moving car. She rails against the world that has created geiko in the first place.[7]

Gion bayashi casts the hanamachi as equally exploitive in 1953 as it was in 1936. Mizoguchi depicts the maiko as having no access to the "unprecedented array of new legal rights, including the right to vote and hold office, to choose their own spouse, and to equal opportunity in education" that the postwar Constitution and Civil Code had accorded women in Japan.[8] Mizoguchi extends this criticism to indict postwar Japan itself as insufficiently democratic. The maiko is at risk because her nation has failed her. The film presents clients as lascivious, teahouse managers complicit, and young women powerless. The plot of the film is simple. After the death of her mother, a former geiko, fifteen-year-old Eiko (Wakao Ayako) persuades Gion geiko Miyoharu (Kogure Michiyo) to train her as a maiko.[9] Eiko has nowhere else to turn: her ill, impoverished father refuses help, and her uncle threatened her with sexual assault. Eiko trains diligently, debuting as the maiko Miyoei. Near the end of the film, when a client shocks Eiko by assaulting her on a trip to Tokyo, she fights back by biting him. This creates the rather comic effect of putting him in the hospital with a huge bandage over his mouth, rendered temporarily unable to speak. But the look on Eiko's face in this famous scene is far from comic, revealing her feelings of betrayal and disillusion (figure 17). In the end, Eiko learns that geiko and maiko, as women disadvantaged by familial backgrounds and financial precarity, exert little control over their lives in the face of wily clients and teahouses managers. Unable to imagine other vocations, they can only bond to help each other. Mizoguchi depicts Gion as a beautiful world of the performing arts, on the one hand, but a shameless exploiter of young women, on the other. As Peter Grilli writes, *Gion bayashi* represents the hanamachi as a world in which "women were still dependent on men who patronized them lavishly before abruptly discarding them, and geisha remained tightly indentured to their houses by social relationships and by the financial debts they could almost never escape."[10]

Mizoguchi explicitly links the maiko's performance to Japanese national identity in one didactic scene. It takes place in a serene tatami room with a view of a garden and a delicate flower arrangement, marking the season, displayed in the tokonoma—a classically beautiful tableau. A group of maiko listen attentively to an older woman who teaches the tea ceremony and ikebana as she expounds on their cultural mission: "As you know, when foreigners come to Japan, they all praise 'Fujiyama and geisha girls' (*geisha gāru*) as symbols of the beauty of Japan. The most beautiful and most representative of these geisha girls are Kyoto's Gion maiko. Just as the tea ceremony and the Noh theater are the pride of Japan, you, too, are a vibrant art. Intangible cultural treasures, we might well say. Have self-respect and take pride in being the symbol of this kind of Japanese beauty, as you study every day."

FIGURE 17. A geiko comforts her maiko sister disillusioned by a trusted client's assault. Mizoguchi Kenji's 1953 film *Gion bayashi* (*A Geisha*). Courtesy of KADOKAWA.

What do the maiko, and by extension, viewers learn from this teacher's speech? The maiko see that theirs is a national mission to perform Japanese culture for the world and that foreigners' opinions should matter. In this era, the term *gaikokujin* (foreigners) calls to mind Anglos, mainly from the United States. By referring to *Fujiyama* and *geisha girls*, terms famously used by foreigners since long before the war, the teacher implies that the foreigner has a naive view, a kind of postcard understanding of Japan. Use of the term *geisha girls* may also invoke for the audience, if not the chaste girls, American soldiers' postwar fraternization with Japanese women, whom they nicknamed "geisha girls."[11] Given the scenes of mistreatment of maiko that follow, this speech underscores the nation's willingness to ignore the reality of the girls' precarity to produce a romantic national image. *Gion bayashi* appeared in August 1953. Although the occupation had ended and Japan had regained its sovereignty, the U.S.-Japan Security Treaty, signed in 1951, tethered the nation to its Cold War alliance with the United States.

Sexual exploitation continued as Japan served as an R&R site for American military men during the Korean War (1950–53). Also, at this time Japan was attempting to rehabilitate its global reputation as a peaceful country devoted to refined arts and culture. Mizoguchi asks audiences to look more closely at the costs of producing this image. Russell argues that adopting this kind of ideological approach placed Mizoguchi within a similar cohort of filmmakers who began careers prewar and who "switched very deftly to the democratic agenda of anti-feudalism after the war."[12]

Debates in the late 1940s and 1950s over outlawing prostitution in Japan prove a critical background to reading *Gion bayashi*, too. As Sarah Kovner explains, a variety of movements led to the enactment of "more than sixty prefectural and municipal ordinances against prostitution" and to Japan's Prostitution Prevention Law of 1956, which went into effect in 1958.[13] Controversy arose over whether geisha and maiko should figure in these prohibitions. In her study of the debates, Caroline Norma notes how conservative male lawmakers "argued vociferously against including geisha venues in the law's provisions" by characterizing them as artists, not prostitutes, provoking the ire of feminist labor activist Yamakawa Kikue. In comments published in the *Yomiuri* newspaper in February 1956 reminiscent of *Gion bayashi*, Japan's justice minister equates geisha and Mt. Fuji as national treasures. Norma observes that his remarks drew swift rebuke as "romanticised propaganda" from Japan Socialist Party member Akamatsu Tsuneko; she argued that women in Japan in particular found the karyūkai (the "flower and willow world" of geisha) "incompatible with social progress."[14] If the justice minister was referring to *Gion bayashi*, he missed the film's criticism of the postwar hanamachi's clients and the exploitation of maiko.

Returning to further scenes in *Gion bayashi*, we see boisterous ozashiki scenes following the teacher's staid lesson, showing older, male clients playing with maiko as though they are dolls. Rather than observing dances, one client stares hungrily at geiko Miyoharu. They do not use the term *geisha girl*, but these Japanese clients, too, see maiko and geiko as sexual prey. These scenes segue to Eiko, now a newly minted maiko, pressing the same teacher during an ikebana lesson about what her rights are. In this scene, Eiko, even as a maiko, embodies a common stereotype of Japanese youth in the 1950s as argumentative, legalistic, and wanting to take things at face value. As film critic Tanaka Chiyoko comments, Eiko's assertiveness reflects a postwar excitement for freedom and democracy, and her après-guerre style attracts clients, even though the "feudalism" of Gion ultimately thwarts her.[15] The older-generation teacher still works within the conservative framework of hanamachi custom, merely paying lip service to the rhetoric of rights. Nothing in this scene informs the audience as to why the teacher has decided to talk about the Constitution. Perhaps she feels it is her duty to give some instruction to the maiko about it, a mere nod to the times. The teacher's ambivalence in the scene recalls the common Japanese terms for surface and depth: it shows the *tatemae* (publicly acceptable position) of the Constitution clashing with the *honne* (one's real feelings) of the hanamachi.[16]

Teacher: That is, today, your freedom is guaranteed by the fundamental human rights established in the Constitution.

Eiko: Teacher.

Teacher: Yes?

Eiko: In that case, if a client starts flirting in a pushy way, he is ignoring our fundamental human rights. Isn't that so?

Teacher: In theory, that is the way it goes, yes.

The teacher concentrates on the flower arrangement on the table in front of her, clearly trying to avoid more of this conversation. But Eiko persists, following her from table to table.

Eiko: Well, then, that goes against the Constitution, doesn't it?

Teacher: That is the case.

Eiko: Well, according to that, it should be all right to complain. That wouldn't be a problem, right?

Teacher (impatiently): *Who* are you asking whether that would be a problem?

Another maiko: That is not something to be asking our teacher of tea and ikebana. You wouldn't get the answer to that unless you asked a lawyer.

Most of the maiko giggle at Eiko's doggedness and the other maiko's retort, but the camera moves to one pensive maiko who is not laughing. We find out why in the next scene when, after the lesson, Eiko walks with this maiko, who confesses that she is being pushed to take a danna. A complete innocent, Eiko responds that she has never heard of this custom and has no idea what a danna is. The other maiko explains that it is the "same as getting married, you become an adult woman." Moreover, her mother, who is her birth mother, is pushing her to do this, so the girl cannot refuse.

Maiko: I must take a danna.

Eiko: It would be wonderful if you liked him!

Maiko: He is a sixty-two-year-old grandfather.

Eiko: Sixty-two! Why don't you refuse?

Maiko: No, my mother told me I had to do this.

Eiko: But she is your real mother, right?

Maiko: Yes, she is, and that is why I cannot refuse. She did the same thing. She debuted as a maiko, then took a danna, and then became a fine geiko. That is the way the custom goes. I complained over and over, but she wouldn't listen. I can't do anything about it. Everyone says that you might hate it at first, but over time, you will be happy.

Arguing that this is, after all, the *shikitari* (custom), the maiko's mother may be looking out for her daughter's long-term financial well-being and imagining the best choice among limited life options. But the film directs our sympathies to the maiko who has no choice in the matter as the system, and all the elders in her life, overpower her. A similar message occurs later in the film when teahouse manager Okimi tells Eiko that "only people with money" have sex with people they love. That is not a luxury maiko Eiko can expect.

As the film ends, we see Eiko, dressed in her maiko finery, walking to an evening ozashiki with her elder geiko sister. The ostracism by clients and teahouses that they had experienced after the Tokyo trip has ended, but at personal cost. To help one powerful client accomplish a major business transaction, geiko Miyoharu had to accede to the sexual demands of the client's customer. The ending shows sisterly bonding and a kind of resignation to the world that they inhabit. *Gion bayashi* leaves no doubt that the danna system is still in place and geiko and maiko have little control over their sexuality or other possibilities for making a living. Here, Mizoguchi points to a masquerade of a different sort, one on a national scale. The arts of the hanamachi are beautiful, but they take place within a world steeped in greed and corruption. Extending the maiko as representative of the beauty of Japan, Mizoguchi argues that the Constitution is only window-dressing and Japan as the so-called "culture nation" does not bear scrutiny. Its refined dance arts rest on the exploitation of young women. The younger generation of maiko recognizes the hypocrisy but is powerless to fight hanamachi customs and patriarchal privilege. Mizoguchi's hanamachi harbors the residue of a past not easily extinguished. Nonetheless, *Gion bayashi* is not a call to action. Rather the film fits well within Mizoguchi's films' sympathy for beautiful, self-sacrificing women, mixing pity with a sense of resignation, and ultimately taking an aesthetic view. As Catherine Russell observes, Mizoguchi's "viewer may be moved to tears at the injustice of their plight, but neither social change nor transformation are ever presented as options."[17]

JANKEN MUSUME: FIFTIES TEENS RESCUE THE MAIKO

Saving the maiko from the clutches of a danna and restoring her to respectability do occur when teens come to the rescue in the 1955 musical comedy *Janken musume*. Like *Gion bayashi*, the film prompts our sympathy for an innocent maiko but stops short of inciting social change. Once the maiko is freed, her problem is resolved in a happy ending, and no thought turns to the others left behind in the hanamachi. Although critical of the danna system, *Janken musume* takes a positive stance toward other aspects of the karyūkai by including a former geisha's passionate defense, casting clients as suave, and mocking a high school teacher who reviles teahouses. Ultimately, the film's take on the karyūkai is ambiguous. The older generation values the geiko's charm and arts, but their disapproving teenage children seek new entertainments and bonds of friendship that transcend class divisions. *Janken musume* affirms teenagers as a new class in themselves.

Janken musume became Toho's biggest hit of 1955.[18] Starring the famous "Three Girls"—singers Misora Hibari, Chiemi Eri, and Yukimura Izumi, the film is famous for promoting girls' fashion and friendships. According to Deborah Shamoon, *Janken musume* and its successful Three Girl sequels, also directed by Sugie Toshio, "mark the first time that film studios begin marketing to a teenage girl demographic."[19] The dilemma of the maiko Hinagiku (Yukimura Izumi) drives much of the *Janken musume* plot. Nearing eighteen, Hinagiku will soon become a geiko and be forced to take a danna, "a bald company president in his fifties." The three girls meet for the first time at a Kyoto teahouse when Ruri (Misora Hibari) and Yumi (Chiemi Eri), Tokyo students on a night's escape from their high school field trip, enjoy a casual ozashiki with Hinagiku and two other maiko. The teahouse manager, a good friend of Ruri's mother, who is a former geisha, arranges the evening.[20] The girls learn how Hinagiku, orphaned as a child and taken in by the hanamachi, has been schooled in traditional arts and music, but adores jazz and dancing the mambo. The other two maiko agree when Hinagiku says, "We are teen-agers (chīn'eijāzu), right?" They also agree when Hinagiku describes theirs as a sad lot. Since Hinagiku smiles as she says this, and the teahouse manager admonishes her to change the topic, we do not descend into Mizoguchi-like tragedy. Instead, a lively mambo dance performed by Hinagiku and Yumi maintains the film's comic pace, changing the focus to lively teenage fun. But, as film scholars Irene González-López and Michael Raine have shown, "teen-agers" was a charged term at this time, connoting as we saw with Mizoguchi's Eiko, a new, questioning generation free of militarism, open to self-expression, and connected to "foreign, unsettling influence."[21] Although much different in tone, A Geisha and Janken musume make the case that generational change is so pronounced, even maiko have changed.

Oddly, Hinagiku's dire situation serves as comic fodder for much of Janken musume. When the three teens meet again in Tokyo, Hinagiku confides the sad tale of her impending match to the aging danna, sharing, too, how she yearns to find a certain Mr. Saitō, a college student in Tokyo. Although she has only met him briefly, Hinagiku is convinced that Saitō loves her and will surely rescue her. A scene of the three girls sobbing over the maiko's plight in Ruri's bedroom as they munch on sweet potatoes is a funny one. Even as they vow to rescue their friend, the melodramatic nature of their protests seems comically sentimental. Eventually, Yumi does discover the handsome Saitō, the son of a wealthy corporate leader, who had merely met the maiko at ozashiki. Too modern to marry without love, the youth rescues Hinagiku by cleverly trick-ing his father into giving him the considerable funds needed to ransom her. In the end, the former maiko reappears in Tokyo, ignorant of the full story of her rescue, but exuberant over reclaiming her legal name and respectability. No longer Hinagiku, she proudly announces, "I am Wada Mitsuko." The film concludes in a famous scene of the Three Girls singing as they ride together on a roller coaster. As Shamoon observes, the absence of any heterosexual romance allows Janken musume to remain focused on girls' friendship, making the film a touchstone for postwar girl culture and the pleasures of homosocial intimacy— a theme we revisit in the Maiko-san-chi no Makanai-san manga ahead.[22]

Only a few scenes in Janken musume ask viewers to take the maiko's fate seriously. At one point, Hinagiku sings a melancholy song alone in her room. In another, when she travels back to Kyoto feeling that all hope is lost, the focus rests on her sad face and drooping posture as she rides by herself on a night train. The reflection of her face in the cold, black windowpane doubles her expression of misery. Yet the vivid pink of her trendy, full-skirted dress and matching hat code her as a privileged young lady—a teen with a bright future—at odds with the reality of her status. In a later scene, the camera pauses on the financial document being exchanged for her freedom. In the other scenes, however, Hinagiku's situation piques comically exaggerated teenage anguish and improbable adventure.

Janken musume plays up generational differences in attitudes toward the maiko in a scene where Yumi describes Hinagiku's tragedy to her parents. Yumi's father is a jovial, modern sculptor specializing in nudes, and her mother, a kindly homemaker. Their old friend Sugimura, a Kyoto artist and regular hanamachi client, is visiting. Yumi relates her story as her parents and Sugimura relax in the living room of her parents' expansive Western-style home, its fireplace adorned by sculptured masks, presumably fashioned by her avant-garde artist father. All three adults burst out laughing at Yumi's naivete and ignorance of the danna system.

Yumi: But, you know, this is the very first time that I have come face to face with social tragedy.

Father: You are exaggerating!

Yumi: But it is a great tragedy! And in a civilized world!

Mother: You're being overly dramatic, silly.

Yumi: No, really, this is the truth! My friend is going to be sold.

Sugimura: What is the situation?

Yumi: Men are tyrants, Mom!

Yumi's mother: What are you talking about?

Yumi: A pretty maiden, only seventeen, will be sold to a hateful, bald company president

A comic exchange ensues about Sugimura's own bald pate, and then they continue with Hinagiku's story.

Sugimura: I like your frankness. So, what is with this bald guy?

Yumi: He buys her freedom for lots and lots of money.

Father: So, what does this girl do?

Yumi: She is a Kyoto maiko.

[All three adults laugh].

Yumi: What is so funny?

Father: That is the custom in the karyūkai.

Yumi: I can't just laugh this off.

The teenager cannot understand the adults' laughter. She wants to do something to rescue Hinagiku. She goes on to describe how Hinagiku has fallen in love with the mysterious Saitō, in effect, transforming her friend's dilemma into a puppy-love story. This tale of teenage infatuation deflects attention from the problem of human trafficking, lightening the mood as the scene concludes. We know that the precocious Yumi will not back down in helping her friend, but the plight has become a comic peril. Similarly, a funny scene in which young Saitō outsmarts his father plays up generational differences. When his son proclaims that he will marry a maiko, old Saitō becomes apoplectic, threatening to disown him as the "third article of the Saitō Family Code forbids marrying a woman of the karyūkai." The father's predictable outrage leads the cunning young Saitō to request money to call off his fictional engagement. He uses the clever scam to ransom Hinagiku. This humorous manner of treating the maiko's dilemma and her marginalized status contrasts with the tragic tone of *Gion bayashi*. The Saitō Family Code, evidence of patriarchal and class privilege, is not held up for criticism.

The absence of any scenes of maiko with older men or ozashiki, save for the girls' party, allows *Janken musume* to take this humorous approach and even launch a defense of the karyūkai. All the older men in *Janken musume* with experience of the hanamachi are genial: the two rakish artists, Yumi's father and his friend as well as Ruri's father, Kitajima, who is Japan's debonair new ambassador to France. Even old businessman Saitō has a soft side. Interestingly, it is the question of Ruri's father and his marginalized status in her life that points to the film's overall ambivalence about the karyūkai. Does Japan need to do away with the karyūkai altogether to free the maiko? Ruri's mother Onobu argues otherwise.

A single mother, former geisha, and innkeeper, Onobu has raised Ruri as a college-bound student and as an accomplished performer of Japanese classical arts, including song and dance. Even though Onobu could not marry Ruri's father, as his wealthy family, like the Saitō clan, forbade their marriage, she defends the karyūkai. She proudly displays a photo of Ruri taken in Hinagiku's maiko costume on the Kyoto trip. But the photo shocks Ruri's

Kyoto field-trip leader and teacher, Kamezawa Sensei (Okamura Fumiko) who spies the picture on a home visit. A frumpish, irritable, middle-aged woman in an unbecoming suit, Kamezawa chides Onobu for permitting her daughter to enter such a "filthy" place as a teahouse. Onobu retorts with an impassioned speech, made all the stronger by the camera moving in closely as she speaks. She argues that if women knew more about geisha charms, their husbands would not be running off to the teahouse, and that young women of today "who think so well of themselves" should emulate what geisha do well.[23] Ruri chides her mother after overhearing this speech, criticizing Onobu as "not in the least bit progressive," asking how she could support the karyūkai after having to end her romance with Ruri's father. Rather than continuing this argument—and confronting the social status of the karyūkai—the conversation turns to Ruri's own relationship with her largely absent father. In the end, *Janken musume* resolves the disparity between bourgeois respectability and the demimonde by evading hard questions and offering the happy twin endings of Wada Mitsuko's rescue and Ruri's tearful reunion with her father, who will formally adopt her.[24] The teens are free to roller-coaster off to a bright future of their own making.

Janken musume's ambivalent stance on the karyūkai calls for one more look at the high school teacher Kamezawa Sensei and the widely publicized mid-1950s debates over prostitution. When Kamezawa marches off to Ruri's and Yumi's homes to complain about their field-trip pranks, playful music signals the audience to laugh at her indignation. Sitting in Yumi's artist father's studio surrounded by images of nudes and in front of his nearly nude male model makes Kamezawa so uncomfortable that she hardly knows where to look. The scene mocks her as prudish. Unsurprisingly, at Onobu's inn, Kamezawa reacts with horror at the sight of Ruri's maiko photograph. This unflattering characterization of Kamezawa draws viewers' sympathies to Onobu's side when she takes on the self-righteous teacher. It is not a stretch to see Kamezawa's outrage aligning her with the anti-prostitution activism of the era led by female legislators and scores of middle-class women who worked locally and nationally to outlaw prostitution. By satirizing Kamezawa Sensei and sympathizing with Onobu's defense, *Janken musume* comes down on the side of karyūkai preservationists here. Yet the film also comments through teenager Ruri that Onobu is "not in the least progressive" and disapproves of Hinagiku's exploitation as sexual prey. Its overall ambivalence may simply reflect discord on the issue at the time. Like *Gion bayashi*, *Janken musume* is no call to social action to end the coercion of maiko. As well, Japanese reviews of both films discuss them in terms of their movie-making skills, but do not problematize the issues maiko face.[25] The question of whether an actress or any of the characters adequately performs maiko-likeness never comes up.

Before leaving maiko representations in 1950s films, I want to comment on director Fukasaku Kinji's *Omocha* (literally, "toy," but commonly translated as "The geisha house"). It is not a coincidence that this title recalls the name of the assertive young geiko in *Gion no shimai* (Sisters of the Gion); *Omocha's* screenwriter is Shindō Kaneto, a Mizoguchi friend and collaborator, who had directed a 1975 documentary on the famous director.[26] Although produced in 1998, *Omocha* is set in 1958 amid the Prostitution Prevention Law taking effect. The film revolves around the plight of the impoverished Tokiko, who wants to become a maiko to earn the money that her parents and younger siblings desperately need. Both parents are in this maiko's life, but they cannot protect her, and neither can her lazy elder brother. Tokiko serves as a shikomi errand girl throughout most of the film. *Omocha* concludes with Tokiko's mizuage, fetishized in every possible Orientalist way with incense games, the Noh mask of a pure young maiden, and antique rituals. At this point, viewers see one scene after another of the maiko's nude body. Although actress Miyamoto Maki, a former Takarazuka female-role player (*musume-yaku*), takes pride in the nude scenes, they strike me as aimed to satisfy the male gaze.[27] *Omocha's* condemnation of the mizuage practice and sympathy for Tokiko devolves into an alibi for voyeurism. The film makes the ritual available to the viewer while also refuting it. It implies that Tokiko, by virtue of owning this opportunity to make money, has retained her self-respect. The final narration of *The Geisha House* invites viewers to imagine the charms of this bygone culture—an ending that strikes me as completely at odds with the corruption evident in the 1950s hanamachi as Fukasaku has conceived it.

KURENAI NIOU: MILLENNIAL VIEW OF THE SIXTIES MAIKO

Our next narrative, although produced in the early 2000s, depicts maiko life in the 1960s. *Kurenai niou* (Crimson fragrance), Yamato Waki's 2003–07 manga, adheres to Iwasaki's 2001 autobiography, but embellishes it with extra characters, scenes, and even a ghost.[28] *Kurenai niou* uses floral imagery in its title and in characters' names—the fictionalized Iwasaki becomes maiko Sakuya, her name embedding the verb *to bloom*—and accentuates happy moments in Sakuya's life by filling the frame with enormous flowers.[29] Flowers in the manga also recall the expression *meika* (celebrated flower) to refer to beautiful courtesans of the pleasure quarters. But this is also a story of maiko grit and resistance. Following Iwasaki, Yamato stresses that the maiko is not up for sale, as represented in *Gion bayashi* and *Janken musume*, arguing that common notions of mizuage, as we saw fetishized in *Omocha*, are mistaken. Nevertheless, *Kurenai niou* dramatizes the maiko's troubles with bullying geiko, harassing clients from Japan and abroad, patriarchal Gion elders, and overwork. Visualizing the high and low points of Iwasaki's autobiography, Yamato characterizes the maiko Sakuya as finding meaning in dance, enjoying refined ozashiki with elegant clients, and falling in love. She also casts Sakuya as a fighter who demands respect. *Kurenai niou* contains scenes of ozashiki as raucous as any in Mizoguchi's *Gion bayashi*, but frames these as aberrations in an otherwise refined world.

Born in 1948, one year before Iwasaki, Yamato is associated with the Year 24 Group of women manga artists born around 1949 (Showa 24), whose stylistic innovations and interior characterizations revolutionized girls comics in the 1970s.[30] A prolific artist, Yamato is best known for two major works—her serialized girls' comic, *Haikara-san ga tōru* (Here comes Miss Modern, 1975–77) and her thirteen-volume rendition of *Asaki yume mishi* (*Tale of Genji*, 1980–1993). Massively popular, both have earned scholarly attention and were adapted for film and the Takarazuka stage.[31] As Alisa Freedman observes, Yamato was "one of the first manga artists to feature working women, a character type that became more common in the 2000s."[32] *Kurenai niou* marked Yamato's first time creating a manga around a living person.[33] In developing Sakuya as a woman pursuing an unusual career, Yamato stresses her increasing confidence and sense of autonomy. *Kurenai niou* employs representational realism and the visual conventions of girls' comics.[34] Caricatures of Sakuya's occasional gaffes create lighter moments. Yamato's lavishly detailed drawings of Gion rhapsodize scenes of cherry blossoms and beautifully patterned kimono.

Iwasaki Mineko's 2001 autobiography, translated into English as *Geisha, a Life*, gave Yamato a richly detailed account of hanamachi life and much personal drama to employ in her manga. Born near Kyoto in 1949, Tanaka Masako (her birth name) was her parents' tenth and final child, and their fourth daughter sent to the Iwasaki okiya. Living in the okiya since age five and formally adopted by the Iwasaki okiya in 1960, Mineko became a maiko in

1965, and a geiko on her twenty-first birthday in 1970, retiring in 1978. Unlike the authors in chapter 3, Iwasaki did not dream of becoming a maiko or feel nostalgic at the end of her apprenticeship. She excelled in dance, achieved fame, and made enormous amounts of money for her okiya while working to exhaustion and inciting jealousy among her cohort. She writes, "The press was claiming I was the most successful geiko to come along in a hundred years."[35]

Kurenai niou opens in 1965 when fifteen-year-old Sakuya is in the process of becoming a maiko, introducing us to the difficult family-okiya negotiations that brought her, as a confused and sometimes even terrified child, to becoming the heir of the "Ishibashi" okiya at age ten. Like the autobiography, the manga concentrates on Sakuya's life as a maiko, showing her geiko transition only in the next-to-last chapter, even though Iwasaki was a geiko for about eight years. It ends in the early 1980s after Sakuya has retired from the Gion, married, and borne a daughter. The last frame depicts a classic pose of two formally dressed maiko facing away from the viewer, our attention drawn to the luxury of their darari obi and to the details of the Gion scenery ahead of them—the street lined with old wooden shops, Yasaka Pagoda in the distance. But Sakuya remains the star of this narrative. Her final speech describes how her presence "lives on in the Gion." She says, "Okoshiyasu! Welcome to the newest maiko. May the path ahead of you bloom with brilliance and sophistication."[36] In taking up this long, complex manga here, I focus on representation of the mizuage, maiko sexuality, and maiko Sakuya's fight against harassment of all kinds. We also see a new attention to the performance of maiko-likeness and the teen's struggle to accomplish this, an aspect of the maiko role that was taken for granted in the 1950s films. This emphasis may reflect Iwasaki's well-known distaste for the sexualized portraits popularized in Golden's Memoirs of a Geisha, still a global best seller at the time she published her first autobiography.

According to Kurenai niou, for the 1960s Gion maiko, love is possible, and intimacy desired. Volume two opens with preparations for the eighteen-year-old Sakuya's mizuage. The narrator explains that a young maiko's charming wareshinobu hairstyle no longer fits a young adult's ezukuroshii quality—that is, her developing womanliness (see chapter 2), but adds that "unlike in red-light districts where the mizuage involves sleeping with a client, in the karyūkai, it is simply about a hairstyle change."[37] In a close-up frame, Sakuya's okiya mother, in one of the manga's many proclamations about women's autonomy, states that she never asks clients for financial support for such occasions, "We are independent career women (*shokugyō fujin*)."[38] When Sakuya embarks on her first intimate relationship, her decision is free of any monetary or hanamachi concern. It is consensual. She falls in love with a handsome singer and sleeps with him only after he complies with her demand to book an ozashiki every night for three years.[39] Yamato Waki romanticizes their first sexual encounter by framing a close-up of the couple kissing amid a profusion of rose petals, as Sakuya exclaims, "I fell in love."[40] Flowers overlay another frame of the couple's lovemaking, the riot of blooms nearly covering them, save for their faces enthralled in passion. Following Iwasaki's autobiography, Yamato depicts Sakuya reaching new expression in dance for having known sexual passion. Here, *Kurenai niou* departs from *Gion bayashi* and *Janken musume* not only for putting the maiko in charge of her sexuality, but by showing her seeking and enjoying lovemaking. Unlike Mizoguchi's Eiko or Sugie's Hinagiku, 1950s maiko who must remain chaste to be sympathetic, Sakuya claims her freedom and pleasure, too. In contrast to *Omocha*'s invitation to gaze at the maiko's nude body, Yamato indicates that both Sakuya and her suitor are nude, but largely covers their bodies with flowers, evoking their consensual desire.

Yamato's depiction of the maiko's interior life shows Sakuya's struggles to produce maiko-likeness. The demand for role perfection replaces the threat of sexual servitude in past narratives. Like Iwasaki, Sakuya always finds performing maiko charm a chore despite her success with clients. The very first frame of *Kurenai niou* introduces Sakuya as admitting to a "tendency toward gloominess."[41] Indeed, the scene depicting her maiko's day off presents one of the few relaxed moments in Sakuya's entire narrative. Wearing her hair down, going without makeup, and enjoying the ease of blue jeans, Sakuya walks Big John, the okiya dog. She greets a local shopkeeper who does not even recognize Sakuya in this day-off look. "I felt like I could be myself," she says.[42] To portray this carefree feeling, Yamato draws an enormous head-shot of Sakuya in profile—eyes closed, chin tilted up, smiling as her long hair blows gently in the wind. This giant Sakuya close-up floats over a detailed drawing of the Kamo River as seen from the Sanjō Ōhashi bridge with buildings on either side and miniature people walking its banks. Freed from constraints, Sakuya can literally expand as much as she likes, transcending the confines of maiko propriety and obligations. In several other scenes, we see how the introverted Sakuya enjoys losing herself in dance, freed from the demands of human interaction. Yamato captures this happiness with huge, blooming peonies framing Sakuya as she dances. Sakuya imagines, "If dance had not been part of my work, I wonder if I could have become a maiko."[43]

Sexual assault and harassment play an even greater role in Sakuya's narrative than in *Gion bayashi*, underscoring how men's mistaken ideas about maiko as playthings cause trouble. One scene captures Iwasaki's experience of sexual assault by her elder sister's son. Stopped from nearly raping Sakuya, the youth sneers, "But she is going to be a geiko anyway."[44] Traumatized by the attack, as the manga amply shows, Sakuya is also shocked by his demeaning comment. She decides to fight back. She admonishes rude clients from abroad excited about "Fujiyama" and "geisha girls" in a manner reminiscent of foreigners imagined in *Gion bayashi*, refusing to excuse "even *gaijin-san*."[45] She fights offensive Japanese clients, too. When one client slyly drives her to a lover's lane, she locks him out of the car and refuses to come out for hours.[46] Most dramatically, when one client grabs her by the legs and drags her about the floor, she flees the room only to return with a huge kitchen knife in her mouth. Suddenly, Sakuya has the knife to his throat (figure 18). Mayhem ensues over several frames, giving readers views of the crisis from different perspectives—above the scene, in close-ups, facing the culprits—magnifying the fright of the cowering client and the malicious geiko who had put him up to the deed. Only Sakuya remains calm and determined, holding the knife steady. She finally puts down the knife, but tells all, "Remember that I am in earnest." A bubble indicates that she thinks, "This was the first time I recognized the vigorous force slumbering within me."[47] At other points, Sakuya fights back by enduring the pain—even a cigarette ground into her palm—to show bullying geiko that they cannot defeat her.[48] Sakuya triumphs by becoming the most popular, highest-income-producing maiko in the Gion. Maiko in *Gion bayashi* and *Janken musume* can do little about their situation. Writing for girls in the early 2000s, Yamato asks them to identify with a young woman stepping outside expected maiko performance, behaving "inappropriately" to resist harassment.

Harassment in Gion of a different sort frustrates Sakuya even more, the abuse of authority much discussed in the Japanese media later in the 2010s as power harassment (*pawa hara*). Here, Sakuya's disenchantment mirrors the criticism of Gion gatekeepers voiced throughout Iwasaki's writings. Even as the most successful geiko in Gion, Sakuya finds herself unable to persuade hanamachi leaders to make any changes on behalf of her colleagues in the hanamachi. She argues for awarding maiko and geiko academic arts degrees

FIGURE 18. Maiko Sakuya shows her fierce demand for respect in Yamato Waki's *Kurenai niou* (Crimson fragrance), vol. 1. Copyright © 2009. Courtesy of Kōdansha.

for their years of study, payment for their performances in public dances, and the rights to commercial use of their likeness (criticisms that Iwasaki voices strenuously in Geisha, a Life). In the end, she retires over her failure to be a voice for innovation. Although Iwasaki describes these Gion elders ambiguously in her autobiography, without reference to gender, Yamato draws them as cranky, old men at the Gion offices and school.[49] A close-up of one angry man shows him literally steaming with anger as he yells, "A geiko has no need for learning, just concentrate on your lessons so you can do well at ozashiki."[50] Another elder in a boiling mad trio of men snarls, "Awful manners, these young geiko today." Chiming in, yet another complains, "So full of herself, convinced she's the top performer (urekko). That's one defiant geiko."[51] In another scene, Sakuya rejects a prospective maiko, arguing that she cannot support an outmoded system by training apprentices. Fighting the system gets her nowhere, and in the end, Sakuya imagines the spirit of one of her deceased elders, a woman that she respected, coming to her in a dream and urging her to blossom (saku) on her own path. The ghost advises, "This is not the place for you. Your brilliance and sophistication cannot thrive here."[52]

Kurenai niou refutes the notion that maiko are associated with sex work but represents the stigma as alive in Japan and abroad in the 1960s and 1970s. The manga brings subjectivity to the maiko, revealing her developing confidence amid internal struggles to perform maiko-likeness. Elderly clients become father figures for her while younger suitors try to woo her. Yamato Waki affirms Sakuya's blossoming sexuality and her fight for maiko and geiko empowerment. Despite its criticism of Gion leadership, Kurenai niou celebrates maiko, geiko, and the hanamachi as Japanese arts worth preserving.

DANDAN: EDUCATING GRANDMOTHER
ABOUT THE GION GEIKO AND MAIKO

In the 2008–09 NHK-TV morning drama Dandan, we find no trace of disorderly ozashiki, bullying geiko, harassing men, or sexual labor. A kindly, rural grandmother is the only character in the drama to harbor negative feelings about the hanamachi and see the maiko as stigmatized. But Gion leaders transform her into an admiring fan. The audience learns, along with the grandmother, that Gion represents fine etiquette, exacting standards for art, and individual responsibility. Ozashiki may be fun, occasionally involving the overconsumption of alcohol, but clients are respectful, avuncular men, part of the larger hanamachi family. And family is what Dandan is all about. Consequently, becoming a geiko in *Dandan* has nothing to do with sexuality and everything to do with maturity. Turning the collar here means achieving artistic excellence, as discussed in chapter 2, but also requires assuming responsibility for the community's prosperity, distinctiveness, and legacy of care.

Broadcast at the height of the maiko boom and the swell in domestic tourism to Kyoto, *Dandan* follows spunky twin sisters—Nozomi (Mikura Kana), the popular Gion maiko Yumehana, and Megumi (Mikura Mana), a high school student from Matsue, a small city near the Japan Sea in Shimane Prefecture.[53] Separated as infants when their parents divorced and never told about the other's existence, the twins discover each other by chance on their eighteenth birthday. Both have a passion for singing, and as a duo, they harmonize magically—an ability that leads to their eventual debut and short career as pop star twins. Their route to stardom is a rocky one, initiated when Nozomi abruptly decides not to become a geiko just ten days before her erikae, striking a terrible blow to the reputation of her Gion okiya/ochaya, the Hanamura. Spurred on by her twin's freedom to choose the life that best suits her, the jibun rashii path, Nozomi insists that she, too, must find her own way. She cannot automatically accept the maiko-geiko path that her mother Makiko, the geiko Hanayuki, had taken and trained her daughter to follow.

Unlike Sakuya, the gregarious Nozomi does not struggle to display maiko-likeness; rather she wrestles with the question of autonomy. Reunited with her fisherman father in Matsue, who had taken his own rebellious journey to self-discovery as a teen, Nozomi sets out to find herself, too. But in the end, after struggling and failing to build a singing career on her own, Nozomi chooses to return to Gion, welcomed by the Hanamura as a kind of prodigal daughter. Incorporating a new maturity in her dance at this point, Nozomi finally decides to become a geiko, fully embracing the role. Unlike Sakuya, whose experience of sexual passion enhances her dance, NHK's chaste Nozomi deepens her dance through a profound sense of personal responsibility. She excels, earning natori status. When the elderly Hanamura manager Hisano falls ill, Nozomi assumes the leadership role. No longer a geiko, she also becomes eligible to marry. (Makiko stipulates that Nozomi must agree to marry at some point to win her approval to move from the geiko career path to becoming the okami). *Dandan* ends by taking the twins into the future, imagining them approaching thirty in 2011, both married and newly pregnant with their first children, and thriving in their respective careers—Megumi as a geriatric nurse on a small island badly in need of young people and Nozomi, as permanent manager of the Hanamura teahouse, training the next generation of maiko.

Only the rural grandmother Hatsue initially stands in the way of this positive Gion picture. At the point where maiko Nozomi decides not to become a geiko and faces ostracism from the Hanamura, she retreats to her father's home in Matsue. There, she finds a sympathetic advocate in her grandmother, Tajima Hatsue (Mitsubayashi Kyōko). Hatsue is a warm character, beloved by her family. But her disgust with the hanamachi resembles the stance adopted by Kamezawa Sensei, caricatured in *Janken musume*. Although *Dandan* would never ridicule this matriarch, it does imply that only a rural granny would misunderstand Gion now. When Hatsue discovers that her long-lost granddaughter has become a maiko, she nearly dissolves into tears, asking, "Why a maiko? Why did they make her a maiko?"[54] We can assume it is the maiko's association with sex work that fuels her concern, although this is unspoken.

Hatsue experiences a radical, almost instant conversion, moving from revulsion to admiration for the hanamachi on her visit to the Hanamura teahouse.[55] She makes the trip to report that Nozomi is doing well in Matsue and to support her choice to leave Gion. Standing outside the Hanamura, Hatsue looks at the teahouse skeptically, loathing to enter. Invited inside, she exchanges pleasantries with matriarch Hanamura Hisano, her counterpart in their blended Matsue-Gion family. But things quickly turn sour as Hatsue offends Hisano by beaming over how well Nozomi is doing since she has "returned to being an ordinary nineteen-year-old girl who can now decide on a life that best suits her." Saving the situation, Nozomi's Gion grandfather, a kimono maker, invites a wary Hatsue to spend time with him the next afternoon. Returning to the Hanamura for this "date," Hatsue is shocked to find the room set up for an ozashiki, and soon a geiko in formal costume appears to welcome her. When her former daughter-in-law and the twins' geiko mother Makiko enters next in full makeup and formal kimono, performing a splendid rendition of the dance *Kurokami* (Black hair), Hatsue instantly realizes the beauty of the Gion arts. The camera captures her look of awe in a close-up. When Makiko falters, overwhelmed by her concern for Nozomi, Hatsue is even more impressed. In tears, moving off her cushion to the tatami floor to bow humbly, Hatsue apologizes to the others; her apology cues one of the drama's triumphant musical themes. "I have said some terribly rude things. Even an amateur like me can understand what rigorous training you have endured. But, more than this wonderful dance, it is Makiko-san's mother's heart that struck me to the core." [Hatsue turns to face Hanamura Hisano.] "Okami-san, I misunderstood Gion. Please forgive me."

Somewhat later in the drama when Hanamura Hisano falls ill, it is Hatsue who sings the praises of the job that the teahouse manager does, extolling how she arranges teahouse parties for captains of industry, heads of state, and royalty.[56] *Dandan* has taken Hatsue from reviling Gion to becoming a well-informed proponent of the hanamachi. As the stigma of sex work is expunged in this story, attention shifts to the geiko as a devoted mother. *Dandan* also works to erase stigma by characterizing clients as uniformly kind to maiko. In fact, they have become part of the family, too, as longtime supporters of the Hanamura and as cultured men. Occasionally, sparring erupts between two older men enamored of Hisano, but the scenes cast sexual tension among elders as funny. There is never a hint of sexual attention to a maiko, who remains a paragon of chastity as the community's cherished daughter.

Raised from childhood to become a maiko, Nozomi performs maiko-likeness easily. More critically, she learns to respect the maiko's uniform as representative of Gion integrity, even when such loyalty costs her dearly. Early in the drama, Hisano chastises Nozomi after Makiko catches her singing in full maiko gear with her twin in a Kyoto "live house," a young people's music hang-out.[57] Chagrined, Nozomi takes this admonition to heart. Much later after her twin leaves their pop duo, causing Nozomi's popularity to falter, the record label gives her only one option—sing in your maiko garb. Unwilling to diminish maiko and Gion as a gimmick, Nozomi quits, losing her pop career.[58] Not only does this scene establish Nozomi's loyalty to Gion, but it also serves to distance Gion from crass commercialism, underscoring its status as a refined arts community.

Unlike *Gion bayashi*'s indictment of the hanamachi and Japan as "feudalistic" and exploitative—a criticism also evident to some degree in *Kurenai niou*—*Dandan* views Gion as one of the nation's saving graces. Unlike *Janken musume*, it does not recommend that wives learn feminine wiles from teahouse culture. Rather *Dandan* depicts Gion as a community of unquestioned integrity, propriety, and traditional arts. As heir to this tradition, the maiko benefits from the wisdom of her elders and the benevolence of her community, including caring clients. Her story is inseparable from *Dandan*'s positive portrait of Japan. Despite the realities of Japan's growing class divides, the rise in unemployment and underemployment, depopulation, and what anthropologist Anne Allison aptly cites as Japan's "care deficit,"

Dandan reassures viewers of the nation's well-being, its procreative future, and their identity as Japanese.[59] The maiko as the quintessential Japanese girl comes to understand her role in maintaining her arts community, sending a powerfully conservative message about the end-goal of girlhood in Japan. In contrast to *Janken musume*'s teenage escape into the future, *Dandan* shows young people helping each other ease back into communal traditions. As they "gradually"—*dandan*—mature and find themselves in conservative, gender-appropriate familial and (re)productive roles, the twins Nozomi and Megumi express gratitude for their families' enduring love. This becomes their jibun rashii path. The drama emphasizes Gion and Matsue as equally rich sites of multigenerational communal living, home cooking, the authenticity of local dialects, and lifelong connections between the extended family and a larger community. *Dandan* presents Japan as a nation where care, including care for the elderly, is abundant and generously given.

MAIKO-SAN-CHI NO MAKANAI-SAN: GIRLS CULTURE BACKSTAGE AT THE OKIYA

Moving up to the late 2010s, we find ourselves in a different maiko narrative altogether. This is the enchanting world of Koyama Aiko's awarding-winning girls comic, *Maiko-san-chi no Makanai-san* (Miss Cook for the maiko girls).[60] Here, charges of exploitation or harassment are gone, scenes of ozashiki are rare, and, as in *Dandan*, clients are gentleman who appear infrequently. The real action of *Maiko-san-chi no Makanai-san* occurs backstage at the okiya where a band of maiko live and interact, revealing themselves as rambunctious teens who must tame their appetites to comport themselves as maiko. The lone geiko character, the charismatic Momoko, inhabits an adult world that the maiko find mysterious and hesitate to discover. The girls do not talk about their long-term futures, nor do they yearn for boyfriends. *Maiko-san-chi no Makanai-san* celebrates their efforts to produce maiko-likeness, their friendship, and their appetites backstage for ordinary home-cooked food. Enormously popular, the series had over one million readers by March 2020; a trailer for the animated version debuted the same month.[61]

Maiko-san-chi no Makanai-san revolves around two sixteen-year-old girls from the northeastern prefecture of Aomori, best friends since childhood, who have ventured to Kyoto, captivated by maiko after meeting one visiting their hometown. The pair take up residence as shikomi in the fictional okiya

Ichi. Readers quickly learn that Sumire, nicknamed Sū-chan, has the flair to become, like Iwasaki/Sakuya, the kind of "maiko seen only once in one hundred years (*hyakunen ni ichido no maiko*)."[62] Sadly, her pal, the pixie-like Kiyo, dances so poorly that the okāsan orders her to return home. At that critical point of dismissal, however, the middle-aged okiya cook falls ill, and Kiyo rises to the occasion, saving the day and her place in the okiya with her cooking talents (figure 19). Able to whip up several meals in record time, Kiyo will stay on as the *makanai*, a term for one who prepares meals for many people, like a cafeteria cook, rather than an elite chef. Since the Ichi hosts an improbably large number of maiko—I count thirteen in one frame—Kiyo has her work cut out for her. As Sū-chan's star rises as the maiko Momohana, Kiyo nourishes her and all the other maiko, and the two remain fast friends. Absent parents enhance the girls' closeness: Sū-chan seems to be an orphan; Kiyo's mother has died, her father travels for work, and her old-fashioned granny has raised her. As loving as *Dandan*'s Hatsue, this granny apparently has no doubts about the hanamachi. Flashbacks to the girls' cozy childhood—playing with the boy Kenta, their favorite Aomori foods, the rural space—add nostalgia and, like *Dandan*, create a complementary countryside-Kyoto binary. There is no mention of the 3.11 disaster.

An experienced manga artist, Koyama draws her maiko in cute, cartoonish ways.[63] But, like Yamato Waki, she renders the hanamachi, inside and out, in exquisite representational detail. Also, like Yamato, Koyama educates her readers about the maiko's training, duties, costumes, and her participation in seasonal events and dances. Unlike *Kurenai niou*, *Maiko-san-chi no Makanai-san* has little character or plot development, which keeps the tone light. Some reader comments on the comic's Amazon site describe enjoying its visuals, one reader noting how the series "soothes"; another feels "calmed."[64] Although the okiya has a mother, most scenes involve only the maiko, recalling the settings of popular prewar stories for girls set at boarding schools and the emphasis on their relationships (see introduction). Unlike in *Dandan*, adults rarely figure in *Maiko-san-chi no Makanai-san*. It is chiefly a girls' world.

Koyama builds almost each episode of her girls' world on a different dish that Kiyo prepares. Close-ups of food preparation, laced with onomatopoeic expressions, snap, crackle, and pop, creating suspense over the mystery meal. Episodes culminate in a detailed drawing of the delectable treat and a note from Koyama about why she likes each dish, especially those from her own childhood in Aomori.[65] Unlike the elegance expected of hanamachi cuisine,

FIGURE 19. Perky cook Kiyo chats with maiko pal Momohana. Cover, *Maiko-san-chi no Makanai-san* (Miss Cook for the maiko girls) by Koyama Aiko, vol. 3. Copyright © 2017. Courtesy of Shōgakukan.

Maiko-san-chi no Makanai-san spotlights teen favorites from savory hot dogs and instant ramen to all kinds of sweets. In Kiyo's kitchen, ordinary foods for girls take on almost magical, healing properties, recalling Yoshimoto Banana's shōjo novel *Kitchin* (Kitchen, 1987) and Grace En-Yi Ting's observations about the feminine escapist fantasies engendered by sweets in shōjo manga.[66] In *Maiko-san-chi no Makanai-san*, cravings are comic. Backstage, the maiko may indulge their yearnings for these foods, but not in public, at least not in maiko garb. One episode depicts the maiko back in Kyoto after their New Year's holiday; still in street clothes, the girls congregate at a fast-food joint, eager to devour hamburgers and fries.[67] This love of the ordinary constantly vexes the girls, complicating their work at maiko-likeness, but it also unites them.

For super-maiko Sū-chan, embodying maiko perfection is her mission. She earns admiration from her cohort and compliments from her elders as the most maiko rashii of all. This does not happen easily. Koyama portrays Sū-chan working harder than anyone else, getting up at dawn to practice dance by the river, and making the rounds of all the teahouses in the afternoon to pay her respects. Even Sū-chan must discipline her appetite; we see her nearly falter in ozashiki, obsessing about garlicky gyōza.[68] One episode epitomizes Sū-chan's mettle, but questions the limits of maiko-likeness at the same time. It occurs one evening in the hanamachi as Sū-chan strolls calmly, maintaining her composure while shutterbug tourists shine lights in her eyes and even try to grab her. Angered, the shikomi Riko escorting Sū-chan glares at these tourists, mystified that Sū-chan does not protest. Scowling all the way back to the okiya, Riko unnerves other tourists and shopkeepers. An unlikely maiko-in-training, Riko is a tall, athletic, short-haired girl who persists in using the slang of school sports teams and retains an outsider's perspective. Catching sight of the indignant shikomi, the dresser, the "wise man" of the hanamachi, lectures Riko on maiko demeanor, explaining how everyone in the hanamachi labors so that "you maiko flowers can show your best face."[69] His comments overlay a frame of an exemplary maiko, giving us the classic view of her ornate hairstyle and darari obi. In the final frames of this chapter, Riko is once again escorting Sū-chan to an ozashiki, reminding herself to smile. But when a tourist steps into the frame, asking to touch Sū-chan's kanzashi, Riko's face lights up, livid.[70] By ending the chapter with Riko's anger, Koyama does not excuse the tourists, disparage Riko, or fault Sū-chan. She does allow the question of the maiko's best response to linger. This is one of the few places in the series where Koyama stages resistance—albeit a gentle resistance given all her endorsements and Sū-chan's success—to maiko-likeness as the endless public performance of compliant femininity.[71]

The lone geiko, Momoko, offers an intriguing counterpoint to maiko innocence. Readers discover the geiko's backstage life when Sū-chan cares for her cat so Momoko may travel. The narrator explains that independent geiko live on their own, develop as artists, and support themselves. Sū-chan's reverie over the geiko's stylish condo ends when the doorbell rings. This starts a procession of one man after another calling on Momoko, visibly annoying

Sū-chan who must deal with each one. First there is a bespectacled man in a kimono, perhaps an artist. Next, a younger man, then an older man. Finally, a cool guy in blue jeans with spiky hair. All are surprised Momoko is out. Back at the okiya kitchen, Sū-chan tells Kiyo how pretty Momoko's apartment is, how darling her cat, "but there were lots of men." In the next frame, Sū-chan pauses to sip a hot drink from a mug, then putting it down, confesses, "I felt kind of nervous."[72] Koyama leaves this glimpse into Momoko's life and Sū-chan's reaction here. Are these men at the door Momoko's clients? Friends? Romantic partners? That the men show up at her apartment indicates familiarity at the least, even hinting at some connection to Momoko's luxury lifestyle. Apparently, it is too much for Sū-chan to contemplate or discuss with Kiyo, and the subject quickly changes to what is for lunch. In a later scene in the same volume, Sū-chan joins other maiko watching the Kyoto marathon on TV, all surprised to see Momoko racing. They are stunned when Momoko blows kisses to men cheering her on. Sū-chan quickly arranges for a bento lunch box to take Momoko and hurries to the finish line. Amazed at Momoko's stamina, Sū-chan learns the geiko intends to work even after "running a full marathon." Momoko replies, "Of course. To perform well at ozashiki—that's why I work myself crazy hard to build stamina. Let's eat this together and both do our best."[73] Watching Momoko run off to get ready, Sū-chan, who had felt discouraged about her dancing, resolves to redouble her own efforts, "I will practice my dance again once more."[74]

Although this marathon scene hints at the geiko's ease with men, *Maiko-san-chi no Makanai-san* gives priority to Momoko's role as a model of physical and emotional strength. Unlike the teenage maiko, all living in a cloistered okiya, the geiko is out in the world, independent, social, and making her own decisions. A glamorous woman, Momoko can perform global sport and Japanese tradition with equal ability. Her sheltered maiko sister finds that Momoko's diligence spurs her on, but her relations with men pose too challenging a vision to ponder. In a sense, Sū-chan stays in the realm of the girl, most comfortable emulating Momoko's example as an accomplished dancer.

What does this manga of teen life at the okiya revolving around home-cooked food tell us about maiko-likeness, the erasure of the stigma of sex work, and Japanese girlhood in the late 2010s? Koyama takes on maiko rashisa as a performance by focusing on the backstage life of maiko and, like Ichimame (chapter 3), capturing the relaxation of a maiko's day off incognito. Although the manga visualizes teens continually (and humorously) chafing at the constraints of their maiko life, none quits. Like *Dandan*, the narrative trajectory of *Maiko-san-chi no Makanai-san* always circles back to the values of hard work, sincerity, gratitude, and perseverance for the greater good. But the friendship among girls replaces *Dandan*'s concentration on the family. The question remains—how will the series conclude? Over the course of thirteen volumes, Sū-chan gradually progresses in rank, coming closer to the erikae decision. In the later volumes, we see Sū-chan, uneasy with sexuality, become secretive and perplexed by romantic feelings developing for Kenta, which may jeopardize her bond with Kiyo and the camaraderie the three have shared since childhood. If Sū-chan follows convention by becoming a geiko or leaving to marry Kenta, the series would likely end there, the realm of girlhood left behind. Since Kiyo's character has not changed over time, she may remain the eternal girl, consigned to Sū-chan's past. Given the popularity of *Maiko-san-chi no Makanai-san*, Koyama may wish to extend Sū-chan's maiko days, slowing her progress and coming up with new foods.

CONCLUSION

Tracing maiko stories from the 1950s through 2020, we have seen a major shift in representations of the maiko's position. The popular 1950s films *Gion bayashi* and *Janken musume* characterized the maiko as a kind of "dame-in-jeopardy," a sexual pawn at the mercy of rich, older men. At the same time, the films sent the message that even maiko identified with the foreign-inflected tastes and attitudes of the postwar teenager. Stories produced in the 2000s—the manga *Kurenai niou*, the NHK-TV drama *Dandan*, and the girls' comic *Maiko-san-chi no Makanai-san*—worked to divorce the maiko from any association with sexual labor. But these stories also increased the expectation that the maiko must be a model Japanese girl—poised, obedient, cheerful, and serious about hanamachi obligations. This charge to perform maiko-likeness presented a new plot line in maiko stories; rather than fearing the clutches of a danna, the girl worried whether she could deliver this idealized performance. Sakuya in *Kurenai niou* and maiko in *Maiko-san-chi no Makanai-san* harbor anxiety about the gap between their "real selves" and their maiko masquerade. For *Dandan*'s Nozomi, consumed with a desire for integrity and a coherent self, the tension resolves when she fully embraces the hanamachi by her own choice to become a geiko and then a teahouse manager. The loss of one or both parents has made the maiko vulnerable—either financially, as in the 1950s stories, or psychologically, as in the later ones—but able to find support in some form in the hanamachi.

The geiko/geisha in these maiko stories take on different positions, too, but do not follow a single trajectory. Her character remains open to various plot lines. In *Gion bayashi*, Miyoharu is powerless to save Eiko, for she, too, is sexual prey. In *Janken musume*, the long-retired geisha and single mother Onobu rallies to the defense of the karyūkai as training ground for femininity and loyalty to old-fashioned morality, but her postwar daughter Ruri dismisses these views as "not progressive in the least." *Kurenai niou* imagines both kind and bullying geiko but dramatizes Sakuya's own geiko career only briefly in the last chapter of volume 3. Focusing on Sakuya's maiko years enables Yamato to delve into the psychological aspects of the young character becoming a woman, representing the maiko as an intensified, unusual experience of girlhood. Once Nozomi turns the collar to become a geiko, *Dandan* quickly moves her into marriage and responsibility as manager of the Hanamura, not lingering on the possibilities for adult independence—financial and sexual—opened by the geiko transition. Girlhood in *Dandan* leads firmly to motherhood and elder care, too. The geiko Momoko in *Maiko-san-chi no Makanai-san* embodies personal freedom, athleticism, career success, and wealth. But maiko Sū-chan feels uncomfortable contemplating her elder sister's life, especially her adventurous romantic life, preferring to remain in the comfortable confines of girlhood. In sum, we can see ambiguities in representations of the geiko/geisha's life and her adulthood; none of these maiko stories moves geiko independence to the foreground or shows maiko looking forward to becoming geiko.[75]

In the next chapter, we continue this exploration of maiko stories by turning to a fantastical series of light novels in which a young teenage boy masquerades on the weekends as the maiko Chiyogiku. Published from 2002 to 2014, these novels follow the maiko's professional development in much the same way as the narratives discussed in this chapter do, with the gentle humor driving *Maiko-san-chi no Makanai-san*. This child, too, lost one of his parents—in this case, his father. But representations of sexuality differ dramatically in the *Chiyogiku* series from what we have seen so far. In this fantasy world, the boy maiko is forever trying to avoid sexual invitations and even blatant sexual harassment by men. Whether or not the men realize—or admit to themselves—that this maiko has a boy's body is a theme that hovers just beneath the plot surface, fitting this series into the Boys Love (BL) genre.

The popularity of this millennial BL maiko series may speak to the success of the cultural work done to divorce the maiko from earlier associations with sexual exploitation. The maiko's sterling reputation in the 2000s allows for the imagination of sexual escapades and gender play in the hanamachi outside the bounds of reality.

CHAPTER 5

Adventures of a Boy Maiko

There Goes Chiyogiku!

"Taking a deep breath, she spoke softly, 'I have been working as a maiko, but I am not a girl. I am a boy.'"

—Chiyogiku confessing in *Jūrokusai no hanayome*, volume 53 of *Shōnen maiko: Chiyogiku ga yuku!*

What happens when a boy assumes the role of Kyoto's quintessential girl? Narratives of maiko artistry take a surprising turn in a popular light novel series that features the precocious Okamura Mikiya masquerading on weekends as the maiko Chiyogiku. Written by Nanami Haruka, *Shōnen maiko: Chiyogiku ga yuku!* (Boy maiko: There goes Chiyogiku!) debuted in 2002 and concluded in 2014 with volume 54.[1] Spinning tales of adventure, romance, furtive sexual exploration, and even blatant sexual harassment, the *Chiyogiku* series plays with technologies of gender and flirts with taboos while educating readers about life in Gion and travel within and beyond Kyoto. The fantasy of the prepubescent boy-maiko Mikiya, his manipulations of language, costume, and behavior as he crosses gender, his romances with beautiful men and youths, and his constant fear of being found out make Chiyogiku an unusual maiko indeed. Yet, maiko, geiko, and their clients are among the series' fans, some having a complete set. Even the staid Gion Kōbu itself boasts about Nanami Haruka, including her along with such literary luminaries as Tanizaki Jun'ichirō and Setouchi Jakuchō, in a magazine article on favored writers associated with the hanamachi.[2] Nanami concludes her series with the lead male characters pledging their love; one voices his belief that Japan will catch up with other "advanced nations" in legalizing same-sex marriage.[3] But, as we shall learn, she does not intend her series as a call for social change. Rather it is the audacious fun of the masquerade, hanamachi lore, and sexual exploration under cover that animates *Chiyogiku* plots.

What does this entertaining fiction tell us about fantasies of the maiko as an icon for gender play in 2000s Japan? What does Chiyogiku reveal about performing maiko-likeness? This chapter begins by considering the *Chiyogiku* series as part of the millennial literary phenomenon in Japan known as the light novel. Reading Nanami's work with the genre's conventions in mind proves useful to interpreting the series' boys' love (BL) themes, including fascination with cross-dressing youth. Turning to the fantasy world of *Chiyogiku*, I analyze its gender masquerades by exploring the author's use of space, language, and behavior. We consider the romantic encounters experienced by the cross-dressed Chiyogiku and her friend Shion, a young woman masquerading as a handsome club host. This look at *Chiyogiku* as gender play takes us, too, to the multiple endings Nanami created for the series, each one presenting a different take on truth-telling, variously resolving the intense love relationship between Mikiya and the wealthy corporate prince, Nirezaki Shin'ichirō, that drives the series. In conclusion, we consider how the Mikiya/Chiyogiku masquerade employs fluid movement between two gendered personas, idealizing maiko-likeness as only a boy can create it.

THE LIGHT NOVEL GENRE

Reading the *Chiyogiku* series offers an apt introduction to an unconventional new genre known as the light novel (*raito noberu*, or for short, *ranobe*). Bound as small paperback books (*bunkobon*), light novels run between 150 and 200 pages.[4] A *Chiyogiku* volume costs between 500 and 600 yen (about US\$4.60–\$5.60 in 2020). Easily accessible to middle and high school students, the major target audience of most light novels, the *Chiyogiku* series mixes conversation with short descriptive passages about characters' fashionable clothing, hanamachi customs, and the history of particular tourist sites.[5] Each volume begins by relating the incident that prompted the boy Mikiya to pose as Chiyogiku in the first place and introduces the other main characters in the series. Although some volumes refer to incidents in previous ones, readers can enter at any point in the series. Every volume concludes with a common feature of the light novel: an *atogaki* (afterword) that is an informal letter from Nanami to her readers, in which she describes her daily life, her latest discoveries about the hanamachi, her travels around Kyoto and its environs, and news about the *Chiyogiku* series or about her letters and gifts from fans.

The entire look of the light novel invites playful, leisurely reading—from its approachable size and easy script to its vibrant covers. Indeed, one of the standout features of light novels is the bright manga-style illustrations adorning their covers, and *Chiyogiku* is certainly no different. *Chiyogiku* illustrator Hori Erio's covers intimate both innocence and sensuality. Gorgeous, fully blooming flowers in vivid pastels or primary colors fill the background of covers later in the series. Most covers feature the wide-eyed, luxuriously coiffed Chiyogiku in resplendent kimono alongside attractive young men in slick suits sporting modish hairstyles. Mikiya occasionally gets cover time, too, depicted as a casually dressed, energetic boy with a rag-taggle ponytail (figure 20). Following the light novel format, Hori's manga-style, black-and-white illustrations within the novel always introduce a few main characters at the outset. Manga also punctuate dramatic scenes within each volume. Extending the light novel's invitation to play, the final *Chiyogiku* volume includes a special *karuta* (Japanese card game of matching words and pictures) section of twenty emotion-packed scenes from the series featuring Chiyogiku and Nirezaki. Additionally, Hori has illustrated *Chiyogiku* stories, also authored by Nanami, as stand-alone manga narratives, publishing these in the monthly *COBALT* magazine. Occasionally, these manga, along with short *Chiyogiku* fiction by Nanami also originally published in *COBALT*, are reprinted in the *Chiyogiku* light novels. Such duplicate publication further connects *Chiyogiku* to the light novel phenomenon, notable for its movement across various commercial platforms including manga, anime, live action films, games, and character goods. Popular narratives can originate in any of these forms before migrating to other ones. I should add that translations into English and other languages offer yet another platform for republishing light novels, many translated by fans and posted online, and others published for sale in the United States.[6] Although *Chiyogiku* is not available in English translation, parts of the series have been published in Chinese and Korean.[7]

The longevity of the *Chiyogiku* series draws attention to the rise of the light novel as a financial boost to Japan's stagnating publishing industry and to emerging scholarly attention to the genre. One can appreciate the influence of light novels by visiting major big-box bookstores in Japan such as Maruzen and Junkudo and viewing the large amount of shelf space devoted to light novels. Satomi Saito views the origins of the term *light novel* as signaling a new trend

FIGURE 20. Mikiya and Chiyogiku appear together with VIP client
Nirezaki on this book cover. Nanami Haruka, *Shōnen maiko: Chiyogiku
ga yuku!* [Boy maiko: There goes Chiyogiku!], vol. 43., *Takasegawa rabu
sutōrī* [Takase River love story]. Illustrator Hori Erio. Courtesy of
Shūeisha. Copyright ©2012.

in "Japan's media ecology" starting in 1990, analyzing its subsequent embrace
by grassroots consumers "to refer to a group of novels that did not properly fit
into conventional genre classifications or age-based market segmentations."[8]
Examining newspaper and magazine attention to the upstart genre, Yamanaka
Tomomi argues that 2004 marked a burst of interest in the new format, generating the so-called "light novel boom."[9] Hoping to exploit this enthusiasm,
publishers developed product lines devoted to the genre and initiated prizes

for first-time writers. In 2000, Shūeisha, for example, one of Japan's major publishers and parent company for the *Chiyogiku* series, established the light novel line, Dash X, aimed at middle and high school students.[10] *Chiyogiku* is published in Shūeisha's Cobalt Bunko, which specializes in "the hugely popular cell phone novels . . . historical love stories and love fantasies [and] covers the spectrum of all possible romances."[11] Even though the initial surge of media curiosity in light novels subsided after a few years, prominent cultural critics took notice. Public intellectuals such as Ōtsuka Eiji, Azuma Hiroki, and Kasai Kiyoshi published criticism of light novels, interweaving this with debate about otaku subculture.[12] When authors of light novels began to win prestigious literary awards, the line between books in these series and high "literature (*bungaku*)" further blurred. Publishers saw advantage in this ambiguity and aimed to attract a "general reader" of broad tastes. Many college students majoring in Japanese literature in Japan have proposed writing their senior theses on light novels, inspiring their faculty to develop critical approaches to the genre. According to Ōhashi Takayuki, this motivated scholars in Japan to establish the new field of Light Novel studies.[13]

Despite this growing respectability, many view light novels such as *Chiyogiku* with skepticism. According to Yamanaka Tomomi, the eye-catching exuberance of their covers can make adults feel uncomfortable at the prospect of being caught shopping in this store section of gaily colored books, manga, and cartoonish characters aimed at kids.[14] But, as publishers hoped, the light novel caught on with readers of all ages. In fact, Nanami counts among her fans, a retired mathematics professor in Kyoto, who often sent her comments about the latest *Chiyogiku* volume, and connoisseurs of the hanamachi.[15]

Critic Kume Yoriko's analysis of the light novel's play with shape-shifting and gender-crossing helps us read *Chiyogiku*. Kume suggests that we can connect themes of same-sex love in light fiction to the prewar era when *shōjo shōsetsu* (novels for girls) were not allowed to show love between members of the opposite sex. Kume also proposes that while censorship in contemporary Japan precludes publication of bare-chested girls, boys crossing as girls can be shown bare-chested, perhaps to bypass these rules.[16] As well, Kume attends to the gender transformations that occur within the "preposterous settings" typically found in light novels, linking the girls dressed as boys to other instances in popular culture such as Takarazuka Revue musicals where women transformed into beautiful men (*dansō no reijin*) win power and position through assuming male gender. Most interesting for reading *Chiyogiku* is

Kume's observation that the feminine attire of cross-dressed male characters (*otoko no ko*) allows them to blend into the familiar *shōjo shōsetsu* worlds of girls, such as girls' academies, like the girls' okiya world in *Maiko-san-chi no Makanai-san* (chapter 4).[17] Pointing to the reported popularity of such light novel series with boys, Kume speculates that they may savor the role of one who is passively led by girls and loved by girls, rather than identifying with the typically heroic male who must initiate and save the day.[18] She finds it unfortunate, however, that these light novels never take the one further step of reflecting on the gender trouble their depictions have staged and fail to ask about the kinds of mobility transgender offers or the role-expectations associated with gender.[19] Rather, they stop at fantasy and affirming messages of self-love and self-acceptance of one's body. In the same way, the entertaining *Chiyogiku* series remains at the level of play, not aiming to politicize gender-role conventions or their disruption.

Boys' love (BL) themes, prominent in manga and light novels aimed at girls, are certainly at work throughout the *Chiyogiku* series, and Nanami herself imagines that among her wide range of readers, many are attracted to what she terms its "soft BL" aspects.[20] Since much fine BL scholarship is available in English, suffice it to say here that boys' love fiction treats the adventures and romantic lives of beautiful young men, and that it may range from including graphic sex scenes to the hints of erotic attraction and play (kissing, hugging) that we find in *Chiyogiku*.[21] BL narratives have drawn criticism for objectifying same-sex relationships for straight readers' consumption, while some scholars have debated why girls enjoy reading tales of love between boys. Scholars have variously proposed that girls feel empowered and liberated in the imaginary role of boys, and/or feel no sense of competition with the main love interest, and/or feel safe since no girl is at risk in such narratives even in fiction.[22] In the case of *Chiyogiku*, whatever their own gender identity, readers can vicariously experience moving between the girl's and boy's perspectives throughout the narrative, viewing the world from two different embodied positions.

THE WORLD OF CHIYOGIKU:
HOW A BOY BECOMES A MAIKO

Although the *Chiyogiku* series was published over nearly thirteen years, the saga within the narrative covers only one year and a half in a young boy's life, taking him from the summer of his thirteenth year to his Christmas and New

Year's holiday celebrations as a fourteen-year-old. Despite the absurdity of Chiyogiku's perfect masquerade and the maiko's unusual life, these stories move slowly at first, with much attention given to the pleasant minutiae of daily life, until the inevitable crisis or puzzle arises, and the pace quickens. The problem upsets the routine school life of Mikiya and weekend ozashiki of Chiyogiku, leading the reader, too, into fraught situations. Often in pursuit of some mystery, Mikiya/Chiyogiku ventures into resplendent Kyoto villas and gardens, views extraordinary artistic performances, and dines on sumptuous meals. Secrets unfold and romance blossoms at every turn. By each volume's end, characters' troubles resolve, and their worlds are righted. With few exceptions, no one guesses Chiyogiku's masquerade, allowing Mikiya's ruse (and the series) to continue. Much like the narrative manga *Kurenai niou* and *Maiko-san-chi no Makanai-san* (see chapter 4), the *Chiyogiku* series educates readers about hanamachi customs, kimono, and architecture, using this world to explore themes of desire and constraint.

How did the Chiyogiku masquerade arise in the first place? The deception that is Chiyogiku emerges as a response to a teahouse crisis: A maiko suddenly disappears! She had been scheduled for several parties celebrating Yoiyama, the July 16 event that occurs the day before the Gion Festival parade of floats. There is no time for the Yoshinoya to find a replacement. All the maiko in Kyoto are fully booked for this evening. Yoshinoya owner and manager, the widow Okamura Hanae is distraught at the thought of disappointing clients on this critical day and fears irreparable harm to the reputation of her teahouse. Her thirteen-year-old son and only child Mikiya volunteers to take the maiko's place, arguing that having grown up in the Yoshinoya, a combined okiya and teahouse, he knows enough to impersonate a maiko for just one evening. When no other solution appears, Hanae agrees. Hanae calls on her nephew, Hiroaki, a handsome graduate student in Greek Philosophy at Kyoto University who also lives at the Yoshinoya, to help with the masquerade. In turn, Hiroaki persuades Masashi, his longtime friend, fellow Shizuoka native, and a hairdresser in the Gion, to aid in costuming Mikiya from head to toe as a *minarai maiko* (see chapter 2). Together, the accomplices (mother Hanae, cousin Hiroaki, hairdresser Masashi, and Mikiya) become "Team Chiyogiku." They are shocked at the transformation. Easily using maiko voice and language, Mikiya automatically goes into maiko mode. He muses, "It was all so natural that even I was surprised."[23] All agree that if anyone notices the resemblance between Chiyogiku and Mikiya, they will be told the two are cousins. Fearful of being found out, Mikiya steels himself to attend four ozashiki the first evening, including one at the elegant inn owned by his best friend Ōsumi Kenta's family. When he realizes that even school chum Kenta does not suspect the ruse, Mikiya realizes he can pull off the masquerade.

Mikiya realizes that there is more to worry about than maintaining this fiction when two American clients, young executive men, sexually harass Chiyogiku on this first evening. Fleeing from them leads Chiyogiku to the fateful encounter with the other main character in the series, Nirezaki Shin'ichirō, a wealthy young man of thirty-two who will soon become enamored of Chiyogiku and near the end of the series, propose marriage. Despite the harrowing evening, Mikiya realizes he enjoys being Chiyogiku, and Hanae learns that clients are thrilled with her. Receiving numerous booking requests for Chiyogiku almost instantly, Hanae exclaims, "This is amazing. If you were a girl, you'd become the most popular maiko in Gion."[24] Mother and son later decide that Mikiya can maintain the masquerade when school starts if he can keep up his studies during the week at St. George's, a private Christian school for boys in Kyoto with an aristocratic European air. After all, Hanae surmises, there is no written rule in the hanamachi that maiko must be girls.[25] Thus, Mikiya begins his adventurous double life and even the geiko and maiko associated with the Yoshinoya have no idea of the ruse. Her misedashi occurs two months later in September. Although mother and son realize that Mikiya will have to quit his maiko impersonation before his voice changes, both seem eager to extend Chiyogiku's existence as long as possible. Chiyogiku's popularity thwarts their initial intentions to maintain a low profile since events conspire to draw her further into Gion celebrity. She becomes an urekko (top-selling) maiko at astonishing speed, winning excellent roles in the annual *Miyako Odori*, and even becoming the model for its printed program. Soon, Chiyogiku is the talk of Gion.

For me, the strangeness of this situation lies not so much in a boy's ability to pass as a heavily made-up, elaborately coiffed, and costumed girl, but in portraits of the ozashiki as drenched in blatant sexual harassment. International and Japanese clients, and especially Nirezaki, make repeated sexual overtures as the series continues. Gone are the strenuous efforts to divorce the hanamachi from associations with harassment that we saw in explanations of maiko training and women's personal accounts (chapters 2 and 3) and film and manga of the 2000s (chapter 4). Whereas the hanamachi took umbrage at filmmaker Mizoguchi's focus on lechery (chapter 4), Gion takes pride in its connection with Nanami's work, as mentioned. Likely it is the fantastical world of the light novel that enables this approach, encouraging readers to take BL genre conventions as such, and not assume that this harassment—or the absurd figure of a boy maiko—offer evidence of Gion reality. Rather, the sexual advances function as a narrative device that puts Chiyogiku in dicey situations where she must think fast to avoid advances and exposure. This also allows Nanami to place Chiyogiku at the sexually and romantically charged center of every plot.

Still, the use of sexual harassment as a narrative device recalls similar, equally troubling scenes in the 1962 comedy *My Geisha* starring Shirley MacLaine as the actress Lucy Dell in geisha masquerade. When her playboy costar Bob Moore (Robert Cummings) makes amorous overtures to her geisha self, Lucy easily outsmarts him, maintaining her masquerade. Lucy assures her producer, who is in on the secret of the masquerade but shocked at Bob that, "I always have that kind of trouble with Bob. . . . There's nothing wrong with Bob. He's just a delayed adolescent, that's all." Produced long before the term "sexual harassment" became a common reference, *My Geisha* frames unwanted sexual attention as harmless and funny, requiring clever responses from women. *My Geisha* dismisses Bob's behavior as comically juvenile, deflecting attention from the reality of sexual harassment in the industry. We may wonder whether a stronger climate in Japan against sexual harassment will affect tropes of harassment in BL narratives, making it impossible to see them as comic. As with Lucy, Chiyogiku outsmarting her harassers also implies that control is possible if ingenious girls remain alert. But, on occasion, Mikiya fumes, asking himself in his boy voice, "*Why* do guys push kisses on Chiyogiku? . . . Five guys—five guys!—even kissed her cheek. Everyone treats [Chiyogiku] like a doll. Shit. I hate it when they do that."[26]

Considering the BL themes in the *Chiyogiku* series also highlights how Mikiya's lack of a father paves the way for the creation of Chiyogiku and her love interests. There is no father to disappoint with the son's crossing, no paternal masculinity to challenge. (Mikiya's father died when he was an infant.) Mikiya develops many close relationships with men and boys, especially with his cousin Hiroaki, who is like an older brother to him. Most of these relationships are charged with an erotic BL quality, displaying affection emotionally and physically, if not sexually. The easy acquiescence of Mikiya's mother also furthers the masquerade. As a single mother, and an outsider from Shizuoka who came into her current position through marriage, Okamura Hanae is depicted as never completely comfortable speaking in the Kyoto dialect, but manages the Yoshinoya ably. Intriguingly, Hanae is excited at Chiyogiku's success as a maiko, feeling almost as if she has had the gift of having a daughter as well as a son. Throughout the series, Mikiya even thinks that sometimes his mother forgets that he is a boy.

From the start, Chiyogiku's girlish innocence is powerfully enhanced by the desiring men that she encounters. It is as though becoming a maiko has placed Mikiya among a veritable beauty contest of handsome male admirers, which the reader may also enjoy contemplating. This attention to men marks *Chiyogiku*'s departure from almost all other maiko narratives of the 2000s; whereas they concentrate on the creation of chaste girls' worlds and girls' performance of maiko-likeness, here we have a bevy of beautiful young men. The prime would-be suitor is the aforementioned Nirezaki, alum of St. George Academy and leader of the Nirezaki conglomerate, who is infatuated with Chiyogiku. Fabulously wealthy, a desirable *batsu-ichi* (once divorced), handsome in form and voice, Nirezaki has an *oresama* (masculine swagger) quality that has great appeal to women in the fictional Gion.[27] Drawn as irresistibly suave, Nirezaki defines salon masculinity (see chapter 1) in the *Chiyogiku* series. As the story goes, Nirezaki's first love was his stepmother, and an early romance with a maiko ended so badly that he had sworn off maiko altogether until meeting Chiyogiku by chance and falling head over heels for her. He becomes jealous, even enraged, when other men spend time with Chiyogiku. In some volumes, it is suggested that Nirezaki knows that Chiyogiku is a boy and that his attraction lies in the boy-costumed-as-girl fantasy.[28] Most of the *Chiyogiku* stories involve some interaction between Chiyogiku and Nirezaki, and while Mikiya is comfortable with a certain amount of intimacy (letting Nirezaki nap with his head in her lap for example), he resists the older man's attempts to seduce Chiyogiku. The series' multiple endings all involve different kinds of resolution with Nirezaki, as we shall see.

Throughout the series, the deception that is Chiyogiku, especially as she becomes the most popular maiko of all, is not only ludicrous; it is the precarious center always threatening to collapse. Mikiya imagines that it would bring ruin and embarrassment to his family and emotional pain to all those who have fallen in love with Chiyogiku if his deception were discovered. Nanami is a creative writer indeed, and her plots always manage to leave the reader wondering how the unveiling will *almost* occur and how things will be righted again so the deception can continue. Yet how Mikiya will eventually extract himself from the ruse without exposing it or hurting anyone becomes a challenge. Near the end of the series, after Mikiya's one year and a half in maiko masquerade, the disappearance of Chiyogiku becomes critical as favored clients press marriage proposals.

Chiyogiku's theme song might be "I like being a girl." Mikiya is in no hurry to grow up and lose the opportunity to be Chiyogiku. It is not simply being a girl that Mikiya enjoys but being a maiko. He often thinks to himself about how he enjoys no end of indulgence from clients and others in the hanamachi. Much like maiko Ichimame, whom we met in chapter 3, Mikiya enjoys meeting celebrities and attending parties to which no ordinary teen has entry. As Mikiya, he envisions only masculine roles in his future. He also feels that, when he leaves his double identity behind, becoming only and always a boy, he must give up his romance with Nirezaki and with his true first love, the teenage professional player of Go, Shidō Kaoru. Mikiya does not express the desire to change his gender permanently; rather he appears to enjoy crossing between genders, experiencing the world in two very different ways, much like the *otoko no ko* typical of other light novels, as Kume has pointed out. When he does imagine his adult future, he hopes that he can work for a supervisor like Nirezaki.[29]

THE SPACES OF CHIYOGIKU'S WORLD

Spaces—the gendered spaces of the boys' school, St. George Academy, and the Yoshinoya teahouse, the elite community of Gion and its environs, and Kyoto and other cities—figure critically in the *Chiyogiku* series. As readers learn from Nanami about the architecture of Kyoto's combined okiya/teahouses, we also see how these spaces aid in Chiyogiku's deception. In Mikiya's case, he lives in a separate building connected to the main house of the Yoshinoya, and shares this space with his older cousin, Hiroaki. It is the only boys' space within the okiya/teahouse. This is where Mikiya does homework, has his personal computer, and often converses with Hiroaki. Chiyogiku, as a weekend maiko (*shūmatsu maiko*), has a small space adjacent to Hanae's own room. It cannot be accessed except by going through the mother's room, thus effectively keeping people out of the Chiyogiku space. As for Mikiya's boy life at St. George, we see many descriptions of the building and gardens that speak to the privilege of the school, and we also learn it is an erotically charged space itself with many boy-couples. Ever the innocent, Mikiya is surprised to learn that many older boys are sexually attracted to him, but his bigger schoolmate Kenta has always kept them away.[30]

As we read about Chiyogiku, we learn about the spaces she and her hanamachi colleagues inhabit. There are teahouses, elegant ryōtei (luxurious Japanese-style restaurants), and the community of the Gion area itself with the vegetable seller, the innkeeper, the hairdresser, and the sweets shops that make it a real community that exists beyond the touristic impression of old Kyoto. Readers are also treated to exotic fictional spaces such as Nirezaki's splendid villa in Northern Kyoto, the host club Moonlight, and the pub Charade where Hiroaki works. Even more ambitiously, the author creates touristic worlds for each *Chiyogiku* adventure. She takes her reader, for example, to Arashiyama in the fall to see the changing leaves and to Nara to see Buddhist statues. She points out aspects of Kyoto geography. For the most part, this information folds into the plot logically and skillfully, and it helps set the stage. Occasionally historical and geographical facts are incorporated into the narratives with the premise being something like Mikiya's research report for school. The *Chiyogiku* series can spur actual travel to the area, according to letters from Nanami's readers that she describes in various atogaki. Adding to the glamorous atmosphere of the locations, many minor characters are the kinds of beautiful people typically found in BL manga, such as an Asian princess in England, a ballerina's son, an opera singer, and an Arab petrol prince who is half-Japanese.

ACTING LIKE A GIRL: PERFORMING THE MAIKO CHIYOGIKU

The *Chiyogiku* series is skillful in depicting gender identity as, in Butler's terms, a series of repetitive gender-coded acts. Chiyogiku succeeds because Mikiya understands that the maiko role is a performance. Although he performs maiko-likeness seamlessly and feels authentic in the role, acting as Chiyogiku requires self-conscious effort. Rather like the onnagata (female-role performers) of Kabuki, Mikiya must create a coherent self that aims above all else to please his audience. No wonder one of the few characters who does guess the Mikiya/Chiyogiku masquerade early on is onnagata Seiemon. Near the end of the series, Seiemon, who asks Chiyogiku to perform the Kabuki dance *Wisteria Maiden* with him, invokes the modern notion of the onnagata as performing an ideal femininity unavailable to actual women to praise Mikiya as an onnagata, too: "Of course, Chiyogiku-chan's dance differs from other maiko's. You know the goal of an onnagata, right? It's 'to be more feminine (*josei rashiku*) than an actual woman'. . . . If the onnagata were to imitate a real (*riaru*) woman, he would fail in comparison. . . . You perform the 'imagined woman.' You embody the 'idealized image of woman' that a flesh-and-blood woman (*namami no josei*) cannot."[31] These remarks make Mikiya realize, "Oh, I know exactly what he means. I guess that is [Chiyogiku]. Performing the 'ideal maiko' (*risō no maiko*) that a flesh-and-blood girl (*shōjo*) cannot express."[32] Thus, the onnagata-like maiko performs maiko-likeness without the interference of a female body. Seiemon also speculates that it is Chiyogiku's imagined femininity that attracted Nirezaki, something other maiko, as girls, could not embody.[33] Yet, as though to keep the tension among reality, illusion, and exposure in play, Nanami imagines the onnagata also cautioning Chiyogiku that dancing reveals one's "naked self," which cannot be disguised.[34]

Ever on the alert when in masquerade, Mikiya must be vigilant to protect the consistency of his Chiyogiku performance.[35] In this regard, he is not so different from those who speak to the importance of continually living up to the maiko image when in uniform (see chapters 2 and 3). It is important to note that, as the narrator often reminds readers, Mikiya is not imitating just any girl, but must, like real girls who take up this path, learn the skill to become the perfect maiko. In his case, memory comes into play, too: Mikiya must always remember what he knows and what Chiyogiku knows that he does not. He may meet Nirezaki in the morning, for instance, but must not hint at their conversation when, as Chiyogiku, he attends an ozashiki with Nirezaki in the evening. Although Mikiya switches roles adeptly, he frequently catches himself about to slip up. This adds to the dramatic tension of most plots, hinting that everything could unravel with the slip of a dialect or an errant clue. The pleasure of the disguise is always positioned against the fear of being found out.

Language is one of the primary means employed by Mikiya to behave in gender-appropriate ways. It is also the key for readers to know when he is speaking as a boy or a girl. As Mikiya, he speaks in standard Japanese, refers to himself as *boku* (the informal masculine pronoun), and freely uses slang (*Yabai!* Crap! *Chō Yabai!* Double Crap!). When he is dressed as Chiyogiku but talking to himself, Mikiya speaks in his male voice, making readers privy

FIGURE 21. Host Shion, masquerading as a man, dances with Nirezaki as Chiyogiku looks on in surprise. Nanami Haruka, *Shōnen maiko: Chiyogiku ga yuku!* [Boy maiko: There goes Chiyogiku!], vol. 8, *Eien no kataomoi* [Eternal unrequited love]. Illustrator Hori Erio. Courtesy of Shūeisha. Copyright ©2004.

coconspirators in their masquerades. As the *Chiyogiku* series concludes, Shion still struggles, unable to expose her secret to Hiroaki.

It is fascinating to see the congruence between the character Shion and the real lives of hosts. As scholar of Japanese host clubs, Akiko Takeyama, has shown, successful hosts do indeed pay attention to performing the masculinity that will attract high-paying female customers.[43] It is also a world that over-turns conventional gender roles in significant ways, positioning men as the ones who must exert themselves to perfect a pleasing appearance, coaxing their clients into conversations, and winning love, while women wield financial power. As a young man out on his own, typically without academic credentials or specialized training, the host occupies an unusual position: Takeyama argues that he is stigmatized for his failed masculinity as one who must rely on women for financial support yet celebrated for his "entrepreneurial profes-sionalism"—that is, his prowess as a neoliberal achiever who depends only on his own sales and charisma, seemingly without need for a safety net. Yet, most hosts live precariously, investing all they have in their appearance, exhaust-ing themselves physically and emotionally, and end up with little savings or accumulated skills. In the lavish world of *Chiyogiku*, however, this host does enjoy financial success. Interestingly, Nanami uses the character of Shion to criticize the romantic failings of Japanese men. Shion tells Mikiya that even one sensitive man may transform a woman, giving her new confidence. Impressed with Shion's stylized brand of salon masculinity, Mikiya has a glimmer of what his post-maiko persona could be.[44]

THE MULTIPLE ENDINGS OF THE CHIYOGIKU SERIES

The *Chiyogiku* series came to an end in 2014, cleverly marketed in not one final volume, but three.[45] The next-to-last volume contains five short stories, each positing a different kind of ending or showing Chiyogiku's farewell to a character that had figured importantly in the series. Although *Chiyogiku* does include stories that end in a wedding, the problem that always must be solved is her disguise. In one ending, Mikiya goes to bed with the flu, but wakes up to find out that Chiyogiku really is a girl and can marry Nirezaki after all.[46] She goes through bridal training at his villa, learning how to cook for him, and ends up in the marital bed with him after their picturesque wedding. Before any wedding-night sex occurs, Mikiya wakes up back in his boy body, aware that he has had a pleasant dream, but remembering none of its details. In another ending, hearing Chiyogiku's confession shocks Nirezaki into a coma; he develops amnesia, forgetting the last year and half—the entire existence of Chiyogiku. This amnesia, in effect, means that there was never a Chiyogiku in his life—something that makes Mikiya too feel a sense of loss.[47] In the series' final story, Mikiya decides to go abroad for two years' study in England. In the last chapter, he and Nirezaki meet six years later at Izumo Shrine (the shrine that *Dandan* depicts, too, as the sacred site that unites people with karmic connection) on Mikiya's twentieth birthday. He is legally an adult. Chiyogiku is long gone, and college-student Mikiya has a low voice, rather ordinary short hair, and wears dark adult casual clothes. He finds himself waiting in the Izumo train station, which looks to him rather like a chapel as it has a stained-glass ceiling. He is hoping against hope that Nirezaki will come. And lo and behold, Nirezaki arrives! He pledges his love to Mikiya as he is, not to the fantasy Chiyogiku, and vows never to part from him. They exchange vows in the chapel-like station beneath the glittering stained glass. They embrace and kiss. Mikiya realizes that it is the first time—he brackets off the name [Mikiya]—has been kissed by Nirezaki.[48] Chiyogiku is gone.

This affirming scene of same-sex union, as Nanami told me in 2017, motivated some gay readers to write her letters of thanks.[49] However, as Mark McLelland and James Welker explain, the "high visibility of BL narratives" may give the misleading impression "that it's easy to be openly gay in Japan."[50] This is not the case; nor is it easy to be transgendered. Activists in Japan hope that the nation's Supreme Court will enact marriage equality, but such sweeping legal affirmation will not likely occur soon. For her part, Nanami states that her goal is to write fantastical fiction, not to engage in politics.[51] In my conversations with her, I asked whether she found inspiration for Chiyogiku in Japanese literary sources such as the twelfth-century *Torikaebaya monogatari* (*The Changelings*), about a brother and sister who switch roles to better fit their sense of their gender identities or Buddhist tales about *chigo* "beautiful boy acolytes."[52] I also wondered whether the number of volumes in her series—fifty-four—was intended as a nod to the legendary romance *Tale of Genji* and its fifty-four episodes. Prince Genji's affair with his father's wife Fujitsubo and his love for the child Murasaki parallels Nirezaki's intimate bond with his stepmother and his fascination with Chiyogiku, a child like the maiko of old. Nanami found these interesting comparisons but said that none had figured in her creation.[53]

CONCLUSION

How does the *Chiyogiku* series—its imaginative author, loyal readers, and the tale itself—contribute to our understanding of the maiko masquerade? The pleasures and perils of the boy Mikiya as he crosses from middle-school student to weekend maiko call our attention to the emphatically gendered and age-bracketed nature of the maiko's role—she is only and always a girl. By manipulating language, costume, body movement, by employing all the strategies of maiko-likeness, Mikiya creates the perfect maiko in Chiyogiku. He resists seeing this persona as a joke or a fake, emphasizing, "I'm not doing *maiko henshin* (the tourist experience of maiko costuming). I'm a real maiko (*honmono no maiko da*)!"[54] Yet Mikiya, the reader, and some characters are always aware of the tension between the fantasy maiko and his physical male body, Mikiya's weekday gender, and his future as a man. Like Kabuki and Takarazuka, the many forms of gender crossing employed in *Chiyogiku* ultimately reinforce a female-male binary. The breach between the ordinary life of the boy and the maiko that Mikiya and Team Chiyogiku have created exaggerates the gap that we saw expressed in the personal accounts of maiko and geiko and in the characters of *Maiko-san-chi no Makanai-san* (chapters 3 and 4). These texts established an "ordinary girl" who must suppress her instincts and behaviors to embody maiko-likeness. Moving back and forth between boy and maiko personalities, however, Mikiya often seems less the creator of Chiyogiku than her twin. This fluidity resists privileging one role over the other until the point in the last tale when adult Mikiya appears, Chiyogiku is gone, and he establishes a mature relationship with Nirezaki.

The Chiyogiku deception enables the fun of seeing the world through two different gendered perspectives and safely allows for fantasies of identification with Chiyogiku and her clients. By the same token, the series allows Chiyogiku's clients to fall in love with a boy while ostensibly enamored of a girl, queering salon masculinity. The idealized girl plays off equally idealized men, everyone searching for some dream of perfect happiness in love. Purportedly, like an onnagata, Mikiya can transcend his boy body, creating maiko-likeness that appeals to men in ways real girls cannot. This parallels *My Geisha*'s Lucy Dell's ability to create her director-husband's perfect geisha fantasy as real Japanese women cannot, which the film satirizes; adamant about filming an authentic *Madame Butterfly*, he rejects all Japanese applicants, unwittingly choosing his own wife in geisha masquerade for the role. Visions of male desire bring us to the disturbing obsession corporate prince Nirezaki harbors for the teenage girl, yet the world of *Chiyogiku* is a safe one where no serious harm comes to anyone. This sense of safety, the blatant fictionality of the series, its backdrop of luxury, and its focus on romance make it possible to spin unconventional tales about sexual desire. For Nanami and her readers that are also fans of the hanamachi and Kyoto, the *Chiyogiku* series creates a maiko experience that brings fiction and tourist reality into close connection, without taking on the full force of gender politics.

In the next chapter, we continue this look at maiko comedy, turning to humorous visual texts found in two prominent Kyoto sites: the legendary textile firm Eirakuya and the Kyoto International Manga Museum. The diversity of maiko images on display in these sites plays with gender identities as *Chiyogiku* does. They also poke fun by placing the maiko in absurd situations and morphing her across different species, with other icons, and even with an alien and a vegetable. As with *Chiyogiku*, this light-hearted view of the maiko makes Kyoto itself a lively space for tourists to imagine the fantastic.

CHAPTER 6

Hit A Homer, Maiko!

Maiko Visual Comedy

Maiko—the culmination of Kyoto's elegant culture. Their demeanor changes with the times. The maiko depicted on tenugui are adorable, and in some respects, humorous.

—Eirakuya, *Irodori tenugui*

A maiko fashioned from a giant daikon radish? Another in full formal gear skiing down a mountain? A maiko with Mr. Spock ears and her own spaceship? Certainly, the maiko represents elegance, but, as the quote above also suggests, Kyoto's visual field allows plenty of room for humorous maiko images. These comic designs often provoke laughter by placing the fully costumed apprentice in unlikely situations such as poised to hit a home run on the baseball field or driving a motor scooter. Others play with elements distinctive to the maiko's uniform but morph her into a new character altogether, creating, for example, a maiko from outer space. These amusing twists on the maiko as icon mute the historical weight of the city's world heritage sites, inviting tourists to experience the old capital as a lighthearted place of leisure. But, as we shall see, some of these comic maiko offer laughter with a bite, satirizing the constraints of maiko-likeness or the pretensions of Kyoto. Others use absurd maiko images to provoke questions about their cultural moment, spoofing the excesses of Cool Japan, celebrity fever, tourism, and even the vogue for modern sports in the 1920s and 1930s.

Investigating some of these diverse, comedic visual representations of the maiko, this chapter delves into images at two prominent Kyoto sites: the maiko designs created by the textile firm Eirakuya in the 1920s and early 1930s as well as in the 2000s, and the *100 Maiko Illustrations* exhibit on permanent display at the Kyoto International Manga Museum since the museum's opening in 2006. Reading these images in their historical and cultural context, I show how artists play with the maiko image to comment on trends and controversies of their times. In turn, we see how their comedy reveals common assumptions about maiko in their day, whether the artist endorses or spoofs them. Unusual maiko images produced in the 2000s, when maiko are revered as Kyoto's quintessential girl, make us think about the pleasures and commodification of girlhood, the appeal and limits of maiko-likeness, the function of masquerade, and the identity of Kyoto. This millennial humor makes us once again aware that the maiko's image must be free of past association with sexual exploitation. Only then can artists re-create the maiko in playful ways. I divide this chapter into two parts, taking up the Eirakuya maiko in the first section and then turning to selected manga in *100 Maiko Illustrations*. The conclusion examines how these comical images figure in the broader terrain of the maiko masquerade.

HIT A HOMER, MAIKO! HUMOR AND THE HAND TOWEL

One finds vivid portraits of maiko at Eirakuya, a Kyoto textile firm dating to 1615, which also uses the romanized name RAAK.[1] Eirakuya stores are in prime shopping and tourist locations in Kyoto. Its *tenugui* (cotton hand towels), well-known souvenirs, offer a range of images, including many lush, detailed prints of the maiko in classic Kyoto settings. The firm's two best-selling tenugui take this approach—one shows a nightscape of a maiko gazing at the moon, the other features a maiko seen walking away from the viewer among the scarlet torii of Fushimi Inari Shrine.[2] But, it is the tenugui featuring maiko playing sports that have always caught my eye, making me curious about their origins. What inspired these absurd visions of maiko in full regalia playing beach volleyball, golfing, skiing, and kicking soccer balls? In fact, the sporting maiko come from two different series: the original series was produced in 1931 amid the vogue for modern, Western-style sports; newer versions come from Eirakuya's revival of the theme in the 2000s.[3] What do we make of these unorthodox renditions of maiko in the early 1930s and as revived in the 2000s? How do these sporting maiko respond to their different cultural moments and what can they tell us of popular assumptions about maiko in each era?

Exploring these questions, I begin with a brief history of the tenugui, examining how Eirakuya positions its products to connect consumers to the vitality of the Edo arts and the nostalgia of its early Showa designs. Moving to the 1930s, I show how the 1931 tenugui designs link to Japanese enthusiasm for modern sports and some concern caused by young women's success in national and world competitions. This takes us in turn to other phenomena of the 1930s hovering in the background of this comedy—the emergence of the modern girl in Japan, also depicted in Eirakuya tenugui designs, and the uncertain status of the geiko amid the influx of new entertainments. I argue that the Eirakuya 1931 sporting maiko express the vogue for new sports—so popular that *even maiko* were doing them—but may also incite some anxiety about how much change in Japan the modern girl and other Western phenomena might bring, affecting *even maiko*. Turning to the 2000s series and closely looking at the scene of sporting maiko at the beach, I show how the fantasy employs a profusion of fun-loving maiko to trade on millennial fascination with girls' culture. The incongruous scene imagines defining maiko-likeness on girls' terms. Although the sports theme in the 2000s appears to reference the earlier Eirakuya series more than women and athletics in millennial Japan, I consider the tensions between notions of femininity and sports that remain and how maiko-likeness may intervene.

TENUGUI: THE COTTON HAND TOWEL AS USEFUL AND ARTISTIC

Popular guides to tenugui in contemporary Japan celebrate its place in material culture historically and recommend new uses for it in the twenty-first century. Literally, the tenugui is something used to "wipe (*nugū*) the hand/s (*te*)." This unhemmed strip of cloth, about one yard long and a foot wide, dates as far back as the Nara period when it was used as a tool for cleaning in shrines and temples. Tenugui became widely available in the Edo period with the advent of mass cotton production. Eirakuya's 2009 book *Irodori tenugui* (Colorful hand towels) cites the frequent appearance of tenugui in ukiyo-e prints as proof of its ubiquity in the lives of commoners. It also refers to the 1784 publication of a humorous volume displaying the results of a tenugui design competition, launched by comic writer Santō Kyōden, which purportedly involved his samurai patrons, courtesans, and literati of the day in Edo, as evidence of early tenugui creativity.[4] Well into the twentieth century, the tenugui served as a common tool in everyday life, used for all kinds of simple kitchen tasks, as a head scarf, and for wrapping and carrying small objects.

Describing the diverse uses for tenugui in Hawaii, Barbara Kawakami deems it "an accessory Japanese immigrants could never have done without" and explains how immigrants returning from visits to Japan would bring back new tenugui as gifts.[5] During the Pacific War, tenugui, along with kimono and other clothing designed with nationalist images, figured as common tools of propaganda.[6] Today tenugui are associated with advertising. Stores have customarily commissioned fresh tenugui to hand out to customers as New Year's greetings and to promote their businesses. Although Western-style towels replaced tenugui in most homes by the 1950s, the vividly designed cloths have enjoyed renewed popularity in recent years for their color and resonance with Edo chic.[7] Eirakuya's *Irodori tenugui* encourages customers to reintegrate tenugui into their daily lives for a cheerful, artistic lift and as an ecological form of wrapping. How-to guides available in bookstore lifestyle sections in Japan offer innovative ways to fold tenugui for use in contemporary life.[8]

The tenugui's continuing importance to performers of traditional arts, including maiko, enhances its identity as a link to the past in the present. Kabuki actors and geiko have occasion to wear tenugui on stage, usually as head gear, and sometimes toss ones printed with their names to audience members. Eirakuya promotions accentuate this connection to Edo-era Japanese performing arts and the vitality of the merchant class that gave rise to them. *Irodori tenugui*, for example, features interviews with a kyōgen actor and a geiko about their use of tenugui. Gion geiko Tamaha describes the tenugui as rooted in her daily life, equally a stage prop, a handy tool, and, on travels abroad, a popular gift. She recalls handing out tenugui at her misedashi and erikae, and even cheering up a friend by gifting an energy drink wrapped in a bright tenugui.[9] The book suggests how readers may introduce a bit of Edo panache into their own lives by including interviews with two career women, who model how tenugui belongs in the repertoire of stylish professionals.[10]

Understanding the tenugui's place in Japanese material culture and its association with the traditional performing arts, we can appreciate why maiko and geiko regularly use them. Learning about the art of crafting tenugui designs for fun and competition since the Edo period makes us aware of their life in visual culture. With both these roles in mind, we take a closer look at the comic 1931 designs of maiko in Eirakuya's souvenir tenugui and view them against the broader visual and cultural field of the times.

SPORTING MAIKO AND MODERN LIFE IN COMIC TENUGUI

Eirakuya's comic 1931 sporting maiko series has fun with the sheer incongruity of formally clad maiko riding horses, rowing crew, and playing tennis. "Yō suberimasu nā" (We're really gliding) pictures two maiko skiing on a snow-covered mountain, their darari obi and long kimono sleeves fluttering behind them as they easily navigate curves with their poles. "Yōidon!" (Ready, go!) captures a lone Gion maiko crouching, poised at the starting line of a race, with four red Gion lanterns dangling from the wire above her. "Kattobasē maiko!" (Hit a homer, maiko!) shows one maiko up to bat, another playing catcher, and a scoreboard recording that even in the bottom of the *tenth* inning the score remains a zero-zero tie (figure 22). It does not appear that any of these maiko is going to get on base, let alone hit a home run.[11]

These sporting maiko contrast radically with the broad visual field of maiko representations in the 1930s. An icon of Kyoto even then and often a child, the maiko depicted in photos of the era look weighted down by their voluminous robes and hair. Artists influential at the time, Yumeji Takehisa and Takabatake Kashō, give her a romantic cast. But we can also view the maiko in contrast to another figure attracting attention in the era's visual culture, even in Kyoto—the modern girl. Associated with Western fashions, cosmetics, new forms of work and entertainment, the modern girl was shaking up notions of gender and Japanese identity. Intriguingly, one early Showa New Year's postcard pairs the maiko and the modern girl as icons of Kyoto, even as it displays the visual gap between them.[12] Artist Suzuki Toshio (1904–1975) inserts a caption in English, "A Happy New Year," followed in Japanese by "Young Misses of Kyoto" (*Kyoto no musume han*).[13] He imagines the two young women on Kyoto's famed Sanjō Ōhashi Bridge. In the foreground, a woman drawn in modernist fashion with short hair and bangs, rouged cheeks, and a smart Western-style coat dress , cloche hat, and handbag walks toward the viewer. Behind her, facing away from the viewer as though gazing at the hills, stands a maiko (figure 23). The classic pose draws the eye to her flowered darari obi and her equally rich hair. The postcard shows that one may expect to see the old and the new in the city. Does the modern woman walking forward hint that she may replace the maiko facing the hills and embodying tradition? For now, at least, both women are in the picture, both have a place in Kyoto, and despite their fashion differences, both are "Young Misses of Kyoto."

FIGURE 22. "Kattobasē maiko!"
(Hit a homer, maiko!). Copyright
©1931. Tenugui design. Courtesy of
Eirakuya, Ltd.

Suzuki's postcard defines the modern girl and the maiko as opposites. But this begs the question in these changing times: if the gap between the two young misses were to close, would the maiko shed tradition and adopt modern tastes, too? How far would she go? Or, is the idea of the maiko escaping from hanamachi traditions too ludicrous to contemplate?

Knowing more about the modern girl helps us appreciate her contrast with the maiko. In many ways a media-generated figure of the 1920s and 1930s, the modern girl sparks nostalgia in millennial Japan as the topic of photo books,

FIGURE 23. Suzuki Toshio's early-Showa New Year's postcard depicts a modern girl and a maiko on Sanjō Ōhashi Bridge. From the collection of Ikuta Makoto. Courtesy of Suzuki Hiroko.

the highlight of art exhibits, and a fashion inspiration.[14] She is romanticized as seeking autonomy in all aspects of life, embodying mobility, and the power of seduction and modern consumerism. Modern girl scholarship has explored the political dimensions of this icon, looking beyond the superficialities of the stereotype. Scholars have examined the phenomenon in relation to women's labor, political protest, the rise of cosmetics and the department store, new forms of transportation, literature, magazines, film, and urban entertain-ment.[15] They have also analyzed the modern girl's roles in forming the cultures of empire and traced her association with modern girls around the world.[16] The modern girl's classic look, often duplicated in the era's visual culture, makes her as recognizable as the maiko. One 1932 Eirakuya tenugui titled "Moga," the casual short form for the Japanese *modan gāru*, captures the stereotype. "Moga" depicts a woman in profile, emphasizing the angularity of her face and her sleek form (figure 24). She has the requisite ruby lipstick, bangs and a short bob, the arched eyebrows and lined eyes. Her Art Deco jewelry, the hints of a slinky dress, and the smoke swirling up from the cigarette held artfully in her hand make cartoon "Moga" the epitome of modern-girl decadence. A blotch of red on her hand makes it look as if she has kissed herself or is intimately involved with another lipstick consumer.

Many other Eirakuya tenugui designs show similar comment on modern life in the 1930s, including maiko as both harbingers of the modern and icons of tradition. Various in tone, Eirakuya's modern designs express cinematic cool, the allure of jazz bands, luxurious leisure, and couples meeting in cafes.[17] Some show ordinary people engaged in skiing, swimming, and team sports. Along with these modern-life designs, Eirakuya also promoted images of older entertainments, offering colorful portraits of Kabuki actors and maiko in conventional poses in the 1930s. One comic series of macabre skeletons, however, bridges tradition and modernity, recalling similar themes in ukiyo-e prints and evoking the early Showa intrigue with the surreal. These tenugui designs imagine viewing maiko and their hosts through X-ray vision. X-ray machines were a fast-growing global business in the early 1930s, including in Japan, as manufactured by Kyoto's Shimadzu Works.[18] "Gaikotsu maiko" (Skeleton maiko, 1931), a scarlet tenugui, depicts a dancing skeleton in black, her distinctive hairstyle identifying her as a maiko.[19] "Gaikotsu keshō" (Skele-ton makeup, 1931) shows a maiko (or perhaps a geiko) seated at her vanity applying cosmetics.[20] Another illustrates the skeleton of a client seated on the floor, the smoke from his cigarette curling upward.[21] Rather than girls having fun with sports, these skeletons recall the art of memento mori—reminders of the inevitability of death, human vanity, and the futility of earthly pursuits—but do so comically as though advocating making the most of life's temporary, sensual pleasures.[22]

Returning to the sporting maiko tenugui of 1931 recalls the strong asso-ciation among modern girls, Western-style sports, and Olympics fever.

FIGURE 24. "Moga" (Modern girl). Copyright © 1932. Tenugui design. Courtesy of Eirakuya, Ltd.

Magazine illustrator Takabatake Kashō created glamorous portraits of feminine beauties suited up for sports.[23] Photographs for the cosmetic firm Shiseido showed women skiing as did tourist ads.[24] As Alison Miller explains, healthy, skiing women enlivened nihonga in the 1930s, too, reflecting "government interest in physical fitness and the gendered body politics of the imperial age."[25] In the late 1920s and early 1930s, star sportswomen like the Olympic medalists runner Kinue Hitomi (1907–1931) and swimmer Maehata Hideko (1914–1995) excited nationalistic pride. Extensive media coverage of the 1932 Summer Olympics in Los Angeles, where Japan placed third for most medals earned, generated much anticipation ahead of the games and thrilled audiences at home. As Frederic A. Sharf has shown, department stores promoted all kinds of products—foods, cosmetics, accessories, and clothing—branded with Olympics enthusiasm.[26] Eirakuya's sporting maiko of 1931 may be an early sign of this wave, too.

But the sight of Japanese women active in sports also fueled apprehension. Dennis J. Frost documents concerns about women athletes' potential loss of femininity, heterosexuality, fertility, and Japanese modesty. Might women lose interest in Japanese men, who felt pressured into more sports performance themselves? Hitomi Kinue's death from illness at age twenty-four exacerbated such fears. Frost includes a 1926 cartoon of Hitomi that encapsulates these anxieties. The comic depicts the sports star as a giant, muscular woman leaping in a single bound over the giant book, *Onna reishiki* (Etiquette for women), while wearing track gear and clutching her enormous trophy. Four women in kimono, all tinier than the book, look up at her.[27] That at least one of these tiny figures seems to express glee implies that women could be attracted to the model of strength and competitive victory that Hitomi embodied.

In contrast to concern over modern girls and Japanese women active in sports in the 1930s, the maiko and geiko might seem the reassuring face of gender tradition. Yet Liza Dalby explains that many in the hanamachi in Kyoto and Tokyo felt pressure to keep up with the times. Pontochō initiated a variety of experiments in modern entertainment (see chapter 1). To describe the uncertainty of the geisha's place in the era, Dalby examines the 1935 *Geigi tokuhon* (The geisha reader), a compendium of advice for geisha given by men from disparate sectors—art and entertainment, industry, politics—that shows the flux in modern tastes. Some wanted the geisha to adapt to modern trends, even wearing a dress rather than a kimono; others saw her as a hopeless anachronism; and still others believed in the geisha's unique value as a symbol of Japanese culture, a portent of the nativism that would take hold in the later 1930s and 1940s. Some *Geigi tokuhon* contributors believed that it was preferable to visit the new cafés, conversing with café girls, another type of modern girl, rather than going through all the ritual and expense of the teahouse.[28] Although no one involved with the book appears to have asked geisha for their thoughts, we do have the 1930 personal account of Tokyo

Shinbashi geisha Hanazono Utako (1905–1982), who was proud of her status as a modern geisha. She embraces the entertainments of the modern era and expresses her frustration with the geisha leaders who are always telling geisha not to wear modern hairstyles, modern clothes, or talk about baseball. In fact, she argues that "the modernization of geisha is the most important requirement for ensuring the prosperity of the karyūkai."[29]

Bringing all these elements together—the modern girl, the geisha in flux, the sporting woman, and the maiko—how can we read the sporty maiko tenugui? Where does the maiko, who was a young teen at this time, fit in this cool new Showa world of modern entertainment, sports, and fashion? One answer is that she does not quite fit, as indicated by Suzuki's postcard that shows the modern girl and the maiko as opposites. By contrasting the maiko to the modern girl, Suzuki makes her the old-fashioned girl facing away as if toward the past, trained in old dance styles, and ensconced in a community set in its ways. Not allowed boyfriends, she may one day marry and leave the community or be matched with a patron. It is absurd to imagine her competing in sports. Or, we can imagine that sports have become so popular that even maiko play them, though this does not necessarily mean that maiko would change in other ways. But still another reading is possible. We can imagine that the Kyoto maiko, like modern Shinbashi geisha Hanazono, are itching to get out there and play ball. Rather than entertaining men at ozashiki, maybe their thoughts are wandering to more modern, active, and self-pleasing activities. Maybe they *do* want to see themselves as batters at the plate. At a quick glance, the incongruity of the sporting maiko must have sparked laughter. Did the comic sight reassure viewers that, after all, some girls would never change, or did it pique the concern that they just might? As historian Barbara Sato writes, "What made the modern girl such a powerful symbol was not that she represented a small percentage of 'real women,' but that she represented the possibilities for what all women could become."[30]

Among the possible readings of Eirakuya's 1931 sporting maiko, there is no hint of a call to rescue maiko as victims of exploitation. These tenugui reflect tacit acceptance of the maiko's marginalized status, perhaps making her imagined escape into sports even more comic. The lack of any reference to maiko sexuality in the 1931 series makes these tenugui easily consumable in the 2000s. Turning our attention to the revived series, we see how fascination with the maiko as well-behaved artist and even representative of girls' culture informs maiko sport comedy in the 2000s.

BEACH VOLLEYBALL MAIKO IN MILLENNIAL JAPAN

The current head of Eirakuya, the fourteenth Hosotsuji Ihee in its history, was born in 1964, entered the firm in 1992, and assumed the top position and lineage name in 2000.[31] Taken with the sporting maiko series of the 1930s, he decided to revive it, creating new images such as maiko on wooden swings amid trees, fishing at a dock, and trios of maiko playing soccer and golf.[32] But the firm also continues to create classic maiko scenes and experiment with new imagery. In the 2000s, some of Eirakuya's most eye-catching tenugui are created in collaboration: Tanaami Keiichi's maiko tenugui reflects his psychedelic pop-art style; painter Osugi Shinji offers his signature big-eyed maiko with an excess of kanzashi atop her head; and in a new spin on sporting maiko, Sanrio contributed its Kitty-Chan, outfitted in kimono and darari obi, popped onto the 1931 Eirakuya design of skiing maiko, zooming downhill herself.

Among the millennial maiko tenugui, one happy beach volleyball scene stands out to me. Titled "Maiko-san-tachi no umi" (Maiko together at the beach, figure 25), the print shows a profusion of maiko, eighteen altogether. All wear formal regalia from red kanzashi in their hair to white tabi on their feet, spending a day at the beach under fluffy white clouds and bright blue skies. Relaxing on beach towels, three pairs of maiko appear to revel in talking with each other as they gaze at the deep blue sea. Six other maiko concentrate on their volleyball match. Another six are playing the old watermelon game as one blindfolded maiko takes whacks at a green ball of fruit while her maiko pals laugh. I translate the Eirakuya website description of the scene as, "The maiko are together on holiday at the seaside. They are playing beach volleyball and the watermelon-splitting game, each merrily enjoying the summer."[33] This tenugui of the eighteen maiko, brilliant in their formal kimono, enjoying beach leisure on a summer day offers a delightful sight. But there is no ocean front in Kyoto, and maiko would never go to the beach in uniform. It's an absurd but enticing fantasy.

"Maiko-san-tachi no umi" crafts a comic vision of girls' culture as safe, free, and fun. Certainly, *Miyako Odori* and other hanamachi dances stage vivid scenes with an abundance of maiko moving in sync. But these beach maiko have gone off script. Basking in the leisure of a sandy day out by themselves and for themselves, they appear to wear kimono for nothing more than their own dress-up play. Hanging out with their maiko friends, talking, and laughing without a care about productivity or for their public appearance

FIGURE 25. "Maiko-san-tachi no umi" (Maiko together at the beach). Copyright © 2014. Tenugui design. Courtesy of Eirakuya, Ltd.

as representatives of Kyoto, they have escaped the constraints of obedient maiko-likeness. Imagined acting on their own terms, these maiko redefine maiko-likeness as fun with girlfriends, visibly free to "waste time." The viewer may take vicarious pleasure. But the comedy here arises from incongruity. Of course, maiko in kimono would no more play beach volleyball than would 1931 maiko play baseball, but neither do maiko in uniform ever have the luxury of avoiding the demands of maiko-likeness in the public eye. Although these beach maiko stage a kind of rebellion, theirs is a gentle one. Cheerful, sweetly funny, "Maiko-san-tachi no umi" does not stray far out of bounds, and that, too, is part of its appeal.

The sight of girls, colorfully dressed, immersed in having fun with each other, without chaperone or boyfriend, resonates with the 2010s "pancake boom," in which young women consumed huge, expensive dessert-like

pancakes at trendy foreign restaurants such as the Hawaiian chain Eggs 'n Things in Harajuku. News media reported on the phenomenon, showing photos of groups of fashionable young women waiting outside in long lines, often for over an hour, for a table. Reportedly, men did not feel comfortable in these sweets-oriented female-spaces. But the young women enjoyed chatting in line and uploading photos of their feasts to Instagram, and they did not hesitate to leave behind the portions they could not eat. This exasperated critics, who took the women to task for their visible excess—they wasted time, wasted money, and wasted food. Comparing criticism of millennial pancake consumers to the irritation modern girls provoked in the 1920s and 1930s with their fashionable, pleasure-seeking forays into public space, Keiko Ishii reads this phenomenon as a "petit rebellion" against the virtues of thriftiness, modesty, and care for others demanded of women in Japan.[34] Like the fantasy of maiko at the beach, the pancake rebels have escaped into girl friendships, leisure, and consumption, indulging in a highly visible and uniquely "girl experience" (*joshi keiken*), to use the common media phrase of the 2000s.[35]

Lingering on the excess of pancake politics, "Maiko-san-tachi no umi," and girl experiences links to one more millennial maiko image—in a trio of colorful posters advertising Kyoto's Keihan Electric Railway nationwide. The poster series "In Kyoto, on Keihan" features an enormous photograph filled with actual maiko—and only maiko—in full regalia waiting for a Keihan train or riding one. The debut 2014 poster, for example, shows an entire train car filled with over twenty maiko, all wearing formal kimono and the yellow-themed kanzashi of March in their hair.[36] Like the beach maiko and pancake rebels, these girls are laughing and chatting with each other, paying no attention to the viewer, who is positioned outside the frame and observing the maiko through the car windows. Like "Maiko-san-tachi no umi," this image, too, invites voyeuristic pleasure. The sheer number of maiko in the frame evokes stories of wealthy men who hired several maiko at a time, for instance, to accompany them to Kabuki, and the spectacle of a spring dance production. But the maiko's concentration on their own conversations in the Keihan posters can tell another story, too, styling Kyoto as a safe place for girls to travel with their pals, making the old capital a site of girls' culture and *joshi keiken*.

Following the strategy for reading the 1931 maiko manga in the historical context of early Showa athletics, it is tempting to view "Maiko-san-tachi no umi" similarly. Although the 2000s Eirakuya sporting maiko allude to the company's earlier series, following this thread shows that some tension still exists about the place of women in sports. Beach volleyball officially became an Olympic sport in 1996. Popular writer Sakai Junko, in her book of comic vignettes on clothing, questions the visual role of the bikinis worn in beach volleyball. She wonders why women's flourishing in sports has led simultaneously to more exposure of the body.[37] Although the maiko are unrealistically garbed in kimono, perhaps not having to bare their bodies and live up to the beautiful body ideal plays a part in their beach-time relaxation. We might also consider how media attention to the 2011 Japanese women's soccer team, the World Cup winners that year, highlighted ways that sporting women have been expected to embody Japaneseness and femininity. The team received its nickname "Nadeshiko Japan" by public vote, becoming identified with the pale pink nadeshiko, a deceptively strong flower that calls to mind feminine beauty, endurance, and self-sacrifice. Winning an international victory only four months after the devastating tragedies of March 2011 made the team a favorite at home and around the world. On their return to Japan after their victory, the athletes received the National Honour Award, along with a set of Japanese makeup brushes from the government, and media attention turned to their personal lives rather than sport.[38] In her discussion of Japan's 2011 World Cup winners, Gitte Marianne Hansen reads the case of Nadeshiko Japan as showing how women in Japan succeeding in masculine-marked sports like soccer "are continually required to confirm their female sex, gender, and heterosexuality."[39] The incongruity of "Maiko-san-tachi no umi" spoofs this demand to perform girlhood appropriately for the nation. But the limits on women's access to certain athletics is real. Even in 2020, women are still not allowed in the professional sumo ring and there are still mountains in Japan that women are not allowed to climb—female impurities being taboo in these sacred spaces.[40] We await an Eirakuya tenugui of maiko taking on this forbidden territory.

Eirakuya's sporting designs of 1931 and the 2000s stand out for making maiko imagery funny. But, as we have seen, this visual maiko comedy also responds to the cultural phenomena of their respective eras. The 1931 sporting maiko designs show that everyone is playing Western sports these days, even maiko. Given the questions swirling about the relevance of the geisha's art in the 1930s, these sporty designs may even be a vote for the maiko and geisha to catch up with the times, taking on sports along with the tango. The laughter the designs provoke may also touch on the anxiety over women succeeding in modern sports in the early 1930s and the sense of changing times produced by young women in visible new forms of urban work and leisure. The modern girl may have been more representation than reality, but her presence in the cultural landscape challenged notions of gender and Japanese identity. In this environment, the sporting maiko may have assuaged anxiety—she might play sports, but after all, she was still a maiko and still inhabited a Kyoto world dedicated to pleasing men. The revival of the sporting maiko series in the 2000s depicts the costumed maiko in some new women's sports—soccer and beach volleyball—as well as fishing and enjoying swings. They are rendered prettier and more colorful than their 1930s predecessors. These 2000s maiko, especially those at the beach, offer fantastic visions of pretty girls at leisure. Rather like *Maiko-san-chi no Makanai-san* and *Janken musume* (chapter 4), these sporting maiko act as a catalyst for immersion in girls' culture as care-free fun. Like women staging petit rebellions through pancake politics, these maiko enjoy "wasting time" by hanging out together, making the beach their own girl space. By extension, they suggest that Kyoto and its hanamachi in the 2000s might be one more playful arena for girls. This interpretation also casts maiko-likeness in a different light. Eirakuya's 2000s sporting maiko embrace their uniform and their girl cohort, spinning maiko-likeness as the embodiment of pleasure by and for girls. The humorous incongruity of the scene—its absurdity—however, depends on the reality of the maiko's containment in a heavy, complex uniform, the symbol of her unusual vocation. She is at once imaginative catalyst for girls' culture and the maiko rashii maiko carefully cultivated to represent Kyoto.

In the next section, we move from Eirakuya's distinctive tenugui comedy to the varied visual field of over one hundred maiko images, each by a different artist, on exhibit at Kyoto's famous manga museum. Here, too, we find the satiric bite of social comment and reassurance, the surprise of maiko in absurd settings, and joyful and even parodic portraits of maiko as representative of contemporary girls' culture. By morphing the maiko with other characters from animals to vegetables, manga artists may endorse the expected meanings of maiko-likeness or redefine it in startling ways.

THE *100 MAIKO ILLUSTRATIONS* EXHIBIT: KYOTO INTERNATIONAL MANGA MUSEUM

The Kyoto International Manga Museum provides a lighter look at maiko through its permanent exhibit *100 Maiko Illustrations*, titled in Japanese, *Hyaku-nin no maiko-ten*.[41] The exhibit title recalls the famous ukiyo-e series *Edo meisho hyakunin bijo* (One Hundred Beautiful Women at Famous Places in Edo) created by Utagawa Kunisada (1786–1865) in which each of his prints celebrates the uniqueness of a location by displaying its notable beauty.[42] A collaboration with The Japan Cartoonists' Association and Kyoto Seika University to commemorate the opening of the museum, *100 Maiko Illustrations* actually features the work of 174 manga artists.[43] Thirty-eight of the artists are women. The museum website praises the collection as featuring "maiko-san with 'rich individuality (*kosei yutaka*)' drawn by over one hundred manga artists." Each manga is about 17 × 11.5 cm, individually framed, and its artist credited—often alongside a miniature of the artist's photo or witty self-portrait. Except for a few manga rendered in color, all are drawn in black ink. The manga hang in even rows along the corridors of the museum, which was once the Tatsuike Primary School, originally opened in 1869. This cozy old elementary school with its dark, wooden floors imbues manga viewing with a kind of nostalgic experience of childhood long past. Although uniform in size, frame, and cream-colored background, the manga present an imaginative diversity of maiko. The exhibit handout gives the names of all the artists in Japanese on one side and as romanized on the other. In English, the handout suggests that viewers, "Find your favorite 'maiko'!!" In Japanese, the handout shifts the attention to the viewer as a fan, "Please do search for the maiko-san drawn by your favorite author" (*daisuki na sakka-san no egaku maiko-san o zehi sagashite mite kudasai*).[44]

Walking these corridors, manga fans will quickly recognize the work of some famous artists. In some instances, it is easy to guess the artist right away from their distinctive style or nod to their own brand. Yanase Takashi (1919–2013), for example, imagines a maiko version of his famous character Anpan-man, the loveable superhero whose bread-head fairly bursts with sweet *an* bean-paste; in 2010, Anpan-man was deemed Japan's most popular character.[45] Smiling at her viewer, this jammy-faced maiko, her kimono emblazoned ANPAN-MAN, soars above the famous Daimonji symbol burning on the Higashiyama hills in mid-August. Like Anpan-man, she is ready to rescue good from evil. In a completely different tone, Shōji Yōko, well-known for her 1970s–80s manga series *Shokun, Seito!* (Attention, Students!), a girl's coming of age story, takes a representational approach. She draws a lifelike teenage maiko with attention to the details of her hair, kanzashi, and kimono. Shōji's maiko looks directly at the viewer, as though caught in the moment when she is brimming with excitement about her costume and her destination. The difference between Yanase's maiko, frankly cartoonish and fantastic, and Shōji's emphasis on the beauty of the maiko's costume and her youth suggests the wide range of images in the exhibit.

Here, I will try to give a sense of the experience of walking in the manga museum and viewing the exhibit, zooming in on several and regretting that I cannot show them all. We see that elements of the maiko's codified look inform every manga to some degree. Often it takes only the suggestion of the maiko's hairstyle, kanzashi, or darari obi to let the viewer recognize the maiko in the manga. American cartoonist and theorist Scott McCloud argues that such "iconic abstraction" allows an artist to focus on specific details by removing others, distilling "an image to its essential 'meaning'" and enabling the artist to amplify its meaning in ways "realistic art can't."[46] Following McCloud, artist

Sarah McConnell explains that "iconic imagery acts as a trigger for the audience to engage their imagination—a reaction that the author-artist actively seeks to encourage."[47] Certainly, *100 Maiko Illustrations* can motivate such active engagement, instilling appreciation for the artist's skill in manipulating iconic abstractions to communicate various views of maiko.

Shared features among some manga in the exhibit make them possible to consider as a group: animal imagery, maiko fashion, other icons of Kyoto, and what I call "maiko-in-motion" themes stand out. It quickly becomes apparent that most manga in the exhibit maintain typical aspects of maiko-likeness in cartoonish fashion. That is, they depict the maiko as a cherubic, doll-like character or a pretty teen, in elaborate costume, exuding femininity, rather like the manga maiko Sū-chan in *Maiko-san-chi no Makanai-san* (chapter 4). Several offer unusual combinations of maiko with surprisingly different images. These odd maiko—morphed with a bearded seal, an American pop star, an unruly teen, and a senior citizen, for some examples—show how manga artists undo maiko-likeness or perform it with satiric bite. They also call on viewers' knowledge of popular culture and references to famous places and signs in Kyoto. Homely, funny, and rude manga maiko reveal the possibility of a different kind of performance. These manga question the maiko's containment in hanamachi tradition and her responsibility to represent Kyoto as its favored girl.

As I sought permissions in spring 2019 to reprint selected manga from the *100 Maiko Illustrations* exhibit, I was surprised and happy to receive comments on their work from five of the artists. Their inspirations lent another interpretation, sometimes different from mine. I include these notes in my discussion of their manga. I should add that the *100 Maiko Illustrations* exhibit does not have wall labels to guide the readers' engagement; other than the broad introduction on the handout described above, the only written texts are those that some artists inserted in their drawing.

ANIMAL MAIKO: KITTENS, MICE, A PARAKEET—AND A BEARDED SEAL

Morphing maiko into animals produces numerous adorable images, but also some that veer from conventional maiko charm. The prevalence of these furry motifs here reminds us of the rich history of animals in Japanese art and their multifarious range, connecting to the zodiac, folktales, political satire, pets, and monsters.[48] They also highlight how manga lends itself to playful renderings

KYOKO WATANABE

FIGURE 26. A parakeet in maiko costume. Copyright © 2006. Kyoto
International Manga Museum. Courtesy of Watanabe Kyoko.

as characters morph into *chibi* size (short, chubby, cute) animals. Most of the
manga artists using an animal theme do so in ways that double the cuteness
of the maiko and her animal twin, emphasizing smallness and vulnerability.
Following Laura Miller's work on animal imagery in Japan, we can look beyond
cuteness alone to see how these zoomorphic maiko broaden their appeal by
averting reference to gender and ethnicity; some lack reference to age, too, while
others clearly infantilize the animal-maiko. The animal's association in Japan
with "naturalness and lack of manipulation" underscores the maiko's link to
the imagined freedom of the shōjo.[49] In this exhibit, cuddly kittens debut most
frequently, but mice, rabbits, and a poodle appear, too. Kyoko Watanabe connects the youthful charm and "dazzling aura of the maiko" with the brilliance
of a small bird, creating parakeet maiko (*inko maiko*) (figure 26).[50] Blending the

charm of petite animals and the maiko, many of these manga mimic childhood toys. Maiko-animals become small pets that comfort, inviting intimacy and identification.[51]

But animals morphed into maiko also produce a few grotesque results, challenging conventional notions of cute and questioning the demand for maiko-likeness. They hint at the aesthetic of grotesque-cute (*gurokawaii*) and creepy-cute (*kimokawaii*) that is "both cute and gross at the same time."[52] Possibly alluding to the shapeshifting fox-women of Japanese folklore, Sakamoto Kiyotoshi draws a half-human creature with seductive, big eyes and dramatic eyelashes, breasts, and a round belly, but also fox ears, long whiskers, and a long bushy tail. Even its kimono sleeves, kanzashi, sandals, and fan don't make a maiko out of this fox. Yashima Kazuo's wild-eyed cat maiko, its kimono covered in paw-print design, looks giant in the frame: Is it a cat that devoured a maiko? Or a maiko behind a ferocious mask? Strange within an exhibit that shows many adorable animal-maiko, the beastliness of these manga turn the tables on the ubiquity of apprentice girlishness. Their unconventional maiko portraits encourage the viewer to re-examine the animal theme.

Among these unconventional animal-maiko, "Tamagawa no Tama-chan, maiko debyū" (Tama-chan of the Tama River, maiko debut) strikes me as both poignant and grotesque.[53] Abe Narumi's close-up visage of a light-gray animal, one of the few manga rendered in color, shows deep soulful brown eyes that gaze out at the viewer. She has red "bee-stung" lips and hot-pink rouge, spikey long whiskers, and huge black nostrils. Colorful kanzashi of all kinds adorn her maiko hairstyle. This manga refers to the male bearded seal first spotted in the Tama River in 2002. Given the diminutive nickname Tama-chan, the seal became a national celebrity. As Christine L. Marran points out, this outpouring of human affection, "domesticating love," transformed this seal into "something onto which anthropomorphizing notions can be projected and through which social standards are maintained."[54] Tama-chan disappeared in 2004, but its celebrity lives on. Like Kyoto's maiko undertaking her own misedashi debut, Tama-maiko of the Tamagawa offers an inviting image of the local, tempting viewers to project fantasies of cross-species love and cross-gender play. As with the maiko, fans were never sure where Tama-chan might pop up. Laura Miller reminds us that animal icons in masquerade occur frequently, and some may inspire viewers to "mask themselves in a character and safely enter a dangerous or unexplored world."[55] Here, it is Tama-chan exploring the mysterious maiko world. Tama-chan's story may also suggest the lure of escape from exhausting celebrity. After all, in maiko cosplay, Japan's most famous seal slips into the costume of a different icon of cute, becoming just one among many nearly identical maiko. In Abe's manga, Tama-chan's outsized celebrity overshadows the maiko morph, turning our attention to the poignancy of seal fame, questioning our expectations for animals.

MAIKO CHIC: KANZASHI, MAID CAFÉS, COSPLAY—AND ATTITUDE

Maiko chic inspires many manga in the exhibit, generating prettiness and some comic visions, too. Some depict a novice maiko tilting her head slightly to the side, allowing her kanzashi cascade of small flowers to flutter.[56] In a different twist on fashion, Minami Ippei uniforms his maiko in kanzashi and kimono but adds the maid café girl's headband and a huge, white ruffled apron, its enormous bow peeking out behind her. This wide-eyed maiko-maid smiles, facing viewers as though poised to welcome us. Akin to the maiko as a maid-enly icon of Japan—in the maid's case, the Cool Japan of otaku, anime, and places like Akihabara—she is imagined as "eternally seventeen." In her faux-French uniform and short frilly apron, the maid delights café customers with her scripted greetings and games (see introduction). Although she smiles, this maiko-maid can hardly move for the layers of her clothing. Minami's manga begs the question: Is there any real girl here or only layers of crafted kawaii packaged as tourist attraction? Taking on layers of cuteness in a different way, Terashima Reiko features a girl, dressed in an under-robe and wearing a skull cap (figure 27). A wig festooned with kanzashi magically hovers above her, as a giant arrow points down toward her head. The caption reads, *Henshin-chū* (In the middle of the maiko makeover). Smiling, she winks at the viewer. Does this girl's wink bring us in on the secret, letting us know that she is about to enjoy a masquerade? For her part, as she wrote me in July 2019, Terashima imagined that her cartoon girl was indeed becoming a maiko, not doing cosplay, but she still hinted at a kind of masquerade. Terashima wrote that her manga "reveals the secret that the maiko is, at heart, an ordinary girl."[57] Terashima's winking maiko plays with notions of authenticity and deception.

Sato Masao's manga blends maiko fashion with social comment (figure 28). One of the few drawn in color, Sato's manga bears the caption, *Kō-sotsu no maiko-san* (High school graduate maiko). On a stroll in Kyoto, this smiling maiko sports teenage chic reminiscent of the 1990s. She embodies a kind of

FIGURE 27. "Henshin-chū" (In the middle of the maiko makeover).
Copyright © 2006. Kyoto International Manga Museum. Courtesy of
Terashima Reiko.

"Japanese Cute-Cool," to use the term coined by Christine Yano to describe
"in-your-face cute as a highly stylized, overwrought visual aesthetic. It is cute
that performs for the street."[58] Sato's high school maiko has rolled her kimono
above her knees, and even hitched up her bright pink darari obi, drawing attention to her bare legs. She wears white tabi, but her pink footwear appears to

FIGURE 28. "Kō-sotsu no maiko-san" (High school graduate maiko).
Copyright © 2006. Kyoto International Manga Museum. Courtesy of
Sato Masao.

mesh okobo with the spice of vintage platform shoes. This maiko loves her
makeup, wearing long, false lashes and bright red lipstick. Her obi sports the
green and yellow "*shoshinsha* mark," the official sign of the beginning driver
that Japan requires new drivers to display on their cars. This girl takes an
inventive approach to maiko hairstyle conventions and kanzashi, too, wearing two enormous combs that jut out from her head. Yet, this maiko wears
her self-fashioned kimono easily, without a hint of self-conscious rebellion

or embarrassment. She is a "beginning driver," after all, perhaps unsure of the rules of the road in the hanamachi, or as a high school graduate, her approaching adult life.

Sato's high school graduate maiko can also evoke the boldness of the kogal trend of the 1990s (see the introduction). These high school girls riled school officials by rolling up the skirts of their school uniforms, bleaching their hair, tanning their skin, and wearing showy makeup and platform shoes. Their look, their slang, their alleged materialism, and association with compensated dating incited moral panic. How different she is from the maiko, who is dressed to code by her elders and schooled in etiquette. In the maiko's case, Japanese tradition *is* the fashion. In contrast, this high school graduate invents a maiko look based on the teen aesthetic popular with her crowd. Identified as a high-school graduate, Sato's maiko signals that an older teen may be less compliant than the middle-school trainee. This perspective points to the humorous juxtaposition of teen virtue with teen delinquency, and maiko containment in hanamachi tradition with out-of-bounds teen behavior. Viewers can read the codes for both here. The sheer impossibility of a maiko redefining maiko-likeness to suit teenage tastes makes this manga funny.

Chic maiko can also have attitude, or at least one does in Manga Tarou's comic. His manga pictures a maiko outfitted in an autumn-themed kimono and obi, wearing a veritable crown of tiny cascading flowers. She appears to be riding down an escalator. Out of the corner of her eye, she notices our gaze, but does not turn around. She is annoyed, the irritation unmistakable in her arched eyebrow. How different from the maiko and geiko authors who wrote about their duty to display pleasant maiko-likeness in public, performing for a constant gaze, and the public perfection of *Maiko-san-chi no Makanai-san*'s Sū-chan (chapter 4). Manga Tarou's maiko refuses compliance. She pushes back, as if to snap, "Outta my face," abandoning propriety and staking out the limits to her performance of maiko-likeness.

KYOTO ICON MASH-UP

Veneration of Kyoto as the old capital calls for appreciation of fine gardens, Buddhist iconography, and romantic sights of the hills framing the city. The manga in *100 Maiko Illustrations* construct a lovable cultural map, as the two manga discussed here show. Artist Hiji Mie's monk maiko (figure 29) resembles the bronze "Maruyama Jizō" statue in front of Daiun-in Temple

FIGURE 29. Hiji Mie gives the jizō statue near Maruyama Park a maiko makeover. Copyright © 2006. Kyoto International Manga Museum. Courtesy of Hiji Mie.

near Gion. Jizō is a bodhisattva "protector and savior, who intervenes and helps those caught in places of suffering."[59] Hiji's maiko has the body of the Jizō statue and holds the iconic staff in one hand, the sacred jewel in the other. Offerings of fruit serve as kanzashi in her maiko hairstyle, her forehead bears the auspicious circular dot (byakugō), her eyes are gently closed, but she smiles. Hiji makes this Buddhist statue maiko-cute, revealing a relaxed approach to religious images in Kyoto, at least in this case, and hinting that Jizō, like the maiko, has become a touristic sign.

Kyoto's pride in its local vegetables earns a manga nod, too. Minami Hiroshi morphs a thick, white daikon radish into a giant maiko, sticking a kanzashi in her leafy "hair" and wrapping her in a loose kimono and darari obi (figure 30). He places his radish maiko on Sannen-zaka, the quaint, hilly street that leads from the Gion to Kiyomizu Temple in the Higashiyama hills. It

FIGURE 30. Minami Hiroshi imagines a daikon radish maiko. Copyright © 2006. Kyoto International Manga Museum. Courtesy of Minami Hiroshi.

would not be unusual to see an elegant maiko photographed at this site. But a giant daikon—the inexpensive garnish to all kinds of Japanese dishes? The humor here encourages the viewer to relax in Kyoto, as though coaxing us not to take it all too seriously.

But Minami sees more in his radish maiko manga than this. In July 2019, Minami wrote to me about his dual inspiration for the radish maiko.[60] Around 2006, the NHK-TV drama *Oshin* was attracting attention beyond Japan; heroine Oshin had become a symbol of the "powerful endurance of Japanese women."[61] About the same time, the media were reporting on wild radishes sprouting in the crevices of Kyoto streets, calling them *dokonjō daikon* (gutsy daikon). Since the maiko, a Japanese girl like Oshin, endured rigorous training, Minami imagined her as a gutsy daikon growing in Sannen-zaka. But

Minami writes that a hint of comedy spices up his manga and relieves this heroic sentiment, observing that the daikon also associates with clumsiness (*daikon bukiyō*). His gutsy girl does not have to be perfect.

MAIKO-IN-MOTION: FRIENDLY SKIES— AND MARTIAN LANDING

Maiko characters in *100 Maiko Illustrations* can morph into speedy girls, too, and even the alien. A host of manga in the exhibit strike me as forming a maiko-in-motion theme. Speedy, gliding, and soaring maiko not only defy convention, but gravity, too. Actual maiko must manage heavy costumes and okobo sandals. They are rooted on the ground in the small neighborhoods of the hanamachi, the mascot of a place. But maiko-in-motion zoom through Kyoto on a motor scooter, ascend to the skies over it, and even venture into outer space. Takenaka Ranko's "Ookini Express" pictures a cute maiko whistling as she rides with her kimono handily bunched up, her okobo firmly planted on the scooter (figure 31). Her romanized *Ookini* (thanks) is zippy; her English "express" contemporary; nothing holds this maiko back. She is going forward. Commenting on her manga in email in July 2019, Takenaka emphasized that the motorbike-riding maiko was a completely fanciful and unrealistic portrait; "it would absolutely never happen." She also spoke to a more serious intent, "This is not a rejection of the traditional cultural role of geiko and maiko, but since this culture originated and developed in a male-dominated society, I believe it is necessary to make changes for a new era. I want to see even manga express this."[62] Takenaka's manga hints that some maiko may want to shed their old-fashioned masquerade, adopting the persona of the ordinary teenager speeding through Kyoto.

Several flying maiko also appear in the exhibit, often their long sleeves or darari obi transformed into wings. Taneda Hideyuki's cute maiko witch soars over Kyoto on her broom. Morimoto Kiyohiko's "monarch maiko" takes wing as a butterfly. Like Tezuka Osamu's famous robot Astro Boy, rocket engines propel maiko by Kosei Ono and Matsuda Masao. The most different of all may be Kosuge Riyako's alien maiko (figure 32). Complete with Mr. Spock ears and antenna growing out of her forehead, this alien maiko smiles at the viewer as she walks across the frame. Images of Saturn and stars dot her kimono and obi. Her robotic hand holds her fan, graced with a moon image. Sturdy space boots replace okobo sandals. A tiny flying saucer stands at the ready. Is she the

FIGURE 31. "Ookini Express" (Thank-You Express). Copyright © 2006. Kyoto International Manga Museum. Courtesy of Takenaka Ranko.

FIGURE 32. Kosuge's maiko comes from outer space. Copyright © 2006. Kyoto International Manga Museum. Courtesy of Kosuge Riyako.

maiko of the future, revving up her costume, or a Martian traveling to Kyoto for the fun of the *maiko henshin* costume experience? These maiko-in-motion manga suggest freedom and escape, pleasures not available to actual maiko.

MAIKO POP: MAIKO JACKSON

One of the most provocative manga in *100 Maiko Illustrations* plays with the idea of blending pop identities, morphing the Kyoto girl with the King of Pop, creating, "Maikō jakuson" (Maiko Jackson) (figure 33).[63] Surely, the reference to Jackson is as recognizable to museum viewers here as any icon on display. Making his first visit to Japan in 1973, the American pop star often returned, enjoying a large and loyal fandom. When he arrived in Japan in 1987 for his sold-out *Bad* tour in the wake of phenomenal sales of *Thriller*, the *Nihon Keizai* newspaper ran the headlines, "Michael Typhoon Lands Today."[64] His legal fights in the United States over charges of child abuse did not dim his popularity in Japan. In May 2006, Jackson received his MTV-Japan Legend Award in person, and the media gave much attention to the outpouring of grief after his death in 2009.[65] In his campy 2006 mash-up, Kojiroh fuses iconic elements of Jackson's look circa the 1987 *Bad* tour with those of the maiko. He blends their signature hairstyles, giving the kimono and obi stars-and-stripes pizzazz. The character grabs the crotch with one hand while lifting a long kimono sleeve above the head with the other. Stray tendrils of hair falling on the forehead, this maiko's arched eyebrows and lined eyes present an unmistakable caricature of Jackson. Kojiroh blends the two icons linguistically as well. He writes "maiko" in characters but adds the katakana mark for extending the vowel, making it sound more like "Michael"; he pens "Jackson" in katakana as *jakuson*. The humor here comes from the pun and crossing two icons that at first glance seem so different. But this manga also calls to mind Michael Jackson's persona as the boy who never grew up, the child star who longed for his lost childhood, and, as we later learned, the man accused by former victims of abusing them as boys.[66] Here Jackson is morphed into the Japanese girl who will also be forever a child. In 2006, when observers might have laughed in surprise at Kojiroh's *Maikō jakuson*, the manga may have made them think twice about the hype that creates the global singing star and the Kyoto maiden alike—and the commodification of childhood. In 2020, we might read the manga as showing a troubled Jackson hiding behind a façade of innocence.

FIGURE 33. "Maikō jakuson" (Maiko Jackson). Copyright © 2006. Kyoto International Manga Museum. Courtesy of Kojiroh.

THE GLEE OF AN ELDERLY MAIKO

The creativity on display at the *100 Maiko Illustrations* exhibit encourages viewers to let their imagination go—really go, using the maiko image to have fun, even imagining being the maiko having fun! As though taking up this invitation, the gleeful oldster of Kuruma Dankichi's manga, fully kitted out in maiko masquerade, cascading kanzashi framing a wrinkled face, beams with delight while strolling in okobo (figure 34). Kuruma's unnamed granny, a staple in his manga repertoire, always knows what she wants and often stoops to trickery to get it.[67] But the way she holds her maiko handbag (*kago*) recalls the amusing trope of the salaryman prancing back home late at night, rosy faced from too much expensive drinking and dining at the sushi bar, with a box of sushi in his hand to appease his family.[68] Perhaps she, too, has stayed out too long tonight—having fun as a girl, breaking the rules like a man. Kuruma's character resonates with popular incarnations of the *rōjo* (elderly woman) created by women writers, too. Like the shōjo, they are marginalized, but equally free of "productive or reproductive obligations."[69] Hiromi

FIGURE 34. Kuruma imagines his granny character in maiko gear. Copyright © 2006. Kyoto International Manga Museum. Courtesy of Kuruma Dankichi.

Tsuchiya Dollase describes, for example, writer Tanabe Seiko's "humorously headstrong" seventy-six-year-old rōjo heroine, the famous Yamamoto Utako, a privileged fashionista "enjoying freedom in the twilight of her busy life."[70] Although Utako defies the stereotype of the elderly as cute, one can imagine her in maiko cosplay as cute-cool. Similarly, Sohyun Chun analyzes how the rōjo narrator in Enchi Fumiko's 1974 story, "Hana kui uba" (The old woman who eats flowers), represents the empowerment of aging women fighting stereotypes as she "comes to identify and reinvigorate the shōjo within her aged body as an expression of unfulfilled desire, love, and passion."[71] She would be a candidate for maiko cute-cool, too. Kuruma's cosplaying senior and these other legendary rōjo characters remind us of Takahara Eiri's definition of girl consciousness as not limited by conventional gender identity or age (see introduction). This elderly maiko basking in her shōjo look expresses a carefree joy in breaking the rules of age-appropriate behavior and defying the gender-neutering effects that accompany old age.

As we have seen, manga in the *100 Maiko Illustrations* present a striking variety of maiko, reminding viewers that we are, after all, in Kyoto, but encouraging us to enjoy the city each in our own way. "Find your favorite maiko!"

The exhibit invites viewers to see how diversely manga artists approach the quintessential mascot of Kyoto, referring to their signature styles, tourist icons, and popular culture. They give us license to take fresh perspectives, too, and devise our own interpretations of the maiko image and frame.

CONCLUSION

Exploring maiko visual comedy, this chapter has discussed how Eirakuya's sporting maiko tenugui series takes us back to the cultural climate of the 1930s—the vogue for sports, the challenge of the modern girl, even surreal play with X-ray machines—and in its revived form, evokes the carefree pleasures associated with girls' culture in the 2000s. We also observed how the *100 Maiko Illustrations* exhibit at the Kyoto International Manga Museum develops maiko imagery in myriad ways, often telling us as much about Japanese popular culture as about maiko. In the 2000s as the stigma of past associations with sexual exploitation receded, as discussed in chapter 4, the maiko became more firmly associated with Japanese etiquette and traditional artistry as well as girlish cheer. This maiko cuteness often verged on the saccharine, as some manga artists have mocked and others embraced, but it also made the maiko's image safe for creative play, parody, and satire. By extension, the humor of tenugui and manga persuade viewers to enjoy Kyoto as a benign touristic space that easily combines the new and old, that promises the freedom to experience the old capital in one's own way.

In sum, this visual play with the apprentice as icon reinforces four major themes evident in representations of the maiko. Firstly, they highlight that the maiko image, when re-created faithfully, does not allow for much variation. While performing maiko-likeness, the maiko is not allowed to play sports, ride a scooter, or alter her costume to suit her personal tastes. She is bound literally by her heavy clothing and hair as well as figuratively by her role in maintaining the cultural traditions of Kyoto. Secondly, several of these images suggest that the maiko is an ordinary girl at heart who might at times prefer to dress up as a kogal, kick a soccer ball, or imagine riding a scooter through Kyoto. No matter how strongly she may want to express her inner self, she must mask those feelings and perform maiko-likeness convincingly for her clients and the public. As we have seen in previous chapters, such imagery idealizes the ordinary self as a masked site of authenticity. Thirdly, the conflict inherent in the maiko masquerade teases the artists, and all of us as viewers of their work, to guess who is behind the mask or, indeed, which persona constitutes the mask. Lastly, artists imply that the gorgeous wardrobe of the maiko, the approval earned for simply being cute can make others—the senior citizen, the bearded seal, and even Michael Jackson—want to take cover in her youthful masquerade and experience girl consciousness, too.

Turning to the concluding chapter, "The Ordinary Girl in the Maiko Masquerade," we consider how representations of the maiko and her foil, the "average girl" (*futsū no ko*) present alternate portraits of girlhood in millennial Japan. What sense of self does the maiko masquerade cover or liberate? What does the future hold for these imagined girls? What are the implications for envisioning adult women's lives in Japan, including Kyoto's geiko?

Conclusion

The Ordinary Girl in the Maiko Masquerade

I am delighted that you, too, sense that my manga "reveals the secret that the maiko is, at heart, an ordinary girl."

—Terashima Reiko, manga artist

We are teenagers (*chīn'eijāzu*), right?

—Hinagiku, maiko character, *Janken musume*

As Japan entered its second decade of economic stagnation in the 2000s, the maiko as Kyoto's quintessential Japanese girl offered reassurance. She stood for the relevance of the hanamachi past in the present. Elaborately coiffed, ornamented, painted, and enrobed, she modeled maiko tradition as Kyoto fashion. This maiko-like maiko displayed fine manners, seamlessly performing the contradictions of a spontaneous teen and the well-schooled apprentice. As we have seen in this book, these representations of the exemplary maiko pique curiosity about the girl behind the mask, presuming an essential self. What girl takes on this role? What is she like when she is not "like a maiko?"

To conclude this book, I take up representations of the girl behind the mask, always depicted in texts as "ordinary," interpreting maiko narratives by shifting the focus to her. After all, without the ordinary girl in this picture, there could be no masquerade, no sense of struggle to perform well, and no evidence of choice. She is always the foil to the maiko, the "before" to the maiko's "after." The texts' emphasis on the maiko's mission, and the diligence required to uphold it tend to eclipse the ordinary girl, but they never erase her.

Indeed, maiko narratives depend on her. Her presence enables the "play with the border between the exotic and the self" that Anne Allision speculates may have intrigued fans of Arthur Golden's *Memoirs of a Geisha* abroad.[1] Most importantly, the ordinary girl in this picture makes the millennial maiko's narrative a story of agency, reinforcing the postwar shift in the maiko's image from victim to artist. It is the ordinary girl who *chooses* to become a maiko. It is the ordinary girl who strives to perform maiko-likeness even when it seems a poor fit. She is the "every girl" in maiko narratives—imagined as unremarkable, uniform, and ubiquitous throughout Japan. It is the ordinary girl character as much as her maiko masquerade that tells us about narratives of girlhood in twenty-first-century Japan.

Storylines involving the maiko and the ordinary girl return us to Gitte Marianne Hansen's concept of contradictory femininity and doppelgänger motifs. Hansen observes how various Japanese cultural texts, produced since the 1980s, employ these motifs to dramatize conflicting messages about femininity. She argues that normative femininity in Japan requires proficiency in navigating among different feminine personas from generous caregiver to corporate manager. The maiko, as a public figure in a role both anachronistic and contemporary, faces a range of femininities to perform, including compliant novice, vivacious girl, dedicated artist, younger sister, elder sister, and Kyoto mascot. These contradictions generate doppelgänger motifs in maiko narratives of all kinds. Not only is the maiko enjoined to represent Kyoto elegantly, but she is also advised to allow her natural self to shine since clients find learning about youthful interests refreshing. But even this natural self must be expressed in a maiko-like way. To reflect on maiko-likeness afresh, this chapter explores the maiko's durable foil, the ordinary girl, as another character among the many roles in the toolkit of contradictory femininity. We may also ask how maiko narratives of the maiko and ordinary girl inform portraits of the geiko in the 2000s.

Reviewing the maiko texts analyzed in *Maiko Masquerade*, we find the ordinary girl has a history, too. In the 1955 film *Janken musume* (or *So Young, So Bright*, as it is was called in the United States), maiko Hinagiku seeks rescue from the "feudalistic" hanamachi and the danna who will buy her contract. Precisely because she identifies as a postwar "teenager" (*chīn'eijā*) with a desire for independence, this maiko yearns to leave the hanamachi and reclaim her legal name. Ordinariness is liberation for her, magically allowing her to join the budding youth culture of her teenage girlfriends. Hinagiku's return to ordinariness points more broadly to the teen liberated from wartime Japan, free to pursue life faithful to a new generation's ethics. Adapting the 1960s maiko life depicted in Iwasaki Mineko's memoir to manga, Yamato Waki imagines Sakuya's dreams of becoming an ordinary girl as truly enormous. They nearly burst the frame in the serialized girl comic *Kurenai niou* (Crimson fragrance). Sakuya adores her rare days off, when she exclaims, "I felt like I could be myself."[2] Yet Sakuya's keen sense of familial and community obligation and passion for dance push her to remain a maiko, and then become a geiko. The 2008–09 NHK-TV drama *Dandan's* maiko Nozomi finds her sister Megumi's ordinary girl life so appealing that twice she masquerades in blue jeans as her twin—first to experience life in rural Matsue with her father's family, then to spend the day as a college student. For Nozomi, her twin's ordinariness promises freedom of choice and interaction with people her own age. Unlike Sakuya, Nozomi leaves the hanamachi to find herself, renouncing her obligation to her okiya, becoming an outcaste as a result, and claiming an ordinary girl's freedom to define her own life. But she does not stay long with this life of "freedom." Once she realizes that a geiko can also walk a *jibun rashii* path within the hanamachi, she heads back to Gion, thus bringing an apt resolution to a millennial NHK story that must endorse both personal freedom and community loyalty. Unlike the 1950s maiko Hinagiku, who escapes the clutches of a lecherous danna, neither Sakuya in the 1960s nor Nozomi in the 2000s faces sexual servitude. Their narratives, however, acknowledge that the stigma of the maiko as a girl for sale lingers.

The freedom of the ordinary girl choosing to become a maiko in the 2000s allows for humorous narratives that call attention to ordinariness as charm and personality. The rambunctious, ravenous maiko of Koyama Aiko's girls' comic *Maiko-san-chi no Makanai-san* (Miss Cook for the maiko girls) and Terashima Reiko's impish cartoon girl, winking as she dons her maiko costume, create the ordinary girl behind the mask as comic relief from the demands of performing maiko-likeness. These and other comic characters may also assuage fears that a girl "loses herself" in the maiko masquerade. Even Koyama's model maiko Sū-chan faces a constant struggle against her appetite at inopportune moments, a sign of her ordinary girl-self who will not be neglected. Accounts by some geiko, such as *A Geisha's Journey* author Komomo, speak to feeling freed by graduating from maiko-likeness, as though "liberated" to express their personalities as geiko rather than conform to maiko "stereotype."

Recalling these varied maiko narratives reveals how the maiko's relationship to ordinariness changes with the choices open to her and with the shifting demands of maiko performance in her era. Narratives shade ordinariness differently by identifying the aspects of the self that must be quelled in the maiko masquerade. Does she wish to escape sexual servitude, familial obligations, lack of career choice, and confining girlishness, or is it simply that she wants to satisfy the demands of her rumbling stomach? The resolutions of the conflict between her maiko and ordinary selves change over time as well. The film *Janken musume* values the liberation of the democratized teenager, leaving the hanamachi in the 1950s while *Dandan* celebrates the return of the prodigal maiko who claims her jibun rashii path as an aspiring Gion leader in the 2000s.

The *Chiyogiku* light novel series strays from the norm of the maiko as an ordinary Japanese girl, imagining an ordinary Japanese boy becoming the top maiko of Gion. Nanami Haruka's vision of the Mikiya-Chiyogiku pair dramatizes a gender binary that resists privileging one gendered role over the other until the end of the series. Rather like Nozomi and Megumi, the boy and his maiko double are almost twins, but gendered foils for each other, too. Likened to an onnagata, Mikiya earns praise for his exemplary maiko-likeness. He has no need to compensate for his lack of female physicality; rather, following modern onnagata ideology, it is precisely this lack that allows him to create a transcendent femininity. Even though *Chiyogiku* stands out among all the texts for its obvious use of masquerade, the fluidity of the movement between boy and girl here appears to be the easiest of transitions. Chiyogiku's maneuvers to escape dicey situations and avoid exposure give the tale a game-like quality, making maiko role-playing fun. Delighting in his gender agility, Mikiya rarely feels any contradiction in performing femininity, especially when costumed, but he denies that he is merely doing maiko cosplay. "I'm a real maiko," he affirms.[3] Taking pleasure in experiencing the world in two gendered personas, Mikiya anticipates a sense of loss when his maturing body will make the disguise impossible. When Chiyogiku is gone, and Mikiya and Nirezaki pledge their love as adult men, the story is over and so is the cross-gendering. The question remains whether Japan will catch up to other "advanced nations," as these two men hope, and make their marriage legal and commonplace.

Returning to the ordinary girl, we see her characterized in hanamachi etiquette texts and discussions of rigorous maiko training as a bit of a slacker. These guides frame the ordinary girl as an overly indulged Japanese teenager inept at communication, unwilling to take direction, and in constant need of praise, who doesn't know how to live communally and can't even sit on tatami mats or use chopsticks properly. She could choose to do better. In contrast, Kiriki Chizu, Komomo, and Kamishichiken Ichimame describe how they—as ordinary girls, too—tried hard, learned to obey their teachers, managed their bodies and emotions, developed resilience, and matured. Their personal accounts and the etiquette guides show how the ordinary girl, even if she does not become a maiko, can draw on a national storehouse of artistry and deportment as preserved in the hanamachi. We might say these texts build on Brian McVeigh's finding that, "Japaneseness and ladylike behavior mutually construct and reinforce one another."[4] In hanamachi texts, maiko-likeness and Japaneseness, inflected by Kyoto traditions, become one and the same. This advice makes women's attempts to transcend ordinariness good, and even patriotic.

Characterizations of the maiko as polished by her mastery of older forms of Japanese etiquette beg the question, "Is the ordinary Japanese girl insufficiently *Japanese?*" A Kyoto-centric pride emerges in many maiko narratives, especially guides on maiko training, that imply that the finest expression of Japanese femininity resides in the hanamachi. That is the secret to transforming the ordinary girl. All maiko texts assume their maiko characters are ethnically Japanese, but not necessarily from Kyoto. As hanamachi elders are quick to note, since 2001, over 90 percent of maiko have come from hometowns elsewhere in Japan. As non-Kyoto girls, the new maiko are undifferentiated "girls who came from elsewhere" (yoso kara kita ko).[5] References in maiko texts to newcomers' habit of slipping into their dialects are what most often signal this diversity and non-Kyoto roots.[6] Unlike the girls of the past born and raised in the hanamachi, these outsiders have much to learn. Born in Shimabara, Arai Mameji remarks of her Gion training in the 1960s, "Since my own home was in the karyūkai, I had already internalized half [the conventions], but that kind of natural, internalized, basic knowledge is gone."[7] "Now, we live in the era when girls come from many places all over the country. Since they haven't internalized instruction from childhood, doesn't that mean I have to be bossy, telling them what to do all the time?"[8] Gion ochaya manager Yoshimura Kaoru voices concerns about outsiders weakening the hanamachi brand, observing, "Ozashiki conversations have really changed."[9] In the past, she explains, maiko from elsewhere always claimed to be from Kyoto if clients asked. "But now, without the slightest hesitation, they respond *Fukuoka dosu* or *Akita dosu* (I'm from Fukuoka, I'm from Akita)."[10] Even though these maiko are speaking in hanamachi dialect, different from their hometown speech, they do not hide their non-Kyoto roots. Arai wonders where this embrace of difference might lead, possibly with girls from other countries applying to become maiko, too. "That might be fun for clients. Certainly, the girls from the provinces (chihō) intrigue guests with that difference, but the topics of conversation turn only to their hometowns. Taking the long view of this, will things endure only by virtue of this curiosity or distinctiveness?"[11]

The task of transforming the ordinary Japanese girl from elsewhere into a maiko circles back to the value placed on maiko-likeness as brand image. If girls refer to their non-Kyoto roots, they change what it means to be maiko rashii, making it both authentic (she looks and speaks like a maiko) and a masquerade (she comes from elsewhere). When I asked a hanamachi insider about the possibility of non-Japanese becoming maiko, she responded, "But you already understand that people come to Kyoto expecting to see the maiko rashii maiko. What would happen to that?" Here, we see how expectations for maiko-likeness prize Kyoto roots, but limit diversity. Even more important than narrowing the possibilities for maiko-likeness, such concerns also constrain what it means to be an "ordinary Japanese girl."

Turning to the comic relief of hijinks in maiko narratives, we observe how often the ordinary girl represents girlhood as carefree. The maiko seems to have the most fun when she gives in to her ordinary girl self that just wants to let go, most often with other girls as in Janken musume and Maiko-san-chi no Makanai-san. Immersed in the teenage culture of friendship, school clubs, and parental indulgence, the ordinary girl appears to have free time, unlimited options for her future, and the freedom to pursue a jibun rashii path to follow her tastes and ambitions. In contrast, the maiko must fulfill a full schedule of lessons, parties, and public appearances while continually supervised and dressed elaborately. She must meet the high expectations for maiko-likeness while the ordinary girl has only to be herself. This binary of the maiko and the ordinary girl inspires admiration for the apprentice while romanticizing ordinary girlhood, giving a sense of what pleasures the maiko has given up for her artistic path. In Suppin geiko (Bare-faced geiko) Yamaguchi wistfully daydreams about a teenage date on the banks of the Kamo River. Iwasaki Mineko regrets her missed chance at a high schooler's life of sports and study. As though living this dream, Dandan's Megumi, the drama's ordinary girl, bikes all over town in high school, hangs out with boys in her band, wears casual clothes, leaves home to attend college, volunteers, and has her evenings to herself for study or seeing friends. She chooses her occupational path as a nurse.

But were we to take the maiko out of this narrative, considering representations of the ordinary girl on her own rather than as a foil, what view of her life would emerge? Inevitably, her life would appear more complicated and less rosy. Pathways to success are often blocked by tiresome gender restrictions, doors remain closed, and some dreams are never even dreamed. We see this kind of difficulty in following both Megumi's journey and Nozomi's experience trying to build a career outside the hanamachi. But in many maiko narratives, the ordinary girl appears coherent and effortless, unchallenged by ubiquitous messages of contradictive femininity directed to women in Japan. On her day-off in boyish clothes, Ichimame feels at home in her typical teen mode, psychologically and physically free to spend time in Kyoto incognito. The myopic view of two forms of girlhood in many texts, narrativized as the maiko and the ordinary girl, entertains and constructs notions of choice, but depoliticizes girlhood in Japan. The maiko and the ordinary girl become almost stock characters. This binary averts attention from the foreclosures effected by gender, class, regional privilege, and ethnicity, and even the hierarchy of high schools in Japan which shape teens' lives. Of course, this is a celebratory literature, not a critical one, and it is appealing for presenting two paths from which a girl can choose.

We may also ask what would happen to the narrative were the ordinary girl to drop out of the frame, leaving only the maiko. According to the literature, a clear career path lies ahead for the maiko who wants to remain within the hanamachi and become a geiko. As an arts professional and entrepreneur, she must develop business skills as well as artistic abilities. She must let go of maiko-like behaviors in favor of developing her jibun rashii adult persona. She will never have to compete with men for promotion. She has a community that has a vested interest in her success and a career path designed to support her on her way to the top. She has the potential to earn considerable income. It is less evident how well the geiko might transfer her knowledge to a career outside the hanamachi, should she choose to leave, especially in realms that require academic pedigree, a concern raised by Iwasaki Mineko. In Gion, the geiko may not marry if she wishes to remain in the profession, but she can become a single mother. Judging by the literature, though, if she remains within the hanamachi, her future is secure to the extent the community remains viable.

Nonetheless, as a single woman devoted to her arts career, the geiko remains outside the orthodox route of marriage and motherhood.

The millennial geiko's social position—inside and outside Japanese society—reminds me of media characterizations of the elite career woman, a popular figure in TV dramas, fiction, and women's magazines in Japan in the 2000s.[12] Single, sophisticated, job-focused and independent, the career-woman character works at getting ahead in competitive men's worlds. She may have a love life but does not aim for marriage. Like the geiko, the career woman, too, bears stigma: conservative criticism has turned against single career women for failing to reproduce the nation, blaming their selfishness for the crisis of Japan's dwindling population. In 2004, critic Sakai Junko's satirical book *Makeinu no tōboe* (The distant howl of the loser dog) famously pushed back at this condemnation.[13] The difficulties women have in forging professional careers and winning top corporate promotions are reminders of Japan's continual low rankings on the Global Gender Gap Report.[14]

Intriguingly, hanamachi literature brings the geiko and the career woman together. Maiko narratives of the 2000s are largely produced by women, focus on women's lives, and are consumed by women. Women professionals—writer Aihara Kyoko, novelist Nanami Haruka, academic Nishio Kumiko, manga artist Yamato Waki, and painter Morita Rieko—have all formed bonds with women in the hanamachi and promote its salon culture. In 2020, half the members of the Ōkini Zaidan support group are women. Iwasaki Mineko writes about how much she enjoyed ozashiki with women who had carved their own career path and writer Hayashi Mariko enthusiastically describes her ozashiki in Kyoto. Even NHK's *Dandan* suggests that the hanamachi will strive to attract more women as clients. As soon as Nozomi assumes the role of teahouse manager, she institutes elegant afternoon ozashiki for ladies. When attention turns to geiko entertaining women, instead of men, and befriending other women professionals, a sense of a woman-friendly space forms, one that takes femininity as pleasure among women. Elegance and affiliation replace stigma, and the idealization of maiko becomes a sentimental bond of imagined girlhoods.

Reflecting on the wide variety of maiko texts and images examined in this book, I am left with some questions. The literature discusses extensively girls' decisions to become maiko and frames their choice to become geiko as means to continue their artistic careers. But we do not learn much about the motivations of those who leave the hanamachi. What happened to maiko who left the hanamachi without becoming geiko? What paths did they take and how did their hanamachi training influence their trajectories? If they reentered lives as ordinary girls in the 2000s, did they face any effects from lingering stigma? Would they recommend becoming a maiko to others? Following Iwasaki Mineko's regret over not having advanced academic degrees, did maiko who went to the hanamachi directly after middle school encounter barriers after they left?

By exploring representations of the maiko as a cultural icon of Japanese girlhood, *Maiko Masquerade: Crafting Geisha Girlhood in Japan* has demonstrated how the erasure of past associations with sex work over the late twentieth century released the maiko's image from victimhood, opening the way for new interpretations. In place of the victim, the representation of the maiko as the epitome of hardworking artist, chaste model of Kyoto etiquette, and good girl of Japan emerged. Analysis of themes of masquerade showed how this paragon of girlhood could motivate guides to Japanese femininity in the manner of maiko, but also subvert norms in the fiction of boy maiko, hungry girl maiko, and morphing manga maiko. I hope this concluding analysis of the maiko and the ordinary girl point to new ways to analyze other transforming figures of femininity, pushing us to ask about the play of ordinariness, masquerade, and transformation operating here. Examining other narratives of girlhood will give us new views on gender, ethnicity, and nation in early twenty-first-century Japan.

ACKNOWLEDGMENTS

Exploring representations of maiko in Japanese media and popular culture has become a fifteen-year journey. My greatest pleasures and discoveries have come from working with people across generations, languages, and geographical locations, gaining new perspectives that challenged me to dig deeper, think more critically, and have more fun. With gratitude, I acknowledge the individuals and institutions who have made this book possible and sustained my work and spirit.

Working with enthusiastic students over the years in my UNC–Chapel Hill course, "The Geisha in History, Fiction, and Fantasy," inspired *Maiko Masquerade*. With gratitude, I dedicate this book to you. I remember each class fondly, from the original first-year seminars to the bigger undergraduate classes. Your close readings, quick repartee, sly humor, and fearless questions made me laugh, think again, and look forward to every discussion. Field trips to the Ackland Art Museum, arranged by Director of Education and Interpretation Carolyn Allmendinger, pushed us to connect our readings and films to prints, paintings, and photographs. Guest speakers, including John Dillon, Aki Hirota, Maki Isaka, and Gaye Rowley, who brought their own engagement with Japanese arts and texts to our class, expanded our view, taking us behind the scenes of creative production. I thank Amy Lorang for her whimsical oil painting, one of her many creative responses to the class; Ash Barnes, for being an active student in one of the seminar's early iterations and a long-time fan of the class; and Princess Small, ever the gregarious student, who went on to teach her own classes on Japan.

I thank my UC Press editor Reed Malcolm for his continual encouragement of this project and steady efforts to keep it on track. I appreciate the attention that editorial assistants Archna Patel and Enrique Ochoa-Kaup devoted to this project. Many thanks to copy editor Gary J. Hamel for his thorough reading and superb suggestions. I took to heart and tried to incorporate the suggestions given by reviewer Bill Tsutsui, who closely read this entire manuscript in its initial draft. Bill's incisive comments helped me see this project anew.

I am filled with admiration for Haruka Kihara, doctoral candidate in Dance Studies at Ochanomizu University, who provided indispensable research assistance. Armed with superb detective skills, social dexterity, fluent Japanese and English, and keen interpretative ability, Haruka helped me fine-tune this research. Her dedication to this project kept everything moving ahead and enabled communication with artists and experts that I could not have achieved on my own. Equally adept at interviews, advising on translations, locating sources, and even finding tasty restaurants in Kyoto and Tokyo, Haruka Kihara truly made research in Japan fun.

Gavin James Campbell, professor of American studies at Doshisha University, cheered on this research. His expert knowledge of the hanamachi helped me understand contemporary aspects of the community, and I appreciated his good humor, ideas, and comments on early drafts of this book. I also thank Gavin for introducing me to graduate student Keiko Ishii, who offered excellent research assistance to me in spring 2017 by helping with correspondence and interviews.

Sharing this research with Jeni Prough, who is completing her own book on Kyoto tourism, helped me see the bigger picture of contemporary maiko fascination, and I appreciated her detailed comments on drafts. Over email and conversations in Tokyo, Alisa Freedman encouraged this project and provided excellent suggestions on my early work. Expert on Japanese women's autobiographies Ron Loftus kindly read my early draft on geiko and maiko memoirs, giving good advice. I kept in mind all your recommendations as I revised this book.

I have enjoyed conversations with Gitte Marianne Hansen and found her innovative work on Japanese literature and popular culture inspiring, especially in crafting the idea of masquerade in this book.

I owe special gratitude to three longtime friends for their substantial contributions to this book. Over four years, Rebecca Copeland read numerous drafts, giving encouragement, spot-on suggestions, brilliant allusions to Japanese literature, devilish jokes, and lines so good that I had to lift them. The Copeland-authored library of books on my shelves will always inspire me. Makiko Humphreys read hanamachi texts of all kinds with me, and many other popular Japanese books, including Marie Kondo's guides. Many of my best research projects started in conversations around Makiko's kitchen table. Thank you for sparking joy. Laura Miller, my ingenious coeditor and coconspirator in many projects, brought her acuity to early drafts, devising clever rephrasings and posing thought-provoking questions. It is always good to have the advice of a "bad girl" scholar.

Conversations in Kyoto and Tokyo and over email with many experts deepened my understanding of the hanamachi and its representations. I enjoyed talking with postcard historian Ikuta Makoto, artist Morita Rieko, management scholar Kumiko Nishio, photographer Naoyuki Ogino, and sisters Yamaguchi Yukiko and Yamaguchi Kimijo. For lively conversations, wonderful walks in Kyoto, and an invitation to an ozashiki, I thank *Chiyogiku* author Nanami Haruka. Kyoko Watanabe, Japan Cartoonists Association (JCA), facilitated communication with artists of maiko manga, explained JCA participation in *100 Maiko Illustrations*, and allowed me to include her perky parrot maiko manga in this book. Eirakuya, led by Hosotsuji Ihee, generously provided images for this book and information about its colorful tenugui. Enomoto Naoki, representative of Kyoto Traditional Musical Art Foundation (Ōkini Zaidan), patiently answered my questions about his organization and Kyoto's hanamachi. Thanks to Keihan Electric Railway Co., Ltd, for information about its delightful maiko travel posters and to Kyoto International Manga Museum for kind responses to my email queries.

For permission to use images from their books and film, I thank the publishers Daiwa Shobō, Kadokawa, Kōdansha, Shōgakukan, and Shūeisha. For their image-permissions, I thank Kintetsu Retailing, Inc., Kyoto Institute, Library and Archives, and Kyoto Municipal Transportation Bureau.

I want to acknowledge several artists for permission to use the superb maiko images that they created. Many thanks to Kanbara Kunie, Katsuyama Keiko, Morita Rieko, and Naoyuki Ogino. I am grateful to manga artists Hiji Mie, Kojiroh, Kosuge Riyako, Kuruma Dankichi, Minami Hiroshi, Sato Masao, Takenaka Ranko, and Terashima Reiko for permission to include their spicy maiko manga. I appreciate Suzuki Hiroko's permission to use Suzuki Toshio's Showa postcard. Many thanks to our good friend Diane Kaczor for permission to use two of her captivating photos from our memorable 2015 trip to Japan. I would be grateful to hear from any copyright holder who is not hereby acknowledged and promise to rectify any errors or omissions in proper credit in future editions of the book.

Generous institutional support made this book possible. As a visiting scholar in Tokyo at the Institute for Gender Studies (IGS), Ochanomizu University in 2018–19, I enjoyed the time, resources, and presentation opportunities critical to completing this manuscript. I thank former IGS Director Masako Ishii-Kuntz, IGS Research Fellow Kumi Yoshihara, and my many colleagues and students there for creating such a welcoming, stimulating environment. Much gratitude to Laura Nenzi and Kazue Sakamoto for introducing me to IGS and Ochanomizu University. My thanks to Ochanomizu University vice president Yasuko Sasaki for her support and convivial dinner parties. A special note of thanks to Ochanomizu 2020 graduate Mizuki Masuyama for many conversations about her musicology research and the politics of Madame Butterfly.

The University of North Carolina at Chapel Hill supported my research, teaching, and academic leadership for twenty-five years. I want to thank Jonathan Hartlyn, who served as senior associate dean for social sciences during my tenure as chair of the Department of Asian Studies, for encouraging my development as an administrator and, equally, as a researcher. My research benefited greatly from UNC–Chapel Hill funding, including a William R. Kenan Jr. Senior Faculty Research and Scholarly Leave; a semester at the UNC Institute for Arts and Humanities; and a 2016 research and study assignment granted by the College of Arts and Sciences. Funds provided me as a Carolina Women's Center Faculty Fellow in 2014–2015 and by The Department of Asian Studies Merrill Fund Grant for Faculty Excellence allowed me to obtain key research materials and conduct research in Japan. A Jimmy and Judy Cox Asia

Initiative Award awarded by the Carolina Asia Center of UNC–Chapel Hill, under the able leadership of Morgan Pitelka, funded my spring research in Kyoto in 2017. I am sincerely grateful for the research time, funding, and encouragement generously provided at Carolina.

This project owes in many ways to study abroad programs in Japan. Thanks to the anonymous maiko who danced for our University of California student group in summer 1971. Like many of the geiko discussed in this book, I first encountered a maiko on my school field trip to Kyoto. I still remember how patiently she answered our questions. Accompanying students to Kyoto in 2003 and 2005, and Osaka in 2011, gave me many more opportunities to learn about maiko and observe their dancing. For their expertise in arranging these programs, I thank Dan Gold, Bob Miles, Lauren Nakasato, and especially Mohácsi Gergely for his superb work in leading our excursions and teaching our students. I thank the founders of the Phillips Ambassadors Program, Kim and Phil Phillips, for their unstinting support of UNC study abroad programs in Asia.

Having the chance to talk with community, student, and faculty audiences proved invaluable to honing my arguments and viewing maiko sources from multiple perspectives. I was honored to present this research at Belmont University, Nashville, Tennessee; Charles B. Wang Center, Stony Brook University, New York; Durham Technical Community College, Durham, North Carolina; Fashion Institute of Technology (FIT), New York; Guilford College, Greensboro, North Carolina; California State University San Diego; New College of Florida–Sarasota; Siena College, Loudonville, New York; Spelman College, Atlanta, Georgia; University of Cincinnati, Ohio; University of Missouri–St. Louis; and Heidelberg University, Germany. For these invitations, I thank Tim E. Cooper, Shannon W. Hahn, Yoshiko Higurashi, Hiroko Hirakawa, Gergana Ivanova, Jinyoung A. Jin, Ronnie Littlejohn, Xuexin Liu, Laura Miller, Kyunghee Pyun, Xia Shi, and Paola Zamperini. For the chance to share this research with community audiences, I thank the Ackland Art Museum; the Osher Lifelong Learning Institute, Duke Continuing Studies; and Carolina Public Humanities. Thanks to the Northeast Asia Council (NEAC) of the Association for Asian Studies for inviting my participation on its Distinguished Speakers Bureau.

Publishing essays on maiko and geisha helped me prepare for this longer project. Thanks to Jeni Prough for inviting me to contribute "Teaching Geisha in History, Fiction, and Fantasy" to the special section that she edited in *ASIA Network Exchange: A Journal for Asian Studies in the Liberal Arts* 17 (2010). Thanks to Steven Heine for the chance to edit the special section, *"Manga, Maiko, Aidoru:* Girl Cool in Japanese Popular Culture" for *Japanese Studies Review* 15 (2011), which included my article, "Maiko Boom: The Revival of Kyoto's Novice Geisha." Inspired by class discussions of Dalby's pioneering work, I published "Liza Dalby's *Geisha:* The View Twenty-Five Years Later" in *Southeast Review of Asian Studies* 31 (2009). Thanks to Hyaeweol Choi for inviting me to participate in her 2011 AAS panel, "Allure and Anxiety: Gamblers, Glamour Girls and New Women in East Asia," which led to a special issue of *Intersections: Gender and Sexuality in Asia and the Pacific,* no. 29 (2012) that included my article, "The New Woman Meets the Geisha: The Politics of Pleasure in 1910s Japan."

My friendships with colleagues in Japanese studies who also work on issues related to gender, media, and popular culture enrich my intellectual life. I admire the integrity, rigor, and joy that they bring to their work. In particular, I thank Tomoko Aoyama, Julia Bullock, Davinder Bhowmik, Michael Cronin, Rachel DiNitto, Hiromi Dollase, Sarah Frederick, Barbara Hartley, Sally Hastings, Laura Hein, Noriko Horiguchi, Maki Isaka, Kinko Ito, Mary Knighton, Mire Koikari, Ryuko Kubota, Vera Mackie, Mark McLelland, Barbara Molony, Christine Marran, Stephen Miller, Masafumi Monden, Sharalyn Orbaugh, Amanda Seaman, Deborah Shamoon, Ann Sherif, Julie Adeney Thomas, James Welker, and Christine Yano. My California mentors, Aki Hirota, Lynne Miyake, and Eri F. Yasuhara deserve warm thanks, too. The Japanese Studies community in North Carolina has been a constant source of friendship and stimulation. I owe a debt of gratitude to my UNC mentors W. Miles Fletcher and the late Larry Kessler, and Japanese studies mentors Eleanor Kerkham and Marlene Mayo at University of Maryland. I thank my generous and skilled colleagues in our UNC Japanese Language Program, Yuki Aratake, Shoko Fukuya (retired), Fumi Iwashita, Yuko Kato, and Katsu Sawamura. I was fortunate to meet Liza Dalby when she spoke at Wake Forest University in spring 2016 and to meet Kelly M. Foreman over email and learn much about geisha from her work. I give hearty thanks to Hsi-chu Bolick, East Asian Studies Librarian at Davis Library, UNC–Chapel Hill, and Kristina Troost, Head of International Area Studies and Japanese Studies Librarian at Perkins Library at Duke University, for their kindness and expertise in locating sources.

Thanks to my friends and family for cheering me on. I enjoyed conversations about this project with Jen Anderson and Chris Gerteis, Cy Bridges, Heather Bridges, Dottie Borei, Inger Brodey, Nancy Dole and John Runkle, Beth Elder, Lori Harris, Joanne Hershfield and Jim Fink, Hiroko Hirakawa, Diane Kaczor, Carl and Penny Linke, Phillip and Susan Lyons, John and Pat Maroney, Sucheta Mazumdar and Vasant Kaiwar, David Phillips, Curtis Selby, Angelika Straus, Marleen Stromme, and Nadia Yaqub. Our "forever neighbors" Irina Olenicheva, Stanislav Shvabrin, and their daughter Sofya gifted me with many dinners and the patience to hear many maiko stories. Visits to Japan in 2019 by the Hobart Contingent (Jeffrey Armstrong, Mark Andersen, Harriet Speed) and Elise and Rob Anderson enlivened our stay indeed. We await Freya Anderson's first visit with glee.

Heartfelt thanks to Phil Bardsley, who was even happier, prouder, and more relieved than I was to see this manuscript off to press. Reading outlines and drafts, making video clips for my talks, watching maiko movies and *Miyako Odori*, and visiting museums with me to scout maiko images, Phil has been there for every bit of this project. His insights, pep talks, home-cooked specialties, and editing advice helped shape this book and make it happen. Our joint adventures stretch back to our teenage years. Onward to the next ones.

Jan Bardsley
Chapel Hill, North Carolina
May 25, 2020

GLOSSARY

DANNA patron of the hanamachi.

DARARI OBI obi worn by maiko with a long portion flowing down the back that reaches almost to the ankles and displays the okiya's crest.

EDO the historic period 1603–1867 when Edo (Tokyo) was the capital of Japan; the era is also known for shogunal rule by the Tokugawa family.

ERIKAE (turning the collar), the ceremonial transition from maiko to geiko.

GEIKO Kyoto dialect; refers to geisha working in Kyoto.

GEISHA independent professional artist working in a hanamachi.

GO-KAGAI all five Kyoto hanamachi together.

HANAMACHI (flower district), licensed community of geiko; home to okiya and ochaya. There are five in Kyoto, each with its own crest displayed on lanterns hanging on the fronts of buildings; may also be pronounced kagai.

IKI insouciant chic or casual elegance associated with geiko/geisha.

JIBUN RASHII feeling and acting like one's authentic self. See *maiko rashii*.

JIKATA geiko who play musical instruments, often samisen, to accompany geiko and maiko dances.

JIMAE GEIKO a geiko who has fully completed her apprenticeship, paid her debts to her okiya, and become a self-employed arts professional.

JOSHI KEIKEN (girls' experience), denotes girls' friendships, leisure, and consumerism.

KABURENJŌ training and performance dance space in each hanamachi.

KAGO a maiko's formal purse with woven base and fabric top.

KANZASHI hair ornaments.

KARYŪKAI (flower and willow world), general term for geisha and teahouse culture.

KATA defined movements that are the basis of traditional arts and etiquette in Japan.

KENBAN administrative offices of the hanamachi.

KOGAL (kogyaru), media label for phenomenon of mid-1990s high school girl culture and fashion.

KUMIAI professional association.

MAID CAFÉ urban cafés where "eternally seventeen" young women clad in faux French maid uniforms serve customers.

MAIKO apprentice geisha.

MAIKO HENSHIN TAIKEN the photo-studio experience of costuming as a maiko.

MAIKO RASHII feeling and acting like a maiko, performing maiko-likeness. See *jibun rashii.*

MINARAI MAIKO the short training period after the shikomi stage and before attaining maiko status.

MISEDASHI a maiko's public debut in her new role.

MIZU SHŌBAI (water trade), an area of nighttime entertainment, which has included sex work.

MIZUAGE a mid-point marker in the maiko's training period; also associated in the past with sexual initiation.

MOTENASHI Japanese hospitality.

NATORI name given by the master of a performing art after the student has achieved a certain level of proficiency.

NIHON BUYŌ traditional Japanese dance genres performed by geiko, Kabuki actors, and other artists.

NIHONGA (Japanese painting), a neo-traditional style.

OBI wide sash worn around the waist to hold the kimono together, tied at the back. See *darari obi* for a description of the obi worn by maiko.

OCHAYA (teahouse), where alcohol is served and exclusive parties occur where maiko and geiko entertain clients.

OFUKU the second hair style that maiko wear, marking progress in the apprenticeship.

OKĀSAN (mother), honorific term that maiko and geiko use to address their okiya head and ochaya managers.

ŌKINI ZAIDAN support organization for all five hanamachi, formally known in English as Kyoto Traditional Musical Art Foundation.

OKIYA (also called "yakata") geisha house where maiko and geiko live.

OKOBO formal high platform sandals that maiko wear.

OMOTENASHI see *motenashi*; the o is honorific.

ONĒSAN (elder sister), honorific term used to address maiko or geiko senior to oneself.

OSHIROI formal white makeup that maiko wear most commonly on their face and neck.

OTOKOSHI male dresser for both maiko and geiko.

OZASHIKI party at ochaya at which maiko and geiko entertain clients.

RYŪ arts guild associated with each hanamachi.

SAMISEN three-stringed instrument associated with geisha. See *shamisen*.

SHAMISEN see *samisen*.

SHIKOMI trainee for first six to twelve months before becoming a maiko.

SHŌJO (girl), between the social roles of childhood and adulthood.

SHOWA the historic period 1926–1989 marked by the reign of Emperor Hirohito, who is known posthumously as the Showa Emperor.

TABI split-toe white socks.

WARESHINOBU the first hair style that maiko wear.

YAKATA see *okiya*.

YUKATA informal, cotton kimono.

NOTES

1. Shigeyuki Murase, "'Maiko' Fever Strikes Kyoto," *The Asahi Shimbun*, April 18, 2008.

2. Masafumi Monden, pegging Lolita fashion to the mid-to-late 1990s and linking its kawaii aesthetics to manga for girls (*shōjo manga*), finds the look "characterized by its self-consciously girlish style, often with extravagant opulence of lace, flounces and ribbon" (109). For wearers, the fashion "also defines their identity and lifestyle" (109). *Japanese Fashion Cultures: Dress and Gender in Contemporary Japan* (London: Bloomsbury Academic, 2015). Proliferating in the mid-2000s, maid cafés served as fantasy spaces where customers, often young male fans of anime and video games, were welcomed by young women in frilly costumes, who would play games, chat, and take pictures with them. For more detail on the maid and comparison with the maiko, see chapter 6, and Patrick W. Galbraith, "Maid in Japan: An Ethnographic Account of Alternative Intimacy," *Intersections: Gender and Sexuality in Asia and the Pacific* 25 (2011), online at http://intersections.anu.edu.au/issue25/galbraith.htm (accessed May 25, 2020). AKB48, a girls' performing group, started in 2005, developed massive popularity in Japan and international notoriety, and became famous for its girl-next-door appeal and ability to attract fan support. Patrick W. Galbraith and Jason G. Karlin, *AKB48* (New York: Bloomsbury Academic, 2020).

3. Linda H. Chance, "*Genji* Guides, or Minding Murasaki," in *Manners and Mischief: Gender, Power, and Etiquette in Japan*, ed. Jan Bardsley and Laura Miller (Berkeley: University of California Press, 2011), 33–34. Chance describes how the anniversary drew attention on local, national, and global scales, inspiring numerous activities.

4. A visit to the Tokyo Metropolitan Central Library in fall 2018 underscored the status of maiko books as popular literature. Although housing over two million

volumes, the library had almost none of my sources; local Tokyo libraries, which cater to lighter tastes, did. Visiting Kyoto in spring 2019, I found few of my old favorites in major bookstores, although new maiko volumes had appeared. The literature of the maiko boom is an ephemeral trend.

5. The Lehman Shock, as the collapse of the Lehman Brothers investment bank is known in Japan, occurred the following autumn in September 2008, initiating the Great Recession.

6. Ayako Kano enumerates the 1990s equity initiatives and traces how disparate supporters of the 2000s backlash sought to reinforce essentialist gender distinctions. "Backlash, Fight Back, and Back-Pedaling: Responses to State Feminism in Contemporary Japan." *International Journal of Asian Studies* 8, no. 1 (2011): 41–62.

7. Focusing on maiko, I confine my investigation to Kyoto. For other geisha communities, see Lisa Dalby, *Geisha* (Berkeley: University of California Press, 1983, 2008); Lesley Downer, *Women of the Pleasure Quarters: The Secret History of the Geisha* (New York: Broadway, 2001), and Kelly M. Foreman, *The Gei of Geisha: Music, Identity, and Meaning* (Aldershot, UK: Ashgate, 2008).

8. Kelly M. Foreman makes this point in "The Perfect Woman: Geisha, Etiquette, and the World of Japanese Traditional Arts," in *Manners and Mischief: Gender, Power, and Etiquette in Japan*, ed. Jan Bardsley and Laura Miller (Berkeley: University of California Press, 2011), 67–79.

9. Liza Dalby, "The Exotic Geisha," in *Geisha: Beyond the Painted Smile*, ed. Peabody Essex Museum (New York: George Braziller, 2004), 74.

10. Dalby, "The Exotic Geisha."

11. The characters for *hanamachi* may also be pronounced *kagai*.

12. Iwasaki Mineko, *Geiko Mineko no hana-ikusa: Honma no koi wa ippen dosu* [The flower battle of Geisha Mineko: True love comes only once] (Tokyo: Kōdansha, 2001). Hereafter, in referring to this book, I will cite its English translation, Iwasaki Mineko and Rande Brown, *Geisha, a Life* (New York: Atria, 2002).

13. Liza Dalby notes that the "Tokyo equivalent, called *han'gyoku*, has completely disappeared." *Geisha*, 183.

14. Andrew L. Maske, "Identifying Geisha in Art and Life: Is She Really a Geisha?," in Peabody Essex Museum, ed., *Geisha: Beyond the Painted Smile*, 44. Maske mentions apprentices in hanamachi elsewhere such as *akaeri* (red collar) and *han'gyoku* (half fee) in Tokyo and Kanazawa in the past. Cecilia Segawa Seigle notes that one can find courtesans' teenage attendants—*shinzō*—in Edo prints. Seigle and Foreman both point to the Edo-era *odoriko* (dancer) as a precursor to geisha; see *Yoshiwara: The Glittering World of the Japanese Courtesan* (Honolulu: University of Hawai'i Press, 1993), 172–73; 180; 232. Kelly Foreman, "Bad Girls Confined: Okuni, Geisha, and the Negotiation of Female Performance Space," in *Bad Girls of Japan*, ed. Laura Miller and Jan Bardsley (New York: Palgrave Macmillan, 2005), 38–39.

15. Kyoko Aihara, *Kyoto maiko to geiko no okuzashiki* [The salon of Kyoto maiko and geiko] (Tokyo: Bungei Shunjū, 2001), 18.

16. The quote is from the caption accompanying a 1925 maiko postcard in Peabody Essex Museum, ed., *Geisha: Beyond the Painted Smile*, 77.

17. Aihara, *Kyoto maiko to geiko no okuzashiki*, 19.

18. Aihara describes how some clients caught on to the maiko's sign language, following the not-so-secret conversation. *Kyoto hanamachi fasshon no bi to kokoro* [The soul and beauty of Kyoto's hanamachi fashion] (Tokyo: Tankōsha, 2011), 8.

19. Aihara, *Kyoto hanamachi fasshon*, 27.

20. Aihara Kyoko, *Maiko-san no odōgu-chō* [Guide to maiko accessories] (Tokyo: Sankaidō, 2007), 46–47.

21. Aihara, *Maiko-san no odōgu-chō*, 47.

22. For example, Mizoguchi Kenji's 1929 silent film *Tokyo kōshinkyoku* (Tokyo marching song) features an impoverished factory girl who becomes a geisha to assist her uncle's family. In a gruesome twist of fate, a client, who turns out to be her father, tries to seduce her.

23. Sayo Masuda, *Autobiography of a Geisha*, translated by G. G. Rowley (New York: Columbia University Press, 2003).

24. Dalby describes older geiko discussing their mizuage with her in the mid-1970s; all expressed relief that "their daughters do not have to submit" to the practice. Dalby sensed that the women talked more freely about sexuality when young women, who would dismiss the mizuage as "feudalistic," were not present. *Geisha*, 110–11.

25. This recalls Higuchi Ichiyō's 1895–96 story, "Takekurabe" (Child's play) in which Midori's new hairstyle indicates her looming debut as a prostitute. Robert Lyons Danly, *In the Shade of Spring Leaves: The Life and Writings of Higuchi Ichiyō, a Woman of Letters in Meiji Japan* (New York: W.W. Norton, 1992), 254–87.

26. Iwasaki believes mizuage as commodified sexual initiation did occur in the pleasure quarters, but not among geiko. Mineko Iwasaki and Rande Brown, *Geisha, a Life* (New York: Atria Books, 2002), 253.

27. Dalby, *Geisha*, 173.

28. Iwashita Takehito, *Gion no hosomichi: Otonbo maiko* [The narrow road to Gion: The youngest child becomes a maiko] (Tokyo: Bungei Shobō, 2009), 32.

29. Caroline Norma, *Comfort Women and Post-occupation Corporate Japan* (London: Routledge, 2019), 75.

30. *Maiko monogatari* (Tale of a maiko, 1954), directed by Yasuda Kimiyoshi (see chapter 4, note 9).

31. "Amerika ni itta maiko-san" [The maiko who went to America], *Shōjo* (April 1954), unnumbered one-page illustration with caption, illustrated by Kinoshita Yoshihisa. The page includes the anecdote of a policeman falling in love at first sight with an adorable maiko, but claims the story is an April Fool's prank. Satō Shigemi, a popular young singer, appears in the illustration as the maiko.

32. A. C. Scott, *The Flower and Willow World: A Study of the Geisha* (London: Heinemann, 1959), 206.

33. Scott, *The Flower and Willow World*.

34. Phenomenally popular in Japan, *Roman Holiday* revolves around the love story of a princess (Audrey Hepburn) masquerading as a commoner who falls in love with an American reporter (Gregory Peck); to honor her royal duties, she relinquishes romance. Directed by Nishiyama Masateru, *Maiko no kyūjitsu* imagines the maiko passing as the daughter of a family prominent in Gion. Striking up a friendship with the Tokyo student, Mitsuko works as his model by day, secretly rushing off to the teahouse at night. Like the princess, she too has obligations that come before romance, but the gap between the social status of the sweethearts is evident, too.

35. Kiriki Chizu, *Aisare jōzu ni naru Gion-ryū: Onna migaki* [The Gion way to skill in becoming loveable: A woman's polish] (Tokyo: Kōdansha, 2007), 210.

36. In "Maiko satsujin jiken" (The maiko murder case), the killer murders a "tourists' maiko," mistaking her identity because he is unable to read the signs that expose the fakery of her costume. Kogiku, an actual maiko, uses her detective skills to help find the killer and prevent the murder of his intended maiko victim. Yamamura Misa, *Miyako odori satsujin jiken* [The Miyako Odori murder case] (1985, repr., Tokyo: Tokuma Bunko, 2004), 5–55. From 1988 to 1990, and again in 1999, TV Asahi broadcast *Maiko-san wa meitantei!* (The maiko is a great detective!), based on Yamamura's maiko mystery stories.

37. David Leheny, *Think Global, Fear Local: Sex, Violence, and Anxiety in Contemporary Japan* (Ithaca, NY: Cornell University Press, 2006), 91.

38. Leheny, *Think Global, Fear Local*, 89

39. Leheny, *Think Global, Fear Local*, 92.

40. Sharon Kinsella, *Schoolgirls, Money and Rebellion in Japan* (London: Routledge, 2014), 197.

41. Noting that the common English gloss *kogal* comes from the Japanese "*kogyaru* (clipped from *kōkōsei gyaru*, high school girls)," Miller finds that the media devised the term as a "generalized, usually derogatory, category" that dismissed the variety of fashion trends invented by girls. Laura Miller, *Beauty Up: Exploring Contemporary Japanese Body Aesthetics* (Berkeley: University of California Press, 2006), 29.

42. Laura Miller, "Bad Girl Photography," in *Bad Girls of Japan*, ed. Laura Miller and Jan Bardsley (New York: Palgrave Macmillan, 2005), 126–41.

43. For kogal fashion, see Miller, *Beauty Up*, 29–30; Kinsella, *Schoolgirls*, ch. 4, "Kogyaru Chic: Dressing Up as a Delinquent Girl."

44. Christine R. Yano, *Pink Globalization: Hello Kitty's Trek across the Pacific* (Durham, NC: Duke University Press, 2013), 53. Yano references discussion of school rules in Merry White, *The Material Child: Coming of Age in Japan and America* (Berkeley: University of California Press, 1993), 223–26.

45. Yano, *Pink Globalization*, 52.

46. Kinsella, *Schoolgirls*, ch. 6, "Girls as a Race."

47. Dalby, *Geisha*, 270.

48. See Anne Allison, *Nightwork: Sexuality, Pleasure, and Corporate Masculinity in a Tokyo Hostess Club* (Chicago: University of Chicago Press, 1994); Akiko Takeyama, *Staged Seduction: Selling Dreams in a Tokyo Host Club* (Stanford, CA: Stanford

University Press, 2016); Elise K. Tipton, "Pink Collar Work: The Café Waitress in Early Twentieth Century Japan," *Intersections: Gender, History and Culture in the Asian Context*, no. 7 (2002). http://intersections.anu.edu.au/issue7/tipton.html (accessed September 26, 2019).

49. Lieba Faier, *Intimate Encounters: Filipina Women and the Remaking of Rural Japan* (Berkeley: University of California Press, 2009); Gabriele Koch, *Healing Labor: Japanese Sex Work in the Gendered Economy* (Stanford, CA: Stanford University Press, 2020); and Rhacel Salazar Parreñas, *Illicit Flirtations: Labor, Migration, and Sex Trafficking in Tokyo* (Stanford, CA: Stanford University Press, 2011).

50. Mark J. McLelland, *Queer Japan from the Pacific War to the Internet Age* (Lanham, MD: Rowman & Littlefield, 2005).

51. See Rieko Morita, *Onnamae: Morita Rieko gabunshū* [Paintings of 'Handsome Women' by Rieko Morita: Onnamae] (Tokyo: Kyūryūdō Art Publishing, 2010). The artist's website is http://www.morita-rieko.com/english/ (accessed May 25, 2020).

52. The artist Osugi's website is http://osugishinji.com/ (accessed May 25, 2020)

53. The artist Tamura's website is http://tamurayoshiyasu.com/en (accessed May 25, 2020).

54. "Mika Ninagawa Exhibition Expresses Aura of Kyoto's Geiko Glamor," *Kyoto Shimbun*, May 27, 2018, https://english.kyodonews.net/news/2018/05/dd8d353022b2-ninagawa-exhibition-expresses-aura-of-kyotos-geiko-glamor.html (accessed June 5, 2020); Yayoi Kusama collaborated with Gion Kōbu, creating an exhibit of her work at the Forever Museum of Contemporary Art in its kaburenjō, May 2018–February 2019. https://fmoca.jp/en/display,(accessed June 5, 2020).

55. Kiriki, *Aisare jōzu ni naru Gion-ryū*, 80.

56. Jennifer Prough, *Revisiting Kyoto: Heritage Tourism in Contemporary Kyoto* (Honolulu: University of Hawai'i Press, forthcoming).

57. Cosplay occurs at other tourist sites in Japan, too. Visitors to the ancient capital of Nara can rent costumes evoking the aristocratic life of children and adults in the Tenpyō Era (729–749), Laura Miller, "Searching for Charisma Queen Himiko," in *Diva Nation: Female Icons from Japanese Cultural History*, ed. Laura Miller and Rebecca Copeland (Oakland: University of California Press, 2018), 60.

58. Kiriki, *Aisare jōzu ni naru Gion-ryū*, 211.

59. Kumiko Nishio, *Kyoto hanamachi no keieigaku* [Business Aspects of the Kyoto Hanamachi] (Tokyo: Tōyō Keizai Shinpōsha, 2007), 114–15; Kumiko Nishio, "Chapter 4, The Life of a Maiko," Jacqueline Kaminski trans., *The Japanese Economy* 37, no. 4 (2010–11): 59–60; Nanami Haruka, Afterword, in *Wakare no warutsu* [The farewell waltz], vol. 23 [9-26] of *Shōnen maiko: Chiyogiku ga yuku!* [Boy maiko: There goes Chiyogiku!] (Tokyo: Shūeisha Cobalt Bunko, 2007), 195–96. The volumes in the series are numbered 9-3 to 9-57. For clarity, I cite both their numerical place in the series as well as the numbers on the book jacket spine.

60. Aimee Major Steinberger, *Japan Ai: A Tall Girl's Adventures in Japan* (Agora Hills, CA: Go!Comi, 2007), 39–50.

61. "Chūgokujin kankōkyaku no maiko taiken" [A Chinese tourist's maiko experience], *Record China*, February 11, 2014. Online at https://www.recordchina.co.jp/b83162-s0-c60-d0035.html (accessed May 25, 2020).

62. Aihara, *Kyoto maiko to geiko no okuzashiki*, 202.

63. The Kyoto café and cosmetics store Yōjiya offers maiko-themed beverages. See https://www.yojiya.co.jp/en/history/ (accessed May 25, 2020).

64. Mizuta Nobuo, dir., *Maiko Haaaan!!!*. Tokyo: NTV, 2007.

65. Sakai Junko, "Sērā fuku" [Sailor uniform], in *Kireba wakaru!* [You'll understand if you wear it]. Tokyo: Bungei Shunjū, 2010), 12–22.

66. Dollase notes that women opposed to the shōjo image and aesthetics have been called *hishōjo* (non-shōjo). Hiromi Tsuchiya Dollase, *Age of Shōjo: The Emergence, Evolution, and Power of Japanese Girls' Magazine Fiction* (Albany: State University of New York Press, 2019), xiv.

67. Analyzing Takahara Eiri's idealization of "girl consciousness," Amanda Seaman argues that Takahara envisions this as "a way of being, open to women seeking to opt out of the competitive and aggressive world of the adult, and even to men who wish to reject the norms and restrictions (gender or otherwise) of everyday society." Seaman, "Women Writers and Alternative Critiques," in *Woman Critiqued: Translated Essays on Japanese Women's Writing*, ed. Rebecca Copeland (Honolulu: University of Hawai'i Press, 2006), 156. Similarly, Patrick W. Galbraith brings attention to men who like shōjo manga in "Seeking an Alternative: 'Male' Shōjo Fans Since the 1970s," in *Shōjo across Media: Exploring "Girl" Practices in Contemporary Japan*, ed. Jaqueline Berndt, Kazumi Nagaike, and Fusami Ogi (New York: Palgrave Macmillan, 2019), 355–90.

68. Sarah Frederick, "Girls' Magazines and the Creation of Shōjo Identities," in *Routledge Handbook of Japanese Media*, ed. Fabienne Darling-Wolf (London: Taylor and Francis, 2018), 22–38.

69. Honda Masuko, "The Genealogy of *Hirahira*: Liminality and the Girl," trans. Tomoko Aoyama and Barbara Hartley, in *Girl Reading Girl in Japan*, ed. Tomoko Aoyama and Barbara Hartley (New York: Routledge, 2010), 27.

70. Dollase, *Age of the Shōjo*, 128.

71. Anne Allison, *Millennial Monsters: Japanese Toys and the Global Imagination* (Berkeley: University of California Press, 2006), 139.

72. Yano, *Pink Globalization*, 63.

73. Yano, *Pink Globalization*, 11.

74. Allison, *Millennial Monsters: Japanese Toys and the Global Imagination*, 16–17.

75. The name of the underground shopping area, Kotochika combines the word for "old capital" (*koto*) with *chika*, the first character in the Japanese word for subway (*chikatetsu*).

76. Yano, *Pink Globalization*, 56.

77. Yano, *Pink Globalization*, 200.

78. Susan J. Napier, *From Impressionism to Anime: Japan as Fantasy and Fan Cult in the Mind of the West* (New York: Palgrave Macmillan, 2007).

79. "Cool Japan" refers to a 2000s government campaign "which emphasized youth-oriented, media-saturated popular culture," and aimed to boost the nation's soft power, Yano, *Pink Globalization*, 257.

80. Seigle, *Yoshiwara*, 117–19.

81. Dalby, *Geisha*, 56.

82. Dalby, *Geisha*, 69.

83. Mio Wakita, "Selling Japan: Kusakabe Kimbei's Image of Japanese Women," *History of Photography* 33, no. 2 (2009): 209–23.

84. For references to geisha in public activities, see Marnie S. Anderson, *A Place in Public: Women's Rights in Meiji Japan* (Cambridge, MA: Harvard University Asia Center, 2010); Elizabeth Dorn Lublin, *Reforming Japan: The Woman's Christian Temperance Union in the Meiji Period* (Vancouver: UBC Press, 2010), and Jan Bardsley, "The New Woman Meets the Geisha: The Politics of Pleasure in 1910s Japan," *Intersections: Gender and Sexuality in Asia and the Pacific* Issue 29 (2012) online: http://intersections.anu.edu.au/issue29/bardsley.htm (accessed May 25, 2020).

85. Dalby, *Geisha*, 82. William Johnston traces the life of one-time geisha Abe Sada, who suffered from advanced syphilis and in 1936 severed her lover's genitalia after killing him. *Geisha, Harlot, Strangler, Star: A Woman, Sex and Morality in Modern Japan* (New York: Columbia University Press, 2005).

86. For more on the geisha's twin status in Japan as model of refinement and mar-ginalized artist, see Foreman, "The Perfect Woman."

87. Dalby, "The Exotic Geisha," 70.

88. Yorimitsu Hashimoto, "Japanese Tea Party: Representations of Victorian Paradise and Playground in *The Geisha* (1896)," in *Histories of Tourism: Representation, Identity, and Conflict*, ed. John K. Walton (Clevedon, UK: Channel View Publications, 2005), 104–24; Yoko Kawaguchi, *Butterfly's Sisters: The Geisha in Western Culture* (New Haven, CT: Yale University Press, 2010); Christopher T. Keaveney, *Western Rock Artists, Madame Butterfly, and the Allure of Japan: Dancing in an Eastern Dream* (Lanham, MD: Lexington Books, 2020); Gina Marchetti, *Romance and the "Yellow Peril": Race, Sex, and Discursive Strategies in Hollywood Fiction* (Berkeley: University of California Press, 1993); Naoko Shibusawa, *America's Geisha Ally: Reimagining the Japanese Enemy* (Cambridge, MA: Harvard University Press, 2006); and Mari Yoshi-hara, *Embracing the East: White Women and American Orientalism* (New York: Oxford University Press, 2003).

89. Arthur Golden, *Memoirs of a Geisha* (New York: Alfred A. Knopf, 1997); Rob Marshall, dir., *Memoirs of a Geisha* (Columbia Pictures, 2005).

90. See Jan Bardsley, "Teaching Geisha in History, Fiction, and Fantasy," *ASIA-Network Exchange: A Journal for Asian Studies in the Liberal Arts* 17, no. 2 (2010): 23–38; and Elisheva Perelman, "The Appropriated Geisha: Using Their Role to Discuss Japa-nese History, Cultural Appropriation, and Orientalism," *Education about Asia* 20, no. 3 (2015): 70–72.

91. Sarah J. Pradt and Terry Kawashima, "Teaching the 'Geisha' as Cultural Criticism," *Education about Asia* 6, no. 1 (2001): 27.

92. Pradt and Kawashima, "Teaching the 'Geisha,'" 27.

93. Pradt and Kawashima, "Teaching the 'Geisha,'" 27.

94. Pradt and Kawashima, "Teaching the 'Geisha,'" 27.

95. Scott Tsuchitani's website displays his parodic geisha poster: http://www.scotttsuchitani.com/sanseigeisha.html (accessed May 25, 2020). Tsuchitani describes the *Memoirs of a Sansei* project in his article, "Making Art, Making Change: The Tactical Use of Guerrilla Intervention." *Social Policy* 43, no. 3 (2012): 27–33.

96. Dalby, "The Exotic Geisha," 67.

97. Nancy Stalker, "Flower Empowerment: Rethinking Japan's Traditional Arts as Women's Labor," in *Rethinking Japanese Feminisms*, ed. Julia C. Bullock, Ayako Kano, and James Welker (Honolulu: University of Hawai'i Press, 2018), 116.

98. Laura Miller argues that MOFA's male leadership packaged the trio as "an uncomplicated aesthetic of cute" with just enough quirky coolness to attract foreign audiences without overturning gender norms or acknowledging girls' own contributions to cultural production. The trio were not teens, but women hired by MOFA to pose as though they were. Laura Miller, "Cute Masquerade and the Pimping of Japan." *International Journal of Japanese Sociology* 20, no. 1 (2011): 26.

99. Dalby, "Preface: Geisha and Anthropology," in *Geisha*, xiii. (This is the preface to the first edition).

100. Efrat Tseëlon, "Introduction: Masquerade and Identities" in *Masquerade and Identities: Essays on Gender, Sexuality and Marginality*, ed. Efrat Tseëlon (London: Routledge, 2001), 4.

101. Eric McCready and Norry Ogata, "Adjectives, Stereotypicality, and Comparison," *Natural Language Semantics* 15, no. 1 (2007): 36.

102. Judith Butler, *Bodies That Matter: On the Discursive Limits of "Sex"* (New York: Routledge, 1993), 2–3.

103. Jennifer Robertson, *Takarazuka: Sexual Politics and Popular Culture in Modern Japan* (Berkeley: University of California Press, 1998), 12. Leonie R. Stickland also analyzes kata in *Gender Gymnastics: Performing and Consuming Japan's Takarazuka Revue* (Melbourne: Trans Pacific Press, 2008).

104. For more on kata, see Jan Bardsley and Laura Miller, "Manners and Mischief: Introduction," in *Manners and Mischief: Gender, Power, and Etiquette in Japan*, ed. Jan Bardsley and Laura Miller (Berkeley: University of California Press, 2011), 8–10.

105. Nanette Gottlieb, *Linguistic Stereotyping and Minority Groups in Japan* (London: Routledge, 2006), 126.

106. Lynne Nakano and Moeko Wagatsuma, "Mothers and Their Unmarried Daughters: An Intimate Look at Generational Change," in *Japan's Changing Generations: Are Young People Creating a New Society?*, ed. Gordon Mathews and Bruce White (London: Routledge, 2004), 138.

107. Ayumi Sasagawa, "Centered Selves and Life Choices Changing Attitudes of Young Educated Mothers," in Mathews and White, *Japan's Changing Generations*, 184.

108. Kiriki, *Aisare jōzu ni naru Gion-ryū: Onna migaki*, 30–31.

109. "Maiko-san no toki kara, Orenifure Satsuki-chan no hibi o shōkai shite kimashita" [We have introduced Satsuki's life from time to time since her maiko days]. *Utsukushii kimono* [Beautiful kimono], Winter 2016 (Tokyo: Hearst Fujingaho Co., Ltd.), 215.

110. Gitte Marianne Hansen, *Femininity, Self-Harm and Eating Disorders in Japan: Navigating Contradiction in Narrative and Visual Culture* (London: Routledge, 2016).

111. Anne Allison, "Memoirs of the Orient," *Journal of Japanese Studies* 27, no. 2 (2001): 394.

112. Allison, "Memoirs of the Orient," 394.

113. Jack Cardiff, dir., *My Geisha* (Los Angeles: Paramount, 1962); Lee Phillips, dir., *An American Geisha* (Interscope Communications TV, 1986).

114. Marchetti, *Romance and the "Yellow Peril,"* 191.

115. Marchetti, *Romance and the "Yellow Peril,"* 200.

116. Marchetti, *Romance and the "Yellow Peril,"* 196.

117. Marchetti, *Romance and the "Yellow Peril,"* 200–201.

118. Alisa Freedman, "Bus Guides Tour National Landscapes, Pop Culture, and Youth Fantasies," in *Modern Girls on the Go: Gender, Mobility, and Labor in Japan*, ed. Alisa Freedman, Laura Miller, and Christine R. Yano (Stanford, CA: Stanford University Press, 2013), 107–28; Laura Miller, "Elevator Girls Moving In and Out of the Box." In Freedman et al., *Modern Girls on the Go*, 41–65.

119. Freedman, National Landscapes (Bus Guides Tour National Landscapes), 127.

120. Miller, "Elevator Girls," 65.

121. Miller, "Elevator Girls," 41.

122. Miller, "Elevator Girls," 64.

CHAPTER 1. THE MAIKO'S HANAMACHI HOME

1. Website of the Kyoto Traditional Musical Art Foundation; nickname, Ōkini Zaidan. https://www.ookinizaidan.com/ (accessed May 22, 2020).

2. Aihara refers to *slow beauty* (*surō na bi*) in *Kyoto hanamachi fasshon*, 126.

3. Anne Allison, *Precarious Japan* (Durham, NC: Duke University Press, 2013), 17.

4. Allison, *Precarious Japan*, 91–93. Allison observes that *ibasho* has become "a catchword of the times," most often in phrases lamenting its absence, 174.

5. Ikuko Takeda (Koito), "Foreword," in *A Geisha's Journey: My Life as a Kyoto Apprentice*, by Komomo and Naoyuki Ogino, trans. Gearoid Reidy and Philip Price (Tokyo: Kodansha International, 2008), 8.

6. Aihara followed her English-language photo book *Geisha: A Living Tradition* (London: Carlton Books, 1999) with the highly informative *Kyoto maiko to geiko no okuzashiki* [The salon of Kyoto maiko and geiko]. Her next book, *Kyoto hanamachi motenashi no gijutsu* [The art of hospitality in Kyoto's hanamachi] (Tokyo: Shōgakukan,

2005), concentrated on etiquette, including anecdotes about how teahouse managers worked with clients and their mutual expectations. Aihara's next two books combined stunning photographs with stories that zoomed in on the maiko's wardrobe and accessories: *Maiko-san no odōgu-chō* [Guide to maiko accessories] (2007) and *Kyoto hanamachi fasshon no bi to kokoro* [The soul and beauty of Kyoto's hanamachi fashion] (2011). Her latest book, *Kyoto hanamachi: Maiko to geiko no uchiake-banashi* [The Kyoto hanamachi: Frank talk from maiko and geiko] (Tokyo: Tankōsha, 2012), intersperses short conversations with maiko with first-person accounts of hanamachi life by longtime teahouse managers and geiko.

7. Nishio based her 2007 book, *Kyoto hanamachi no keieigaku* on her 2006 dissertation at Kobe University Graduate School of Business Administration. Nishio conducts scholarship on women's careers and institutions related to career building. The English translation by Jacqueline Kaminski [Business Aspects of the Kyoto Hanamachi] was published as separate chapters in the journal *The Japanese Economy*, 2010–11, as listed in this book's bibliography. In citing Nishio's *Kyoto hanamachi no keieigaku*, I will also refer readers to Kaminski's translation.

8. Nishio's two recent books, intended for a general audience, are *Maiko no kotoba: Kyoto hanamachi hitosodate no gokui* [Maiko language: Training secrets from the Kyoto hanamachi] (Tokyo: Tōyō Keizai Shinpōsha, 2012) and *Omotenashi no shikumi: Kyoto hanamachi ni manabu manejimento* [The mechanisms of hospitality: Management skills learned in Kyoto hanamachi] (Tokyo: Chūōkōron Shinsha, 2014).

9. Mizobuchi Hiroshi, *Kyoto no kagai; The Kagai in Kyoto: Legendary Beauty of Geiko and Maiko* (Kyoto: Mitsumura Suiko Shoin Publishing, 2015); Judith Clancy, *The Alluring World of Maiko and Geiko*, Photographs by Mizobuchi Hiroshi (Kyoto: Tankōsha, 2016).

10. Mizobuchi, *The Kagai in Kyoto*, 301–3.

11. Ōta Tōru and Hiratake Kōzō, eds., *Kyō no kagai: Hito, waza, machi* [Kyoto's hanamachi: People, arts, towns] (Tokyo: Nippon Hyōronsha, 2009). The contributors (three men, two women) are: Ōta Tōru, owner of Kamishichiken sweets shop Oimatsu, author of books related to the tea ceremony, professor at Ikenobo Academy and lecturer at Kyoto Women's University among others; Hiratake Kōzō, deputy chief secretary of Kyoto City Government for Culture and Art Policy; Hamasaki Kanako, who has lectured at Kyoto Seika University and authored books on Japanese literature and culture; Inoue Eriko, architecture scholar and associate professor, Kyoto Women's University; and Kanbayashi Kenji, a lecturer at Kyoto Seika University and listed as director of the NPO dedicated to preserving the Gion area (246).

12. The historical Shimabara district, established in 1640 as a licensed pleasure quarter, appears on some maps of the hanamachi, always with the caveat that it no longer functions as one (see, for example, Dalby, *Geisha*, 25). In its heyday, Shimabara was associated with literati culture, famous courtesans and educated, upper-class men. Writer and painter Yosa Buson frequented the Shimabara; Ihara Saikaku referred to it in his 1687 *Nanshoku ōkagami* (*The Great Mirror of Male Love*). One *ageya* (a house

where courtesans received and performed for guests) remains: dating back to 1641, the Sumiya has been converted into a museum and was designated an Important Cultural Property in 1952. According to Aihara, one may still see performers in full costume reenact courtesan (*tayū*) dances there, *Kyoto maiko to geiko no okuzashiki*, 27. The Shimabara teahouse Wachigai-ya is still in operation. For more on the history of Shimabara, see C. Andrew Gerstle, ed., *18th Century Japan: Culture and Society* (Richmond, VA: Curzon, 2000).

13. According to Aihara, all the okiya in Kamishichiken and Miyagawa-chō are combined with ochaya. *Kyoto maiko to geiko no okuzashiki*, 37.

14. All the hanamachi schools focus on arts training. According to Nishio, the smaller hanamachi—Kamishichiken and Gion Higashi—arrange for instructors to come to the hanamachi. *Kyoto hanamachi no keieigaku*, 178. In the case of Pontochō, lessons take place in Kamogawa Gakuen, housed in the hanamachi's fine old kaburenjō. Two hanamachi schools are listed among Kyoto's vocational and technical schools http://www.kyosen.or.jp/fields.html, (accessed May 24, 2020): Miyagawa-chō's Higashiyama Joshi Gigei Gakkō, established in 1968 and accredited the following year, trains maiko and geiko in the Hanayanagi-ryū of dance, the samisen and other musical instruments, Edo-era songs, and the tea ceremony. Gion Kōbu's Yasaka Nyokōba Gakuen, which provides similar arts training, opened its doors in 1873, thanks to public and private funding. Its early curriculum included sewing, spinning, and samisen-making, becoming the model for other schools for geiko and prostitutes opening in Japan in the 1870s. In her account of the school's founding, Amy Stanley analyzes how Kyoto politicians and Gion leader and Ichiriki teahouse owner, Sugiura Jirōemon employed the rhetoric of enlightenment and productivity, the new ideal of motherhood, and civic engagement in shaping the school's purpose. Amy Stanley, "Enlightenment Geisha: The Sex Trade, Education, and Feminine Ideals in Early Meiji Japan." *Journal of Asian Studies* 72, no. 3 (2013): 539–62.

15. One photo-guide to shops in Kyoto promises to tell readers about the "iki places that geiko and maiko frequent." It promotes expensive bars and eateries along with casual dining at ramen and noodle shops, Japanese sweets, and souvenirs. Yasuda Yōko, Kaneda Chikako, and Fukuoka Yūko, eds., *Kyoto hanamachi no meiten* [Famous shops in the Kyoto hanamachi] (Kyoto: Seigensha Art Publishing, 2010).

16. In the finale, the group of twenty maiko representing each hanamachi dances to the famous song, "Gion kouta" (Song of the Gion). The brainchild of the Association of the Kyoto Hanamachi (Kyoto Kagai Kumiai Rengōkai) and the Kyoto City Office of Tourism, and originally intended to inspire respect for Kyoto's traditional performing arts, *Miyako no nigiwai* became performed annually. Sugita Hiroaki and Mizobuchi Hiroshi, *Kyō no kagai, Gion* [Gion, hanamachi of the old capital] (Kyoto: Tankōsha, 2003), 52.

17. Kitano Tenmangū was erected in 947 to appease the vengeful spirit of Heian-era scholar and poet Sugawara no Michizane, now known as the god of learning, whose unjust exile fueled his wrath even after death. On February 25, Kamishichiken maiko and geiko, in formal dress and makeup, serve tea at the Plum Blossom Festival (Baikasai)

that commemorates Michizane's love of plum blossoms, and again on December 1, at the Kitano Tea Dedication Festival (Kitano kenchasai). The latter event pays homage to the spectacular 1587 Grand Kitano Tea Gathering held at the shrine by famed samurai leader Toyotomi Hideyoshi for which teahouses in the area served as resting spots.

18. Aihara, *Kyoto maiko to geiko no okuzashiki*, 23–24.

19. Aihara, *Kyoto maiko to geiko no okuzashiki*, 24.

20. Aihara interview with Nakamura Yasuko, manager of the legendary Kamishichiken ochaya Nakazato. Aihara, *Kyoto hanamachi: Maiko to geiko no uchiake-banashi*, 53–54.

21. The Kamishichiken Kabukai (the association that manages the hanamachi) website gives a brief account of its history and public dances; recruits prospective maiko; and advertises its beer garden and kaburenjō: http://www.maiko3.com/index.html (accessed May 22, 2020).

22. Kristin Surak succinctly defines the hierarchical master-disciple iemoto system, found in schools of Noh, the tea ceremony, ikebana, dance, and other Japanese arts: "Fusing the characters *ie*, meaning house or family, and *moto*, meaning origin or root, the term *iemoto* refers to the person who simultaneously heads a school or style of an aesthetic activity and a family that has passed down for generations the authority to define this style" (93). Surak explains that this system may combine "real and fictive familial relationships to control the preservation of cultural authority and the transmission of specialized knowledge" (93). *Making Tea, Making Japan: Cultural Nationalism in Practice* (Stanford, CA: Stanford University Press, 2013).

23. For example, Mizobuchi's book depicts geiko, maiko, and other women surrounding Inoue Yachiyo V at their annual July festivity at Yasaka Shrine known as *Miyabi-kai* where they "pray for dance skills and the prosperity of their group." Mizobuchi Hiroshi, *The Kagai in Kyoto*, 143. A 2003 photo book on the Gion devotes one chapter to the Inoue ryū, including short biographies of all five women who have held the iemoto position. Sugita and Mizobuchi, *Kyō no kagai, Gion*, 77–88.

24. According to Kelly M. Foreman, the unshakable prominence of the Inoue ryū in the Gion dates to the first performance of *Miyako Odori* in 1872. *Miyako Odori* was one of several events meant to draw tourism back to Kyoto after Tokyo became the capital. Foreman explains that the Inoue ryū's stylistic proximity to the venerated Noh theater linked it firmly to Kyoto traditions rather than the arts of Edo. "The result was that Gion was promoted heavily by the Kyoto government as 'the geisha headquarters of Japan,' and *Miyako Odori* played a large role in this partnership because the Inoue ryū operates exclusively in Gion." *Gei of Geisha*, 52. Mariko Okada discusses early performances of *Miyako Odori*, its function as war propaganda in the 1930s, and contributions to international tourism and nation branding in the postwar. "Prolegomenon to Geisha as a Cultural Performer: Miyako Odori, the Gion School, and Representation of a 'Traditional' Japan." *The Institute for Theater Research, the 21st Century COE Program, Waseda University* 1 (2003), 159–65, and "Before Making Heritage: Internationalisation of Geisha in the Meiji Period," in *Making Japanese Heritage*, ed. Christoph Brumann and Rupert Cox (London: Routledge, 2010), 31–43. The Gion Kōbu Kabukai

maintains an English website advertising *Miyako Odori*: http://miyako-odori.jp /english/, accessed May 22, 2020.

25. Aihara, *Kyoto maiko to geiko no okuzashiki*, 16.

26. Aihara, *Kyoto hanamachi: Maiko to geiko no uchiake-banashi*, 8.

27. Aihara, *Kyoto hanamachi: Maiko to geiko no uchiake-banashi*.

28. Lesley Downer, *Women of the Pleasure Quarters: The Secret History of the Geisha* (New York: Broadway, 2001), 202.

29. Iwasaki and Brown, *Geisha, a Life*, 59.

30. Hanamikōji, which leads to Kenninji Temple, opened in 1874, but its cobblestone paving and its buried telephone poles are Heisei-era innovations, Ōta, "Hanamachi no rekishi" [History of the hanamachi], in Ōta and Hiratake, *Kyō no kagai*, 62.

31. Gion Corner maintains a website in several languages: http://www.kyoto-gioncorner.com/global/en.html (accessed May 22, 2020). In Japanese, the name is given in katakana, Gion kōnā; its English name reflects the theater's origins as entertainment for European-language-speaking tourists from abroad. For more on Gion Corner, see Laurence R. Kominz, "The Impact of Tourism on Japanese 'Kyōgen': Two Case Studies," *Asian Folklore Studies* 47, no. 2 (1988): 195–213.

32. Occasionally, if no maiko is available for the Gion Corner performance, a minarai (trainee close to her maiko debut) will be pressed into service. Arai Mameji, *Gion Mameji: Chotto mukashi no Gion machi* [Mameji of the Gion: The Gion of recent past] (Tokyo: Asahi Shimbun Publications, 2015), 127.

33. As part of an elaborate plot to avenge the death of his lord, rōnin leader Ōishi Kuranosuke Yoshio assumed deep cover by playing the part of a dissolute for two years, frequenting the Ichiriki. After Ōishi and the other masterless samurai (rōnin) killed their lord's enemy in Edo, they were arrested and ordered to commit ritualized suicide (*seppuku*), which they did on March 20, 1703. The event inspired the tale *Chūshingura* (*The Treasury of Loyal Retainers*), taking form in plays, film, TV, literature, woodblock prints, and manga. The Ichiriki hosts a private ceremony in honor of Ōishi on the anniversary of the suicide, serving guests soba noodles in memory of the last meal consumed by the avenging rōnin. Sugita and Mizobuchi, *Kyō no kagai, Gion*, 40–41; Lorie Brau, "Soba, Edo Style: Food, Aesthetics, and Cultural Identity," in *Devouring Japan: Perspectives on Japanese Culinary Identity*, ed. Nancy Stalker (New York: Oxford University Press, 2018), 72.

34. The Gion Higashi district's website lists the names of its teahouses, including a map of their locations. http://www.gionhigashi.com/intro (accessed May 22, 2020).

35. Foreman explains that after completing its theater in 1949, the hanamachi changed its name to Gion Higashi Shinchi (Gion East). Foreman, *Gei of Geisha*, 53. Gion Higashi maintains a website in Japanese: http://gion-east.jp/gion-east/ (accessed May 22, 2020).

36. Hamasaki Kanako, "Hanamachi no nen-chū gyōji" [Annual festivals in the hanamachi] in Ōta and Hiratake, *Kyō no kagai*, 104–5.

37. Nishio, *Kyoto hanamachi no keieigaku*, 23; Chapter 1: The Kyoto Hanamachi," trans. Jacqueline Kaminski, *The Japanese Economy* 37, no. 4 (2010–11): 11.

38. In a sidebar in Mizobuchi's book on the district, Tsubokura Rikio, president of the Miyagawa-chō Ochaya Union, provides a brief history. Mizobuchi Hiroshi, *Kyō maiko: Miyagawa-chō* (Kyoto: Mitsumura Suiko Shoin, 2013), 13.

39. Mizobuchi, *Kyō maiko*, 13.

40. For more information on Miyagawa-chō, see the district's bilingual English-Japanese website: http://www.miyagawacho.jp/ (accessed September 2, 2020).

41. Dalby, *Geisha*, 57.

42. Dalby, *Geisha*, 80–81.

43. Aihara, *Kyoto maiko to geiko no okuzashiki*, 18–19.

44. Percival Densmore Perkins, *Geisha of Pontocho: Photos* (Tokyo: Tokyo News Service, 1954).

45. Perkins, *Geisha of Pontocho*, 168.

46. I discuss media interest in women's leadership in the 1950s in Jan Bardsley, *Women and Democracy in Cold War Japan* (London: Bloomsbury Academic, 2014).

47. The Pontochō website is https://www.kamogawa-odori.com/ (accessed September 2, 2020).

48. Dalby, "The Exotic Geisha," 75.

49. Dalby, *Geisha*, 82; 181.

50. Iwasaki and Brown, *Geisha, a Life*, 51.

51. Dalby, *Geisha*, 93; 181.

52. Aihara, *Kyoto hanamachi: Maiko to geiko no uchiake-banashi*, 142.

53. Hiratake Kōzō and Hamasaki Kanako, "Hanamachi wa ima" [The hanamachi now] in Ōta and Hiratake, *Kyō no kagai*, 33.

54. Iwasaki and Brown, *Geisha, a Life*, 163.

55. Aihara, *Kyoto hanamachi motenashi no gijutsu*, 152.

56. Kiriki, *Aisare jōzu ni naru Gion-ryū*, 210.

57. Arai Mameji, *Gion Mameji: Chotto mukashi no Gion machi* [Mameji of the Gion: The Gion of recent past] (Tokyo: Asahi Shimbun Publications, 2015), 31.

58. Hiratake and Hamasaki, "Hanamachi wa ima," 33; Murase, "'Maiko' Fever Strikes Kyoto"; Nishio, *Kyoto hanamachi no keieigaku*, 27; "Chapter 1: The Kyoto Hanamachi," 13.

59. Mizobuchi, *The Kagai of Kyoto*, 301.

60. Yamato and Iwasaki, *Kurenai niou*, 3:207.

61. Hiratake and Hamasaki, "Hanamachi wa ima," 37.

62. Hiratake and Hamasaki, "Hanamachi wa ima," 33; Murase, "'Maiko' Fever Strikes Kyoto."

63. Aihara, *Kyoto hanamachi motenashi no gijutsu*, 152.

64. In an email dated May 20, 2020, the Ōkini Zaidan gave me the numbers of teahouses, geiko, and maiko by district as of April 30, 2020, which I cite with its permission:

Gion Higashi: 7 teahouses; 11 geiko; 8 maiko; Gion Kōbu: 55 teahouses; 66 geiko; 31 maiko; Kamishichiken: 10 teahouses; 14 geiko; 5 maiko; Miyagawa-chō: 29 teahouses;

36 geiko; 28 maiko; and Pontochō: 21 teahouses; 38 geiko; 9 maiko. In total, there were 122 teahouses, 165 geiko, and 81 maiko in April 2020.

65. Dalby, "The Exotic Geisha," 75.

66. Aihara, *Kyoto hanamachi: Maiko to geiko no uchiake-banashi*, 123. Also see the Ōkini Zaidan website cited in note 1.

67. Hamasaki Kanako, "Hanamachi e no akusesu (Ōkini Zaidan)" [Access to the hanamachi (The Ōkini Zaidan)], in Ōta and Hiratake, *Kyō no kagai*, 237.

68. Hamasaki, "Hanamachi e no akusesu," 237.

69. Hamasaki, "Hanamachi e no akusesu," 238. Foreman explains that despite their talents, geiko and geisha are not eligible for the award National Living Treasure, an honor that gives considerable financial support and recognition to (male) performers in arts such as Noh and Kabuki. Foreman speculates that such government agency recognition of geisha would not win public support due to perceived links between geisha and prostitution and past controversies involving geisha and politicians (*Gei of Geisha*, 92).

70. Foreman, *Gei of Geisha*, 102–3.

71. Foreman, *Gei of Geisha*, 103.

72. Hamasaki, "Hanamachi e no akusesu," 238.

73. According to my email communication May 19, 2020, with the Ōkini Zaidan, cited with permission, Friends' Group membership is about 320, with women and men equally represented; membership costs 33,000 yen per year (approximately US$300 in spring 2020).

74. Objecting to the Orientalist connotations of the word *teahouse*, Nishio prefers to use the term *guest house* when writing in English about this system (Nishio, *Kyoto hanamachi no keieigaku*, 51). To be sure, *teahouse* conjures notions of exotic sexuality from the late nineteenth century in Pierre Loti's *Madame Chrysanthème* to the postwar American comedy *Teahouse of the August Moon*. While I take Nishio's point, I find that *guest house* mistakenly implies that the ochaya functions as a kind of hotel. I prefer to use both *teahouse* and *ochaya* interchangeably in this book, providing numerous examples from contemporary Japanese writing to clarify their function. I notice that Kaminski also suggests "members-only teahouse" in her translation. "Chapter 2: Geiko, Maiko, Ochaya, and Okiya," *The Japanese Economy* 37, no. 4 (2010–11): 26–27.

75. Aihara, *Kyoto hanamachi motenashi no gijutsu*, 105.

76. Taniguchi Keiko, *Gion, uttoko no hanashi: "Minoya" okami, hitori katari* [Gion, stories of our place: Thoughts from the manager of the Minoya] (Tokyo: Heibonsha, 2018), 20.

77. Nishio, *Kyoto hanamachi no keieigaku*, 51–52; "Chapter 2: Geiko, Maiko, Ochaya, and Okiya," 27.

78. Nishio, *Kyoto hanamachi no keieigaku*, 51; "Chapter 2: Geiko, Maiko, Ochaya, and Okiya," 27.

79. In her 2015 memoir, *Gion Mameji*, Gion teahouse manager Arai Mameji recounts her days as a maiko and geiko in Gion, her love of dance, and stories of life in the

hanamachi in the Showa era so that young people will appreciate its history and traditions. Arai was born in 1954 in Shimabara, where her mother and elder sister were geiko. The 2017 NHK-TV documentary, *Gion onna-tachi no monogatari: Ochaya hachidai-me okami* [Stories of Gion women: The eighth-generation teahouse manager] features Ōta Kimi, who was born in 1940 and in 1974 became the eighth-generation manager of the Gion teahouse Tomiyo, one of the most well-known and oldest in the area and dating back over two hundred years. The film explores how Ōta chose to pursue this career rather than marrying; at the end, we see her handing over the reins to her daughter. Another view of the manager's career appears in Taniguchi Keiko's 2018 biography of Yoshimura Kaoru [Taniguchi, *Gion, uttoko no hanashi*], who was born in 1950 and became the okami-san of the Gion teahouse Minoya. *Gion, uttoko no hanashi* describes a day in the busy life of the manager, her preparations for ozashiki, and her Buddhist sensibilities; it also zooms out to talk about Kyoto's changing seasons and changes over time in Gion life. Publisher Heibonsha runs a short statement from famed author Setouchi Jakuchō, who wrote the novel *Kyō mandara* [Mandala of the old capital, 1971–72] modeled on Yoshimura's mother: Setouchi praises the biography as communicating "the gentleness, beauty, and sensuality as told in the iki language of the Gion," explaining "teahouse customs and all about maiko and geiko from their make-up to their kimono." She exclaims, "Read this one volume, and you will feel as though you have become a connoisseur (tsū) of the Gion." https://www.heibonsha.co .jp/book/b372268.html (accessed May 22, 2020).

80. Aihara, *Kyoto hanamachi: Maiko to geiko no uchiake-banashi*.

81. Aihara, *Kyoto maiko to geiko no okuzashiki*, 205–6.

82. Mizobuchi, *Kyō maiko*, 92–93.

83. Kiriki, *Aisare jōzu ni naru Gion-ryū*, 77.

84. Nishio, *Kyoto hanamachi no keieigaku*, 52; "Chapter 2: Geiko, Maiko, Ochaya, and Okiya," 27

85. Nishio, *Kyoto hanamachi no keieigaku*, 51; "Chapter 2: Geiko, Maiko, Ochaya, and Okiya," 27

86. Nishio, *Kyoto hanamachi no keieigaku*, 126; "Chapter 5: No Wallet Required," trans. Jacqueline Kaminski, *The Japanese Economy* 37, no. 4 (2010–11): 65.

87. The kenban of each hanamachi records the earnings of maiko and geiko. The kenban also figures the taxes and monthly fees owed by the teahouses, and then reports what the teahouse must pay the okiya for the maiko and geiko's time (Iwasaki and Brown, *Geisha, a Life*, 139). Nishio and Iwasaki both praise this system for its transparency. Nishio, *Kyoto hanamachi no keieigaku*, 28.

88. An email communication from Ōkini Zaidan, October 20, 2019, cited with permission.

89. For more detail on maiko and geiko earnings, see chapter 2.

90. See Foreman, "The Perfect Woman," for more on expectations for clients, and her *Gei of Geisha* for ozashiki protocols.

91. Iwasaki often recounts stories about her favorite clients, including Morita Akio, cofounder of Sony Corporation; Tsukamoto Kōichi, the founder of Wacoal, a famous

lingerie company; Yukawa Hideki, who received the Nobel Prize for Physics in 1949; and Kyoto philosopher of aesthetics Tanigawa Tetsuzō. See, for example, Iwasaki Mineko, *Gion no kagai jugyō* [Lessons outside of class in the Gion] (Tokyo: Shūeisha, 2004).

92. Aihara, *Kyoto hanamachi: Maiko to geiko no uchiake-banashi*, quotes responses from various maiko when queried about their favorite clients, 145–48.

93. Komomo and Naoyuki Ogino, *A Geisha's Journey*, 38.

94. "The Age of the Dandy," ch. 5 in Seigle, *Yoshiwara*, 129–68.

95. Jan Bardsley, "The *Oyaji* Gets a Makeover: Guides for Japanese Salarymen in the New Millennium," in *Manners and Mischief: Gender, Power, and Etiquette in Japan*, ed. Jan Bardsley and Laura Miller (Berkeley: University of California Press, 2011), 114–35.

96. Bardsley, "The *Oyaji*," 114–15.

97. Taniguchi, *Gion, uttoko no hanashi*, 157.

98. Aihara, *Kyoto hanamachi motenashi no gijutsu*, 93.

99. Aihara, *Kyoto hanamachi: Maiko to geiko no uchiake-banashi*, 101.

100. Iwasaki and Brown, *Geisha, a Life*, 136.

101. Aihara, *Kyoto hanamachi motenashi no gijutsu*, 84; 90–91.

102. Kiriki, *Aisare jōzu ni naru Gion-ryū*, 130–31.

103. Aihara, *Kyoto hanamachi motenashi no gijutsu*, 90–91.

104. Kelly Foreman, "The Perfect Woman," 67–79.

105. Nishio mentions hearing of a case where an individual's rude behavior at an ozashiki resulted in his abrupt job transfer out of Kyoto. *Kyoto hanamachi no keieigaku*, 84; "Chapter 3: No First-Time Customers," trans. Jacqueline Kaminski, *The Japanese Economy* 37, no. 4 (2010–11): 40.

106. Kiriki, *Aisare jōzu ni naru Gion-ryū*, 78.

107. Christina Liao, "An Inside Peek at Kyoto's Secretive Geisha Culture," *Vogue*, March 21, 2017, https://www.vogue.com/article/geisha-culture-kyoto-japan-how-to-see-geiko-maiko (accessed May 22, 2020).

108. Aihara, *Kyoto hanamachi motenashi no gijutsu*, 84.

109. Aihara, *Kyoto hanamachi motenashi no gijutsu*, 94.

110. Nishio, *Kyoto hanamachi no keieigaku*, 64; "Chapter 2: Geiko, Maiko, Ochaya, and Okiya," 33.

111. Aihara, *Kyoto maiko to geiko no okuzashiki*, 81–82.

112. Aihara, *Kyoto maiko to geiko no okuzashiki*, 80.

113. Aihara, *Kyoto maiko to geiko no okuzashiki*, 86–87.

114. Nishio, *Kyoto hanamachi no keieigaku*, 65; "Chapter 2: Geiko, Maiko, Ochaya, and Okiya," trans. Jacqueline Kaminski, 34.

115. Iwasaki describes that, despite her taciturn demeanor at ozashiki, Ariyoshi Sawako wrote sensitively about Gion women in her 1970 novel *Shibazakura* [The flocks]. Iwasaki Mineko, *Gion no kyōkun: Noboru hito noborikirazuni owaru hito* [Lessons from the Gion: Those who succeed, those who never do] (2003, rpt., Tokyo: Daiwa Shobō, 2007), 38–39. Ariyoshi followed *Shibazakura* with the sequel, *Boke no hana*

[The Quince, 1973]; the narrative "traces the lives of two women from their teenage years as apprentice geishas to postwar years during which they become successful entrepreneurs." Yoshiko Yokochi Samuel, "Ariyoshi Sawako (1931–1984)," in Chieko Irie Mulhern, ed., *Japanese Women Writers: A Bio-Critical Sourcebook* (Westport, CT: Greenwood Press, 1994), 13.

Hayashi Mariko effuses over the feminine beauties found "only in Gion" in *Bijo wa nan demo shitte iru* [The beauty knows all] (Tokyo: Magajin Hausu, 2010), 227–31.

116. Iwasaki Mineko, *Gion no kyōkun*, 38.

117. Iwasaki and Brown, *Geisha, a Life*, 169–70.

118. Nishio, *Kyoto hanamachi no keieigaku*, 3. Kaminski translates this sentiment well as "the elegant entertainment and restrained splendor of the Kyoto hanamachis' local color that Japanese people somehow find highly fascinating have continued all the way down to the present day." In my translation, I want to capture Nishio's use of "we Japanese" and the deep, emotional pull of the hanamachi for Japanese that she imagines. "Business Aspects of the Kyoto Hanamachi: Introduction," *The Japanese Economy*, 37, no. 4 (Winter 2010–11): 4.

119. Aihara, *Kyoto hanamachi motenashi no gijutsu*, 130.

120. Koichi Iwabuchi, "Cultural Policy, Cross-Border Dialogue and Cultural Diversity," in Fabienne Darling-Wolf, ed., *Routledge Handbook of Japanese Media* (London: Taylor & Francis 2018), 370.

121. Iwabuchi, "Cultural Policy," 370.

CHAPTER 2. THE WELL-MANNERED CAREER PATH

1. Komomo and Naoyuki Ogino, *A Geisha's Journey: My Life as a Kyoto Apprentice* (Tokyo: Kodansha International, 2008); *Komomo: Nihongo ban* (Komomo: The Japanese language version) (Tokyo: Kodansha International, 2008). A nine-year collaborative effort by photographer Naoyuki Ogino and Miyagawa-chō geiko Komomo, *A Geisha's Journey* includes the perspective of Koito, former geiko, manager of the okiya Kaden, and Komomo's mentor.

2. Cynthia Dickel Dunn, "Bowing Incorrectly: Aesthetic Labor and Expert Knowledge in Japanese Business Etiquette Training, " in *Japanese at Work: Politeness, Power, and Personae in Japanese Workplace Discourse*, ed. Haruko Minegishi Cook and Janet S. Shibamoto-Smith (New York: Palgrave Macmillan, 2018), 16.

3. Iwashita, *Gion no hosomichi*, 123.

4. Nanami Haruka, *Hanamikōji ni okoshiyasu* [Welcome to Hanamikōji], vol. 1 [9-3] of *Shōnen maiko: Chiyogiku ga yuku!* (Tokyo: Shūeisha Cobalt Bunko, 2002), afterword, 197–98.

5. Nishio, *Maiko no kotoba*, 151.

6. Aihara, *Kyoto hanamachi motenashi no gijutsu*, 164.

7. Aihara, *Kyoto hanamachi motenashi no gijutsu*, 165–66.

8. Takie Sugiyama Lebra, *Japanese Women: Constraint and Fulfillment* (Honolulu: University of Hawai'i Press, 1984), 42.

9. Lebra, *Japanese Women*, 44–45.

10. Brian J. McVeigh, *Life in a Japanese Women's College: Learning to Be Ladylike* (London: Routledge, 1997), 83.

11. McVeigh, *Life in a Japanese Women's College*, 83.

12. Aihara, *Kyoto hanamachi motenashi no gijutsu*, 161. For more on the concept of shugyō, see Maki Isaka, "Box-Lunch Etiquette: Conduct Guides and Kabuki *Onnagata*" in *Manners and Mischief: Gender, Power, and Etiquette in Japan*, ed. Jan Bardsley and Laura Miller (Berkeley: University of California Press, 2011), 48–66.

13. Dunn, "Bowing Incorrectly," 17.

14. Dunn, "Bowing Incorrectly," 17 (emphasis in original).

15. Foreman, "The Perfect Woman," 67–68.

16. Yoshimura Kaoru observes that non-Kyoto girls agonize over learning hanamachi dialect. Taniguchi, *Gion, uttoko no hanashi*, 15.

17. Dalby, "Preface to the 25th Anniversary Edition," *Geisha*, 2008, xxii–xxiii.

18. Aihara, *Kyoto maiko to geiko no okuzashiki*, 38.

19. Nishio, *Kyoto hanamachi no keieigaku*, 54; "Chapter 2: Geiko, Maiko, Ochaya, and Okiya," 29.

20. Komomo and Ogino, *A Geisha's Journey*, 56 .

21. Iwasaki and Brown, *Geisha, a Life*, 77–78.

22. Aihara, *Kyoto hanamachi motenashi no gijutsu*, 143.

23. See Dalby, *Geisha*, ch. 3, 15–47; Nishio, *Kyoto hanamachi no keieigaku*, 59–62; "Chapter 2: Geiko, Maiko, Ochaya, and Okiya," 31–33.

24. Aihara, *Kyoto hanamachi motenashi no gijutsu*, 178.

25. Aihara, *Kyoto hanamachi motenashi no gijutsu*, 183.

26. Aihara, *Kyoto hanamachi motenashi no gijutsu*, 167.

27. Hamasaki Kanako and Ōta Tōru, "Hanamachi o sasaeru mono to waza" [Things and arts that support the hanamachi], in Ōta and Hiratake, eds., *Kyō no kagai*, 157; John Paul Foster, *Now a Geisha* (Tokyo: IBC Publishing, 2017), 177–78.

28. Hamasaki and Ōta, "Hanamachi o sasaeru mono to waza" 158–59.

29. Arai, *Gion Mameji*, 29–30.

30. Iwasaki and Brown, *Geisha, a Life*, 80.

31. Koyama Aiko, *Maiko-san-chi no Makanai-san* [Miss Cook for the maiko girls] (Serialized girls' comic) (Tokyo: Shōgakukan, 2018), vol. 6, episodes 58, 71.

32. Aihara, *Kyoto hanamachi motenashi no gijutsu*, 180.

33. In 2022, the age of adulthood will change to eighteen in Japan, although alcohol, smoking, and gambling privileges remain reserved until turning twenty. Tomohiro Osaki, "Japan's Diet OKs law lowering age of adulthood to 18," *Japan Times*, June 13, 2018, https://www.japantimes.co.jp/news/2018/06/13/national/crime-legal/japan -enacts-law-lower-adulthood-age-18/#.XLGT-OgzYuU (accessed May 23, 2020).

34. Koito, "Foreword," in Komomo and Ogino, *A Geisha's Journey*, 7.

35. Komomo and Ogino, *A Geisha's Journey*, 13.

36. Komomo and Ogino, *A Geisha's Journey*, 19.

37. Aihara, *Kyoto hanamachi motenashi no gijutsu*, 172.

38. Aihara, *Kyoto hanamachi: Maiko to geiko no uchiake-banashi*, 49.

39. Aihara, *Kyoto hanamachi: Maiko to geiko no uchiake-banashi*, 56.

40. Aihara, *Kyoto hanamachi: Maiko to geiko no uchiake-banashi*, 55–57.

41. Koito, "Foreword," in Komomo and Ogino, *A Geisha's Journey*, 8.

42. Aihara, *Kyoto hanamachi motenashi no gijutsu*, 137.

43. Nishio, *Kyoto hanamachi no keieigaku*, 165; "Chapter 6. The Hanamachi Evaluation System," trans. Jacqueline Kaminski, *The Japanese Economy*, 37, no. 4 (Winter 2010–11): 84.

44. With the exception of Nishio's descriptions of active maiko and geiko bringing in equal income from ozashiki. See below, note 93. The difference is that all the maiko's income, except for tips from customers, goes to her okiya.

45. Aihara, *Kyoto maiko to geiko no okuzashiki*, 48.

46. Aihara, *Kyoto hanamachi motenashi no gijutsu*, 141–43.

47. Nishio, *Maiko no kotoba*, 27 .

48. Nishio, *Maiko no kotoba*, 14.

49. Komomo and Ogino, *A Geisha's Journey*,19.

50. Komomo and Ogino, *A Geisha's Journey*, 20.

51. Arai, *Gion Mameji*, 210.

52. Komomo and Ogino, *A Geisha's Journey*, 24.

53. Komomo and Ogino, *A Geisha's Journey*, 22.

54. Nishio, *Maiko no kotoba*, 37.

55. Nishio, *Maiko no kotoba*, 43.

56. Ogino and Komomo, *A Geisha's Journey*, 35.

57. For *misedashi*, books consulted for this study use the characters for "store opening," meaning that the maiko can now be hired. However, Nishio explains that during the course of her research, she observed the characters for "showing the face," also pronounced misedashi, used in the hanamachi for the maiko's debut. This usage also avoids the sense of the maiko as commodified. *Kyoto hanamachi no keieigaku*, 94; "Chapter 4: The Life of a Maiko," trans. Jacqueline Kaminski, *The Japanese Economy*, 37, no. 4 (Winter 2010–11): 60n2. (Nishio does not number the footnotes in the Japanese version; Kaminski does in her translation.)

58. Dalby, "Geisha in the Twenty-First Century." Preface to the 25th Anniversary Edition," *Geisha*, 2008, xxiii.

59. Komomo and Ogino, *A Geisha's Journey*, 24.

60. Arai, *Gion Mameji*, 35.

61. Mizoguchi Kenji, dir., *Gion bayashi* (*A Geisha*), Daiei, 1953; Suo Masayuki, dir., *Maiko wa redi* (*Lady Maiko*), Toho, 2014.

62. Komomo and Ogino, *A Geisha's Journey*, 34.

63. Nishio, *Maiko no kotoba*, 92.

64. Hiratake and Hamasaki, "Hanamachi wa ima," 32.

65. Arai, *Gion Mameji*, 87.

66. Arai, *Gion Mameji*, 88.

67. Nishio, *Maiko no kotoba*, 62.

68. Aihara, *Kyoto hanamachi motenashi no gijutsu*, 145.

69. Komomo and Ogino, *A Geisha's Journey*, 46.

70. Nishio, *Maiko no kotoba*, 132.

71. Nishio, *Maiko no kotoba*, 127–28.

72. Nishio, *Maiko no kotoba*, 131.

73. Nishio, *Kyoto hanamachi no keieigaku*, 98; "Chapter 4: The Life of a Maiko," 51.

74. Hiratake and Hamasaki, "Hanamachi wa ima," 27.

75. Aihara, *Kyoto maiko to geiko no okuzashiki*, 72.

76. Hiratake and Hamasaki, "Hanamachi wa ima," 28n19.

77. Changes in the maiko's collars mark her progress in the apprenticeship. Initially, she will wear a red silk collar embroidered with white and metallic thread. As time passes, "the appliqué becomes heavier until little red (a symbol of childhood) can be seen." Iwasaki, *Geisha, a Life*, 153.

78. Nishio, *Maiko no kotoba*, 142. In her translation of *Kyoto hanamachi no keieigaku*, 96, Kaminski romanizes Nishio's expression for "turning the collar" as *erigae* "Chapter 4: The Life of a Maiko," 50. I find *erikae* the common usage; Aihara, Dalby, and Iwasaki all use *erikae* in their English publications.

79. Ogino and Komomo, *A Geisha's Journey*, 104.

80. Aihara, *Kyoto maiko to geiko no okuzashiki*, 61.

81. Foster, *Now a Geisha*, 8.

82. Prior to their erikae transition to becoming geiko, maiko follow different costuming, makeup rituals, and dance practices depending on the customs of their hanamachi. See Komomo and Ogino, *A Geisha's Journey*, 94–101, for Komomo's preparations.

83. Komomo and Ogino, *A Geisha's Journey*, 104.

84. Nishio, *Maiko no kotoba*, 143.

85. Liza Dalby, *Kimono: Fashioning Culture* (Seattle: University of Washington Press, 1993, 2001), 325.

86. Hiratake and Hamasaki, "Hanamachi wa ima," 35.

87. Nishio, *Kyoto hanamachi no keieigaku*, 30. "Chapter 1: The Kyoto Hanamachi," 15.

88. Ogino and Komomo, *A Geisha's Journey*, 107.

89. Aihara, *Kyoto maiko to geiko no okuzashiki*, 63–65.

90. Arai, *Gion Mameji*, 69.

91. Aihara, *Kyoto maiko to geiko no okuzashiki*, 63.

92. Hiratake and Hamasaki, "Hanamachi wa ima," 33.

93. Kiriki, *Aisare jōzu ni naru Gion-ryū*, 89.

94. Hiratake and Hamasaki, "Hanamachi wa ima," 36. Foreman, "Bad Girls Confined," 34.

95. Hiratake and Hamasaki, "Hanamachi wa ima," 33.

96. In contrast to jikata (seated one), geiko, as dancers, are tachikata (standing ones). For more nuanced discussion of these terms, see Foreman, *Gei of Geisha*, 78.

97. Kiriki, *Aisare jōzu ni naru Gion-ryū: Onna migaki*, 95.

98. Hiratake and Hamasaki, "Hanamachi wa ima," 28.

99. Gion website: http://miyako-odori.jp/jikata/ and Pontochō website: https://www.kamogawa-odori.com/recruit/ (accessed May 23, 2020).

100. Foreman, "The Perfect Woman," 67.

CHAPTER 3. LIFE IN THE HANAMACHI

1. Yamaguchi Kimijo, *Suppin geiko: Kyoto Gion no ukkari nikki* [Bare-faced geiko: My haphazard diary of Gion, Kyoto] (Tokyo: LOCUS, 2007), 69.

2. Yamaguchi, *Suppin geiko*, 68–69.

3. An early example of a geisha autobiography is Ishii Miyo's 1916, *Geisha to machiai* [Geisha and teahouses], reprinted in Kōra Rumiko and Iwami Teruyo, eds., *Josei no mita kindai* [Modernity as seen by women] *Onna to rōdō* [Women and labor], vol. 21 (Tokyo: Yumani Shobō, 2004). Describing her Shinbashi teahouse life in Tokyo, Ishii rebuffs Japanese ladies' disparagement of geisha, observing how Western ladies enjoy talking with them on visits to Japan. Similarly, in 1957, Masuda Sayo describes stigmatization as a former geisha. Masuda, *Autobiography of a Geisha*.

4. From 2001 through 2018, several books by geiko, former geiko, and Kyoto teahouse managers appeared in Japanese, including two in English translation, that gave voice to the experiences of maiko and geiko. The most prolific, retired Gion geiko Mineko Iwasaki, collaborated with Rande Brown on *Geisha, a Life*, based on her 2001 autobiography in Japanese, revealing her maiko-geiko life in the late 1960s and 1970s (see chapter 4). Photographer Naoyuki Ogino collaborated with geiko Komomo, creating the 2008 photo essay *A Geisha's Journey*, and in Japanese, *Komomo* (see chapter 2). In 2015 and 2018 respectively, books about the careers of hanamachi elders—okiya manager and former geiko Arai Mameji, and teahouse manager Yoshimura Kaoru—gave views of maiko life in the 1960s and the 2000s (see chapters 1 and 2).

5. See Mary C. Brinton, *Women and the Economic Miracle: Gender and Work in Postwar Japan* (Berkeley: University of California Press, 1993).

6. I use the term "personal accounts" in categorizing these books to allow for the varied formats: Kiriki's is an autobiographical lifestyle guide; Yamaguchi's offers humor; and Ichimame's guide to maiko etiquette is also a recruiting tool. For concise discussion of reading strategies for postwar Japanese women's autobiographies, see Ronald P. Loftus, *Changing Lives: The "Postwar" in Japanese Women's Autobiographies and Memoirs* (Ann Arbor, MI: Association for Asian Studies, 2013), 3–5. Through discussion and partial translation of several memoirs, *Changing Lives* sheds light on women's experiences of postwar Japan in varied walks of life.

7. Kiriki, *Aisare jōzu ni naru Gion-ryū*, 174

8. See Jan Bardsley, "Transbeauty IKKO: A Diva's Guide to Glamour, Virtue, and Healing," in *Diva Nation: Female Icons from Japanese Cultural History*, ed. Laura Miller and Rebecca Copeland. (Berkeley: University of California Press, 2018), 133–50.

9. Kiriki's *Aisare jōzu ni naru Gion-ryū* parallels the language and femininity advice in the best-selling lifestyle guide for women, Bandō Mariko's *Josei no hinkaku* [The

Dignity of the woman] (Tokyo: PHP Shinsho, 2006). Born in 1946, Bandō built a stellar career, serving as consul general of Japan in Brisbane, Australia, the first woman to hold such a post, the first director general of the Japanese Cabinet Office's Gender Equality Bureau, and president of Showa Women's University. Much like Kiriki, Bandō emphasizes deploying femininity as the way to get ahead. She, too, stresses "lovability," also advising women to concentrate on showing love to receive love. Although readers likely were not surprised by a former geiko promoting lovability, superwoman Bandō's readers were "irritated to find that this art of "lovability" [was] presented as a matter of feminine virtue, rather than as a strategy for surviving discriminatory conditions." Hiroko Hirakawa, "The Dignified Woman Who Loves to Be 'Loveable,'" in *Manners and Mischief: Gender, Power, and Etiquette in Japan*, ed. Jan Bardsley and Laura Miller (Berkeley: University of California Press, 2011), 137.

10. Kiriki, *Aisare jōzu ni naru Gion-ryū*, 21 . Laura Miller also found *mai pēsu* used to identify new personality types in late twentieth-century Japanese women's magazines, explaining how such new typologies may enable readers more freedom in reflecting on their own life choices. Laura Miller, "People Types: Personality Classification in Japanese Women's Magazines." *Journal of Popular Culture* 31, no. 2 (1997): 153; 156–57.

11. Kiriki, *Aisare jōzu ni naru Gion-ryū*, 88.

12. See Julia C. Bullock, *Coeds Ruining the Nation: Women, Education, and Social Change in Postwar Japanese Media* (Ann Arbor: University of Michigan Press, 2019).

13. MEXT (Ministry of Education, Culture, Sports, Science, and Technology) report, *Gakkō kihon chōsa* [Basic survey on schools], https://www.mext.go.jp/b_menu/toukei/chousa01/kihon/1267995.htm (accessed May 15, 2020).

14. Kiriki, *Aisare jōzu ni naru Gion-ryū*, 212.

15. Kiriki, *Aisare jōzu ni naru Gion-ryū*, 217, 219.

16. Hiratake and Hamasaki, "Hanamachi wa ima," 34–35.

17. Kiriki, *Aisare jōzu ni naru Gion-ryū*, 6.

18. Kiriki, *Aisare jōzu ni naru Gion-ryū*, 17.

19. Kiriki, *Aisare jōzu ni naru Gion-ryū*, 18.

20. According to her website, Kiriki presented a paper comparing geiko and Korean kisaeng at a comparative literature conference at Kyushu University in 2008, and in 2010, collaborated with Kyoto University professor Maruhashi Yoshio to publish another paper. She notes that this was the first academic publication based on the experience of a geiko. http://c-kiriki.com/index.html (accessed May 24, 2020).

21. Kiriki, *Aisare jōzu ni naru Gion-ryū*, 210.

22. Kiriki, *Aisare jōzu ni naru Gion-ryū*.

23. Kiriki, *Aisare jōzu ni naru Gion-ryū*, 76, 224–25.

24. Kiriki, *Aisare jōzu ni naru Gion-ryū*, 220, 223.

25. Kiriki, *Aisare jōzu ni naru Gion-ryū*. 223

26. Kiriki, *Aisare jōzu ni naru Gion-ryū*.

27. Kiriki, *Aisare jōzu ni naru Gion-ryū*.

28. Kiriki, *Aisare jōzu ni naru Gion-ryū*, 122–25.

29. *Tokushū: Gion* [Special issue on Gion], *Taiyō* [*The Sun*] (June 1972): 51, 86–87.

30. Kiriki, *Aisare jōzu ni naru Gion-ryū*, 220. Kiriki notes that she was twenty-two at the time of the 1975 PARCO poster sensation, but she must have been about twenty-four.

31. Kiriki, *Aisare jōzu ni naru Gion-ryū*, 221.

32. Kiriki, *Aisare jōzu ni naru Gion-ryū*, 221–22.

33. Kiriki, *Aisare jōzu ni naru Gion-ryū*, 11.

34. Kiriki, *Aisare jōzu ni naru Gion-ryū*,10.

35. Kiriki, *Aisare jōzu ni naru Gion-ryū*, 94.

36. Kiriki, *Aisare jōzu ni naru Gion-ryū*, 28.

37. Kiriki, *Aisare jōzu ni naru Gion-ryū*.

38. Kiriki, *Aisare jōzu ni naru Gion-ryū*, 220.

39. Geisha must pass rigorous exams to earn the natori, that is, "taking the name" of their respective dance school. Foreman explains that the natori "firmly establishes a performer's position as an official member of that performing tradition." She notes that geisha typically have several natori, since they gain proficiency in multiple arts (Foreman, *Gei of Geisha*, 76).

40. Kiriki, *Aisare jōzu ni naru Gion-ryū*, 184–85.

41. Kiriki, *Aisare jōzu ni naru Gion-ryū*.

42. Kiriki, *Aisare jōzu ni naru Gion-ryū*, 185.

43. Kiriki, *Aisare jōzu ni naru Gion-ryū*.

44. Kiriki, *Aisare jōzu ni naru Gion-ryū*, 185–87.

45. Kiriki, *Aisare jōzu ni naru Gion-ryū*, 233.

46. For historical context on women's ikebana careers, see Stalker, "Flower Power."

47. Kiriki, *Aisare jōzu ni naru Gion-ryū*, 236.

48. Kiriki, *Aisare jōzu ni naru Gion-ryū*.

49. Kiriki, *Aisare jōzu ni naru Gion-ryū*, 241.

50. Kiriki Chizu's website and blog are lavish with color photos. http://www.c-kiriki.com/ (accessed May 18, 2020).

51. For Japanese women's embrace of Korean popular culture, see Bardsley, "Transbeauty IKKO," 143–45.

52. Kiriki, *Aisare jōzu ni naru Gion-ryū*, 30.

53. Kiriki, *Aisare jōzu ni naru Gion-ryū*, 30–31.

54. MEXT report, *Gakkō kihon chōsa* data cited note 13.

55. Mary C. Brinton, *Lost in Transition: Youth, Work, and Instability in Postindustrial Japan* (Cambridge: Cambridge University Press, 2011). See chapter one, "The Lost Generation."

56. Nishio, *Kyoto hanamachi no keieigaku*, 26; "Chapter 1. The Kyoto Hanamachi," 13.

57. I thank Kimijo's sister Yamaguchi Yukiko, who collaborated in the writing of *Suppin geiko*, for meeting with me in Tokyo on June 12, 2019, to discuss the book and her permission to cite this conversation.

58. Mikiko Ashikari, "Urban Middle-Class Japanese Women and Their White Faces: Gender, Ideology, and Representation," *Ethos* 31, no. 1 (2003): 5.

59. Yamaguchi, *Suppin geiko*, 73.

60. Yamaguchi, *Suppin geiko*, 89–90.

61. Yamaguchi, *Suppin geiko*, 143–44.

62. Yamaguchi, *Suppin geiko*, 4. Popularized throughout Japan in the mid-twentieth century, Shichigosan is a mid-November Shinto festival that marks a rite of passage for children ages seven (*shichi*), five (*go*), and three (*san*), with most attention centered on girls at three and seven, and boys at age five. Melinda Papp, *Shichigosan: Change and Continuity of a Family Ritual in Contemporary Urban Japan* (New York: Palgrave Macmillan, 2016), 1–2.

63. Yamaguchi, *Suppin geiko*, 4

64. Yamaguchi, *Suppin geiko*, 4.

65. Yamaguchi, *Suppin geiko*, 4.

66. Yamaguchi, *Suppin geiko*, 6.

67. Yamaguchi, *Suppin geiko*, 5.

68. Yamaguchi, *Suppin geiko*, 96.

69. Yamaguchi, *Suppin geiko*, 6 (emphasis in the original).

70. Yamaguchi, *Suppin geiko*, 10.

71. Yamaguchi, *Suppin geiko*, 10.

72. Yamaguchi, *Suppin geiko*, 96.

73. Yamaguchi, *Suppin geiko*, 96.

74. Yamaguchi, *Suppin geiko*, 97–98.

75. Yamaguchi, *Suppin geiko*, 98.

76. Yamaguchi, *Suppin geiko*, 83.

77. Yamaguchi, *Suppin geiko*, 52.

78. Yamaguchi, *Suppin geiko*, 84

79. Yamaguchi, *Suppin geiko*, 19.

80. Yamaguchi, *Suppin geiko*, 158.

81. Yamaguchi, *Suppin geiko*, 12–13.

82. Yamaguchi, *Suppin geiko*, 13.

83. Yamaguchi, *Suppin geiko*, 92.

84. Yamaguchi, *Suppin geiko*, 65.

85. Yamaguchi, *Suppin geiko*, 93.

86. Yamaguchi, *Suppin geiko*, 93–94.

87. Yamaguchi, *Suppin geiko*, 87.

88. Yamaguchi, *Suppin geiko*, 87.

89. Yamaguchi, *Suppin geiko*, 88.

90. Yamaguchi, *Suppin geiko*, 88.

91. Yamaguchi, *Suppin geiko*, 88.

92. Yamaguchi, *Suppin geiko*, 36–37.

93. Yamaguchi, *Suppin geiko*, 100.

94. Yamaguchi, *Suppin geiko*, 150.

95. Galbraith and Karlin, *AKB48*, 57.

96. Nishio, *Kyoto hanamachi no keieigaku*, 26; "Chapter 1. The Kyoto Hana-machi," 13.

97. Kamishichiken Ichimame, *Maiko no osahō* [Maiko etiquette] (Tokyo: Daiwa Shobō, 2007). This passage appears on an unnumbered page in the Introduction.

98. Ichimame's book displays a screen shot of her blog and gives its address on page 26, but the site is no longer maintained.

99. Ichimame, *Maiko no osahō*, 25.

100. Posted on February 1, 2007, on the website, ThingsAsian, AFP correspondent Daniel Rook's interview with Ichimame mentions her blog. Ichimame explains that the Ichi teahouse encouraged her to keep the blog; a son in the Ichi family, whom she refers to as "older brother," took photos for the blog and helped her with it. See http://thingsasian.com/story/ichimame-apprentice-geisha (accessed May 15, 2020).

101. Ichimame, *Maiko no osahō*, author profile, unnumbered page.

102. The website Giappone in Italia is maintained by the Associazione Culturale. Francesca Gambera posted "Maiko Ichimame" describing Ichimame's 2008 maiko blog on January 11, 2011. https://www.giapponeinitalia.org/?s=Ichimame (accessed May 15, 2020).

103. Ichimame, *Maiko no osahō*, 44.

104. Ichimame, *Maiko no osahō*, 98.

105. Ichimame, *Maiko no osahō*, 124.

106. Ichimame, *Maiko no osahō*, 6.

107. Ichimame, *Maiko no osahō*, 6.

108. Ichimame, *Maiko no osahō*, 8.

109. Ichimame, *Maiko no osahō*, 34.

110. Ichimame, *Maiko no osahō*, 30, 32.

111. Ichimame, *Maiko no osahō*, 32.

112. Ichimame, *Maiko no osahō*, 31, 33.

113. Ichimame, *Maiko no osahō*, 20.

114. Ichimame, *Maiko no osahō*, 53.

115. Ichimame, *Maiko no osahō*, 40.

116. Ichimame, *Maiko no osahō*, 109.

117. Ichimame, *Maiko no osahō*, 68.

118. Ichimame, *Maiko no osahō*, 72.

119. Ichimame, *Maiko no osahō*, 42.

120. Ichimame, *Maiko no osahō*, foreword, unnumbered page.

121. Ichimame, *Maiko no osahō*, 36.

122. Ichimame, *Maiko no osahō*, 90.

123. Ichimame, *Maiko no osahō*, 90–92.

124. Ichimame, *Maiko no osahō*, 92.

125. Ichimame, *Maiko no osahō*, 94–95.

126. Ichimame, *Maiko no osahō*, 94.

127. Ichimame, *Maiko no osahō*, 88.
128. Ichimame, *Maiko no osahō*, 94.
129. Ichimame, *Maiko no osahō*, 101.
130. Ichimame, *Maiko no osahō*, 108.
131. Ichimame, *Maiko no osahō*, 27.

CHAPTER 4. FROM VICTIM TO ARTIST

1. Based on a 1934 novel by Nagata Mikihiko, Mizoguchi's *Gion bayashi* earned critical acclaim in Japan and internationally. The film title is also translated as "Gion festival music." *Janken Musume* was released in the United States as *So Young, So Bright* in 1963. Sugie Toshio, *Janken musume*, Toho, 1955.

2. Aoki Shin'ya, prod., *Dandan* (Japan: NHK-TV, 2008–09). Moriwaki Kyōko wrote the script.

3. Catherine Russell, *Classical Japanese Cinema Revisited* (London: Bloomsbury, 2011), 59.

4. Yoshii Isamu, "*Gion bayashi* o mite" [Watching *Gion bayashi*], in *Kyō no uta goyomi* [Seasonal poems of the old capital] (Tokyo: Daviddosha, 1957), 102–5; Noborikawa Naoki, "*Gion bayashi*," *Kinema junpō* 72 (1953): 56–57; Matsuura Hisaki, "Ōga to kenryoku: Mizoguchi Kenji, *Gion bayashi*" [Reclining and Power: Mizoguchi Kenji, *Gion bayashi*], *Shineteikku* 1 (1993): 120–44; Sugiyama Hei'ichi, "*Gion bayashi*," *Eiga hyōron* 10 (1953): 76–78.

5. Aihara, *Kyoto maiko to geiko no okuzashiki*, 16–17.

6. Keiko I. McDonald, *Reading a Japanese Film: Cinema in Context* (Honolulu: University of Hawai'i Press, 2006), 31.

7. Reading the cinematic strategies employed in this scene, McDonald finds that Mizoguchi "was afraid to take a firmly objective view of the sisters' plight" (*Reading a Japanese Film*, 32). Peter M. Grilli, however, sees the ending as a powerful indictment, "Through Omocha's passionate outcry at the end of this film, Mizoguchi protests not only the specific plight of a geisha, but also the repression of all women everywhere." Grilli, "Geisha on Stage and Screen," in Peabody Essex Museum, *Geisha: Beyond the Painted Smile*, 145. Mizoguchi, *Gion shimai* [Sisters of the Gion] (Daiichi Eiga, 1936).

8. Julia C. Bullock, "Beauvoir in Japan: Tracing the Impact of *The Second Sex* on Japanese Women," Keynote speech. Institute for Gender Studies, Ochanomizu University, May 19, 2019.

9. Wakao Ayako played the lead maiko role the following year in the lesser-known film *Maiko monogatari* [Tale of a maiko, 1954], directed by Yasuda Kimiyoshi. Quitting music school in Tokyo and becoming a maiko to help pay the medical expenses of her dying geiko mother, Tomeko falls victim to others' greed and sexual license. Like Eiko in *A Geisha*, she has no father to save her. A vampirish scene shows her prospective danna kneeling at the sleeping Tomeko's bed, about to take his prey, when he suddenly realizes that she has ingested an overdose of medicine to kill herself. Luckily, after Tomeko is rushed to the hospital, a handsome young doctor saves her and marries her

to boot. Although the film recognizes Tomeko's maiko transformation as visually splendid, the narrative shows her happiest in street clothes, wearing a trendy pinafore, her hair in a ponytail. *Maiko monogatari* does not extend to broad critique about maiko exploitation but does support the new era's idealization of love marriage.

10. Grilli, "Geisha on Stage and Screen," 145.

11. For more on this aspect of occupation culture, see Shibusawa, *America's Geisha Ally.*

12. Russell, *Classical Japanese Cinema Revisited*, 53.

13. Sarah Kovner, *Occupying Power: Sex Workers and Servicemen in Postwar Japan* (Stanford, CA: Stanford University Press, 2012), 16.

14. Norma, *Comfort Women and Post-occupation Japan*, 86.

15. Tanaka Chiyoko, "Wakao Ayako: Jisen 11 sakuhin, kaisetsu" [Wakao Ayako: Her eleven recommended works, an interpretation]," in *Joyū: Wakao Ayako* [Actress: Ayako Wakao], ed. Harada Masaaki and Aoki Shin'ya (Tokyo: Kinema Junpōsha, 2012), 7.

16. See Ellen V. Fuller, *Going Global: Culture, Gender, and Authority in the Japanese Subsidiary of an American Corporation* (Philadelphia: Temple University Press, 2009), 45–47.

17. Russell, *Classical Japanese Cinema Revisited*, 54.

18. Jim Hillier and Douglas Pye, *100 Film Musicals* (London: Palgrave Macmillan, 2011), 113–14; Stuart Galbraith IV, *The Toho Studios Story: A History and Complete Filmography* (Lanham, MD: Scarecrow Press, 2008), 115.

19. Deborah Shamoon, *Passionate Friendship: The Aesthetics of Girls' Culture in Japan.* (Honolulu: University of Hawai'i Press, 2012), 91.

20. It is unclear whether Ruri's mother Onobu was a Kyoto geiko or Tokyo geisha. Since she uses the term *geisha* in her speech to Kamezawa, I refer to Onobu as a former geisha. Actress Naniwa Chieko played both *Janken Musume*'s Onobu and *Gion Bayashi*'s Okimi.

21. Irene González-López, "Marketing the *Panpan* in Japanese Popular Culture: Youth, Sexuality, and Power," *U.S.-Japan Women's Journal* 54 (2018), 32–33; Michael J. Raine, "Youth, Body, and Subjectivity in Japanese Cinema, 1955–1960." PhD diss., University of Iowa, 2002.

22. Shamoon, *Passionate Friendship*, 91–92.

23. Onobu's suggestion that middle-class women learn from geisha echoes advice found in 1920s women's magazines as analyzed in Aiko Tanaka, "'Don't Let *Geisha* Steal Your Husband': The Reconstruction of the Housewife in Interwar Japan," *U.S.-Japan Women's Journal* 40 (2011): 122–46.

24. Shamoon explains that the father's decision to adopt Ruri offers narrative closure in the film and notes that 1950s narratives about children with missing or deceased parents were common. *Passionate Friendship*, 92.

25. Reviews of *Gion bayashi* (cited above in note 3) do not call attention to the plight of maiko nor dispute expectations for their sexual servitude. Reviews located for *Janken musume* analyze the film as a musical, focusing on the three leads' talents; they do not

discuss the maiko's situation: Okada Kiichirō, *Showa kayō eigakan* [Showa popular song films] (Tokyo: Chūkō Shinsho, 2009), 144–48; "Ninki sutā: Jūhachi musume ga sannin yoreba" [Popular stars: The eighteen-year-old three girls], *Shūkan Yomiuri* (November 1955): 26–29; Izawa Jun, "Nihon eiga hihyō" [Japanese film review]. *Kinema junpō* 132 (1955): 89.

26. Shindō Kaneto, dir., *Aru eiga-kantoku no shōgai* [Kenji Mizoguchi: The life of a film director] (Criterion Collection, 1975).

27. "Miyamoto Maki," *Kinema junpō* 1275 (1999): 18–19; 94–99.

28. *Kurenai niou* was initially serialized in 2003–07 in the bimonthly girls manga magazine *BE LOVE*. In 2004, Kōdansha Comic released the manga as a four-volume series. In 2009, Kōdansha reprinted the manga in three volumes for its Kōdansha Manga Bunko Series. I cite the 2009 version here. Iwasaki Mineko's *Geiko Mineko no hana-ikusa* was later translated as *Geisha, a Life*.

29. *Kurenai niou*, an expression used in the ancient poetry collection, *Manyōshū*, can also refer to dyeing something red, perhaps used here to imply Sakuya's deepening maturity and sensuality.

30. For more on the Year 24 Group and the history and production of girls' comics, see Jennifer S. Prough, *Straight from the Heart: Gender, Intimacy, and the Cultural Production of Shōjo Manga*. Honolulu: University of Hawai'i Press, 2011.

31. For analysis of Yamato Waki's manga of *Tale of Genji*, see Akiko Hirota, "The Tale of Genji: From Heian Classic to Heisei Comic," *Journal of Popular Culture* 31, no. 2 (1997): 29–68, and Haruo Shirane, ed., *Envisioning "The Tale of Genji": Media, Gender, and Cultural Production* (New York: Columbia University Press, 2008), 334–40.

32. Alisa Freedman, "Romance of the Taishō Schoolgirl in Shōjo Manga: Here Comes Miss Modern," in *Shōjo across Media: Exploring 'Girl' Practices in Contemporary Japan*, ed. Jaqueline Berndt, Kazumi Nagaike, and Fusami Ogi (New York: Palgrave MacMillan, 2019), 33.

33. "Supesyaru tōku" [Special talk], a conversation between Yamato and Iwasaki appended to *Kurenai niou*, 2009 edition, volume 3, unnumbered page.

34. Shamoon identifies "interior monologue, open frames, layering, symbolic imagery, and emotive backgrounds" as comprising "the visual grammar of the shōjo manga." *Passionate Friendship*, 114.

35. Iwasaki, *Geisha, a Life*, 281.

36. Yamato, *Kurenai niou*, volume 3, "Saishū hanashi" (Final episode), unnumbered pages.

37. Yamato, *Kurenai niou*, volume 2, episode 7, unnumbered page.

38. Yamato, *Kurenai niou*, volume 2, episode 7.

39. In *Geisha, a Life*, Iwasaki relates this demand to her suitor, entertainer Katsu Shintarō (1931–97) to an ancient tale. Legendary Heian poet Ono no Komachi demanded Officer Fukakusa visit her for one hundred consecutive nights "before she would give him her hand." Iwasaki does not mention that the strain killed Fukakusa, who died on the ninety-ninth night. Iwasaki, *Geisha, a Life*, 226.

40. Yamato, *Kurenai niou*, volume 2, episode 15, unnumbered page.

41. Yamato, *Kurenai niou*, volume 1, episode 1, unnumbered page.

42. Yamato *Kurenai niou*, volume 2, episode 8, unnumbered page.

43. Yamato, *Kurenai niou*, volume 2, episode 10, unnumbered page.

44. Yamato, *Kurenai niou*, volume 1, episode 1, unnumbered page.

45. Yamato, *Kurenai niou*, volume 3, episode 12, unnumbered page.

46. Yamato, *Kurenai niou*, volume 3, episode 13, unnumbered page.

47. Yamato, *Kurenai niou*, volume 1, episode 4, unnumbered page.

48. Yamato, *Kurenai niou*, volume 1, episode 4, unnumbered page.

49. Iwasaki, *Geisha, a Life*, 276–77.

50. Yamato, *Kurenai niou*, volume 3, Final Episode, unnumbered page.

51. Yamato, *Kurenai niou*, volume 3, Final Episode, unnumbered page.

52. Yamato, *Kurenai niou*, volume 3, Final Episode, unnumbered page.

53. NHK (Nippon Hōsō Kyōkai) is Japan's national broadcasting organization. Several excellent articles in English analyze the NHK-TV morning drama, its history, goals, format, and notable series. See, for two examples, Christine R. Yano, "Gazing upon Sakura: Imaging Japanese Americans on Japanese TV," in *Gender and Globalization in Asia and the Pacific: Method, Practice, Theory*, ed. Kathy Ferguson and Monique Mironesco (Honolulu: University of Hawaiʻi Press, 2008), 101–20, and Paul A. S. Harvey, "Interpreting Oshin: War, History and Women in Modern Japan," in *Women, Media and Consumption in Japan*, ed. Lise Skov and Brian Moeran (Honolulu: University of Hawaiʻi Press, 1995), 75–110.

54. *Dandan*, episode 7.

55. *Dandan*, episode 66.

56. *Dandan*, episode 109.

57. *Dandan*, episode 37.

58. *Dandan*, episodes 106, 108.

59. Anne Allison, *Precarious Japan* (Durham, NC: Duke University Press, 2013), 40.

60. *Maiko-san-chi no Makanai-san* originally appeared in Shōgakukan's comic magazine *Shūkan Shōnen Sandei* (Weekly Youth Sunday) in December 2016, an unusual placement for a manga about girls since this publication features comics for boys. In April 2017, Shōgakukan also began publishing the series in book form (*tankōbon*). I found the tankōbon versions shelved in bookstores in the girls' comics section, but the series won Shōgakukan's sixty-fifth award in 2019 for excellence in the division of manga aimed to boys. I cite the tankōbon version here.

61. The volume 13 book jacket (2020) announces that the series "broke one million" readers. NHK announced its upcoming animated version on March 31, 2020. https://www6.nhk.or.jp/anime/special/special.html?i=8132 (accessed May 27, 2020).

62. Koyama, *Maiko-san-chi no Makanai-san*, vol. 2, episode 11, page 30.

63. Koyama divulges little about herself other than that she is an Aomori native who grew up in Yokohama. She has authored two other successful Shōgakukan manga series, one about middle-school students in sports, *Ping Pong Rush* (2009–10), and *Chirori* (2011–15), a beautifully drawn comic about a young woman working in a coffee shop in the late Meiji era.

64. Comment on the "calming" nature of volume 5 posted by deepest puddle, August 10, 2018, and "soothing" aspect by Reimy, May 9, 2018. Reader comments' site https://www.amazon.co.jp, (accessed May 1, 2020).

65. Food manga constitute a genre in themselves, as discussed in Lorie Brau, "*Oishinbo*'s Adventures in Eating: Food, Communication, and Culture in Japanese Comics," *Gastronomica: The Journal for Food Studies* 4, no. 4 (2004): 34–45.

66. Ting explains how writer Fukuda Ricca reads sweets in shōjo manga as fashioning "a space of enjoyment for readers to freely indulge in a world driven by forms of 'feminine' desire." Grace En-Yi Ting, "The Desire and Disgust of Sweets: Consuming Femininities through *Shōjo* Manga," *U.S.-Japan Women's Journal* 54 (2018): 62.

67. Koyama, *Maiko-san-chi no Makanai-san*, volume 3, episode 27, 92–93.

68. Koyama, *Maiko-san-chi no Makanai-san*, volume 5, episode 50, 103–13.

69. Koyama, *Maiko-san-chi no Makanai-san*, volume 6, Episode 58, 71.

70. Koyama, *Maiko-san-chi no Makanai-san*, volume 6, Episode 58, 74.

71. Following Laura Miller's argument that her scripted persona shielded the vulnerability of the elevator girl, we may also see Sū-chan's unshakable poise as a similar strategy, though Koyama makes no comment on this. Miller, "Elevator Girls," 64–65, as discussed in the introduction.

72. Koyama, *Maiko-san-chi no Makanai-san*, volume 5, episode 42, 13.

73. Koyama, *Maiko-san-chi no Makanai-san*, volume 5, episode 43, 26.

74. Koyama, *Maiko-san-chi no Makanai-san*, volume 5, episode 43, 26.

75. For the purposes of this study, I focused only on major films featuring maiko. Other prominent films in the 1950s centered story lines on geisha such as Naruse Mikio's *Bangiku* (*Late Chrysanthemums*, 1954) and *Nagareru* (*Flowing*, 1956). Close study of these and other geiko/geisha and maiko films might elaborate on their representations over time.

CHAPTER 5. ADVENTURES OF A BOY MAIKO

1. Nanami Haruka, *Shōnen maiko: Chiyogiku ga yuku!* [Boy Maiko: There Goes Chiyogiku!], 54 vols. (Tokyo: Shūeisha Cobalt Bunko, 2002–2014). The first volume in the series is numbered 9-3; the last is 9-57; for clarity, I will cite volumes by indicating both their numerical place in the series along with the number designated on the book jacket spine: 9-3 through 9-57. Nanami Haruka is the penname of Yokoyama Yachiyo; she created the name "Chiyogiku" by combining part of her given name with *kiku* (chrysanthemum) As she told me in an interview in Kyoto, May 27, 2017, cited with her permission.

2. See Gion Kōbu Kumiai, Noguchi Masanori, ed., "Gion to bungakusha" [The Gion and literati], *Gion* 226 (2016): 19–26.

3. This exchange on same-sex marriage occurs in a short story within the volume of the same name. Nanami Haruka, "Futari dake no kekkonshiki" [Wedding for only two], in *Futari dake no kekkonshiki, Shōnen maiko: Chiyogiku ga yuku!*, vol. 54 [9-57] (Tokyo: Shūeisha Cobalt Bunko, 2014), 77–78.

4. *Bunkobon* (paperbacks in a series) are packaged in the international paper size A6. *Tankōbon*, in contrast, are considered "stand-alone" books and, while generally larger than bunkobon, they may be printed in a variety of sizes.

5. Nanami includes difficult Chinese characters (*kanji*), adding syllabic characters (*furigana*) to guide readers to their pronunciation.

6. It is the custom in the world of amateur translation of manga and light novels for fan-subs (fans' translations) to be retracted when the publisher puts out an authorized translation.

7. "Shinshun tokushū: Bundan de katsuyaku suru Shimada-bito: Shōsetsuka Yokoyama Yachiyo" [New Year's Special Section: Shimada resident active in the literary world: Novelist Yokoyama Yachiyo], *Shimada Life* 87 (2009): 4.

8. Satomi Saito, "Narrative in the Digital Age: From Light Novels to Web Serials," in *Routledge Handbook of Modern Japanese Literature*, ed. Rachael Hutchinson and Leith Morton (New York: Routledge, 2016), 315. For more on the light novel genre in English, see also Senko K. Maynard, *Fluid Orality in the Discourse of Japanese Popular Culture* (Amsterdam: John Benjamins, 2016).

9. Yamanaka Tomomi charts the number of light novel–related articles in major newspapers and magazine articles, showing attention to the topic in 2004 through 2009, with *Asahi Shimbun* and *Yomiuri Shimbun* exhibiting the highest and most sustained interest overall. Yamanaka Tomomi, *Raito noberu yo, doko e iku? 1980 nendai kara zero nendai made* [The light novel, where will it go? From the 1980s to the 2000s] (Tokyo: Seikyūsha, 2010), 11.

10. Dash-X aimed to provide "front-line entertainment in the form of love & fantasy, school dramas, slapstick and comedy action, and full-scale sci-fi." http://www.shueisha .co.jp/english/books/ (accessed May 20, 2020).

11. In 2011, Cobalt Bunko celebrated its 35th anniversary. http://www.shueisha.co .jp/english/books/ (accessed May 20, 2020).

12. Yamanaka, *Raito noberu yo*, 8.

13. According to Ōhashi Takayuki, these scholarly initiatives led to the influential *Raito noberu kenkyū josetsu* [Introduction to light novel research] edited by Ichiyanagi Hirotaka and Kume Yoriko (Tokyo: Seikyūsha, 2009). Ōhashi, *Raito noberu kara mita shōjo/shōnen shōsetsushi: Gendai Nihon no monogatari bunka o minaosu tame ni* [The history of novels for young adults as seen in light novels: Rethinking modern Japanese narrative culture] (Tokyo: Kasama Shoin, 2014), 9.

14. Yamanaka, *Raito noberu yo*, 7.

15. In her final atogaki, Nanami writes, "The *Chiyogiku* series has readers that vary in age from elementary school students to those in their nineties, including both men and women," afterword, *Futari dake no kekkonshiki*, 264.

16. Kume Yoriko, "Toraburu to shite no sekushuaritī: Otoko no ko hyōshō to shōjo komyunitī shikō" [Sexuality as trouble: Representations of the *otoko no ko* and preference for *shōjo* community], in Ichiyanagi and Kume, *Raito noberu sutadīzu* [Light Novel Studies] (Tokyo: Seikyūsha, 2013) 73, 77.

17. Sharon Kinsella's research on the *otoko no ko* phenomenon of the "uncertain 2000s" tracks a range of media, activities, and products extending well beyond manga and light novels, including magazines, TV, campus beauty contests, cosmetics, cute fashion, and clubs. Observing that the cute mode of the *josō shōnen* (cross-dressed youth) is a hobby or commercial enterprise for many, and "not so clearly correlated with sexual orientation or preferences at all," Kinsella proposes the phenomenon "could be understood as a means of opening up to new and unknown directions and futures," a response to "moments of social upheaval and 'category crisis.'" Even the term *otoko no ko*, as used for cross-dressed youth, queers the word for boy (*otoko no ko*) by using the character *musume* (daughter) for the final ko. Kinsella, "Cuteness, *josō*, and the Need to Appeal: *Otoko no ko* in Male Subculture in 2010s Japan," *Japan Forum* 3, no. 32 (2019): 432–58.

18. Kume, "Toraburu to shite no sekushuaritī," 80.

19. Kume, "Toraburu to shite no sekushuaritī," 79.

20. In one of her last atogaki, Nanami writes, "The *Chiyogiku* series has many types of readers.... Some read it because they enjoy Kyoto, some because they like maiko, others because they like soft BL (*sofuto* BL)—I imagine that everyone that finds it fun has a different reason." Afterword, Nanami Haruka, *Jūrokusai no hanayome* [The Sixteen-year-old Bride], vol. 53 [9-56]. *Shōnen maiko: Chiyogiku ga yuku!* [Boy Maiko: There Goes Chiyogiku!] (Tokyo: Shūeisha Cobalt Bunko, 2014), 252.

21. Popular since the 1970s, BL narratives involve romance and sexual relationships between beautiful men who rarely identify as gay. Although BL readership includes numerous girls and women, boys and men are among the fans, too. For an in-depth, wide-ranging discussion of BL—historical resonances, readership, marketing, and regulatory agendas—see Mark J. McLelland, Kazumi Nagaike, Katsuhiko Suganuma, and James Welker, eds., *Boys Love Manga and Beyond: History, Culture, and Community in Japan* (Jackson: University Press of Mississippi, 2015).

22. Deborah Shamoon discusses debate over BL readers' perspectives in *Passionate Friendship*, chapter 5, "The Revolution in 1970s Shōjo Manga." Ishida Hitoshi questions whether BL's use of male-male love feeds female fans' subconscious homophobia in "Representational Appropriation and the Autonomy of Desire in *Yaoi/BL*," in McLelland et al., *Boys Love Manga and Beyond*, 210–32.

23. Nanami Haruka, *Hanamikōji ni Okoshiyasu* [Welcome to Hanamikōji], *Shōnen maiko: Chiyogiku ga yuku!*, vol. 1 [9-3] (Tokyo: Shūeisha Cobalt Bunko, 2002), 37.

24. Nanami, *Hanamikōji ni Okoshiyasu*, 185.

25. Nanami, *Hanamikōji ni Okoshiyasu*, 28.

26. Nanami Haruka, *Minoshirokin wa haha no koibumi* [The ransom, mother's love letter], *Shōnen maiko: Chiyogiku ga yuku!*, vol. 2 [9-4] (Tokyo: Shūeisha Cobalt Bunko, 2002), 109.

27. Japanese media culture has represented the once-divorced man positively in the 2000s since he shows interest in long-term heterosexual relationships, even if he failed once. For example, the 2008 TV drama *Around 40* presents divorce as increasing

the desirability of an affluent designer; he, too, is now *batsu-ichi*. See Alisa Freedman and Kristina Iwata-Weickgenannt, "'Count What You Have Now. Don't Count What You Don't Have': The Japanese Television Drama *Around 40* and the Politics of Women's Happiness," *Asian Studies Review* 35, no. 3 (2011): 295–313.

28. Talking with Shion, the woman cross-dressing as a host, Chiyogiku realizes that if Nirezaki discovered Shion's hidden female body, he has probably also learned that his favorite maiko is a boy. Nanami Haruka, *Eien no kataomoi* [Eternally unrequited love] *Shōnen maiko: Chiyogiku ga yuku!*, vol. 8 [9-10] (Tokyo: Shūeisha Cobalt Bunko, 2004), 235. But, in the final story, *Futari dake no kekkonshiki*, Nirezaki wonders why he never dreamed Mikiya and Chiyogiku were the same person, 67.

29. Nanami, *Minoshirokin wa haha no koibumi*, 83.

30. Nanami, *Hanamikōji ni Okoshiyasu*, 75.

31. Nanami Haruka, "Ninin Fuji Musume" [The two wisteria maidens], story in *Jūrokusai no hanayome*, 188. Leonard Pronko describes the kabuki dance *Wisteria Maiden*, about a woman's anguish over a faithless lover, as requiring "a mingling of chastity with eroticism," which seems befitting of Chiyogiku. Leonard C. Pronko, "The Wisteria Maiden: *Fuji Musume*," in *Kabuki Plays on Stage, Volume 3: Darkness and Desire, 1804–1864*, ed. James Brandon and Samuel L. Leiter (Honolulu: University of Hawai'i Press, 2002), 169. Maki Isaka discusses the history of the idealization of femininity in relation to the onnagata's male body in *Onnagata: A Labyrinth of Gendering in Kabuki Theater* (Seattle: University of Washington Press, 2016); Ayako Kano takes up the twentieth-century politics of the issue in *Acting Like a Woman in Modern Japan: Theater, Gender and Nationalism* (New York: Palgrave Macmillan, 2001).

32. Nanami, "Ninin Fuji Musume," 188.

33. Nanami, "Ninin Fuji Musume," 190.

34. Nanami, "Ninin Fuji Musume," 183

35. In this regard, Mikiya's masquerade recalls Nomachi Mineko's comedic book, *O-kama dakedo OL yattemasu* [I am queer, but I'm an office lady] (Tokyo: Take Shobō, 2006). In her analysis of Nomachi's book, Vera Mackie describes how working as an office lady (OL) in a corporate office continually makes the narrator fear that coworkers will "discern the gap between *his* sexed body and *her* performance of feminine gendered identity" (413). The narrator's adoption of technologies of femininity in speech, movement, and appearance "reveal the constructedness of masculinity and femininity" (414). Mackie shows how the narrator's performance requires the deployment of "embodied memories"—that is, girlhood experiences to share with women in the office. This foregrounds how "gender identity is about the narration of shared experiences" (414). Although Chiyogiku produces a feminine demeanor, she rarely faces the challenge of girl talk since most scenes take place in the company of boys or men and her experience of the rituals, training, and costuming associated with the maiko provide her cover story. In fact, Chiyogiku does have a girlhood—a maiko girlhood. Vera Mackie, "How to Be a Girl: Mainstream Media Portrayals of Transgendered Lives in Japan." *Asian Studies Review* 32, no.3 (2008): 411–23.

36. Nanami, *Eien no kataomoi*, 232.

37. Nanami, *Eien no kataomoi*, 89–90, 91.

38. Nanami, *Eien no kataomoi*, 91.

39. Nanami, *Eien no kataomoi*, 85.

40. Nanami, *Eien no kataomoi*, 85.

41. Nanami, *Eien no kataomoi*, 128.

42. Nanami, *Eien no kataomoi*, 117–18.

43. Takeyama, *Staged Seduction*.

44. Mikiya imagines becoming an *ii otoko*, literally, a "good man." Here, the term implies more than virtue, connoting fine appearance and sophistication, too. By the same token, references to *ii onna* (good woman) in this conversation evoke ideal femininity, the polished persona produced in a woman by host Shion's attention. Nanami, *Eien no kataomoi*, 93.

45. The final three volumes were published in quick succession in August, October, and December 2014.

46. Nanami, "Jūrokusai no hanayome," 7–105.

47. Nanami, "Ninin Fuji Musume," 169–243.

48. Nanami, "Futari dake no kekkonshiki," 170.

49. Interview with author, May 27, 2017.

50. Mark J. McLelland and James Welker, "An Introduction to 'Boys Love' in Japan," in McLelland et al., *Boys Love Manga and Beyond*, 3.

51. Interview with author, May 27, 2017.

52. Rosette F. Willig, *The Changelings: A Classical Japanese Court Tale* (Stanford, CA: Stanford University Press, 1983); McLelland and Welker, "An Introduction to 'Boys Love' in Japan," 6. In *Age of Shōjo*, Dollase discusses Himuro Saeko's retelling of this classic in her 1983 novel, *Za chenji* [The change], arguing that gender-role reversal in *Za chenji* "resonated with women who had started entering the workforce, traditionally a male sphere, in the 1980s" (97).

53. Interview with author, May 27, 2017.

54. Nanami Haruka, *Eien no kataomoi*, 12.

CHAPTER 6. HIT A HOMER, MAIKO!

1. Eirakuya sells various cloth products. One can see numerous maiko designs on the company's website http://www.eirakuya.jp/ (accessed May 19, 2020). The location of Eirakuya's main store on Muromachi Street in Kyoto, the former home of kimono sellers, cloth sellers, and cloth cleaners, reflects a connection to the textile merchant culture of the past.

2. Interview with Eirakuya representative in Kyoto, May 27, 2017; cited with permission. The representative explained that tenugui, as sustainable items, had been popular souvenirs of Kyoto for decades. Tenugui customers tend to be tourists in their forties and fifties with disposable income; in May 2020, the price for one tenugui in the maiko series is generally equivalent to US$18. The representative noted that the sporting maiko tenugui have been more popular with domestic travelers while those from abroad tend

to prefer the classic maiko designs. He speculated that since Japanese were familiar with the maiko, they felt comfortable with the playful designs, whereas the classic maiko image came closer to international tourists' conceptions of Kyoto. The firm initiates new ideas each year, employing an in-house "team design" format where a group of artists trades ideas to create new designs.

3. Eirakuya had an in-house team of three designers employed by the firm in the 1930s who created one hundred designs per year. Eirakuya maintains an archive of its designs. Although little information exists on the inspiration for the sporting maiko tenugui, the design of skiing maiko likely reflected a new vogue for the sport. Interview with author, May 27, 2017.

4. Eirakuya Hosotsuji Ihee Shōten, eds., *Irodori tenugui* (Colorful hand towels) (Tokyo: Graphic-sha Publishing, 2009), 58. In her discussion of Santō Kyōden's 1784 *Tanagui awase* (tenugui competition), Seigle explains that scholarly disagreement exists over whether this competition, in fact, occurred. Seigle, *Yoshiwara*, 201, 267n60.

5. Barbara F. Kawakami, *Japanese Immigrant Clothing in Hawaii, 1885–1941* (Honolulu: University of Hawai'i Press, 1993), 125.

6. Jacqueline M. Atkins, "Wearing Propaganda: Textiles on the Home Front in Japan, Great Britain, and America during the Greater East Asian War, 1931–45," *Textile: The Journal of Cloth & Culture* 2, no. 1 (2004): 34.

7. *Tenugui: Japanese Hand Towels* (Tokyo: Airy Rhyme, 2014).

8. For one example, Katō Atsuko's picture guide *Tenugui tsukaikonashi bukku* [Tenugui mastery guide] (Tokyo: Shufunotomo-sha, 2018) offers eighty ways for using tenugui to beautify daily life, explaining its origins and linking it to a Japanese sense of seasonal change, celebration, and greetings.

9. Eirakuya, *Irodori tenugui*, 8–13. Eirakuya is not affiliated with any single hanamachi, although the firm does support dance productions by purchasing advertising space in the printed programs. It sometimes hires geiko and maiko to appear in its advertisements. Eirakuya also designs custom kimono for maiko and geiko. Interview with author, May 27, 2017.

10. Eirakuya, *Irodori tenugui*, 20–25.

11. These three 1931 images appear in Eirakuya, *Irodori tenugui*, 69–70.

12. The postcard is reproduced in Ikuta Makoto, *Modan gāru daizukan* [Big picture book of the modern girl] (Tokyo: Kawade Shobō Shinsha, 2012), 117. I thank Mr. Ikuta for his scan of the original.

13. *Musume* may be translated as "daughter," "young unmarried woman," and "girl"; in Kyoto, *han* replaces the standard honorific suffix *san*. Thus, I translate *musume han* as "young misses." The Adachi Museum of Art in Shimane, Japan, exhibits Suzuki's work. https://www.adachi-museum.or.jp/ (accessed May 19, 2020).

14. Photo books in Japanese on the modern girl include Ikuta, *Modan gāru daizukan*; Ikuta Makoto, *Joryū sakka no modan Tokyo* [The modern Tokyo of women writers] (Tokyo: Kawade Shobō Shinsha, 2015); Yayoi Museum and Nakamura Keiko, *Showa modan kimono: Jojōga ni manabu kikonashi jutsu / Shouwa Modern Kimono* (Tokyo: Kawade Shobō Shinsha, 2005). Exhibits such as Osaka City History Museum's

permanent exhibit, *Dai Osaka no jidai* (The age of greater Osaka) features the modern girl. In the United States, too, exhibits related to the modern girl have led to books: Kendall H. Brown, Sharon Minichiello, Letitia Burns O'Connor, and Lorna Price, *Taishō Chic: Japanese Modernity, Nostalgia, and Deco* (Honolulu: Honolulu Academy of Arts, 2001) and John W. Dower, Anne Nishimura Morse, Jacqueline M. Atkins, and Frederic A. Sharf, *The Brittle Decade: Visualizing Japan in the 1930s* (Boston: MFA Publications, 2012).

15. Sarah Frederick, *Turning Pages: Reading and Writing Women's Magazines in Interwar Japan* (Honolulu: University of Hawai'i Press, 2006); Alisa Freedman, Laura Miller, and Christine R. Yano, eds., *Modern Girls on the Go*; Barbara Hamill Sato, *The New Japanese Woman: Modernity, Media, and Women in Interwar Japan* (Durham, NC: Duke University Press, 2003); and Miriam Rom Silverberg, *Erotic Grotesque Nonsense: The Mass Culture of Japanese Modern Times* (Berkeley: University of California Press, 2006).

16. Frequently cited among comparative modern girl studies is *The Modern Girl around the World: Consumption, Modernity, and Globalization*, compiled by the Modern Girl around the World Research Group (Durham, NC: Duke University Press, 2008). For comparative examination of the modern girl in East Asia, see Tani E. Barlow, Itō Ruri, and Sakamoto Hiroko, eds., *Modan gāru to shokuminchi-teki kindai: Higashi Ajia ni okeru teikoku, shihon, jendā* [The modern girl and colonial modernity: Empire, capital, and gender in East Asia] (Tokyo: Iwanami Shoten, 2010).

17. For Eirakuya tenugui designs of modern girls, cafés, cars, and romance, see Hamada Nobuyoshi, ed., *Kyō no fūryū, Eirakuya no machiya tenugui / Eirakuya's Tenugui: The refined tastes of Kyoto* (Kyoto: Seigensha, 2014), 162–91.

18. Pierre-Yves Donzé, "Siemens and the Business of Medicine in Japan, 1900–1945," *Business History Review* 87 (2013): 203–28.

19. Hamada, *Eirakuya's Tenugui*, 142.

20. Hamada, *Eirakuya's Tenugui*, 144.

21. The design is dated as "early Showa," Hamada, *Eirakuya's Tenugui*, 143. In our May 2017 interview, the Eirakuya representative mentioned that Eirakuya was not the only tenugui shop to make skeleton maiko; others, too, made use of this theme. He related this to similar themes in ukiyo-e.

22. I thank postcard art historian Ikuta Makoto for this suggestion in our interview in Tokyo, July 12, 2019; cited with permission.

23. Barbara Hartley, "Performing the Nation: Magazine Images of Women and Girls in the Illustrations of Takabatake Kashō, 1925–1937." *Intersections: Gender and Sexuality in Asia and the Pacific* 16 (2008), http://intersections.anu.edu.au/issue16/hartley.htm (accessed May 16, 2020).

24. Gennifer Weisenfeld, "Selling Shiseido: Cosmetics Advertising and Design in Early 20th-Century Japan," MIT, Visualizing Cultures, 2009, https://visualizingcultures.mit.edu/shiseido_01 (accessed May 16, 2020).

25. Alison J. Miller, "Wintry Women: Skiing, Modern Girls, and Imperial Body Politics as Represented in 1930s Nihonga." *Journal of Japanese Studies* 47, no. 2 (2021), forthcoming.

26. Historian Frederic A. Sharf describes the extensive media coverage of "Olympic-mad" Japan starting in summer 1932, explaining how clothing, accessories, and novelty items, branded with the five-color rings, brightened department store windows, and that Olympics fans could also buy themed "ashtrays, children's toys and even chocolates." "Shōwa Sophistication," in Dower, et al., *The Brittle Decade*, 167.

27. Dennis J. Frost, *Seeing Stars: Sports Celebrity, Identity, and Body Culture in Modern Japan* (Cambridge, MA: Harvard University Press, 2010), 137

28. Dalby, *Geisha*, 82–91. For more on the café girl, see ch. 4, "The Café Waitress Sang the Blues," 73–107 in Silverberg, *Erotic Grotesque Nonsense* and Tipton, "Pink Collar Work."

29. Hanazono Utako, *Geigi tsū* [Geisha chic]. Tokyo: Shiroku Shoin, 1930. Reprinted in the series *Josei no mita kindai* [Modernity as seen by women] as *Onna to rōdō* [Women and labor], vol. 24, edited by Kōra Rumiko and Iwami Teruyo (Tokyo: Yumani Shobō, 2004), 37.

30. Sato, *The New Japanese Woman*, 49.

31. The full name of the firm is Eirakuya Hosotsuji Ihee Shōten. The website does not give the birth name of the current Hosotsuji Ihee, who assumed this lineage name. See http://www.eirakuya.jp/ (accessed May 16, 2020).

32. Eirakuya, *Irodori tenugui*, 68–71.

33. The original Japanese as romanized is *maiko-san-tachi ga minna de umi de bakansu. Bīchi barē ya suika wari, sorezore ga tanoshige ni natsu o tanoshinde imasu.* See https://eirakuya.shop-pro.jp/?pid=85952543 (accessed May 16, 2020).

34. Keiko Ishii, "Pancake Politics: Gender, Identity and Petit Rebellion in Japanese Pancake Cafes." MA thesis, Doshisha University, 2018.

35. According to Baba and Ikeda, the term *joshi*, as opposed to other Japanese words for girl (*onna no ko; shōjo*), frequently appeared in fashion magazines and other media in the 2000s to denote young women forming friend networks and seeking their own pleasures without concern for men or the male gaze. Baba Nobuhiko and Ikeda Taishin, "*Joshi" no jidai!* [The age of "girls"] (Tokyo: Seikyūsha, 2012). Taking a more critical view, Aya Hirata Kimura likens "joshi power" to the discourse on "girl power" in the United States. In both cases, positive views of female friendships and hip consumerism abide, but ultimately reinforce conventional gender roles. She notes that "the image of these empowered girls or women still resides squarely within hegemonic standards of beauty and acceptability" (96). Kimura explains how joshi requirements for "cheerful, friendly, and unthreatening femininity" circumscribe women's social activism (97). *Radiation Brain Moms and Citizen Scientists: The Gender Politics of Food Contamination after Fukushima* (Durham, NC: Duke University Press, 2016), 94–98.

36. The three Keihan posters featuring groups of formally dressed maiko debuted nationwide successively in 2014, 2015, and 2018; the third poster continues through 2020. The 2014 poster's caption plays with Kyoto (its first character, *kyō*, meaning imperial capital) and the word for "today" (*kyō*): "Kyō mo yoroshū, Keihan de" (Today, too, we are relying on you, Keihan). Email communication from Keihan Electric Railway Co., Ltd, October 31, 2019 and May 25, 2020, cited with permission.

37. Sakai questions whether the demands on women to display bodily perfection forced the early retirement of Japanese beach volleyball stars Saeki Mika and Asao Miwa. Sakai Junko, "Bīchi bare" [Beach volleyball], in *Kireba wakaru*, 104–14.

38. Hansen, *Femininity, Self-Harm and Eating Disorders in Japan*, 107.

39. Hansen, *Femininity, Self-Harm and Eating Disorders in Japan*, 108.

40. As Motoko Rich reported, sexism in sumo even threatened a man's life in 2018 when referees ordered women out of the ring after they rushed to assist a politician who had collapsed while delivering a speech. "Women Barred from Sumo Ring, Even to Save a Man's Life," *New York Times*, April 5, 2018, https://www.nytimes.com/2018/04/05 /world/asia/women-sumo-ring-japan.html (accessed May 16, 2020). Yumi Wijers-Hasegawa reported that citizens' groups in Japan protested the Japanese government's application to designate the Kii mountain range a UNESCO world heritage site since it included sites off limits to women. "UNESCO heritage bid challenged over gender bias," *Japan Times*, May 1, 2004. https://www.japantimes.co.jp/news/2004/05/01 /national/unesco-heritage-bid-challenged-over-gender-bias/#.XsskhWhKjD4 (accessed September 17, 2020). In 2014, Amy Chavez reported that the UNESCO designation had been approved, thus including these sites of sexist discrimination in Japan with those in "Burma, India, and Greece." "4 Things Women Are Banned from Doing in Japan." *Huffington Post*, July 8, 2015; updated December 6, 2017, https://www .huffpost.com/entry/4-things-women-are-banned_b_7733704 (accessed May 16, 2020).

41. The Kyoto International Manga Museum lists the names of all the cartoonists who participated in this exhibit, see https://www.kyotomm.jp/en/event/per-exh _maiko/

42. Museum holdings of individual prints in this Kunisada series are widely available online.

43. To celebrate the establishment of the Kyoto International Manga Museum, which opened in November 2006, the Japan Cartoonists Association (JCA) planned an exhibit. Aiming to let museum visitors "get to know Kyoto through manga," JCA invited its members to submit their signed single-frame manga of a maiko character (*maiko-san kyara*). Makino Keiichi, a professor at Kyoto Seika University at that time and a JCA director, led the project. The JCA issued the call to its membership twice, receiving over 170 manga, not all of which are exhibited; some manga artists submitted more than one cartoon for consideration, but only one each could be used. The call stated that human maiko and animal maiko were both acceptable. A spokesperson for the JCA, Watanabe Kyoko, informed me that the JCA had collaborated on similar manga exhibits for other locations such as Kamakura, Tsukuba, and Yokohama. She noted that among the maiko manga, there were those with "an ingenuous twist or social satire. The maiko riding a scooter is one example of this. Since the theme was maiko, we initially expected that all the works would be maiko, but there are some that do not appear very maiko-like." Watanabe Kyoko, email message to author, July 29, 2019; cited with permission.

44. Manga are associated with Japan the world over. Much excellent scholarship exists on manga from introductory guides to studies of specific manga genres and

themes. For an overview see Mark Wheeler Macwilliams, ed., *Japanese Visual Culture: Explorations in the World of Manga and Anime* (Armonk, NY: M.E. Sharpe, 2008).

45. Hiroko Tabuchi, "In Search of Adorable, as Hello Kitty Gets Closer to Goodbye," *New York Times*, May 14, 2010, https://www.nytimes.com/2010/05/15/business /global/15kitty.html (accessed May 16, 2020).

46. Scott McCloud, *Understanding Comics: The Invisible Art* (New York: Harper Perennial, 1993), 30.

47. Sarah McConnell, "Illustration in Motion: Sequential Momentum in Children's Illustrated Books," in *A Companion to Illustration: Art and Theory*, ed. Alan Male (Hoboken, NJ: John Wiley & Sons, Inc., 2019), 142.

48. Philip Kennicott, "Cute puppies and octopus sex: A Japanese art exhibition reveals our fascination with animals." *Washington Post*, May 30, 2019, https://www .washingtonpost.com/entertainment/museums/cute-puppies-and-octopus-sex-a -japanese-art-exhibition-reveals-our-fascination-with-animals/2019/05/29/7b4c0c8e -8221-11e9-933d-7501070ee669_story.html (accessed May 16, 2020).

49. Laura Miller, "Japan's Zoomorphic Urge," *ASIANetwork Exchange* 17, no. 2 (2010), 74.

50. Email communication with author, March 10, 2020; cited with permission.

51. This recalls the "enchanted commodities" that Allison discusses in *Millennial Monsters* (see introduction).

52. Rachel B., "Kimokawaii: Both Cute and Gross at the Same Time." *Tofugu*, June 18, 2013, https://www.tofugu.com/japan/kimokawaii/ (accessed May 16, 2020); Nancy K. Stalker, *Japan: History and Culture from Classical to Cool* (Oakland: University of California Press, 2018), 377.

53. I was unable to contact the late artist's family for permission to include this manga.

54. Christine L. Marran, "Beyond Domesticating Animal Love," *Mechademia* 6 (2011), 43.

55. Miller, "Japan's Zoomorphic Urge," 76.

56. Manga by Makino Kazuko, Seki Yoshimi, and Shiga Kimie feature this common pose.

57. Terashima Reiko, email message to author, July 29, 2019; cited with permission.

58. Christine Yano, *Pink Globalization*, 3.

59. Jan Chozen Bays, *Jizo Bodhisattva: Modern Healing and Traditional Buddhist Practice* (Boston: Tuttle Publishing, 2002), xix.

60. Minami Hiroshi, email message to author, July 29, 2019; cited with permission.

61. Broadcast from April 1983 to March 1984, this morning drama narrated modern Japanese history through the rags-to-riches rise of heroine Oshin. Considering its global reach, Koichi Iwabuchi writes, "The drama was distributed free of charge to many Asian countries as well as the Middle East and South America under the cultural exchange program of the Japan Foundation." Iwabuchi, "Cultural Policy, Cross-Border Dialogue and Cultural Diversity," 366. For analysis and reception of *Oshin*, see Harvey, "Interpreting *Oshin*."

62. Takenaka Ranko, email message to author, July 29, 2019; cited with permission.

63. Kojiroh gives "maiko" in characters (kanji) and Jackson in katakana as *ja.ku.so .n*, defining the two icons linguistically as native and other.

64. "Michael Jackson Arrives in Japan for 13-Concert Tour." *New York Times*, September 10, 1987, https://www.nytimes.com/1987/09/10/arts/michael-jackson -arrives-in-japan-for-13-concert-tour.html (accessed May 16, 2020).

65. Yuri Kageyama, "Michael Jackson Had Loyal, Generous Fans in Japan," *San Diego Tribune*, June 26, 2009, https://www.sandiegouniontribune.com/sdut-japan -michael-jackson-062609-2009jun26-story.html (accessed May 16, 2020).

66. The accusers appear in the 2019 documentary *Leaving Neverland*, directed by Dan Reed and distributed by HBO.

67. Kuruma's granny features in his comics for Hagimoto Kin'ichi's book, *Kinchan no jinsei konto dayo* [Kin-chan's life is a comedy!] (Tokyo: Jitsugyō no Nihon-sha, 2004).

68. The sight of the inebriated salaryman returning home with his sushi offering associates with the postwar Showa era. The manga and anime website NeoApo captures Namino Norisuke, a salaryman character in the famous *Sazae-san* comics in this predicament: http://neoapo.com/characters/8148 (accessed May 16, 2020).

69. Dollase, *Age of Shōjo*, 115.

70. Dollase, *Age of Shōjo*, 120.

71. Sohyun Chun, "The Shōjo in the Rōjo: Fumiko Enchi's Representation of the Shōjo Who Refused to Grow Up," in *Shōjo across Media: Exploring "Girl" Practices in Contemporary Japan*, ed. Jaqueline Berndt, Kazumi Nagaike, and Fusami Ogi (New York: Palgrave Macmillan, 2019), 135.

CONCLUSION

1. Allison, "Memoirs of the Orient," 394.

2. Yamato, *Kurenai niou*, volume 2, episode 8, unnumbered page.

3. Nanami, *Eien no kataomoi*, 12.

4. McVeigh, *Life in a Japanese Women's College*, 83.

5. Taniguchi, *Gion, uttoko no hanashi*, 15.

6. In *Suppin geiko* Yamaguchi Kimijo describes maiko returning to Kyoto after New Year's vacations back home, armed with local delicacies and fully back in their hometown dialects (129). In *Dandan*, falling into local dialect distinguishes a maiko's non-Kyoto roots and denotes an authentic self—the one masquerading as a maiko. In Nozomi's case, the reverse is true: when exposed masquerading as her twin, she reverts to hanamachi dialect, her authentic voice. The 2014 film *Maiko wa redī* (*Lady Maiko*) pokes fun at staid hanamachi mothers trying to teach a new maiko their dialect, using the disparity between rural dialects and the hanamachi's own to spice up the comedy, and ignoring the hierarchy of dialect privilege in Japan.

7. Arai, *Gion Mameji*, 84.

8. Arai, *Gion Mameji*, 88.

9. Taniguchi, *Gion, uttoko no hanashi*, 162.

10. Taniguchi, *Gion, uttoko no hanashi*, 162.

11. Arai, *Gion Mameji*, 136–37.

12. For discussion of media characterizations of career women, see Jan Bardsley and Hiroko Hirakawa, "Branded: Bad Girls Go Shopping," and Freedman and Iwata-Weickgenannt, "'Count What You Have Now.'"

13. Sakai Junko, *Makeinu no tōboe* [The distant howl of the loser dog] (Tokyo: Kōdansha, 2004).

14. According to the *Global Gender Gap Report 2020*: "Japan's gender gap is by far the largest among all advanced economies and has widened over the past year. The country ranks 121st out of 153 countries on this year's Global Gender Gap Index, down 1 percentage point and 11 positions from 2018." The report remarks on a "widening of the political gender gap," noting that, "At 10%, female representation in the Japanese parliament is one of the lowest in the world (135th) and 20% below the average share across advanced economies." World Economic Forum, *Global Gender Gap Report 2020* (Geneva: World Economic Forum, 2019), 31, http://www3.weforum.org/docs/WEF _GGGR_2020.pdf (accessed May 28, 2020). Women in Japan, however, report a higher level of happiness than men; reasons are explored in Gill Steel, ed., *Beyond the Gender Gap in Japan* (Ann Arbor: University of Michigan Press, 2019).

BIBLIOGRAPHY

Aihara, Kyoko. *Geisha: A Living Tradition*. London: Carlton Books, 1999.

———. *Kyoto maiko to geiko no okuzashiki* [The salon of Kyoto maiko and geiko]. Tokyo: Bungei Shunjū, 2001.

———. *Kyoto hanamachi motenashi no gijutsu* [The art of hospitality in Kyoto's Hanamachi]. Shōgakukan, 2005.

———. *Maiko-san no odōgu-chō* [Guide to maiko accessories]. Tokyo: Sankaidō, 2007.

———. *Kyoto hanamachi fasshon no bi to kokoro* [The soul and beauty of Kyoto's hanamachi fashion]. Tokyo: Tankōsha, 2011.

———. *Kyoto hanamachi: Maiko to geiko no uchiake-banashi* [The Kyoto hanamachi: Frank talk from maiko and geiko]. Tokyo: Tankōsha, 2012.

Allison, Anne. *Nightwork: Sexuality, Pleasure, and Corporate Masculinity in a Tokyo Hostess Club*. Chicago: University of Chicago Press, 1994.

———. "Memoirs of the Orient." *Journal of Japanese Studies* 27, no. 2 (2001): 381–98.

———. *Millennial Monsters: Japanese Toys and the Global Imagination*. Berkeley: University of California Press, 2006.

———. *Precarious Japan*. Durham, NC: Duke University Press, 2013.

Anderson, Marnie S. *A Place in Public: Women's Rights in Meiji Japan*. Cambridge, MA: Harvard University Asia Center, 2010.

Aoki Shin'ya, prod. *Dandan*. Televised serial novel. Japan: NHK-TV, 2008–09.

Arai Mameji. *Gion Mameji: Chotto mukashi no Gion machi* [Mameji of the Gion: The Gion of recent past]. Tokyo: Asahi Shimbun Publications, 2015.

Ashikari, Mikiko. "Urban Middle-Class Japanese Women and Their White Faces: Gender, Ideology, and Representation." *Ethos* 31, no. 1 (2003): 3–37.

Atkins, Jacqueline M. "Wearing Propaganda: Textiles on the Home Front in Japan, Great Britain, and America during the Greater East Asian War, 1931–45." *Textile: The Journal of Cloth & Culture* 2, no. 1 (2004): 24–45.

B., Rachel. "Kimokawaii: Both Cute and Gross at the Same Time." *Tofugu*, June 18, 2013. https://www.tofugu.com/japan/kimokawaii/ (accessed May 16, 2020).

Baba Nobuhiko and Ikeda Taishin. "*Joshi" no jidai!* [The age of "girls"]. Tokyo: Seikyūsha, 2012.

Bandō Mariko. *Josei no hinkaku* [The Dignity of the woman]. Tokyo: PHP Shinsho, 2006.

Bardsley, Jan. "The New Woman Meets the Geisha: The Politics of Pleasure in 1910s Japan." *Intersections: Gender and Sexuality in Asia and the Pacific* 29 (2012), online: http://intersections.anu.edu.au/issue29/bardsley.htm (accessed May 25, 2020).

———. "The *Oyaji* Gets a Makeover: Guides for Japanese Salarymen in the New Millennium." In *Manners and Mischief: Gender, Power, and Etiquette in Japan*, edited by Jan Bardsley and Laura Miller, 114–35. Berkeley: University of California Press, 2011.

———. "Teaching Geisha in History, Fiction, and Fantasy." *ASIANetwork Exchange: A Journal for Asian Studies in the Liberal Arts* 17, no. 2 (2010): 23–38.

———. "Transbeauty IKKO: A Diva's Guide to Glamour, Virtue, and Healing." In *Diva Nation: Female Icons from Japanese Cultural History*, edited by Laura Miller and Rebecca Copeland, 133–50. Oakland: University of California Press, 2018.

———. *Women and Democracy in Cold War Japan*. London: Bloomsbury Academic, 2014.

Bardsley, Jan, and Hiroko Hirakawa. "Branded: Bad Girls Go Shopping." In *Bad Girls of Japan*, edited by Laura Miller and Jan Bardsley, 110–25. New York: Palgrave Macmillan, 2005.

Bardsley, Jan, and Laura Miller. "Manner and Mischief: Introduction." In *Manners and Mischief: Gender, Power, and Etiquette in Japan*, edited by Jan Bardsley and Laura Miller, 1–28. Berkeley: University of California Press, 2011.

Barlow, Tani E., Itō Ruri, and Sakamoto Hiroko, eds. *Modan gāru to shokuminchi-teki kindai: Higashi Ajia ni okeru teikoku, shihon, jendā* [The modern girl and colonial modernity: Empire, capital, and gender in East Asia]. Tokyo: Iwanami Shoten, 2010.

Bays, Jan Chozen. *Jizo Bodhisattva: Modern Healing and Traditional Buddhist Practice*. Boston, MA: Tuttle Publishing, 2002.

Brau, Lorie. "*Oishinbo's* Adventures in Eating: Food, Communication, and Culture in Japanese Comics." *Gastronomica: The Journal for Food Studies* 4, no. 4 (2004): 34–45.

———. "Soba, Edo Style: Food, Aesthetics, and Cultural Identity." In *Devouring Japan: Perspectives on Japanese Culinary Identity*, edited by Nancy K. Stalker, 65–80. New York: Oxford University Press, 2018.

Brinton, Mary C. *Lost in Transition: Youth, Work, and Instability in Postindustrial Japan*. Cambridge: Cambridge University Press, 2011.

———. *Women and the Economic Miracle: Gender and Work in Postwar Japan*. Berkeley: University of California Press, 1993.

Brown, Kendall H., Sharon Minichiello, Letitia Burns O'Connor, and Lorna Price. *Taishō Chic: Japanese Modernity, Nostalgia, and Deco*. Honolulu: Honolulu Academy of Arts, 2001.

Bullock, Julia C. "Beauvoir in Japan: Tracing the Impact of *The Second Sex* on Japanese Women," Keynote speech. Institute for Gender Studies, Ochanomizu University, May 19, 2019.

———. *Coeds Ruining the Nation: Women, Education, and Social Change in Postwar Japanese Media.* Ann Arbor: University of Michigan Press, 2019.

Butler, Judith. *Bodies That Matter: On the Discursive Limits of "Sex."* New York: Routledge, 1993.

Cardiff, Jack, dir. *My Geisha.* Los Angeles: Paramount, 1962.

Chance, Linda H. "*Genji* Guides, or Minding Murasaki." In *Manners and Mischief: Gender, Power, and Etiquette in Japan*, edited by Jan Bardsley and Laura Miller, 29–47. Berkeley: University of California Press, 2011.

Chavez, Amy. "4 Things Women Are Banned from Doing in Japan." *Huffington Post*, December 6, 2017. https://www.huffpost.com/entry/4-things-women-are-banned_b_7733704 (accessed May 16, 2020).

"Chūgokujin kankōkyaku no maiko taiken" [A Chinese tourist's maiko experience]. *Record China.* February 11, 2014. Online at https://www.recordchina.co.jp/b83162-s0-c60-d0035.html (accessed May 25, 2020).

Chun, Sohyun. "The Shōjo in the Rōjo: Fumiko Enchi's Representation of the Shōjo Who Refused to Grow Up." In *Shōjo across Media: Exploring "Girl" Practices in Contemporary Japan*, edited by Jaqueline Berndt, Kazumi Nagaike, and Fusami Ogi, 133–53. New York: Palgrave Macmillan, 2019.

Clancy, Judith. *The Alluring World of Maiko and Geiko.* Photographs by Mizobuchi Hiroshi. Kyoto: Tankōsha, 2016.

Dalby, Liza. "The Exotic Geisha." In *Geisha: Beyond the Painted Smile*, edited by Peabody Essex Museum, 67–79. New York: George Braziller, 2004.

———. *Geisha.* Berkeley: University of California Press, 1983, 2008.

———. *Kimono: Fashioning Culture.* Seattle: University of Washington Press, 1993, 2001.

Danly, Robert Lyons. *In the Shade of Spring Leaves: The Life and Writings of Higuchi Ichiyō, a Woman of Letters in Meiji Japan.* New York: W.W. Norton, 1992.

Dollase, Hiromi Tsuchiya. *Age of Shōjo: The Emergence, Evolution, and Power of Japanese Girls' Magazine Fiction.* Albany: State University of New York Press, 2019.

Donzé, Pierre-Yves. "Siemens and the Business of Medicine in Japan, 1900–1945." *Business History Review* 87 (2013): 203–28.

Dower, John W., Anne Nishimura Morse, Jacqueline M. Atkins, and Frederic A. Sharf. *The Brittle Decade: Visualizing Japan in the 1930s.* Boston: MFA Publications, 2012.

Downer, Lesley. *Women of the Pleasure Quarters: The Secret History of the Geisha.* New York: Broadway, 2001.

Dunn, Cynthia Dickel. "Bowing Incorrectly: Aesthetic Labor and Expert Knowledge in Japanese Business Etiquette Training." In *Japanese at Work: Politeness, Power, and Personae in Japanese Workplace Discourse*, edited by Haruko Minegishi Cook and Janet S. Shibamoto-Smith, 15–36. New York: Palgrave Macmillan, 2018.

Eirakuya Hosotsuji Ihee Shōten, eds. *Irodori tenugui* [Colorful hand towels]. Tokyo: Graphic-sha, 2009.

Faier, Lieba. *Intimate Encounters: Filipina Women and the Remaking of Rural Japan.* Berkeley: University of California Press, 2009.

Foreman, Kelly M. "Bad Girls Confined: Okuni, Geisha, and the Negotiation of Female Performance Space." In *Bad Girls of Japan*, edited by Laura Miller and Jan Bardsley, 32–47. New York: Palgrave Macmillan, 2005.

———. *The Gei of Geisha: Music, Identity and Meaning.* Aldershot, UK: Ashgate, 2008.

———. "The Perfect Woman: Geisha, Etiquette, and the World of Japanese Traditional Arts." In *Manners and Mischief: Gender, Power, and Etiquette in Japan*, edited by Jan Bardsley and Laura Miller, 67–79. Berkeley: University of California Press, 2011.

Foster, John Paul. *Now a Geisha.* Tokyo: IBC Publishing, 2017.

Frederick, Sarah. "Girls' Magazines and the Creation of *Shōjo* Identities." In *Routledge Handbook of Japanese Media*, edited by Fabienne Darling-Wolf, 22–38. London: Taylor and Francis, 2018.

———. *Turning Pages: Reading and Writing Women's Magazines in Interwar Japan.* Honolulu: University of Hawai'i Press, 2006.

Freedman, Alisa. "Bus Guides Tour National Landscapes, Pop Culture, and Youth Fantasies." In *Modern Girls on the Go: Gender, Mobility, and Labor in Japan*, edited by Alisa Freedman, Laura Miller, and Christine R. Yano, 107–28. Stanford, CA: Stanford University Press, 2013.

———. "Romance of the Taishō Schoolgirl in Shōjo Manga: Here Comes Miss Modern." In *Shōjo across Media: Exploring "Girl" Practices in Contemporary Japan*, edited by Jaqueline Berndt, Kazumi Nagaike, Fusami Ogi, 25–48. New York: Palgrave Macmillan, 2019.

Freedman, Alisa, and Kristina Iwata-Weickgenannt. "'Count What You Have Now. Don't Count What You Don't Have': The Japanese Television Drama *Around 40* and the Politics of Women's Happiness." *Asian Studies Review* 35, no. 3 (2011): 295–313.

Freedman, Alisa, Laura Miller, and Christine R. Yano, eds. *Modern Girls on the Go: Gender, Mobility, and Labor in Japan.* Stanford, CA: Stanford University Press, 2013.

Frost, Dennis J. *Seeing Stars: Sports Celebrity, Identity, and Body Culture in Modern Japan.* Cambridge, MA: Harvard University Press, 2010.

Fuller, Ellen V. *Going Global: Culture, Gender, and Authority in the Japanese Subsidiary of an American Corporation.* Philadelphia: Temple University Press, 2009.

Galbraith, Patrick W. "Maid in Japan: An Ethnographic Account of Alternative Intimacy." *Intersections: Gender and Sexuality in Asia and the Pacific* 25 (2011). Online at http://intersections.anu.edu.au/issue25/galbraith.htm (accessed May 25, 2020).

———. "Seeking an Alternative: 'Male' Shōjo Fans Since the 1970s." In *Shōjo across Media: Exploring "Girl" Practices in Contemporary Japan*, edited by Jaqueline Berndt, Kazumi Nagaike, and Fusami Ogi, 355–90. New York: Palgrave Macmillan, 2019.

Galbraith, Patrick W., and Jason G. Karlin. *AKB48.* New York: Bloomsbury Academic, 2020.

Galbraith, Stuart, IV. *The Toho Studios Story: A History and Complete Filmography.* Lanham, MD: Scarecrow Press, 2008.

Gerstle, C. Andrew, ed. *18th Century Japan: Culture and Society.* Richmond, VA: Curzon, 2000.

Gion Kōbu Kumiai, Noguchi Masanori, ed., "Gion to bungakusha" [The Gion and literati]. *Gion,* 226 (2016): 19–26.

Golden, Arthur. *Memoirs of a Geisha.* New York: Alfred A. Knopf, 1997.

González-López, Irene. "Marketing the *Panpan* in Japanese Popular Culture: Youth, Sexuality, and Power." *U.S.-Japan Women's Journal* no. 54 (2018): 29–51.

Gottlieb, Nanette. *Linguistic Stereotyping and Minority Groups in Japan.* London: Routledge, 2006.

Grilli, Peter M. "Geisha on Stage and Screen." In *Geisha: Beyond the Painted Smile,* edited by Peabody Essex Museum, 139–47. New York: George Braziller, 2004.

Hagimoto Kin'ichi. *Kinchan no jinsei konto dayo* [Kin-chan's life is a comedy]. Tokyo: Jitsugyō no Nihonsha, 2004.

Hamada Nobuyoshi, ed. *Kyō no fūryū, Eirakuya no machiya tenugui / Eirakuya's Tenugui: The refined tastes of Kyoto.* Kyoto: Seigensha, 2014.

Hamasaki Kanako. "Hanamachi no nen-chū gyōji" [Annual festivals in the hanamachi]. In *Kyō no kagai: Hito, waza, machi* [Kyoto's hanamachi: People, arts, towns], edited by Ōta Tōru and Hiratake Kōzō, 92–109. Tokyo: Nippon Hyōronsha, 2009.

———. "Hanamachi e no akusesu (Ōkini Zaidan)." [Access to the hanamachi (The Ōkini Zaidan)]. In *Kyō no kagai: Hito, waza, machi* [Kyoto's hanamachi: People, arts, towns], edited by Ōta Tōru and Hiratake Kōzō, 237–38. Tokyo: Nippon Hyōronsha, 2009.

Hamasaki Kanako and Ōta Tōru. "Hanamachi o sasaeru mono to waza" [Things and arts that support the hanamachi]. In *Kyō no kagai: Hito, waza, machi* [Kyoto's hanamachi: People, arts, towns], edited by Ōta Tōru and Hiratake Kōzō, 138–64. Tokyo: Nippon Hyōronsha, 2009.

Hanazono Utako. *Geigi tsū* [Geisha chic]. Tokyo: Shiroku Shoin, 1930. Reprinted in the series *Josei no mita kindai* [Modernity as seen by women] as *Onna to rōdō* [Women and labor], vol. 24, edited by Kōra Rumiko and Iwami Teruyo. Tokyo: Yumani Shobō, 2004.

Hansen, Gitte Marianne. *Femininity, Self-Harm and Eating Disorders in Japan: Navigating Contradiction in Narrative and Visual Culture.* London: Routledge, 2016.

Hartley, Barbara. "Performing the Nation: Magazine Images of Women and Girls in the Illustrations of Takabatake Kashō, 1925–1937." *Intersections: Gender and Sexuality in Asia and the Pacific* 16 (2008). http://intersections.anu.edu.au/issue16/hartley.htm (accessed May 16, 2020).

Harvey, Paul A. S. "Interpreting Oshin: War, History and Women in Modern Japan." In *Women, Media and Consumption in Japan,* edited by Lise Skov and Brian Moeran, 75–110. Honolulu: University of Hawai'i Press, 1995.

Hashimoto, Yorimitsu. "Japanese Tea Party: Representations of Victorian Paradise and Playground in *The Geisha* (1896)" In *Histories of Tourism: Representation, Identity, and Conflict*, edited by John K. Walton, 104–24. Clevedon, UK: Channel View Publications, 2005.

Hayashi Mariko. *Bijo wa nan demo shitte iru* [The beauty knows all]. Tokyo: Magajin Hausu, 2010.

Hillier, Jim, and Douglas Pye. *100 Musical Films*. London: Palgrave Macmillan, 2011.

Hirakawa, Hiroko. "The Dignified Woman Who Loves to Be 'Lovable.'" In *Manners and Mischief: Gender, Power, and Etiquette in Japan*, edited by Jan Bardsley and Laura Miller, 136–55. Berkeley: University of California Press, 2011.

Hiratake Kōzō and Hamasaki Kanako. "Hanamachi wa ima" [The hanamachi now]. In *Kyō no kagai: Hito, waza, machi* [Kyoto's hanamachi: People, arts, towns], edited by Ōta Tōru and Hiratake Kōzō, 18–41. Tokyo: Nippon Hyōronsha, 2009.

Hirota, Akiko. "*The Tale of Genji*: From Heian Classic to Heisei Comic." *Journal of Popular Culture* 31, no. 2 (1997): 29–68.

Honda, Masuko. "The Genealogy of *Hirahira*: Liminality and the Girl." Translated by Tomoko Aoyama and Barbara Hartley. In *Girl Reading Girl in Japan*, edited by Tomoko Aoyama and Barbara Hartley, 19–37. New York: Routledge, 2010.

Ichiyanagi Hirotaka and Kume Yoriko, eds. *Raito noberu sutadīzu* [Light novel studies]. Tokyo: Seikyūsha, 2013.

Ikuta Makoto. *Joryū sakka no modan Tokyo* [The modern Tokyo of women writers]. Tokyo: Kawade Shobō Shinsha, 2015.

———. *Modan gāru daizukan* [Big picture book of the modern girl]. Tokyo: Kawade Shobō Shinsha, 2012.

Isaka, Maki. "Box-Lunch Etiquette: Conduct Guides and Kabuki *Onnagata*." In *Manners and Mischief: Gender, Power, and Etiquette in Japan*, edited by Jan Bardsley and Laura Miller, 48–66. Berkeley: University of California Press, 2011.

———. *Onnagata: A Labyrinth of Gendering in Kabuki Theater*. Seattle: University of Washington Press, 2016.

Ishida Hitoshi. "Representational Appropriation and the Autonomy of Desire in *Yaoi/BL*." In *Boys Love Manga and Beyond: History, Culture, and Community in Japan*, edited by Mark J. McLelland, Kazumi Nagaike, Katsuhiko Suganuma, and James Welker, 210–32. Jackson: University Press of Mississippi, 2015.

Ishii, Keiko. "Pancake Politics: Gender, Identity and Petit Rebellion in Japanese Pancake Cafes." MA thesis, Doshisha University, 2018.

Ishii Miyo. *Geisha to machiai* [Geisha and teahouses]. Tokyo: Nihon Shoin, 1916. Reprinted in the series *Josei no mita kindai* [Modernity as seen by women] as *Onna to rōdō* [Women and labor], vol. 21, edited by Kōra Rumiko and Iwami Teruyo. Tokyo: Yumani Shobō, 2004.

Iwabuchi, Koichi. "Cultural Policy, Cross-Border Dialogue and Cultural Diversity." In *Routledge Handbook of Japanese Media*, edited by Fabienne Darling-Wolf, 365–74. London: Taylor & Francis, 2018.

Iwasaki Mineko. *Geiko Mineko no hana-ikusa: Honma no koi wa ippen dosu* [The flower battle of Geisha Mineko: True love comes only once]. Tokyo: Kōdansha, 2001.

———. *Gion no kagai jugyō* [Lessons outside of class in the Gion]. Tokyo: Shūeisha, 2004.

———. *Gion no kyōkun: Noboru hito noborikirazuni owaru hito* [Lessons from the Gion: Those who succeed, those who never do]. 2003, rpt. Tokyo: Daiwa Shobō, 2007.

Iwasaki Mineko and Rande Brown. *Geisha, a Life*. Translated by Rande Brown. New York: Atria, 2002.

Iwashita Takehito. *Gion no hosomichi: Otonbo maiko* [The narrow road to Gion: The youngest child becomes a maiko]. Tokyo: Bungei Shobō, 2009.

Izawa Jun. "Nihon eiga hihyō" [Japanese film review]. *Kinema junpō* 132 (1955): 89.

Johnston, William. *Geisha, Harlot, Strangler, Star: A Woman, Sex, and Morality in Modern Japan*. New York: Columbia University Press, 2005.

Kageyama, Yuri. "Michael Jackson Had Loyal, Generous Fans in Japan," *San Diego Tribune*, June 26, 2009. https://www.sandiegouniontribune.com/sdut-japan-michael-jackson-062609-2009jun26-story.html (accessed May 16, 2020).

Kamishichiken Ichimame. *Maiko no osahō* [Maiko etiquette]. Tokyo: Daiwa Shobō, 2007.

Kano, Ayako. *Acting Like a Woman in Modern Japan: Theater, Gender and Nationalism*. New York: Palgrave Macmillan, 2001.

———. "Backlash, Fight Back, and Back-Pedaling: Responses to State Feminism in Contemporary Japan." *International Journal of Asian Studies* 8, no. 1 (2011): 41–62.

Katō Atsuko. *Tenugui tsukaikonashi bukku* [Tenugui mastery guide]. Tokyo: Shufunotomo-sha, 2018.

Kawaguchi, Yoko. *Butterfly's Sisters: The Geisha in Western Culture*. New Haven, CT: Yale University Press, 2010.

Kawakami, Barbara F. *Japanese Immigrant Clothing in Hawaii, 1885–1941*. Honolulu: University of Hawai'i Press, 1993.

Keaveney, Christopher T. *Western Rock Artists, Madame Butterfly, and the Allure of Japan: Dancing in an Eastern Dream*. Lanham, MD: Lexington Books, 2020.

Kennicott, Philip. "Cute puppies and octopus sex: A Japanese art exhibition reveals our fascination with animals." *Washington Post*, May 30, 2019. https://www.washingtonpost.com/entertainment/museums/cute-puppies-and-octopus-sex-a-japanese-art-exhibition-reveals-our-fascination-with-animals/2019/05/29/7b4c0c8e-8221-11e9-933d-7501070ee669_story.html (accessed May 16, 2020).

Kimura, Amy Hirata. *Radiation Brain Moms and Citizen Scientists: The Gender Politics of Food Contamination after Fukushima*. Durham, NC: Duke University Press, 2016.

Kinsella, Sharon. "Cuteness, *josō*, and the Need to Appeal: *Otoko no ko* in Male Subculture in 2010s Japan." *Japan Forum* 3, no. 32 (2019): 432–58.

———. *Schoolgirls, Money and Rebellion in Japan*. London: Routledge, 2014.

Kiriki Chizu. *Aisare jōzu ni naru Gion-ryū: Onna migaki* [The Gion way to skill in becoming loveable: A woman's polish]. Tokyo: Kōdansha, 2007.

Koch, Gabriele. *Healing Labor: Japanese Sex Work in the Gendered Economy*. Stanford, CA: Stanford University Press, 2020.

Kominz, Laurence R. "The Impact of Tourism on Japanese 'Kyōgen': Two Case Studies," *Asian Folklore Studies* 47, no. 2 (1988): 195–213.

Komomo and Naoyuki Ogino. *A Geisha's Journey: My Life as a Kyoto Apprentice*. Translated by Gearoid Reidy and Philip Price. Tokyo: Kodansha International, 2008.

———. *Komomo: Nihongo ban* [Japanese-language version of *A Geisha's Journey: My Life as a Kyoto Apprentice*]. Tokyo: Kodansha International, 2008.

Kovner, Sarah. *Occupying Power: Sex Workers and Servicemen in Postwar Japan*. Stanford, CA: Stanford University Press, 2012.

Koyama Aiko. *Maiko-san-chi no Makanai-san* [Miss Cook for the maiko girls]. Serialized girls' comic. Tokyo: Shōgakukan, 2017–2020.

Kume Yoriko. "Toraburu to shite no sekushuaritī: *Otoko no ko* hyōshō to *shōjo* komyunitī shikō [Sexuality as Trouble: Representations of the *otoko no ko* and preference for *shōjo* community]." In *Raito noberu sutadīzu* [Light Novel Studies], edited by Ichiyanagi Hirotaka and Kume Yoriko, 69–83. Tokyo: Seikyūsha, 2013.

Lebra, Takie Sugiyama. *Japanese Women: Constraint and Fulfillment*. Honolulu: University of Hawai'i Press, 1984.

Leheny, David. *Think Global, Fear Local: Sex, Violence, and Anxiety in Contemporary Japan*. Ithaca, NY: Cornell University Press, 2006.

Liao, Christina. "An Inside Peek at Kyoto's Secretive Geisha Culture." *Vogue* March 21, 2017. https://www.vogue.com/article/geisha-culture-kyoto-japan-how-to-see -geiko-maiko (accessed May 22, 2020).

Loftus, Ronald P. *Changing Lives: The "Postwar" in Japanese Women's Autobiographies and Memoirs*. Ann Arbor, MI: Association for Asian Studies, 2013.

Lublin, Elizabeth Dorn. *Reforming Japan: The Woman's Christian Temperance Union in the Meiji Period*. Vancouver: UBC Press, 2010.

Mackie, Vera. "How to Be a Girl: Mainstream Media Portrayals of Transgendered Lives in Japan." *Asian Studies Review* 32, no. 3 (2008): 411–23.

Macwilliams, Mark Wheeler, ed. *Japanese Visual Culture: Explorations in the World of Manga and Anime*. Armonk, NY: M.E. Sharpe, 2008.

"Maiko-san no toki kara, Orenifure Satsuki-chan no hibi o shōkai shite kimashita." [We have introduced Satsuki's life from time to time since her maiko days]. *Utsukushii kimono* [Beautiful kimono]. (Winter 2016): 215.

Marchetti, Gina. *Romance and the "Yellow Peril" Race, Sex, and Discursive Strategies in Hollywood Fiction*. Berkeley: University of California Press, 1993.

Marran, Christine L. "Beyond Domesticating Animal Love." *Mechademia* 6 (2011): 39–50.

Marshall, Rob, dir. *Memoirs of a Geisha*. Columbia Pictures, 2005.

Maske, Andrew L. "Identifying Geisha in Art and Life: Is She Really a Geisha?" In *Geisha: Beyond the Painted Smile*, edited by Peabody Essex Museum, 37–49. New York: George Braziller, 2004.

Masuda, Sayo. *Autobiography of a Geisha*. Translated by G. G. Rowley. New York: Columbia University Press, 2003.

Matsuura Hisaki. "Ōga to kenryoku: Mizoguchi Kenji, *Gion bayashi*" [Reclining and Power: Mizoguchi Kenji, *Gion bayashi*]. *Shineteikku* 1 (1993): 120–44.

Maynard, Senko K. *Fluid Orality in the Discourse of Japanese Popular Culture*. Amsterdam: John Benjamins, 2016.

McCloud, Scott. *Understanding Comics: The Invisible Art*. New York: Harper Perennial, 1993.

McConnell, Sarah. "Illustration in Motion: Sequential Motion in Children's Illustrated Books." In *A Companion to Illustration: Art and Theory*, edited by Alan Male, 140–59. Hoboken, NJ: John Wiley & Sons, Inc., 2019.

McCready, Eric, and Norry Ogata. "Adjectives, Stereotypicality, and Comparison," *Natural Language Semantics* 15, no. 1 (2007): 35–63.

McDonald, Keiko I. *Reading a Japanese Film: Cinema in Context*. Honolulu: University of Hawai'i Press, 2006.

McLelland, Mark J. *Queer Japan from the Pacific War to the Internet Age*. Lanham, MD: Rowman & Littlefield, 2005.

McLelland, Mark J., Kazumi Nagaike, Katsuhiko Suganuma, and James Welker, eds. *Boys Love Manga and Beyond: History, Culture, and Community in Japan*. Jackson: University Press of Mississippi, 2015.

McLelland, Mark J., and James Welker. "An Introduction to 'Boys Love' in Japan." In *Boys Love Manga and Beyond: History, Culture, and Community in Japan*, edited by McLelland et al., 3–20. Jackson: University Press of Mississippi, 2015.

McVeigh, Brian J. *Life in a Japanese Women's College: Learning to Be Ladylike*. London: Routledge, 1997.

"Michael Jackson Arrives in Japan for 13-Concert Tour." *New York Times*, September 10, 1987. https://www.nytimes.com/1987/09/10/arts/michael-jackson-arrives-in-japan -for-13-concert-tour.html (accessed May 16, 2020).

"Mika Ninagawa Exhibition Expresses Aura of Kyoto's Geiko Glamor." *Kyoto Shimbun*, May 27, 2018. https://english.kyodonews.net/news/2018/05/dd8d353022b2-ninagawa -exhibition-expresses-aura-of-kyotos-geiko-glamor.html (accessed June 5, 2020).

Miller, Alison J. "Wintry Women: Skiing, Modern Girls, and Imperial Body Politics as Represented in 1930s Nihonga." *Journal of Japanese Studies* 47, no. 2 (2021).

Miller, Laura. "Bad Girl Photography." In *Bad Girls of Japan*, edited by Laura Miller and Jan Bardsley, 126–41. New York: Palgrave Macmillan, 2005.

———. *Beauty Up: Exploring Contemporary Japanese Body Aesthetics*. Berkeley: University of California Press, 2006.

———. "Cute Masquerade and the Pimping of Japan." *International Journal of Japanese Sociology* 20, no. 1 (2011): 18–29.

———. "Elevator Girls Moving In and Out of the Box." In *Modern Girls on the Go: Gender, Mobility, and Labor in Japan*, edited by Alisa Freedman, Laura Miller, and Christine R. Yano, 41–65. Stanford, CA: Stanford University Press, 2013.

———. "Japan's Zoomorphic Urge." *ASIANetwork Exchange* 17, no. 2 (2010): 69–82.

———. "People Types: Personality Classification in Japanese Women's Magazines." *Journal of Popular Culture* 31, no. 2 (1997): 143–59.

———. "Searching for Charisma Queen Himiko." In *Diva Nation: Female Icons from Japanese Cultural History*, edited by Laura Miller and Rebecca Copeland, 51–76. Oakland: University of California Press, 2018.

Miller, Laura, and Jan Bardsley, eds. *Bad Girls of Japan*. New York: Palgrave Macmillan, 2005.

"Miyamoto Maki." *Kinema junpō* 1275 (1999): 18–19; 94–99.

Mizobuchi Hiroshi. *Kyō maiko: Miyagawa-chō*. Kyoto: Mitsumura Suiko Shoin, 2013.

———. *Kyoto no kagai; The Kagai in Kyoto: Legendary Beauty of Geiko and Maiko*. Kyoto: Mitsumura Suiko Shoin Publishing, 2015.

Mizoguchi, Kenji, dir. *Gion bayashi* [A Geisha]. Tokyo: Daiei Co., 1953.

———. *Gion shimai* [Sisters of the Gion]. Tokyo: Daiichi Eiga, 1936.

Mizuta Nobuo, dir. *Maiko Haaaan!!!*. Tokyo: NTV, 2007.

Modern Girl around the World Research Group. *The Modern Girl around the World: Consumption, Modernity, and Globalization*. Durham, NC: Duke University Press, 2008.

Monden, Masafumi. *Japanese Fashion Cultures: Dress and Gender in Contemporary Japan*. London: Bloomsbury Academic, 2015.

Morita Rieko. *Onnamae: Morita Rieko gabunshū* [Paintings of 'Handsome Women' by Morita Rieko: Onnamae]. Tokyo: Kyūryūdō Art Publishing Co., 2010.

Murase, Shigeyuki. "'Maiko' Fever Strikes Kyoto." *The Asahi Shimbun*, 18 April, 2008.

Nakano, Lynne, and Moeko Wagatsuma. "Mothers and Their Unmarried Daughters: An Intimate Look at Generational Change." In *Japan's Changing Generations: Are Young People Creating a New Society?*, edited by Gordon Mathews and Bruce White, 137–53. London: Routledge, 2004.

Nanami Haruka. *Shōnen maiko: Chiyogiku ga yuku!* [Boy maiko: There goes Chiyogiku!]. 54 vols. Tokyo: Shūeisha Cobalt Bunko, 2002–2014.

Napier, Susan J. *From Impressionism to Anime: Japan as Fantasy and Fan Cult in the Mind of the West*. New York: Palgrave Macmillan, 2007.

NHK (Nippon Hōsō Kyōkai). *Gion onna-tachi no monogatari: Ochaya hachidai-me okami* [Stories of Gion women: The eighth-generation teahouse manager]. TV documentary. Tokyo: NHK, 2017.

"Ninki sutā: Jūhachi musume ga sannin yoreba." [Popular Stars: The eighteen-year-old three girls]. *Shūkan Yomiuri* (November 1955): 26–29.

Nishio Kumiko. "Business Aspects of the Kyoto Hanamachi: Introduction." Translated by Jacqueline Kaminski. *The Japanese Economy* 37, no. 4 (2010–11): 3–5.

———. "Chapter 1. The Kyoto Hanamachi." Translated by Jacqueline Kaminski. *The Japanese Economy* 37, no. 4 (2010–11): 6–19.

———. "Chapter 2: Geiko, Maiko, Ochaya, and Okiya." Translated by Jacqueline Kaminski. *The Japanese Economy* 37, no. 4 (2010–11): 20–35.

———. "Chapter 3. 'No First-Time Customers.'" Translated by Jacqueline Kaminski. *The Japanese Economy* 37, no. 4 (2010–11): 36–46.

———. "Chapter 4. The Life of a Maiko." Translated by Jacqueline Kaminski. *The Japanese Economy* 37, no. 4 (2010–11): 47–60.

———. "Chapter 5. No Wallet Required." Translated by Jacqueline Kaminski. *The Japanese Economy* 37, no. 4 (2010–11): 61–73.

———. "Chapter 6. The Hanamachi Evaluation System." Translated by Jacqueline Kaminski. *The Japanese Economy* 37, no. 4 (2010–11): 74–89.

———. *Kyoto hanamachi no keieigaku* [Business Aspects of the Kyoto Hanamachi]. Tokyo: Tōyō Keizai Shinpōsha, 2007.

———. *Maiko no kotoba: Kyoto hanamachi hitosodate no gokui* [Maiko language: Training secrets from the Kyoto hanamachi]. Tokyo: Tōyō Keizai Shinpōsha, 2012.

———. *Omotenashi no shikumi: Kyoto hanamachi ni manabu manejimento* [The mechanisms of hospitality: Management skills learned in Kyoto hanamachi]. Tokyo: Chūōkōron Shinsha , 2014.

Nishiyama Masateru, dir. *Maiko no kyūjitsu* [Maiko holiday]. Kyoto: Kyoto Daiei, 1961.

Noborikawa Naoki. "Gion bayashi," *Kinema junpō* 72 (1953): 56–57.

Nomachi Mineko. *O-kama dakedo OL yattemasu* [I am queer, but I'm an office lady]. Tokyo: Take Shobō, 2006.

Norma, Caroline. *Comfort Women and Post-occupation Corporate Japan*. London: Routledge, 2019.

Ōhashi Takayuki. *Raito noberu kara mita shōjo/shōnen shōsetsushi: Gendai Nihon no monogatari bunka o minaosu tame ni* [The history of novels for young adults as seen in light novels: Rethinking modern Japanese narrative culture]. Tokyo: Kasama Shoin, 2014.

Okada Kiichirō. *Showa kayō eigakan* [Showa popular song films]. Tokyo: Chūkō Shinsho, 2009.

Okada, Mariko. "Before Making Heritage: Internationalisation of Geisha in the Meiji Period." In *Making Japanese Heritage*, edited by Christoph Brumann and Rupert Cox, 31–43. London: Routledge, 2010.

———. "Prolegomenon to Geisha as a Cultural Performer: Miyako Odori, the Gion School, and Representation of a 'Traditional' Japan." *The Institute for Theater Research, the 21st Century COE Program, Waseda University*, 1 (2003): 159–65.

Osaki, Tomohiro. "Japan's Diet OKs law lowering age of adulthood to 18." *Japan Times* June 13, 2018. https://www.japantimes.co.jp/news/2018/06/13/national/crime-legal/japan-enacts-law-lower-adulthood-age-18/#.XLGT-OgzYuU (accessed May 23, 2020).

Ōta Tōru and Hiratake Kōzō, eds. *Kyō no kagai: Hito, waza, machi* [Kyoto's hanamachi: People, arts, towns]. Tokyo: Nippon Hyōronsha, 2009.

Papp, Melinda. *Shichigosan: Change and Continuity of a Family Ritual in Contemporary Urban Japan*. New York: Palgrave Macmillan, 2016.

Parreñas, Rhacel Salazar. *Illicit Flirtations: Labor, Migration, and Sex Trafficking in Tokyo*. Stanford, CA: Stanford University Press, 2011.

Perelman. Elisheva. "The Appropriated Geisha: Using Their Role to Discuss Japanese History, Cultural Appropriation, and Orientalism." *Education about Asia* 20, no. 3 (2015): 70–72.

Perkins, Percival Densmore. *Geisha of Pontocho*. Photos. Tokyo News Service, 1954.

Phillips, Lee, dir. *An American Geisha*. Interscope Communications TV, 1986.

Pradt, Sarah J., and Terry Kawashima. "Teaching the 'Geisha' as Cultural Criticism." *Education about Asia* 6, no. 1 (2001): 26–31.

Pronko, Leonard C. "The Wisteria Maiden: *Fuji Musume*." In *Kabuki Plays on Stage, Volume 3: Darkness and Desire, 1804–1864.*, edited by James Brandon and Samuel L. Leiter, 164–73. Honolulu: University of Hawai'i Press, 2002.

Prough, Jennifer S. *Straight from the Heart: Gender, Intimacy, and the Cultural Production of Shōjo Manga.* Honolulu: University of Hawai'i Press, 2011.

———. *Revisiting Kyoto: Heritage Tourism in Contemporary Kyoto.* Honolulu: University of Hawai'i Press, forthcoming.

Raine, Michael J. "Youth, Body, and Subjectivity in Japanese Cinema, 1955–1960." PhD diss., University of Iowa, 2002.

Reed, Dan, dir. *Leaving Neverland.* Distributed by HBO, 2019.

Rich, Motoko. "Women Barred from Sumo Ring, Even to Save a Man's Life." *New York Times*, April 5, 2018. https://www.nytimes.com/2018/04/05/world/asia/women-sumo-ring-japan.html (accessed May 16, 2020).

Robertson, Jennifer. *Takarazuka: Sexual Politics and Popular Culture in Modern Japan.* Berkeley: University of California Press, 1998.

Russell, Catherine. *Classical Japanese Cinema Revisited.* London: Bloomsbury, 2011.

Saito, Satomi. "Narrative in the Digital Age: From Light Novels to Web Serials." In *Routledge Handbook of Modern Japanese Literature*, edited by Rachael Hutchinson and Leith Morton, 315–27. New York: Routledge, 2016.

Sakai Junko. *Kireba wakaru!* You'll understand if you wear it]. Tokyo: Bungei Shunjū, 2010.

———. *Makeinu no tōboe* [The distant howl of the loser dog]. Tokyo: Kōdansha, 2004.

Samuel, Yoshiko Yokochi. "Ariyoshi Sawako 1931–84." In *Japanese Women Writers: A Bio-Critical Sourcebook*, edited by Chieko Irie Mulhern, 8–18. Westport, CT: Greenwood Press, 1994.

Sasagawa, Ayumi. "Centered Selves and Life Choices: Changing Attitudes of Young Educated Mothers." In *Japan's Changing Generations: Are Young People Creating a New Society?*, edited by Gordon Mathews and Bruce White, 171–87. London: Routledge, 2004.

Sato, Barbara Hamill. *The New Japanese Woman: Modernity, Media, and Women in Interwar Japan.* Durham, NC: Duke University Press, 2003.

Scott, A. C. *The Flower and Willow World: A Study of the Geisha.* London: Heinemann, 1959.

Seaman, Amanda. "Women Writers and Alternative Critiques." In *Woman Critiqued: Translated Essays on Japanese Women's Writing*, edited by Rebecca L. Copeland, 153–205. Honolulu: University of Hawai'i, 2006.

Seigle, Cecilia Segawa. *Yoshiwara: The Glittering World of the Japanese Courtesan.* Honolulu: University of Hawai'i Press, 1993.

Shamoon, Deborah. *Passionate Friendship: The Aesthetics of Girls' Culture in Japan.* Honolulu: University of Hawai'i Press, 2012.

Sharf, Frederic A. "Shōwa Sophistication." In Dower et al., *The Brittle Decade: Visualizing Japan in the 1930s*, 145–70. Boston: Museum of Fine Arts, 2012.

Shibusawa, Naoko. *America's Geisha Ally: Reimagining the Japanese Enemy*. Cambridge, MA: Harvard University Press, 2006.

Shindō Kaneto, dir. *Aru eiga-kantoku no shōgai* [Kenji Mizoguchi: The life of a film director]. Criterion Collection, 1975.

"Shinshun tokushū: Bundan de katsuyaku suru Shimada-bito: Shōsetsuka Yokoyama Yachiyo" [New Year's Special Section: Shimada resident active in the literary world: Novelist Yokoyama Yachiyo]. *Shimada Life* 87 (2009): 3–5.

Shirane, Haruo, ed. *Envisioning "The Tale of Genji": Media, Gender, and Cultural Production*. New York: Columbia University, 2008.

Shiromoto Satomi. "Ōta Kimi-San (Gion Kōbu)." In *Kyō no kagai: Hito, waza, machi* [Kyoto's hanamachi: People, arts, towns], edited by Ōta Tōru and Hiratake Kōzō, 214–15. Tokyo: Nippon Hyōronsha, 2009.

Silverberg, Miriam Rom. *Erotic Grotesque Nonsense: The Mass Culture of Japanese Modern Times*. Berkeley: University of California Press, 2006.

Stalker, Nancy K. "Flower Empowerment: Rethinking Japan's Traditional Arts as Women's Labor." In *Rethinking Japanese Feminisms*, edited by Julia C. Bullock, Ayako Kano, and James Welker, 103–18. Honolulu: University of Hawai'i Press, 2018.

———. *Japan: History and Culture from Classical to Cool*. Oakland: University of California Press, 2018.

Stanley, Amy. "Enlightenment Geisha: The Sex Trade, Education, and Feminine Ideals in Early Meiji Japan." *Journal of Asian Studies* 72, no. 3 (2013): 539–62.

Steel, Gill, ed. *Beyond the Gender Gap in Japan*. Ann Arbor: University of Michigan Press, 2019.

Steinberger, Aimee Major. *Japan Ai: A Tall Girl's Adventures in Japan*. Agoura Hills, CA: Go!Comi, 2007.

Stickland, Leonie R. *Gender Gymnastics: Performing and Consuming Japan's Takarazuka Revue*. Melbourne: Trans Pacific Press, 2008.

Sugie Toshio. *Janken musume* [So Young So Bright]. Tokyo: Toho, 1955.

Sugita Hiroaki and Mizobuchi Hiroshi. *Kyō no kagai, Gion* [Gion, hanamachi of the old capital]. Kyoto: Tankōsha, 2003.

———. 2010. *Pontochō no subete* [Everything about Pontochō]. Kyoto: Tankōsha.

Sugiyama Hei'ichi. "Gion bayashi." *Eiga hyōron* 10 (1953): 76–78.

Suo Masayuki, dir. *Maiko wa redī* [Lady Maiko]. Tokyo: Toho, 2014.

Surak, Kristin. *Making Tea, Making Japan: Cultural Nationalism in Practice*. Stanford, CA: Stanford University Press, 2013.

Tabuchi, Hiroko. "In Search of Adorable, as Hello Kitty Gets Closer to Goodbye." *New York Times*, May 4, 2010. https://www.nytimes.com/2010/05/15/business/global/15kitty.html (accessed May 16, 2020).

Takeda, Ikuko (Koito). "Foreword." In *A Geisha's Journey: My Life as a Kyoto Apprentice*, by Komomo and Naoyuki Ogino, 7–9. Tokyo: Kodansha International, 2008.

Takeyama, Akiko. *Staged Seduction: Selling Dreams in a Tokyo Host Club*. Stanford, CA: Stanford University Press, 2016.

Tanaka, Aiko. "'Don't Let *Geisha* Steal Your Husband': The Reconstruction of the Housewife in Interwar Japan." *U.S.-Japan Women's Journal* 40 (2011): 122–46.

Tanaka Chiyoko. "Wakao Ayako: Jisen 11 sakuhin: kaisetsu" [Wakao Ayako: Her eleven recommended works, an interpretation]." In *Joyū: Wakao Ayako* [Actress: Ayako Wakao], edited by Harada Masaaki and Aoki Shin'ya, 6–27. Tokyo: Kinema Junpōsha, 2012.

Taniguchi Keiko. *Gion, uttoko no hanashi: "Minoya" okami, hitori katari* [Gion, Stories of our place: Thoughts from the manager of the Minoya]. Tokyo: Heibonsha, 2018.

Tenugui: Japanese Hand Towels. Volume 1 of Free-Wrench Everyday Masterpieces of Japanese Craft. Tokyo: Airy Rhyme, 2014.

Ting, Grace En-Yi. "The Desire and Disgust of Sweets: Consuming Femininities through *Shōjo* Manga." *U.S.-Japan Women's Journal* 54 (2018): 52–74.

Tipton, Elise K. "Pink Collar Work: The Café Waitress in Early Twentieth Century Japan." *Intersections: Gender, History and Culture in the Asian Context* 7 (2002). http://intersections.anu.edu.au/issue7/tipton.html (accessed September 26, 2020).

Tokushū: Gion [Special issue on Gion]. *Taiyō* [*The Sun*] (June 1972): 5–116.

Tseëlon, Efrat. "Introduction: Masquerade and Identities." In *Masquerade and Identities: Essays on Gender, Sexuality and Marginality*, edited by Efrat Tseëlon, 1–17. London: Routledge, 2001.

Tsuchitani, Scott. "Making Art, Making Change: The Tactical Use of Guerrilla Intervention." *Social Policy* 43, no. 3 (2012): 27–33.

Wakita, Mio. "Selling Japan: Kusakabe Kimbei's Image of Japanese Women." *History of Photography* 33, no. 2 (2009): 209–23.

Weisenfeld, Gennifer. "Selling Shiseido: Cosmetics Advertising and Design in Early 20th-Century Japan." MIT, Visualizing Cultures, 2009. https://visualizingcultures.mit.edu/shiseido_01 (accessed May 16, 2020).

White, Merry. *The Material Child: Coming of Age in Japan and America*. Berkeley: University of California Press, 1993.

Wijers-Hasegawa, Yumi. "UNESCO heritage bid challenged over gender bias." *Japan Times*, May 4, 2004. https://www.japantimes.co.jp/news/2004/05/01/national/unesco-heritage-bid-challenged-over-gender-bias/#.XsskhWhKjD4 (accessed May 16, 2020).

Willig, Rosette F. *The Changelings: A Classical Japanese Court Tale*. Stanford, CA: Stanford University Press, 1983.

World Economic Forum. *Global Gender Gap Report 2020*. Geneva: World Economic Forum, 2019. http://www3.weforum.org/docs/WEF_GGGR_2020.pdf (accessed May 28, 2020).

Yamaguchi Kimijo. *Suppin geiko: Kyoto Gion no ukkari nikki* [Bare-faced geiko: My haphazard diary of Gion, Kyoto]. Tokyo: LOCUS , 2007.

Yamamura Misa. *Miyako Odori satsujin jiken* [The Miyako Odori murder case]. 1985, rpt, Tokyo: Tokuma Bunko, 2004.

Yamanaka Tomomi. *Raito noberu yo, doko e iku? 1980 nendai kara zero nendai made* [The light novel, where will it go? From the 1980s to the 2000s]. Tokyo: Seikyūsha, 2010.

Yamato Waki and Iwasaki Mineko. *Kurenai niou* [Crimson fragrance]. Serialized manga. 2003–07, rpt Tokyo: Kōdansha, 2009.

Yano, Christine R. "Gazing upon Sakura: Imaging Japanese Americans on Japanese TV." In *Gender and Globalization in Asia and the Pacific: Method, Practice, Theory*, edited by Kathy Ferguson and Monique Mironesco, 101–20. Honolulu: University of Hawai'i Press, 2008.

———. *Pink Globalization: Hello Kitty's Trek across the Pacific*. Durham, NC: Duke University Press, 2013.

Yasuda Kimiyoshi, dir. *Maiko monogatari* [Tale of a maiko]. Tokyo: Toho, 1954.

Yasuda Yōko, Kaneda Chikako, and Fukuoka Yūko, eds. *Kyoto hanamachi no meiten* [Famous shops in the Kyoto hanamachi]. Kyoto: Seigensha Art Publishing, 2010.

Yayoi Museum and Nakamura Keiko. *Showa modan kimono: Jojōga ni manabu kikonashi jutsu / Shouwa Modern Kimono*. Tokyo: Kawade Shobō Shinsha, 2005.

Yoshihara, Mari. *Embracing the East: White Women and American Orientalism*. New York: Oxford University Press, 2003.

Yoshii, Isamu. "*Gion bayashi* o mite" [Watching *Gion bayashi*]. In *Kyō no uta goyomi* [Seasonal poems of the old capital], 102–5. Tokyo: Daviddosha, 1957.

INDEX

Founded in 1893,
UNIVERSITY OF CALIFORNIA PRESS
publishes bold, progressive books and journals
on topics in the arts, humanities, social sciences,
and natural sciences—with a focus on social
justice issues—that inspire thought and action
among readers worldwide.

The UC PRESS FOUNDATION
raises funds to uphold the press's vital role
as an independent, nonprofit publisher, and
receives philanthropic support from a wide
range of individuals and institutions—and from
committed readers like you. To learn more, visit
ucpress.edu/supportus.

www.ingramcontent.com/pod-product-compliance
Lightning Source LLC
Chambersburg PA
CBHW031056280326
41928CB00049B/488